William F. Tolmie at FORT NISQUALLY

LETTERS, 1850-1853

Fort Nisqually's Chief Trader Dr. William Fraser Tolmie with his son Alexander, circa 1865. *Courtesy of the Magedanz Collection*

William F. Tolmie at FORT NISQUALLY

LETTERS, 1850-1853

COMPILED AND EDITED BY

Steve A. Anderson

INTRODUCTION BY

Jerry V. Ramsey, PhD

WSU PRESS

Washington State University Press
Pullman, Washington

Washington State University Press
PO Box 645910
Pullman, Washington 99164-5910
Phone: 800-354-7360
Email: wsupress@wsu.edu
Website: wsupress.wsu.edu

© 2019 by the Board of Regents of Washington State University
All rights reserved
First printing 2019

Printed and bound in the United States of America on pH neutral, acid-free paper. Reproduction or transmission of material contained in this publication in excess of that permitted by copyright law is prohibited without permission in writing from the publisher.

Library of Congress Cataloging-in-Publication Data

Names: Tolmie, William Fraser, author. | Anderson, Steve A., 1955- editor. | Ramsey, Jerry V., writer of introduction.
Title: William F. Tolmie at Fort Nisqually : letters, 1850-1853 / compiled and edited by Steve A. Anderson ; with an introduction by Jerry V. Ramsey.
Description: Pullman, Washington : Washington State University Press, [2019] | Includes bibliographical references and index.
Identifiers: LCCN 2019015010 | ISBN 9780874223712 (alk. paper)
Subjects: LCSH: Tolmie, William Fraser--Correspondence. | Fort Nisqually (DuPont, Wash.)--Biography. | Hudson's Bay Company--Biography. | Fur traders--Washington (State)--Puget Sound--Biography. | Physicians--Washington (State)--Puget Sound--Biography. | Hudson's Bay Company--History--19th century. | Fort Nisqually (DuPont, Wash.)--History--19th century. | Puget Sound Region (Wash.)--History--19th century | Frontier and pioneer life--Washington (State)--Puget Sound.
Classification: LCC F897.P9 T65 2019 | DDC 979.7/703092 [B] --dc23 LC record available at https://lccn.loc.gov/2019015010

Published with the generous assistance of the Fort Nisqually Foundation.

On the cover: Fort Nisqually's Chief Trader Dr. William Fraser Tolmie, circa 1865. *Courtesy of the Magedanz Collection*

Dedicated to my "American Columbia" wintering partners,
Jerry and Elaine Ramsey

Contents

Maps and Illustrations

Preface

Widely accepted histories of Fort Nisqually have been a part of Washington State's communal memory since the late nineteenth century. I encountered a number of these as I began administering Fort Nisqually Living History Museum (located in Point Defiance Park, Tacoma, Washington) in May 1980. As part of my job, I assessed these time-honored narratives. Ultimately, many raised several concerns.

A good percentage of them remained contextually shallow or had been taken out of context altogether. Some had been repackaged for a more sensational impact. Many had not been academically challenged or verified. Parts were missing—important parts. And then there were the unchecked biases and the wonderful but piecemeal memories of "old graying pioneers"—reminiscences that pushed and pulled incessantly at my historian's credibility meter. It was as if a good many authors of the early twentieth century did not wish to step "outside the vogue" already established. Or, did the absence of additional primary source material impede accurate histories? That ominous possibility—that documentation regarding Fort Nisqually, Puget Sound's earliest Euro-American settlement, had somehow been destroyed or scattered to the winds—increased my anxiety. Fortunately, much of it has been found safe, having landed in distant archives.

I first became aware of Dr. William F. Tolmie's letters in 1983. During a trip to Seattle, I visited the University of Washington's Suzzallo Library. There, within the Clarence B. Bagley, Edward Huggins, and William F. Tolmie Collections I found hundreds of individual documents produced at the fort, some typescripts and many originals in Tolmie's own hand.

By 1984 I learned of the vast and nomadic Nisqually Papers. Nisqually Tribal Historian Cecelia Carpenter alerted me to this more than 2,000-page archive which had made its way from DuPont to Seattle in the 1920s, and then to San Marino, California, in the 1950s. It now resides as a part of the larger Soliday Collection in the Huntington Library. I found the first Fort Nisqually "letterbook" in this archive. Here was a singular volume, covered in marbled paper, containing copies of Dr. Tolmie's letters from late 1855 through 1858. I transcribed it jacket to jacket in 1993.

During a research sabbatical to Victoria's Royal British Columbia Museum and Archives in 1986, I spent a week looking into the physical structure of the 1843 fort site. Dr. Tolmie's original diary and many letters surfaced there as well.

After leaving the fort's employment in 1990, many questions about its past remained unanswered, at least in my mind. Throughout the next two decades, I continued writing short stories using the material I had gleaned throughout the

1980s. Around 2012, I discovered two more Fort Nisqually letterbooks at the Manitoba Provincial Archives in Winnipeg. Taking up a meager inch or two of shelf space in that monumental Hudson's Bay Company Archives, the fragile pages had never been transcribed, yet they possessed a fairly complete record of Fort Nisqually's outgoing (and some incoming) correspondence during the early 1850s.

Perusing these new volumes, letters that covered 1850 through late 1855, and then revisiting those from the Nisqually Papers letterbook, I had become privy to nearly a decade of Tolmie's private conversations. Here were the weighty business decisions he faced, the prittle-prattle gossip of the day, eyewitness accounts, political intrigue, patterns of commerce, and critical assessments of the fort's business. Even after thirty-odd years of exploring this subject matter, I found the letters new, edifying, and an enormous "value-added" component to the homogeneous narratives I had encountered in the early 1980s.

The good doctor's correspondence had reached a critical mass. In my mind, they were crying out for more exposure. So, after the transcription process had been completed, Dr. Jerry Ramsey urged me to publish them all. That has led to the creation of this first book. Hopefully, others will follow containing later correspondence.

Over the years, various people and institutions have provided me with moral support, crucial information, and hands-on assistance. These include several family members, especially my love (and this work's copy editor), Lynn Doggett Anderson, and my folks Ed and Loraine Anderson. My sister Connie supported me throughout her lifetime in all ventures of this sort, and brother Mark continues to do so now.

My gratitude extends to others as well, including:

The Hudson's Bay Company Archives, a division of the Archives of Manitoba, in Winnipeg, specifically Heather Beattie, Holly McElrea, and Judith Hudson Beattie Valenzuela, who provided several of the Fort Nisqually letterbook copies; and researcher Murray Peterson for his most welcomed assistance in their fair city.

Nisqually Tribal Historian Cecelia S. Carpenter, who opened doors for me that I could not have possibly discovered on my own. Her only request was that I share this history with the nation. That is a promise I intend to keep.

My mentor David K. Hansen and colleague Doreen Beard who remain supportive of my work long after we had departed each other's company. You two . . . please remember this about Pacific Northwest fur trade history: "You may check out any time you like, but you can never leave."

Doug Magedanz, a big tip of the hat for his sharing of several wonderful images within this work.

Scott Rook of the Oregon Historical Society, for permission to use their image of Peter Skene Ogden.

The DuPont Historical Society's board—in the past, Lorraine Overmyer and Karl Krill; and in the present, Lee McDonald, president, and her board, for steadfastly believing in the necessity of my pursuits over the years—and the latter for financially supporting this work so that it would be published.

Marianne Bull of the Steilacoom Historical Society for use of several images unique to that town's history.

The Fort Nisqually Living History Museum's Claire Keller-Scholz, in Tacoma, for her assistance in obtaining copies of letters and the James Douglas image in their collection; and the Fort Nisqually Foundation, Dana Repp, president, for its supportive role in this work's publication.

The University of Washington Libraries, Special Collections Division, including former staff members Karyl Winn, Janet Ness, and Jo Lewis, for their help in the 1980s obtaining copies of letters in their collection.

Ed Nolan and Eileen Price of the Washington State Historical Society for permission to print Tolmie letters I found in their collection.

The Huntington Library, Art Collections and Botanical Gardens' Peter Blodgett, for continued access and permission to use items from that institution's Nisqually Papers.

The family of Hewitt Jackson (daughter Eileen Dvorak and her son James), whose sketch of the HBC's steamer *Beaver* they've permitted to be used in this work. I met Mr. Jackson in the 1980s and found his maritime artistry amazing. The *Beaver*'s sketch depicts the vessel's appearance when it was seized by customs officials in the early 1850s. My thanks to you all.

The Royal British Columbia Museum and Archives' Diane Wardle and Kelly-Ann Turkington in Victoria, for providing copies and permissions to publish Tolmie's private letters.

Past and present authors, researchers, scholars, and experts in the field who continue to challenge me with historical insights and academic support: Bruce M. Watson, Joseph Huntsman, Nancy Anderson, Harvey Steele, Seattle Pacific University's Richard Scheuerman, University of Washington's John M. Findlay, and Robert Clark and the staff and editorial board of Washington State University Press in Pullman.

Finally, I dedicate this book to Jerry and Elaine Ramsey. It was Jerry who prodded me throughout the last six years to take this work to the next level and make it public. His book, *Stealing Puget Sound, 1832–1869*, should be considered a companion piece, as it continues to open eyes to an "augmented" history of Puget Sound.

Thank you all for your support and for allowing this work to shed light on a portion of Washington State's "dark ages."

Steve A. Anderson
Cape Carteret, North Carolina

Editorial Principles

Many letters and documents created by Hudson's Bay Company (HBC) traders have been published. The Hudson's Bay Record Society (HBRS) and Champlain Society (CS) began their extensive transcription and publication efforts in the 1930s. Since then, they have made many valuable contributions to researchers' bookshelves. Yet, curiously, they have never dealt specifically with Fort Nisqually's documents en masse. However, their efforts and this present work have a similar goal: replicate as closely as possible historical documents and make them available to a wider audience.

Aside from the considerable financial and academic support provided to the work of the HBRS and CS, the book before you differs in just a few ways. Theirs was an academic effort accomplished in a defined, and much shorter, period. My work has taken over 30 years to accumulate and understand. The former transcribers had access to primary documentation, while I depended on copies of originals, or typescripts that were retained in a variety of institutions. Similar to HBRS's work, I have introduced my own commentary as chapter summaries, letting contemporary voices fill in where possible.

This work has been made easier by my familiarity with many of the correspondents and the phraseology they employed; nineteenth century idioms such as the use of "instant" when referencing the present month, "ultimo" for the month just passed, and "proxo" for the month to come. Letters of this time period also made liberal use of abbreviations, including "inst" for instant, "ult" for ultimo, and many others. These abbreviations have been left, except in particularly obscure cases; for these, brackets add missing information. Spelling has been left uncorrected. Acronyms, euphemisms, and obscure nineteenth century words have been deciphered and footnoted when necessary. Good examples of this include the phrase "Indian opportunity," which is an unexpected but immediately available native mail courier; the term "poor" when used to describe one's "poor health"; or the word "thereanent" which is in reference to that matter, subject, or affair previously spoken about.

As the correspondences' headers and salutations ranged from elaborate to austere, I standardized the lot, giving each document a chapter and number (i.e., Document 1:01). Next came the document's structure (i.e., a letter, memo, report, etc.), followed by the document's originator and physical location; the intended recipient and physical location; and finally, the date the document was written. Where locations were impossible to determine, they were left blank.

Place names, which changed over time, have been left as originally penned; "Nasqually," "Nesqually," and "Nisqually" are good examples. Capitalization of common words remains unaltered. Like the fur traders, I capitalize the word "Company" when referring to the Hudson's Bay Company or Puget's Sound Agricultural Company (HBC/PSAC). "Coy" is often used as an abbreviation for "Company"; PSC, PS Ag. Co., and others all refer to Puget's Sound Agricultural Company. Ship names, italicized in modern convention, were not underlined or otherwise set apart in the letters and therefore have been left unitalicized. Occasionally I have interpreted the "dash" of a pen stroke to be a period. Sometimes I perceived the writer was just recharging his quill, so the sentence is allowed to move on unabated. I have [bracketed] breaks in the text where decryption was impossible or original text was lost. Where conceivable, I [bracketed in] the lost text based on context, and included all words that had been struck by their authors. Some letters were moved to more chronologically appropriate locations, which allowed the following letters to make more sense. In all cases, footnotes mark the changes and sources.

Sometimes an incomplete letter from one archive was made whole by a copy from another. These, too, are appropriately footnoted as to source. Later nineteenth and twentieth century side notes (not the original author) were also included as footnotes, as they often added depth or an explanation to the discussion at hand.

Standard letter closures are fully included as they reflect the rank or position of the document's writer to its recipient. In most cases, I have nudged these sometimes lengthy parting gestures up into the preceding paragraph, primarily to save space.

I have briefly introduced Tolmie's primary correspondents in each chapter's summary. With the exception of chapter one, I have allied this book's chapters to the business cycle of the HBC's supply "outfit" or "fur trading outfit." Beginning on June 1, it progressed through to May 31 of the following year. At that juncture in the calendar, Company servants (the HBC's word for employees) anticipated the arrival of the eastern brigade, a possible advancement in rank or pay, the engagement of new employees, the retention or retirement of older employees, the requisition and/or inventory of goods, and the delivery of supplies. Thus, June 1, 1849, marked the end of Outfit 1849 and the beginning of Outfit 1850.

After weighing the political turbulence that surrounded Dr. Tolmie's Fort Nisqually in early 1850 against the relative calm that had taken hold by late May 1853, I concluded that the end of Outfit 1853 made for a suitable date to end this present work.

Abbreviations in Text and Notes

CS—Champlain Society
HBC, HB Coy, HB Co—Hudson's Bay Company
HBRS—Hudson's Bay Record Society
HBCA—Hudson's Bay Company Archives
NWC—North West Company
PFC—Pacific Fur Company
PSAC, PSC, PS Ag. Co, PS Co, et al.—Puget's Sound Agricultural Company
RAFC—Russian American Fur Company

Introduction

Jerry V. Ramsey, PhD

Since retiring as a high school and college educator, I have been troubled by the reduction of history-related coursework in Washington State's public school system (especially studies pertaining to the Pacific Northwest). Even now, an ever-shrinking curriculum consumed with our nation's wars, the development of the eastern half of the United States, the California Gold Rush, and Oregon Trail dominates class time. Until very recently, the same could be said of academia. Add to this imbalance the state's published histories, historic sites, and museums that have finally initiated their discussions of Puget Sound's past using more than references to a small group of American settlers arriving at Tumwater in 1845. Within the state's narratives, such as Tacoma's winning of a railroad terminus and Seattle's rise to prominence, one typically finds the veneration of Caucasian, male, financially, militarily, and/or politically successful *American* settlers. Those equally deserving, but deficient in these prerequisites, are left haunting the darkened corners of our state's past.

A recent book provides us with a good example. In *Songs Upon the Rivers: The Buried History of the French-Speaking Canadiens and Métis from the Great Lakes and the Mississippi across to the Pacific*, co-author Robert Foxcurran takes umbrage with the fact that "Lewis and Clark never downplayed the role of the [French-Canadians] in their expedition who had served as guides and translators in the land they mapped, [yet] editors and historians have written out of their accounts the contributions of the Canadien, Creole, and Métis members of [the Corp of Discovery]."[1]

There is little doubt that William F. Tolmie's role in Washington State's history has also been marginalized by these same "editors and historians." When mentioned, he is rarely characterized as an early settler or pioneer. Critics quickly point out that this "agent of a foreign corporation" was bereft of historical veneration for he was never an American citizen, nor did he arrive via "pioneer-honored" modes of travel. Furthermore, during his lifetime, cultural boundaries involving class and miscegenation framed "civilized" society. Tolmie crossed that line as well, marry-

1 Robert Foxcurran, Michel Bouchard, and Sébastien Malette, *Songs Upon the Rivers: The Buried History of the French-Speaking Canadiens and Metis from the Great Lakes and the Mississippi across to the Pacific* (Montreal: Baraka Books, 2016), 22.

ing a woman of mixed descent. He also championed lost causes: the rights of first peoples (Indians); the rights of a large but foreign corporation (by treaty); the rule of law (protection against those in power); and the promotion of free education for children.[2] In his time, these were socially unpopular (and failed) endeavors. Finally, Tolmie and his descendants did not remain, or prosper, in the United States.

Fort Nisqually, Tolmie's place of residence while living on Puget Sound, fares little better. Throughout the twentieth century, it has either been portrayed as a graveyard of ambition, a den of iniquity, "a dark cloud over Pierce County's past," or a contentious pawn on the volatile chess board of national conquest and regional settlement. Given these harsh facts, why should we remember (much less celebrate) this itinerate Scotsman who came and went, like so many others before and after him?

In sharp contrast to his detractors, this work's documents reflect not only Dr. Tolmie's position in our territorial history, but also the fort's role as a vital communications center—one that linked American and British settlements up and down the Pacific Coast. Bolstered by the infusion of California gold and hard currency, the fort became a financial center as well, one of the few on Puget Sound with enough ready cash to not only fund United States government payrolls, but also for personal and business loans. In essence, it was British money that capitalized some of the earliest businesses in the settlements of Portland, Steilacoom, Tumwater, San Francisco, and Olympia. Thus the doctor was at the center of the development of some of the first equitable (and in some cases failed) credit practices in the region. Unmistakably, Pierce County's agricultural history started at Fort Nisqually in 1833—long before the settlers came. While he resided at the fort, Tolmie not only bore witness to the birth of Oregon and Washington Territories, but vigorously participated in the development of trade, agriculture, banking, government, and business throughout the Pacific Northwest.

The time has come to set aside preconceived, deeply flawed notions of the past. Instead, let us reintroduce Dr. William Fraser Tolmie into Washington State's historical narrative, especially as it concerns the Puget Sound Agricultural Company and his work at Fort Nisqually. This present work, I trust, will help stimulate the discussion.

Background

In January 1850, William F. Tolmie, the principal correspondent of this work, was a medically trained physician holding the rank of chief trader in one of the oldest companies in North America: the Hudson's Bay Company (HBC) of London, England.[3]

Chartered in 1670 by King Charles II of England, the HBC had been created in response to the increased demand for beaver pelts used in the manufacture of fur hats and clothing for European, American, and Asian markets. This royal charter gave "the Company" proprietary rights to exploit the fur reserves of the Hudson's Bay watershed (then called Rupert's Land). Initially consisting of a string of fortified trading posts that dotted the bay's southerly shores, the HBC acquired pelts

2 Walter H. Stuart, "Some Aspects of the Life of William Fraser Tolmie" (master's thesis, University of British Columbia, Vancouver, 1948).

3 For further reading see Peter C. Newman's masterful trilogy *Company of Adventurers* and John S. Galbraith's *The Hudson's Bay Company as an Imperial Factor*.

by trading steel knives, axes, guns, glass beads, wool blankets, and much more to the indigenous tribes with whom they had contact.

For over 100 years, the Company was unrivaled as it expanded its operations southward. In 1784, however, its success attracted a group of Montreal Scotsmen who formed the North West Company (NWC).[4] These "Norwesters" challenged the HBC's supremacy using "murder, arson, Indian warfare, and pitched battles ... to say nothing of a smothering blanket of arrests, legal actions, and court proceedings," noted fur trade historian John Hussey.[5] By the early nineteenth century, the aggressive NWC had bested its older rival by extending operations beyond the Rocky Mountains and to the rugged shoreline of the Pacific Ocean.

Then, following Lewis and Clark's successful Corps of Discovery, American businessmen joined the British and Scottish traders in the collection of animal pelts. While the HBC and NWC battled each other to the north, Americans quietly ascended the Missouri River both individually and in organized groups or "brigades." Though largely comprised of autonomous "mountain men," New York and St. Louis-based entrepreneurs had soon broached the high passes of the Rocky Mountains. Some had even made it to the Pacific Ocean.[6] By 1812 John Astor's Pacific Fur Company (PFC) had erected Fort Astoria at the mouth of the Columbia River. And the pressure did not stop there. Working their way out of present-day Alaska, the Russian American Fur Company (RAFC) had extended its trade all the way into today's northern California.

By 1821, and now wholly destabilized by a never-ending trade war, the HBC and NWC sought a truce. Retaining the HBC title, the new "coalition" incorporated many of the NWC's practices and personnel. Shareholders consisted of the governors, chief factors, and chief traders of both firms—the latter two "classes" being referred to as "wintering partners." Comprised of learned, powerful English, Irish, Scottish, and some French Canadian businessmen, they had all gained financially from the companies' amalgamation. Below them in ranked order worked the clerks, apprentice clerks, and postmasters—again, literate men who, if they showed promise, ascended to the ranks above. Below them were the illiterate classes comprised of craftsmen, laborers, and various "servants" or *milieu*—on whose backs the bulk of the physically demanding (and dangerous) work transpired.[7] In this, the largest group of the Company's personnel, one found a cosmopolitan mix of English, Scottish, Irish, French Canadian, métis (mixed bloods or "half-breeds"), Hawaiians (aka Sandwich Islanders/Kanakas), and local Indians. These working-class men and women trapped and traded the furs, farmed the land, had families, and were lucky to get a small stipend, if anything, at the end of their employment.

In 1821 the Company's new North American governor, George Simpson, was a harsh administrator, so much so that he earned the title "Little Emperor."[8] Divid-

4 The North West Company's history is well documented. See especially Thomas Douglas Selkirk's *British Fur Trade in North America*.

5 John A. Hussey, *The History of Fort Vancouver and Its Physical Structure* (Tacoma: Washington State Historical Society, 1957), 8.

6 Washington Irving's classic *Astoria* offers an excellent account.

7 One way to interpret the HBC's Latin motto, *Pro Pelle Cutem*, "skin for a skin," is that the company was willing to risk its employees lives (or the lives of others) to acquire pelts.

8 For more on Simpson see James Raffan, *Emperor of the North: Sir George Simpson and the Remarkable Story of the Hudson's Bay Company* (New York: HarperCollins Canada, 2010), and Arthur S. Morton,

ing today's modern Canada into four departments (Canadian, Southern, Northern, and Columbia) and various sub-districts, Simpson reinvigorated his firm against his emboldened American and Russian counterparts. By the middle 1820s this "opposition" was peddling furs deep into *his* Columbia Department (today's British Columbia and the states of Washington, Idaho, and Oregon).

After consolidating the Columbia and Snake River watershed districts, Simpson and the HBC's governing council were forced to align their business practices with British foreign policy. The Treaty of 1818 had already been signed by representatives of the United States and Great Britain. It effectively opened the new Oregon County to "joint occupancy" by citizens and subjects of both nations. Each nation would eventually colonize the region peacefully, but in its own unique fashion.

Fort Vancouver, erected by 1825 on the north bank of the Columbia River in today's Vancouver, Washington, was the HBC's primary depot and the Columbia Department's administrative headquarters. Former "Norwester" Chief Factor Dr. John McLoughlin, that depot's headstrong administrator, was placed in charge of the vast lands west of the Rocky Mountains to the ocean, south of today's Alaska and north of today's California.

Somewhat of a maverick, McLoughlin favored the expansion of local, privatized, large-scale farming within the context of the fur trade. He proposed that independent and Company farmers could produce grains, vegetables, and livestock that the HBC could then consume or buy at lower-than-importation prices. This idea was objected to by the Company's governors who had no desire to see their chief factor's talents being spent on anything other than the fur trade.[9] By 1839, however, McLoughlin's cost saving idea had given rise to the Company's agricultural subsidiary, the Puget's Sound Agricultural Company (PSAC) (alternately referred to as the Puget's Sound Association [PSA] in this work). Aside from small-scale farming at most of the HBC's trading posts, two sites were chosen for large scale operations: Fort Nisqually for livestock and Cowlitz Farm (near today's Toledo, Washington) for the growing of produce. An arrangement with the Russians was reached whereby the HBC/PSAC would provide them with foodstuff in return for access to several areas under Russian control, and no further incursions southward by the RAFC.

Actively expanding the Company's physical presence along the Pacific Northwest Coast, McLoughlin had begun a building program in the late 1820s, one that included the erection of Fort Nisqually on lower Puget Sound in 1833–1834 (today's DuPont, Washington). Austere in appearance, the 100-by-100-foot palisaded enclosure served primarily as a southern port and way station between Vancouver and Fort Langley (1828) on the Fraser River. Constructed 250 feet above sea level, and about 150 yards from a deep water anchorage, the fort was connected to the beach by the region's first wagon road. The site also provided ample level ground on which to build and farm. However, its personnel had no direct access to fresh water.

Sir George Simpson, Overseas Governor of the Hudson's Bay Company: A Pen Picture of a Man of Action (Toronto, Vancouver: J. M. Dent & Sons, 1944).

9 E. E. Rich, ed. *John McLoughlin's Fort Vancouver Letters, Series One, Two, and Three, 1825–1846* (London: Hudson Bay Record Society, 1941, 1943, 1944). Hereafter cited as *McLoughlin's Vancouver Letters*. Dr. McLoughlin was a consummate promoter of his "Oregon Tallow and Hide Company" idea, a scheme to raise and sell beef cattle on a private level. The London directors did not buy this early plan, but later approved the idea of an in-house or "joint stock" farming concern. This was the idea that eventually created the Puget Sound Agricultural Company.

By 1840, a majority of the fort's operation had been transferred to the new PSAC. Its trade shop, while still receiving furs from the Coast Salish, remained deferential to the fort's ever-expanding farm operation. In spite of the vast resources of the HBC and McLoughlin's personal attentions, Fort Nisqually at first prospered under creditable leadership, but soon suffered under the shortcomings of those less competent. In the three years prior to Dr. Tolmie's arrival, it experienced not only its highest rate of managerial turnover, but also exhibited a pronounced physical decay, growing dissent amongst its labor force, and disarray within its operation.

This hard reality was Dr. Tolmie's to manage in July 1843.

Born in Inverness, Scotland, William Fraser Tolmie (1812–1886) advanced through Inverness Academy and Perth Grammar School. Eventually, he spent two years in medical school at the University of Glasgow.[10] Reared largely by his aunt (his mother died when he was a toddler), and with an education financed by an uncle, Tolmie excelled in physics, botany, chemistry, and French. A voracious appetite for classic literature, natural history, mathematics, geography, history, ornithology, politics, aboriginal cultures, and religion rounded out the young Scot's expansive mind. Despite a brief period of postgraduate study in France that furthered his medical education in 1842, most Tolmie biographers maintain that he never earned a physician's license. Instead, he received a diploma as "Licentiate of the Faculty of Physicians and Surgeons of Glasgow." Even so, in 1831 the largely honorary designation of "doctor" became his for a lifetime.

While a severe illness sidelined his education in 1831, Tolmie's recovery allowed him to work as a clerk at a Glasgow cholera hospital. However, it would be his relationship with the renowned botanist William J. Hooker and also Dr. John Scouler that brought him to the HBC's governors' attention. Contracted as a "clerk and surgeon," Tolmie spent his first ten years (1833–1843) in the Company's service working as an Indian trader and physician all along the Pacific Northwest Coast of North America.

After a furlough to Europe in 1842–43, he returned to the Oregon Country and, in his tenth year with the HBC, assumed the management of Fort Nisqually. There, he supervised the same mix of servants spoken of earlier—including a contingent of Coast Salish Indians from throughout the region—contracted for long- or short-term jobs. Of the 30-odd laborers under his watch, some retained high hopes (or high opinions) of themselves. A few were extremely good at their jobs, while others were complete bunglers. Alcoholics and "tea-totalers" came and went, as did butchers, shepherds, gardeners, clerks, and couriers. There were illiterates who spoke in nothing but vulgarities. Earnest, healthy "servants" worked alongside those plagued with colds, diabetes, fever, and disease. Aboriginals and children bore the highest mortality rate—some are buried there still. Puget Sound's long, overcast winters caused depression and suicides. And while a select few died at the hands of others, many quit the region and were never heard from again. However, some stayed and became American citizens.

---

10 W. Kaye Lamb, "Tolmie, William Fraser," in *Dictionary of Canadian Biography*, vol. 11, University of Toronto/Université Laval, 2003–, www.biographi.ca/en/bio/tolmie_william_fraser_11E.html.

On his arrival that July day in 1843, Dr. Tolmie immediately began rallying this mixture of humanity into a viable workforce. As a result, within a year, the fort's removal to a site a half a mile inland had begun. This second site proved better suited to agriculture, was within 15 yards of Sequalitchew Creek's fresh water, and adjacent to pasturelands that stretched miles eastward to the foothills of the Cascade Range. The fort's size also more than doubled, now a 250-by-250-foot enclosure. In 1848, its warehouses, dwellings, sales shops, and other buildings specifically designed to support agriculture were surrounded by a 20-foot-high stockade.

By January 1850, Dr. Tolmie's Fort Nisqually was a large-scale, international commodities supplier. In ten short years, over 12,000 head of sheep, 10,000 head of cattle, 600 horses, and oxen had been amassed on 161,000 acres, or 252 square miles. All land between the Nisqually and Puyallup Rivers, including today's downtown Tacoma, the Puyallup Indian Reservation, Fife, Puyallup, and all towns extending south through Kapowsin and the Ohop Valley and west to Puget Sound, belonged to the HBC/PSAC. Literally thousands of horses, cattle, and sheep, tons of salted beef and salmon, mutton, wool and hides, and farm produce (butter, potatoes, peas, other vegetables, and animal fodder) were being shipped annually from its anchorage. This produce (as well as imported trade goods) made their way to trading posts east of the Cascades, the Russian America Fur Company post at Sitka, speculators in San Francisco, and markets in the Sandwich Islands (Hawai'i). Annual shipments of Nisqually wool arrived on London's docks having been carefully packed alongside thousands of cowhides, hooves, and horns. Under consideration by the HBC's management in 1850 was the profitability of lumber sales to boom town San Francisco.

Treaty of 1846

The Oregon Treaty in 1846 established the 49th parallel as an international boundary between British North America and the United States. The Columbia Department was separated into American Columbia (today's Washington, Idaho, and Oregon) and what became today's Province of British Columbia. Aside from its Puget Sound holdings, the HBC/PSAC at that time occupied lands in the fertile Cowlitz River Valley, on the north bank of the Columbia River at Fort Vancouver, and northward into the San Juan Islands. Dr. Tolmie quickly realized that all of it, his employer's businesses and his home, were now on foreign soil.

Allaying fears of exploitation by newly arriving settlers from the United States, the treaty's authors had identified the Company's right to retain "ownership and operations north of the Columbia River [and south of the boundary] until compensated for all properties surrendered, if required by the United States." Unfortunately, that $650,000 payday would not take place until 1870. In the meantime, the treaty merely implied that the Company could continue business with unfettered access to its deep water ports on Puget Sound and in the Columbia River.[11]

11 The Company's port on the Columbia was at Fort Vancouver. A good reference on the fort is Dorothy Morrison's *Outpost: John McLoughlin and the Far Northwest* (Portland: Oregon Historical Society Press, 1999). For a comprehensive sketch, see Bruce M. Watson, *Lives Lived West of the Divide: A Biographical Dictionary of Fur Traders Working West of the Rockies, 1793–1858*, 3 vols (Kelowna, BC: Centre for Social, Spatial, and Economic Justice, UBC Okanagan, 2010), 3:1052–56. Hereafter cited as Watson, *Lives Lived.*

By 1849 the relationship between the American settlers and Britons south of the new boundary deteriorated. Legal, nationalistic, and regulatory problems had been unknowingly spawned by the treaty. It also complicated the HBC/PSAC's long-standing business practices and shipping routes while fostering increasingly bad blood between the two nations. In truth, the Treaty of 1846 failed on several critical points unrecognized by its original signatories.

First, its language provided no framework for governing a mixture of American citizens, British subjects, and first peoples of the region. Second, it did not propose an all-encompassing legal system to aid in that endeavor. In *Beyond the Reservation: Indians, Settlers, and the Law in Washington Territory*, author Brad Asher acknowledged this by stating, "the resources of the national government tended to be concentrated in areas where local interests were influential enough to demand federal action or . . . triggered military responses."[12]

A third component involved the Native Americans' centuries-old systems of settling disagreements—both civil and criminal. Coast Salish law-ways were usually not acceptable to the HBC's hierarchy. Nor were the Company's corporate policies (which aligned with British common law) recognized by the settlers. Clearly, many settlers had only a layman's grasp of justice based on a legal system operating over 3,000 miles behind them. So, initially, there was no legal system, authority, or process in place. It was either the Company's judgement or first people's common laws that carried the day.

Thus, the Oregon Country's first "American judiciary" manifested itself via the circuit courts and the U.S. Army. It was a system that typically miscarried justice, and when the army turned a blind eye to the questionable legal practices of the settlers, conflicts arose. "These struggles pitted settlers against Indians, authorities against citizens, federal officials against local officials, and ultimately Indians against Indians" notes Asher. Completely ignored were the Company's grievances, all of which were legally stonewalled by an ungoverned and largely unregulated administrative bureaucracy. It was "a state of courts and parties," not an era of hands-off, laissez-faire.[13] Today, one might call it "governance by a single-minded special interest group" devoid of any adopted legal code.

This asymmetrical approach to justice, under which Tolmie struggled, was girded externally by "malice of purpose" reporting or plain old shoddy journalism. In the *Oregon Spectator* "Extra Edition" of November 4, 1846, the new treaty's approval was announced . . . without details. The following year, on March 4, 1847, that paper published its own version of the treaty, omitting any mention of the "possessory rights" awarded to the British corporations. One month later an authentic and complete version was published, only to be challenged editorially. Finally, on April 15, 1847, it was announced that the Company had a copy that matched the newspaper's authentic version. By then, the agreement was nearly a

---

12 Brad Asher, *Beyond the Reservation: Indians, Settlers, and the Law in Washington Territory, 1853–1889* (Norman: University of Oklahoma Press, 1999).

13 Stephen Skowronek, *Building a New American State: The Expansion of National Administrative Capacities, 1877–1920* (New York: Cambridge University Press, 1982).

year old and officially exchanged with London on July 17, 1847.[14] This confusing piecemeal diaspora of facts meant that few settlers knew of, or would honor, the Company's interests and rights, as detailed in its Articles III and IV. Even worse: the treaty admitted no protection to the Company, but merely preserved the status quo until the U.S. government's payment was confirmed.[15]

In his 1905 book *In the Beginning*, Clarence Bagley of Seattle noted: "This international dispute became *a personal one* between the American citizens of Old Oregon on one side, and the officers and adherents of the Hudson's Bay Company on the other. Since the wars of the revolution and of 1812 down to recent years, it was a favorite pastime of the individual and collective Yankee to 'twist the tail of the British lion,' and the early immigrants from the valley of the Mississippi to the valley of the Willamette and the shores of Puget Sound kept alive the national custom."[16] Ameliorating the vast cultural, political, racial, ideological, and historical prejudices that divided the settlers from their British neighbors proved (in many cases) insurmountable. Even so, as with any backward glance in history, one cannot simply paint all with malicious aspersions. Following are three categories of settlers that (I feel) emerged as the conflict widened.

A small but educated minority empathized with the Briton's plight, recognized the Company's possessory rights, and did what they could to defuse the two groups' highly charged encounters. Moving through this work's documents, they are easily recognized by their steady, supportive voices, clear-headed thinking, and positive attitudes in confronting the challenges.

A much larger group was guilty of woeful ignorance: they simply did not understand the basis of the struggle. Their comprehension was limited to bullet points: the treaty was signed; the boundary set; the territory was American soil; land was cheap; and the foreigners should leave. Jenny Williams, whose family squatted on PSAC lands southwest of the U.S. Army's leased lands near Steilacoom, provides us with one contemporary's view. During the International Boundary Commission's hearings in 1866, she was asked if she ever received legal title to her claim. Her truthful answer exposes this group's obliviousness to the facts:

> No, I never received [a title]. Do you know why? Because of this company of squatters. They called us squatters—a name that was really theirs. They gave up the right to this land south of the forty-ninth parallel when they signed the treaty of 1846. I want to say right here and now that I have always had my doubts that the farms hereabouts ever had been granted this company. Since we came to this county in 1853 and took out our claims we have been worried for fear we'd never own them; we've been pestered with trespasser notices; we've been forbidden to survey our claims, and because we never received title to our land we couldn't sell or transfer. If that company needs help in packing its bag and baggage, we settlers shall be glad to help them on their way out.[17]

---

14 Oregon Spectator Index Project at http://hdl.handle.net. Gerald W. Williams Collection.

15 Article III stated: "the possessory rights of the Hudson's Bay Company . . . shall be respected." Article IV agreed to arbitration to determine the value of land and other property.

16 Clarence B. Bagley, *In the Beginning: Early Days on Puget Sound* (Everett, WA: Historical Society of Seattle and King County, 1905, reprint 1980), 1.

17 Della Gould Emmons, *Nothing In Life is Free* (Minneapolis: The Northwestern Press, 1953), 305.

A third group of settlers was hot-blooded, even violent. Possessing a herculean sense of self-importance, they appeared hell-bent on disrupting the Company's operations by any means at their disposal. These were often "petty" public officials—men whose actions and policies hinged on personal vendetta, illegal financial gain (i.e., bribes/blackmail), political agenda, or a narrow, ideological bend. Legal codes? International treaties? The rule of law? To them, such declarations meant little or nothing. Excising British subjects from American soil was their unifying ambition.

Except for the first (and smallest) of the aforementioned groups, many settlers detested the Company's continued presence on "their land." As with Jenny Williams' example, many had designs on the seemingly vast, arable acreage then under Tolmie's control. Thus, by the early 1850s, a quiet little war erupted on Puget Sound. The armed threats, the movement of gun-toting men, the use of military tactics, the seizure of private property, politically opposing views, and a disregard for the rule of law made it a cold war—but a war none the less. From Tolmie's perspective, the settlers, representatives to the U.S. Congress, decorated army officers, (today's) historically celebrated public officials, and educated lawyers exhibited the most severe, even aggressive, behavior.

The first assaults blindsided the Britons. Using stealth, deception, racism, and the pretext of federal authority, the settlers struck. At first, the "foreigners" could only watch slack-jawed as events unfolded. Typically, the settlers cried wolf in the face of the most trivial infractions of new, confusing, and in some cases undisclosed customs regulations. Once, the highly polished bayonets of the U.S. Army were employed. Threats were made and actions taken, but no casualties occurred—unless you consider relations between Great Britain and the United States. Emboldened by their politicians' lies, armed settlers appropriated the Company's land, seized property and vessels, and sealed up HBC warehouses. The Company's shipping routes would be blockaded, its livestock killed or stolen, fencing plundered, and prime farmlands occupied by squatters.

In 1849, four events greatly impacted the work of Dr. Tolmie and other Company officials.

First, the Englishman Joseph T. Heath died of natural causes on March 7, 1849.[18] A "gentleman farmer," he had been brought to Puget Sound by the Company in 1844 to farm on shares for the PSAC. Eventually, he developed two fallow 1841 Red River Settler's farms (just six miles north of the fort) into one, referring to them collectively as "Steilacoom Farm."[19] Following his death, the inventory and appraisal of the site's assets fell to Tolmie and Heath's executor, an Irish squatter and member of the Oregon Territory's judiciary, Thomas M. Chambers.[20]

18 Joseph Thomas Heath (1804–1849), arrived on the Columbia and was assigned a farm at what became Fort Steilacoom, on Chambers Creek. On January 1, 1845, Heath started farming operations. Early in 1849 he died from heart problems and pneumonia. See biographical sketch in Heath, *Memoirs of Nisqually* (Fairfield, WA: Ye Galleon Press, 1979).

19 It is presumed that he named the farm after one of his best workers, Steilacoom, an Indian laborer who lived at the mouth of today's Chambers Bay with wife Lavielle, daughter Nancy, and son Streeas.

20 A good general biography of Thomas M. Chambers (1796–1876) can be found in Linda Perez, "Judge Thomas M. Chambers, Father of Western Washington Industry," *Steilacoom Historical Museum Quarterly* 12, no. 4 (1983). See also: *Told by The Pioneers; Tales of Frontier Life in Washington, Volume 1*

The appraisal was briefly interrupted by a second event, the violent May 1, 1849, skirmish at Fort Nisqually's small northern gate.[21] Initiated by visiting Snoqualmie Indians, the clash has historically been interpreted as either an attempt to murder all whites and loot the fort or the settling of a personal grudge between two Salish tribal headmen. In either case, the ensuing melee inflicted half a dozen casualties, including a settler named Leander C. Wallace who was shot and killed in the crossfire after ignoring calls to get inside the palisades.

This violence prompted a third event: the arrival of the United States Army on lower Puget Sound that August. Officers and soldiers of Company M, 1st Artillery Regiment, retrofitted Heath's farm site for military use—legitimately leasing the land from the Company for $50 a month.[22] Dr. Tolmie enjoyed a cooperative relationship with the army's officers, principally Captain Bennett H. Hill[23] (founding commander), Dr. John Haden[24] (surgeon), and 2nd Lieutenant John Dement[25] (liaison officer). By December 1849, the army occupied the eastern portion of Heath's former lodgings referring to it alternately as either Fort Steilacoom or Steilacoom Barracks.[26]

As the army's compound took shape, Heath's crops were harvested and his livestock auctioned off at a £300 profit. Through it all, Tolmie and Judge Chambers maintained a professional rapport, but one must concede that no love was lost between them. With the estate's matters nearly concluded, Tolmie discovered Chambers' son staking off (for himself) the westernmost portions of Heath's former lands. As the standard "notice of trespass" was delivered, Judge Chambers reportedly placed a loaded firearm on the newly constructed fence rail; a hint none too subtle. He then threw down a thinly veiled legal gauntlet regarding the conclusion of the estate's business. Tolmie viewed it as a stalling tactic; one that provided Chambers' son time to fence in several more acres.

The California Gold Rush was the fourth event. During 1848–1849, "gold fever" had decimated the HBC/PSAC's labor force, including those employed in

---

([Olympia, Washington]: 1937), 147. Hereafter cited as *Told by The Pioneers*.

21 Edward Huggins, "Reminiscences of Puget Sound," *Portland Oregonian*, September 30, 1900.

22 The United States Army's Company M, 1st Artillery, arrived at Puget Sound on August 23, 1849. Company M remained at Fort Steilacoom Barracks for the rest of its tour in the territory. In February 1853 Captain Hill turned over Fort Steilacoom to the 4th Infantry and returned to Vancouver. George Dickey, "Company M. 1st Artillery in Oregon Territory 1849–53." Np. Nd.

23 Bennett Hoskin Hill was the founding officer of Fort Steilacoom. For a biography see www.historicfortsteilacoom.org/bennett-h.-hill.html.

24 John Miller Haden (1825–1892) was born in Mississippi (Monroe County), graduated from the Medical College of Louisiana in 1847, and joined the U.S. Army as an assistant surgeon in December of that same year. Attached to Company M, 1st Artillery, Dr. Haden's name appeared in the 1850 Census of Lewis County, Oregon Territory, indicating that he was now serving at Fort Steilacoom Barracks. While there he conducted surgeries and reported on diseases and injuries among the soldiers in the Pacific Northwest. At that time he was single and 25 years old. Dr. Haden returned to the states by 1856, and resigned from the U.S. Army at the outbreak of the Civil War. He served as surgeon for the Confederate Army from 1861 to the end of the war. He died in October 1892 at the age of 67 in Philadelphia, Pennsylvania. freepages.genealogy.rootsweb.ancestry.com/~katy/haden/b3962.html.

25 2nd Lieutenant John Dement (1823–c. 1865) of Company M, First Artillery, was born in Washington, D.C., in 1823. He was a career soldier in the United States Army, and 27 years old when posted at Steilacoom Barracks/Fort Steilacoom. In his time there, he acted as quartermaster.

26 "Steilacoom Barracks" is used in this work as the nineteenth century use of the term "fort" often infers the presence of a stockade or otherwise secured enclosure—which never existed at this U.S. Army post.

its maritime service. Many deserted, and though some prospered in the mines, rumors persisted that there had been deaths, and murder.

In mid-October 1849, the Company's "Board of Management" on the Pacific Northwest coast received word from London "that the *Norman Morison*[27] [skippered by Captain David Wishart[28]] with 65 passengers for Fort Victoria sails from Gravesend tomorrow morning [October 20th, 1849]. Mr. [Sebastian] Helmcken,[29] the only cabin passenger, acts as surgeon to the ship on the voyage out, and is to be permanently attached to the establishment at Fort Victoria. The passengers in the steerage are Mr. [William] Parsons,[30] the miller, and his wife; Mr. [Alexander McFarlane] Macfarland,[31] [who is] Capt[ai]n [Walter Colquhoun] Grant's[32] schoolmaster; and a young man of the name of [Edward] Huggins,[33] who has taken a grant of 20 acres of land [on Vancouver Island]. Between decks there are sixty passengers. . . ."[34] Huggins, then just 18 years old, would become Dr. Tolmie's right hand man at Nisqually. No doubt the doctor was relieved to hear that help was on the way.

Elevated to the rank of chief factor in 1855, Tolmie played the role of peacemaker during the Puget Sound Indian War, and in 1859, removed his family permanently to Cloverdale Farm on Vancouver Island. There, he would live out his days, though continuing as an active member of the HBC's Western

---

27 *Norman Morison*, HBC barque. See Watson, *Lives Lived*, 3:1121–22.

28 David Durham Wishart. See Watson, *Lives Lived*, 3:987.

29 John Sebastian Helmcken. See Watson, *Lives Lived*, 2:451.

30 William Parsons came out on the *Norman Morison*, and took over the management of the HBC sawmill at Colwood, one of four large farms established by the Hudson's Bay Company in the 1850s to supply Fort Victoria's personnel with foodstuffs and building material.

31 Alexander McFarlane never made it to Vancouver Island. After his vessel, the *Norman Morison*, got far out to sea, fellow passenger John Sebastian Helmcken (HBC physician), noted that "this very quiet, worthy old Highlander" died at sea on January 21, 1850. The vessel had experienced a rough trip for all and especially so for schoolmaster McFarlane, who reportedly died of cancer. "When dying, he gave me his fishing rod, with which he had hoped to catch salmon in the rivers of Sooke" noted Helmcken. Jim Hume, "Bats Blessed, But Broom Has Him On a Sticky Wicket: Grant's Legacy of Scotland's Prolific Shrub Cursed to this Day By Farmers, Gardeners," *Times Colonist*, July 27, 2008 at www.pressreader.com/canada/times-colonist/20080727/282071977678252.

32 Walter Colquhoun Grant (1822–1861) was a retired British Army officer from Scotland who, in 1849, was the first colonist to buy 200 acres of land from the HBC at Sooke Harbor (25 miles west of Fort Victoria). Though somewhat lacking in ability, he nevertheless became the HBC's first surveyor on the island, but resigned, lured away by California's gold fields. It is rumored that he was also responsible for bringing Scotch broom to the Pacific Northwest.

33 Edward Huggins (1832–1907) grew up in London and graduated from Queen Elizabeth Grammar School. His employment in a London brokerage office eventually led him to the Fenchurch Street storefront of the HBC—just a few blocks away. After switching employers, Huggins's voyage to North America began in 1849. Douglas, all too aware of Dr. Tolmie's personnel shortages, sent Huggins, who began as an 18-year-old apprentice-clerk working in Fort Nisqually's Indian trade shop. He became an American citizen and homesteaded on the fort site after 1870. For more see Watson, *Lives Lived*, 2:471.

34 Archibald Barclay to HBC Board of Management, October 19, 1849, HBCA London Correspondence Outwards, A. 6/28, fo. 67. In another letter from Barclay to Douglas, dated London, December 17, 1849, Edward Huggins is mentioned again as having been granted land. "You have been informed of your appointment as Agent of the Hudson's Bay Company for the sale of lands &c in Vancouver's Island. Hitherto the only sub-grants made are 100 acres to Captain Grant, and 20 acres to Mr. Huggins, to be selected by them from any land not already appropriated." HBCA, 6/28. fo. 90d. According to the Vancouver Island land sales (BCARS C/AA/30. 7/2), Huggins purchased lots 768, 769, 770, and 771 on October 27, 1858, for £ 41/13/4. This information provided courtesy of Bruce M. Watson.

Department Board of Management. Still championing the "lost causes" spoken of earlier, he often returned to Fort Nisqually, now much-diminished, to see old friends and relatives.

The PSAC ceased to exist as a corporate entity in the early 1930s, when its real estate holdings were acquired by a land developer in Victoria, and its paper value liquidated on London's stock market. The HBC exists as a Canadian department store today, having withdrawn northward in 1870 after the U.S. Government paid for all of the Company's possessions.

Tolmie biographer Walter Stuart summed up the doctor's life this way: "Within the span of half a century, Dr. Tolmie had seen civilization on the Northwest Coast develop from a few isolated trading posts in the primordial wilderness to a complex community of closely-linked towns and villages. In that growth he had been both an interested by-stander and a willing worker. Although a commissioned officer in two organizations whose best interests were served by a consistent denial of the territory to independent [American] settlers, he had grown with the new rapidly forming society to become, at his retirement, an integral part of that society."[35] He passed away in 1886 at the age of 74 years old.

With a few exceptions (the fort's *Journal of Occurrences* as one example), Fort Nisqually's documents have never been presented en masse as they are here. The amateur historian *and* professional scholar will find a gold mine of material in this work. Our hope (and the reason behind this publication) is for the readers to draw their own conclusions and/or formulate new arguments using its contents.

It is my fervent hope that you will enjoy the consistently interesting, highly nuanced, and occasionally contentious documents contained herein. Steve Anderson's work provides a rare glimpse into Washington's State's nineteenth century British and American history. It opens in early 1850 as Company flagged vessels and property are seized and placed under the American settlers' lock and key. But not for long.

With that bit of foreshadowing, I remain, Your Most Obedient Servant,

Jerry V. Ramsey, PhD
Tacoma, Washington

---

35 Stuart, "Some Aspects of the Life of Tolmie," 214–15.

CHAPTER ONE

January 1st, 1850–May 31st, 1850

"Having lately got married to Jane, eldest daughter of C.F. Work, I have ceased thinking of revisiting the Land o' Cakes [Scotland] and look forward to ending my days as a settler on Vancouver's Island."
—William Tolmie to Archibald Barclay, March 2, 1850

In the first days of 1850, Doctor Tolmie's itinerary was teeming with matrimonial plans. Between January 19 and February 26, he was on Vancouver Island getting married to Jane Work,[1] the eldest daughter of Chief Trader John Work and Josette Legace, a mixed-heritage woman of the Spokane tribe.[2] Chief Trader John Tod[3] was in charge of the fort during Tolmie's absence. By March, the doctor had requested a promotion and, as noted in the passage above, announced his desire to finish out his days as a settler on Vancouver Island.

That March, important individuals arrived at Nisqually. HBC Governor Eden Colvile[4] and Vancouver Island's Governor Richard Blanchard[5] stepped ashore, having been carried south by the H.M.S. Steamer *Driver*. In April, the *Norman Morison*[6] finally arrived at Victoria, its hold containing several men who would help strengthen Tolmie's much-depleted work force.

The most alarming news would be customs agents' seizure of the HBC's schooner *Cadboro*.[7] Right after that, they did the same with Captain Richard

1 Jane Work Tolmie (1827–1880).

2 For Work see Watson, *Lives Lived*, 3:989–90. Also see William R. Sampson, "Work, John," in *Dictionary of Canadian Biography, vol. 9*, University of Toronto/Universite Laval, 2003–, www.biographi.ca/en/bio/work_john_9E.html.

3 For Tod see Watson, *Lives Lived*, 3:929–30.

4 For Colvile see Watson, *Lives Lived*, 1:280.

5 Blanchard [var. Blanshard] was appointed Governor of Vancouver Island in 1849. He was not respected nor liked by many HBC officials. For more see en.wikipedia.org/wiki/Richard_Blanshard.

6 *Norman Morrison*, HBC barque. See Watson, *Lives Lived*, 3:1121–22.

7 See Watson, *Lives Lived*, 3:1100–1101.

Henderwell's[8] floating warehouse, the bottom ship *Albion*.[9] Having just arrived at Nisqually aboard the soon to be seized *Cadboro*, apprentice clerk Edward Huggins vividly recalled that the next morning "we were surprised at the appearance of Captain [James] Sangster, who informed [us] . . . that a detachment of United States troops, commanded by Lieutenant [John] Dement, had arrived in a boat, and formally seized the schooner for violating the revenue law, and had also seized the goods in the [beachfront] store and placed them in charge of a non-commissioned officer and a few men. The charge was smuggling goods into the United States, and landing passengers before entering at a custom-house."[10]

A month prior to these seizures, Tolmie had learned of the mass exodus of soldiers from the army's Vancouver Barracks to California's gold fields. Next, he was informed that two of Steilacoom Barracks' soldiers had previously stowed away on the *Cadboro*, revealing their presence only as anchors were dropped in Victoria's inner harbor. Considered a petty incident by Company officials, the deserters' actions inadvertently put Tolmie and his superiors on a collision course with not only the U.S. Army, but also with territorial officials in Oregon City. When the Company could legally do nothing about the desertions, the settlers misinterpreted its inaction as collusion.[11] At first, a rumor was leaked that "the Cadboro . . . will be seized for landing British Goods in the Am[erican] Territory without paying duties." As revealed in this chapter's letters, the *Cadboro*'s role in the deserters' escape (and eventual seizure by customs officials) had become inexorably tied into one giant knot of complicity.

Yet, from Puget Sound Customs Inspector Eben May Dorr's[12] perspective, the seizures had effectively cut off several foreign (and illegal) smuggling rings (those of Captains Henderwell and Sangster). Company officials should have anticipated this eventuality according to historian and retired customs agent Harvey Steele. He noted that the " . . . Company had watched with concern the aggressive actions

8 At anchor on northeastern tip of the Olympic Peninsula in what is now Jefferson County, the crew of Captain Henderwell's [var: Hinderwell, Henderson] *Albion* was busily loading giant spars from densely timbered forests that pressed the shoreline. Within eight days, his ship was similarly boarded, seized, sailed to Port Steilacoom, anchored next to the *Cadboro*, and its crew sent ashore with all their personal belongings. With no means to return home to England, many set off to California's gold fields. As for the *Cadboro*, Edward Huggins remembered: "After Captains Brotchie and Hinderwell were so summarily dismissed from [the *Albion*] they came up to Fort Nisqually, where Hinderwell remained a few weeks to watch the proceedings of the custom house authorities. He then obtained funds from the Company to take him home to England. Captain Brotchie remained with us for some time, and I shared my room with him, for in these days, our accommodations were quite limited." See Huggins, Edward, "The Seizure, Condemnation and Sale of the British Ship *Albion*, by the Puget Sound Customs," *Portland Oregonian*, October 14, 1900.

9 The *Albion* was owned by John Lidgett & Company, London. Principal cargo was logs and spars. After seizure and auction to an Olympia concern, it was renamed American bottom ship *Elizabeth*, loaded with spars, sailed to San Francisco, and sunk as part of a new jetty.

10 Edward Huggins, "The Seizure of the Hudson's Bay Company Schooner *Cadboro*," *Portland Oregonian*, October 28, 1900.

11 As explained in the letters, this was now a matter for the civil courts to handle, not the Company's.

12 A native New Yorker born in 1822, Dorr (1822–1902) was Puget Sound's first officially appointed customs inspector. He would prove to be a worthy adversary to Dr. Tolmie and a constant thorn in the side of the HBC/PSAC.

of the first Customs Collector in the Pacific Northwest, John Adair,[13] who was appointed to the Astoria post in 1848 and began operations in 1849. The HBC's London officials, relying on the treaty of 15 June 1846, were confident that their navigation rights to the Columbia River and Puget Sound were legally protected. [The seizures] had caused them to temper their optimism."[14] Even so, no evidence suggests that HBC officials in Oregon had ever been apprised of, much less provided a copy of, the new customs regulations. And, with the regular traffic of Company goods and personnel now linked to the charge of smuggling, Tolmie and his superiors realized that their operations were vulnerable to attack by any customs official, men with guns who could interpret the treaty's language in whatever manner they pleased, or political agenda they backed.

Throughout the spring and early summer, these "extraordinary proceedings" dominated Tolmie's correspondence and attentions, especially his travel. Face-to-face consultations with his immediate superiors became a necessity.

North on Vancouver Island at Fort Victoria lived Chief Factor James Douglas.[15] He had joined the fur trade in 1819 and who was now Tolmie's supervisor in all matters relative to the PSAC's farming operation in Oregon, and later, Washington Territories. Anticipating the U.S. Government's buyout of his employer's properties, Douglas had moved the HBC/PSAC's primary headquarters north of the new boundary line to Fort Victoria in May 1849—taking with him his family and five wagons; one loaded with California gold.[16] Tolmie and Douglas met, confirmed by the latter's letter to the HBC's London office on May 20, 1850, when he noted that "Chief Trader Tolmie arrived here lately; but could give no further intelligence in regard to this painful subject [of the seizures] . . . We drew up the two Protests against these proceedings, as per copies herewith, which Mr. Tolmie was to deliver immediately on his return to Nisqually."[17]

13 "General" John Adair Jr. (1808–1888) was born near Harodsburg, Kentucky, the youngest of eleven children of Governor John Adair Sr. and Catherine Palmer Adair. He was educated at Danville College in Kentucky, West Point, and Harvard, after which he studied law for two years under his brother-in-law, Judge Thomas Monroe, in Frankfort, Kentucky. In 1848 President Polk appointed Adair Collector of United States Customs—the first such position on the Pacific Coast—for the port of Astoria, Oregon Territory. For more see Harvey Steele's *Hyas Tyee: The United States Customs Service in Oregon, 1848–1889* (Washington, D.C.: Department of the Treasury United States Custom Service, Pacific Region, 1990), 4.

14 Harvey Steele, "Fort Nisqually Besieged," *Occurrences: The Journal of Activities of Fort Nisqually Historic Site* 12 (1994), (Metropolitan Park District of Tacoma, Washington), 2:8–13.

15 South America-born Douglas apprenticed to the Northwest Company in 1819, continuing with the HBC after the two companies' 1821 amalgamation. Throughout the 1830s and 1840s he served under Chief Factor John McLoughlin at Fort Vancouver—rising to the elevated rank of chief factor in the mid-1840s. Following McLoughlin's retirement in 1846, Douglas became the principal administrator of the Company's business on the Pacific Coast. He also served as principal liaison to the British Government and later became the "Governor of the Colony of Vancouver Island." For more see Watson, *Lives Lived*, 1:340–41.

16 Douglas arrived at Nisqually on Friday, May 25, 1849, with that wagon. George Dickey, ed., *The Journal of Occurrences at Fort Nisqually: commencing May 30, 1833; ending September 27, 1859* [Tacoma, WA?]: Fort Nisqually Association, [1988]. Hereafter cited as Dickey, ed., *Nisqually Journal.*

17 James Douglas to Archibald Barclay, May 20, 1850, Hartwell Bowsfield, ed., Fort Victoria Letters: 1846–1851 (Manitoba: Hudson's Bay Company Records Society, 1979), 96–97. Hereafter cited as Bowsfield, ed., Victoria Letters.

South on the Columbia River at Fort Vancouver lived Chief Factor Peter Skene Ogden.[18] Ogden had made the fur trade his life's work since 1817 and was now Tolmie's supervisor in that aspect of Fort Nisqually's business. Nearing retirement, the Quebec-born chief factor was answerable only to Douglas but often apprised Tolmie of facts and rumors emanating from Oregon City and other American settlements along the lower Columbia River. However, written exchanges between the two typically involved the fur trade.

Dr. Tolmie did not limit his correspondence to immediate superiors. Occasionally, he went above their heads and communicated directly with Archibald Barclay, secretary to the HBC's governors in London.[19] Such correspondence continued through the first half of 1850 while the *Cadboro* and the Company's beach front warehouse at Nisqually remained under the customs house's seals.

Occasionally, Tolmie corresponded with fellow colleagues and friends. This included the English Clerk George Roberts[20] who was then operations manager of the 11-year-old "Cowlitz Farm" (near present day Toledo, Washington). Roberts's letters dealt with many topics: the hit and miss mail service of the day, the passage of people along the portage, personal news, details of the Willamette River flood, married life, whispered gossip, shop talk, market rates of commodities, the comings and goings of shared acquaintances, and current events, including desertions.

Archibald McKinley[21] is another of Tolmie's regular correspondents. Working at the HBC's store in Oregon City, McKinley often discussed matters of Company business in that quarter and apprised Tolmie of the increasingly volatile markets in San Francisco.

When Douglas and Tolmie finally arrived back at Fort Nisqually in late May, they found Captains Henderwell and William Brotchie of the *Albion* in residence, their seized vessel still anchored next to James Sangster's *Cadboro* at the mouth of today's Chambers Bay. Hoping to expedite the *Cadboro*'s release, Douglas continued southward on a "grand tour" to Vancouver and other points. He also sought the legal opinion of the Company's attorney and to meet with customs officials. By the end of May, Dr. Tolmie administered to the washing and shearing of thousands of sheep. His sheep processing team was comprised of 30–40 men, women, and children; white, metis, and Indian, all engaged in the annual commotion of raised voices, bleets, and sweat.

Here then are Tolmie's letters from a majority of the last half of Outfit 1850.

---

18 Quebec-born Ogden joined the Northwest Company in 1817, but his future was in question when his employer merged with the HBC in 1821. Retained by the latter fur company, his activities during the 1820s, '30s, and '40s ranged from the desolate "Snake Country" of the Great Basin to the chilly Northwest Coast. For more see Watson, *Lives Lived*, 2:733–34.

19 For a complete biographical sketch of HBC Secretary Barclay's (1806–1855) involvement, see www.gov.mb.ca/chc/archives/hbca/biographical/b/barclay_archibaldus.pdf.

20 Born in Suffolk, England, George Barber Roberts had attended the prestigious Greenwich Royal Naval School and was thereafter assigned a seven-year apprenticeship to the HBC. Working at Fort Vancouver on the Columbia River in the 1830s, Roberts first labored in the warehouses and then was appointed as school master. He eventually returned to England in 1843 where he got married and returned to Fort Vancouver in 1844. The couple resided at Cowlitz Farm by 1850. For more see Watson, *Lives Lived*, 2:821.

21 For McKinley see Watson, *Lives Lived*, 2:663.

Document 1:01: A letter from Thomas M. Chambers, Steilacoom, to William F. Tolmie, Nisqually, January 15, 1850.[22]

Dear Sir,

In answer to your note of the 13th Inst[ant], I have the honour to inform you that I am not prepared to close the Accounts of the farm of Steilacoom lately in occupation of Mr. Jos[eph] Tho[ma]s Heath—deceased. I might detail at length the reasons that influence me in thus declining further proceedings in the business in question, but this will suffice.

The demise of Mr. Heath having taken place after the passage of the law of Congress of the United States of America extending the jurisdiction of the same over this territory; consequently all matters of administration of the Estates of deceased persons as well as decent and distribution of property will be made according to the laws of the Country. It will not be controverted that the Administration of the Estates of all persons belongs to the Country in which the demise of the deceased took place. And that Administration must be conducted by some person appointed by a Court having probate powers conferred on it by the Law-making powers of the Country.

I am well satisfied that no Administrative power[s] have been conferred on you by the same so as to give authority to the assumption of the powers and duties of an Administrator in the premises. That the business conducted with the Estate of the late Mr. Heath deceased—as far as conducted—is Extra Judicial and without Authority of law, I shall take the earliest opportunity that presents itself to place in the possession of the proper Court all papers and copies of all papers now in my possession relative to the Estate of the late Mr. Heath as well as what information I possess on the subject and pray said Court for the Appointment of a proper Administrator for said Estate. In Answer to your [inquiry?], I would say that I decline making a charge for assisting in valuing the property on the farm at Steilacoom until I can present the same to the proper Court for Allowance.

[Yours Very Truly, &c., &c., Signed Thomas M. Chambers]

Document 1.02: A report of transactions between Thomas M. Chambers and William F. Tolmie, relative to the settlement of the late Joseph T. Heath affairs with the Puget's Sound Agricultural Company, Fort Nisqually, January 18, 1850.

On the 10th February 1849, the late Mr. J[oseph Thomas] Heath, being then in a very low state of health, removed from his residence at Steilacoom to Fort Nisqually in order to be nearer to his medical adviser and to have the advantage of being attended upon by more careful and intelligent persons than he could have obtained at home.

On the 18th Feby [18]49, finding himself getting worse, the deceased Mr. Heath made his will, extracts from which bearing on the matters in questions are herewith

22 William Fraser Tolmie Papers, University of Washington Libraries Special Collections, Seattle, Accession 4577, Box 1 Folder 1. Hereafter cited as UW Library, Tolmie Papers Acc. 4577-001.

forwarded. In said Will, the deceased appointed Mr. T[homas] M. Chambers as his representative to see to the valuation of the Buildings, Live Stock, &c., &c., on the Farm at Steilacoom which the deceased had occupied, in accordance with the fifth article of an Agreement made by the deceased with the Agents of the Puget's Sound Agricultural Company in London, wherein provision was made for the contingency of Mr. Heath's demise. Mr. Chambers, arriving at Ft Nisqually on the 19th February, agreed to undertake the office assigned to him in said Will.

Subsequently to the 18th February, the late Mr. Heath experienced a slight amendment in health and at times entertained faint hopes of partial recovery. When speaking of his temporal affairs he always expressed a wish that operations should be closed on the Steilacoom farm and the business wound up, as speedily as possible in order to avoid unnecessary expense.

Immediately after Mr. Heath's decease which took place on the 7th March [18]49, I had an Inventory taken of the agricultural implements and other moveables at Steilacoom and had [the] deceased's private effects carefully collected and sent to [Fort] Vancouver for sale, as directed in his Will. I also placed a trustworthy person in the employ of the Company as a resident at Steilacoom to see to the safety of the premises.

In June and July [18]49, Mr. Chambers and myself were engaged at different dates in valuing the Buildings, Fence poles, Live Stock &c., on the Farm at Steilacoom. In only one instance had we occasion to refer a disputed point to a third person and his decision was in favor of Mr. Chambers in the case submitted.

As soon as the Wheat was thrashed out and delivered to the Company the working Indians were paid off and the expense of looking after the premises and fields [livestock, and] crop at Steilacoom thereafter was defrayed by the Company, in whose possession the farm was considered to be.

Towards the end of July, by which period it was deemed safe to spean the lambs, the sheep belonging to Steilacoom farm were valued, and transferred to the Coy.

On the 25th July, the implements of husbandry, and a lot of miscellaneous articles belonging to Steilacoom farm were sold here by public auction, Mr. Chambers officiating as Auctioneer. I was inclined to have offered part of the Live Stock for sale by auction likewise but deferred in this matter to Mr. C[hambers] who thought that in the existing state of the country it would be more advantageous to the heirs of the deceased to have the whole of the Livestock transferred at a fair valuation to the Puget's Sound Company.

On the 27th July, Mr. Chambers and myself, after fixing the value of the Wheat, Pease, and potatoes transferred to the Coy since the 7th March, added up the amounts of the different valuations, he having a statement priced in dollars and cents and I using one valued in pounds, shillings, and pence. Mr. Chambers was on the same day furnished, by his own request, with a copy of the valuations in Dollars and Cents, the original remaining in my possession.

The business of winding up the late Mr. Heath's affairs was thus on the 27th July [18]49 brought very nearly to a close, there being only yet to ascertain whether certain articles sold at the public auction had, when supplied from the HBC stores at Vancouver, been charged against deceased Farm or private Account, for which purpose a detailed account of supplied to the Farm from the commencement had to be obtained from Vancouver and for which I wrote early in August.

Mr. Chambers on the 27th July and some previous occasions contended that the profits realized by the Farm at Steilacoom ought not to be equally divided between the heirs of the late Mr. Heath and the Puget's Sound Company, but should belong entirely to the former, and he proposed taking the opinion on the matter of the first eligible person, conversant with business, who might visit Nisqually, saying that his desire was to be set right if in error. I, on the other hand, invariably maintained that the agreement and correspondence between the parties and the late Mr. Heath's receipt for the Live Stock delivered to him in 1845—wherein he acknowledged receiving said Livestock on the terms of his agreement with the P[uget] S[ound] C[ompany]—as well as the tenor of his last Will and Testament, all made it perfectly clear to me that an equal division should take place. I, moreover, stated that altho' not conceiving myself empowered to submit such a question to arbitration, I was perfectly willing to exhibit the documents bearing upon it, and to explain my own views thereupon, to any gentleman Mr. Chambers might select.

In August, J[essie] Quinn Thornton,[23] Esquire of Oregon City, late Supreme Judge of Oregon Territory, coming to Nisqually in his capacity of Indian Agent, Mr. Chambers proposed our explaining each his views and showing the documents to that gentleman, by whose decision Mr. Chambers professed himself willing to abide. This was accordingly done, Mr. Walter Ross, Clerk,[24] in the HB Co's [Hudson's Bay Company's] employ being present, when Judge Thornton, after a careful investigation of the matter, by reference to the documents, and verbal enquiry,[25] declared it as his opinion, that the profits of the farm at Steilacoom should be equally divided betwixt the heirs of the late Mr. Heath, and the Puget's Sound Co agreeably to the stipulations of the agreement entered into between the late Mr. H[eath] and the agents of the said Comp[an]y in London.

On receiving in December from Vancouver the detailed account of supplies to Steilacoom Farm, I wrote Mr. C[hambers] on the 20th of that month that I was now ready to close the accounts of the Farm, and hope he could make it convenient to be here in time to admit of my forwarding a statement to England by the first of January Mail from Steilacoom Barracks. Mr. C[hambers] replied that, health & weather permitting he would be here about the 1st January [1850]. He came on the 10th and on my introducing the subject of the Farm Account, he postponed doing anything 'till his return from Steilacoom, which happened on the 13th. He then, when addressed on the subject, informed me that he had ascertained when the Court sat at Steilacoom for the trial of the Indian Murderers on the 1st October [18]49, that he had acted illegally in having officiated as the late Mr. Heath's representative, that the whole would have to be done over again, and the proceedings customary in the United States in such cases adopted as soon as courts came to be

23 Thornton (1810–1888) was an influential settler involved in Oregon Territory's early political, legal, and educational spheres. As the 5th Supreme Court Judge of the Provisional Government of Oregon, Thornton brought petitions to the U.S. Congress to get Oregon Territory established. He also served in the Oregon Legislature and wrote the state's motto. He was a staunch opponent to the HBC/PSAC's existence on U.S. soil and did everything in his power to oust the Company and negate their rights as established in the Treaty of 1846. For more see en.wikipedia.org/wiki/Jesse_Quinn_Thornton.

24 For Ross see Watson, *Lives Lived*, 2:837.

25 The word "enquiry" is the 19th century equivalent to "inquiry," and is used throughout the letters as such.

held in this country.

Surprised at the course adopted by Mr. Chambers and at his having so long concealed his scruples from me altho, since the 1st October [18]49 we had several times met, I resolved to make out a report of the Steilacoom Farm Transactions from the commencement and to have advice as to my future proceedings so in order to give Mr. C[hambers] an opportunity of stating his own case. I requested his reasons in writing for refusing to act, but these he declined giving on paper being, as he said, unwilling to commit himself, and added that he would communicate his reasons by letter to Mr. T. W[illiam] Heath,[26] brother to the deceased, and his executor in England. Mr. [John] Tod, Mr. W[alter] Ross, and a Mr. [Isaac N.] Ebey[27] were present during my conversation with Mr. Chambers.

On the following morning, January 14th, I handed Mr. C[hambers] a note, wherein he was requested to subscribe with me the valuation of the Steilacoom Farm property we had jointly made, as well as the account of sales by public Auction, at which he himself had officiated as Auctioneer. Likewise, I suggested in said note that Mr. C[hambers] should look over the accounts to satisfy himself that all was correct, and concluded by asking him to present his [bill] for having acted as Valuator, &c., &c. Mr. C[hambers] pocketed the note without perusal saying he would read it after reaching home, and reply when he should return to this quarter after the rivers became passable for horses.

It can easily be shown that any attempt to disturb the arrangements already made of the Steilacoom Farm affairs would lead to inextricable confusion for the buildings were rented in September last to the United States Government, for the use of the military, and have since been greatly altered, and improved. The Sheep have been assorted and distributed amongst the Company's flocks, while of the horses and Cattle, some have since died, and others have been sold and variously disposed of. The only person, moreover, who knew all the Steilacoom Farm Cattle as distinguished from those belonging to the Co and who pointed them out when the valuation was made has since left the country.

It is but just to state that in doing his part in the valuations last summer, Mr. Chambers showed a very praiseworthy desire to promote as far as possible the interests of the deceased, Mr. Heath's heirs, and in refusing to proceed further in the business, as he did on the 13th Inst, he may have been actuated by the purest motives. Nevertheless, it ought not to be overlooked on the other hand that Mr. C[hambers] has on several occasions shown himself immically [negatively] disposed towards the Puget's Sound Company and he has since last September been occasionally improving at first for his son, and latterly for himself, a tract on Steilacoom prairie

26 For Heath see Watson, *Lives Lived*, 2:450.

27 Ebey (1818–1857) was born in Columbus, Ohio, and during childhood his family moved to Missouri. There, Ebey was trained in the law. At age 25, he married Rebecca Davis and they later had two sons. Temporarily leaving his family, Ebey came to the Northwest in 1848 and two years later took a donation claim on the west side of Whidbey Island, one mile south of Penn's Cove. He was the first attorney on Puget Sound, and later became Prosecuting Attorney and Collector of Customs. Ebey was murdered by Northern Indians in 1857. Gary Fuller Reese, ed. *Nothing Worthy of Note Transpired Today: The Northwest Journal of August Kautz* (Tacoma, WA: Tacoma Public Library, 1978), 516. See also Edward Huggins, *Reminiscences of Puget Sound*, ed. Gary Fuller Reese (Tacoma, WA: Tacoma Public Library, 1984), 340–50. For more information see en.wikipedia.org/wiki/Isaac_N._Ebey.

and on the lands claimed by the Puget's Sound Co under the Treaty stipulations which though latterly forming a part of the sheep walk of Steilacoom Farm, was formerly occupied by a farmer who held under the P[uget] S[ound] Co by a nearly similar agreement to that made with the late Mr. J[oseph Thomas] Heath, and Mr. C[hambers], for the temporary security of said claim against being rejumped, has newly roofed the abandoned dwelling house still standing upon it. The land tha[t is] being improved by Mr. Chambers closely adjoins the Steilacoom Farm, and it is not improbable that his south boundary line may intersect one of the enclosures.

As I have stated, nothing in the foregoing pages but what can be fully substantiated and as I forwarded more than two month ago a copy of the valuations to the Agents of the P[uget] S[ound] Co in London, and gave them, as well as the relatives of the late Mr. Heath, to understand that the business would very soon be wound up and the accounts forwarded. I desire now a legal opinion as to whether, notwithstanding Mr. C[hambers] withdrawal, I would not be justified in making good that promise, and closing the accounts; first of all submitting them to the inspection of two competent persons who should examine, and certify to their correctness. Hereafter likewise, when county Courts may be held in Lewis Co[unty], I could, if required, submit to the proper authorities all the documents[28] bearing upon the settlement of the late Mr. Heath's affairs. Neither at the time of his death nor subsequently have there been officers enough in the County to constitute a Court.

[Signed] William Fraser Tolmie, Agent, Puget's Sound Agricul Co

Document 1.03: A letter from George B. Roberts, Cowlitz Farm, to William F. Tolmie, Nisqually, January 15, 1850.[29]

Sir,

I duly received your letter & ac[counts] sent by Dr. [John] Hayden, tho' we had not the pleasure of seeing the doc. You must have been surprised at not hearing from me by Corporal Handy,[30] & I must at once apologize for the seeming neglect. The Brave Corporal in truth, from the time he left this until his return here, was scarcely in his wits from drink & it was only upon his arriving here that he apparently came to fully understand his position, & was determined to push on instantly, so I could not get him to wait for a letter.

This being the dead season of the year, & having some little business at Oregon City, I undertook the trip there where I found myself in the holidays & amidst the greatest kinds of merry-making. I found all well & jovial notwithstanding the losses by [the Willamette River] flood. There were a number of kind enqui-

28 Here is a list of documents forwarded with this letter that bear on this report but that are not included here: 1) Extracts from the will of late Joseph T. Heath; 2) Copy of receipt from Joseph T. Heath for livestock delivered to him on the terms of his agreement with Puget's Sound Agricultural Company, October 27, 1845; 3) Correspondence between Joseph T. Heath & Archibald Barclay Esquires, August & September 1843; 4) Agreement of Joseph T. Heath with agents of the Puget's Sound Agricultural Company, London, September 21, 1843.

29 UW Library, Tolmie Papers Acc. 4577-001, Box #2, Folder #1.

30 No information was found regarding this soldier.

ries for Mr. Tolmie. Judge [Jesse Quinn] Thornton,[31] with his compliments, sent you a few more [news]papers which shall be sent you soon. Had I premeditated going to O[regon] City I should have offered my services to have done anything there for you. Dr. [John] McLoughlin[32] suffered but little loss from the high water. Friend Daniel Harvey[33] was looking well & busying about the Grist Mill. It contained 12,000 bus[hels of] wheat at the time of the flood, which fortunately escaped unwetted. The Company's [Oregon City] store, purchased last summer by [Archibald] McKinlay,[34] was swept away. The one they now occupy, as well as the house belonging to the Old Gentleman [McLoughlin], & in seeing that the lease is about to expire, &c., will not be renewed.

Now for a little news which by the way may be all stale to you.

[Captain Charles] Humphreys[35] was in California with a ship of his own, the Volunteer,[36] [and he has apparently gone] stark mad, running about without Shoes or Hat on & Mrs. H[umphreys] was onboard.

Two of the murdering Taloquist & another of the Kayouse [Cayuse of the Whitman Massacre] were lately shot by their own people.

[Narcisse] Raymond[37] was at the Falls [Dalles] & thought nearly all would have been cut off 'ere spring.

Mr. Richard Grant[38] was at death's door with the gout.

Rob[er]t Logan[39] has just arrived at Van[couve]r.

[Thomas] Lowe[40] and Banby [?] leave this spring, "certain" [of success]—as the Frenchmen say.

[Archibald] McKinlay suffered a small loss by the wreck of the Josephine.[41]

Colonel [William W.] Loring[42] & a party of gentlemen will be this way en route to Steilacoom [Barracks] 'ere long.

---

31 A native of Illinois, Thornton arrived in the Oregon Territory around 1846. He had been active in political, legal, and educational circles, and was, by 1849, officially "Indian Agent for Oregon Territory."

32 For McLoughlin see Watson, *Lives Lived*, 2:673. Dr. John McLoughlin, who now lived as a private businessman in Oregon City, had resigned from the HBC March 20, 1846. See also William R. Sampson, *Dr. [John] McLoughlin's Business Correspondence, 1847–1848* (Seattle: University of Washington Press, 1973), xli.

33 For Harvey see Watson, *Lives Lived*, 2:445–46.

34 For McKinlay see Watson, *Lives Lived*, 2:663.

35 For Humphreys see Watson, *Lives Lived*, 2:472–73.

36 *Volunteer*, American ship. Roberts mistakenly observes that this was Humphreys' ship. Actually, the *Volunteer* was a part of a fleet owned by American shipping magnate William Fletcher Weld (1800–1881). During the "Golden Age of Sail" this Bostonian made millions which he later invested in railroads and real estate. He greatly multiplied his family's fortune. en.wikipedia.org/wiki/William_Fletcher_Weld.

37 For Raymond see Watson, *Lives Lived*, 2:807–8.

38 For Grant see Watson, *Lives Lived*, 2:416–17.

39 For Logan see Watson, *Lives Lived*, 2:601.

40 For Lowe see Watson, *Lives Lived*, 2:605.

41 *Josephine*, British brig, sank in 1849 at the mouth of the Columbia River.

42 Colonel Loring (1818–1886), the one-armed hero of the Mexican War, was born in Wilmington, North Carolina, and was a career army officer. He had arrived in the Pacific Northwest with the Regiment of Mounted Rifles in 1849 and was, by 1850, Commander in Chief of the U.S. Army in Oregon Territory. He retained that post for the next two years. He later served the Confederacy during the Civil War. For more on his career and life, see en.wikipedia.org/wiki/William_W._Loring.

Col [James] Taylor[43] met with a heavy loss in the [Calamity/Willamette Flood—mostly to his saw] Mills.

Gov [Joseph] Lane[44] also [lost much] in the escape of an immense number of saw logs, [when] he, [in order] to save the Saw Mills, cut away a portion of the Dr.'s [McLoughlin's] breakwater, which he has to put in repair at considerable outlay. They have determined upon not selling lumber under $200.00 p[er] M [thousand board feet].

Flour was up to $30, & probably $40 'ere this [reaches you], Salt at $5 & $6 dollars the bushel; the J.W. Catu[45] was also selling at this price.

Wheat was only at $1.50 to $2.00 at Oregon City, a large purchase was made at this low price.

Property [in Oregon City] has attained an almost unheard of price during my stay. Dr. McL[oughlin] sold ½ a lot 16 feet x 25 at $3,000 to [Judge J. Quinn] Thornton & was mortified to think he let it go at this, for the Judge took him at his word & unthinkingly [paid that price]. [Francis] Ermatinger's[46] old house was sold the other day for $4,000. Quesnel's Rock, Knightin's, now designated Pacific City, was sold at $20,000.

I saw [Doctor Elijah] White, who enquired kindly after you; he is speculating largely.

[Nathaniel] Crosby[47] & [Jacob] Smith[48] bought [Simon Plomondon] Plamondin's[49] Mill for $5,000, partly paid in goods, a very cheap bargain. Old Cunningham [?] is here to fix it & starts in a day or two for Newmarket [today's Tumwater] where he is to be busily engaged putting up Mills. [Nathaniel] Crosby, [who] told me he should move over [to Newmarket] in the Spring—Bag & baggage, lamented that he could not get his ships [the brigantines *O.C. Raymond* and *Grecian*] insured for the Columbia; the [Puget] Sound is now the universal cry & a good claim

43 "Colonel" Taylor settled in Oregon City in 1845 and established the sawmill that was seriously damaged by the flood mentioned here.

44 Joseph Lane (1801–1881) was a veteran of the Mexican–American War, and entered politics as a state legislator as a Democrat representing Evansville, Indiana. President James K. Polk appointed Lane as the first Governor of Oregon Territory and later, in 1859, gained the job as one the young state's first senators. For more information see en.wikipedia.org/wiki/Joseph_Lane.

45 *J.W. Catu*, American ship. Nothing was found regarding this ship or its captain in Portland.

46 For Ermatinger see Watson, *Lives Lived*, 2:362–63.

47 In 1850, Roberts is likely referring to Nathaniel Crosby, who was "one of a family of sea captains, [and in 1847] in command of the brig *O.C. Raymond*, to take supplies to relieve the distress of those [Oregon Trail] immigrants, who, illy prepared, as were all too many, had joined the wild rush to seek their fortunes on the Pacific Coast. So impressed was Capt. Crosby with this land of opportunities, he decided to have his kinsmen join him. Clanrick Crosby, an elder brother, bought the brig *Grecian*, 270 tons capacity, and sailed in 1849. Clanrick was captain of the brig, with a brother-in-law, Washington Hurd first officer, and Alfred Crosby second officer." Mrs. George E. (Georgiana) Blankenship, ed., *Early History of Thurston County, Washington; Together with Biographies and Reminiscences of those Identified with Pioneer Days* (Olympia, WA: 1914), 267.

48 Indiana native Jacob Smith and his family crossed the Oregon Trail in the late 1840s. They first settled on Whidbey Island before moving to Chambers Prairie. Their large family included four daughters and three sons. Jacob Smith died in 1879. Priscilla Smith remained in the house on Chambers Prairie until her death in 1894. She was remembered fondly. The *Morning Olympian* described her as "known far and wide for her charity and hospitality." www.masonicmemorialpark.com/index.php/9-notables/20-jacob-smith-family.

49 For Plomondon see Watson, *Lives Lived*, 783–84.

taken near Port Townsend or New Dungeness could be worth a fortune to you. The others told [me] in half confidence that "the Sound, the Sound, [is] the place!"

We have had a [great] deal of liquor in this settlement lately, chiefly thro[ugh] Plamondin.

Old [Thomas] Cooper[50] is gone over to Newmarket, engaged at $5.00 a day, but his pay had not commenced until he began to work at Newmarket, probably [as a] cook for the hands who will shortly number 30. Old Cooper hung on to Crosby's Kitchen at Portland & I assure you that the old scamp did not earn a dollar the whole time he was there.

Kenneth Logan[51] & young Lewis[52] are employed by Crosby.

[Louis] Ledoux[53] left a day or two after my return home [from Oregon City]—his loss I don't deplore.

[John] Sutherland,[54] I see, is unsettled & I have no doubt will leave in the spring. They are all obedient & respectful, but when there is liquor to be had, I am very uncomfortable about them.

We are glad to hear of poor [Charles] Forrest's[55] amended health, & sincerely hope he may continue to improve. Mrs. [Martha] R[oberts] is in excellent health, [and] expects to present me with another little one sometime next month. We are uneasy at the thought of being so remote from aid at such a time but we hope all will be well.

Old [George] Patterson[56] has settled a few miles above Willow Point on the South Side of the [Cowlitz] river. A number of families have begun to settle at the mouth of the river. Gardening is all the rage now. [Peter S.] Ogden made a bargain with Colonel Loring to supply land & seed, the Col's hands & sentries [are] to work the Vancouver Garden, Sharing equally [in] the produce.

---

50 For Cooper see Watson, *Lives Lived*, 1:286.

51 For Logan see Watson, *Lives Lived*, 2:600–601.

52 With no further information to flesh out his identity, this individual could be any number of Lewis's employees at this point in time.

53 Louis Ledoux (aka Daunt) [variations: Ladue/Ladu/Ledieu/Ladew] (c.1821–?). French-Canadian Louis Ledoux, from Montreal, joined the Hudson's Bay Company in circa 1839 and arrived on November 1 to begin his career with the Puget Sound Agricultural Company. He worked mostly as a farmhand and was an active participant for he appeared regularly in the Fort Nisqually journals. He claimed he became a U.S. citizen on October 15, 1849, and on January 1, 1850, he deserted, most likely for the gold fields of California. He appears to have re-enlisted but then changed his mind and deserted once again on June 15, 1851. On September 20, 1854, he settled on a claim of 640 acres in Lewis Co[unty]. Ledoux, according to Munnick, later served as a private under Captain Henry Peers in the Cowlitz Rangers from November 1855 to January 1856. Ledoux had one wife and two recorded children. Mysteriously, in the 1850 Lewis County census, he was listed as having no family. On February 5, 1852, he married Margaret Wood. Hudson's Bay Company Archives (hereafter HBCA) York Factory Abstracts of Servants' Accounts; HBCA Fort Vancouver [Columbia] Abstracts of Servants' Accounts; Dickey, ed., *Nisqually Journal*, January 1, 1846–April 20, 1847; Munnick, Harriet Duncan, et al., *Catholic Church Records of the Pacific Northwest, Vancouver, 1838–1844*, 76, 77 and *Vancouver, 1842–1856*, 116; Washington Territory Donation Land Claims, Olympia office entry #643 (microfilm roll 101, 926), Seattle Genealogical Society, 1980, 150; Anderson, *The Physical Structure of Fort Nisqually*, 167–71. Courtesy of Bruce M. Watson.

54 For Sutherland see Watson, *Lives Lived*, 3:898.

55 For Forrest see Watson, *Lives Lived*, 1:387–88.

56 For Patterson see Watson, *Lives Lived*, 2:758.

Mr. [George] & Mrs. Abernethy, Annie & William,[57] were to have taken passage 'ere this time for the States by the Louisianna. Abernethy [was] to return in August next. [However,] the Louisianna, which is one of [Nathaniel] Crosby's, was unfortunately grounded by Crosby on the bank at Portland at the top of the freshet, so there she must lay 'till next June if not 'till this time next year.

The Mail left for the States about the end of the month: .64 Cents is the charge [for] England. I find I have scarcely space to say Mrs. R[oberts] joins me in wishing you & the gentlemen at Nisqually many happy returns of the season. I am, Sir, Very respectfully yours,

Geo[rge] B. Roberts

[P.S.:] Our sheep are considerably reduced, & we have now 7 In[che]s [of] snow [on the ground]. We have 150 bus[hels of] wheat only sown. Many of the settlers have not ploughed an acre yet—[Simon] Plamondin & Marcel [Bernier][58] & others, the [Michel Cottonoire] Cottentires,[59] merely sowed this summer's fallows. [John R.] Jackson[60] has done nothing yet. Flour is selling here at $10.00 the barrel—a spec[ulation] might be made in this by some of the enterprising people of the Sound. Crosby has up [to] several hundred Bbls. [barrels] from Plamondin at $20.00 intended for Newmarket. This is well, as the [grist] Mills will be paid to him mostly in goods for the Cowlitz Market.[61]

Tell Mr. [Charles] Forrest [that] our little store at the Water side was entirely swept off by the high water. The Settler's store stands now on the very brink of the [Cowlitz] river & destruction. The Water was up to the upper part of the door of Plamondin's granary at the Water side's lower landing. By the Bye, I spoke to Mr. Ogden about his scandalous behavior to me with regard to the Claim there. He throws all the blame on Mr. [James] Douglas & Mr. Douglas told me he was sorry for me, & washed his hands of the matter. I never knew during my residence in the country a more shameless thing—I have not done with this—& all for the reason that I had, [there was] nowhere to appeal for protection. Dare [I say] this injury [would] have been done me if a British Man of War or Consul had been here? Voila! No! No! No! I had the misfortune to have been born in England. Shame! Shame! Shame! I ask no more than justice. [Peter S.] Ogden did all in his power to spread the report that I had jumped Plamondin's Claim.[62]

You may have heard that I was bargaining for Laramie's claim, and probably should have had it but that he tied me for the payment too close—15th Janu-

57 Abernethy (1807–1877) was Oregon's first governor under the provisional government. He was a Methodist missionary, but became involved in politics and was known to have founded the *Oregon Spectator*, the first newspaper printed west of the Rocky Mountains.

58 For Bernier see Watson, *Lives Lived*, 1:197.

59 For Cottonoire see Watson, *Lives Lived*, 1:291–92.

60 A naturalized American citizen, Jackson was formerly a British butcher, and is credited with establishing the first American land claim north of the Columbia River on the Jackson Prairie, just north of Cowlitz Farm, in 1845.

61 The market rates quoted by Roberts presumably helped Dr. Tolmie set Nisqually's prices when settlers made inquiries about purchasing PSAC livestock and produce.

62 This "shame, shame, shame" commentary relates to a failed land transaction involving Roberts and Simon Plomondon, a former Company employee, and which Ogden apparently advocated as claim jumping by Roberts.

ary—$25.00 for Lock, Stock and barrel. Plamondin has taken it, payment deferred 'till May next. I would have bought it for Mr. [John] Dement if he had authorized me to do so. I [offered] to make enquiry about it for him, but he was gone [for] such an unconscionable time that Plamondin & Laramie came to me together and said since I had first spoken I should have first choice, but that if I declined Plamondin would take it forthwith. I was to pay by the 15th January or the bargain [would] be null, paying any expense that might have been incurred. Dr. McL[oughlin] was very kind to me at the [Willamette] Falls & gave me some good advice [on this matter].

This letter goes by Thomas Chambers, & as it is uncertain when it may reach you I shall defer sending the Government ac[counts] for the present. These other Chaps [present] are unpleasant and unbusiness-like & I sincerely hope I may be more punctual in [the] future.

[Your Most Obedient Servant, George B. Roberts]

Document 1.04: A letter from George B. Roberts, Cowlitz Farm, to William F. Tolmie, Nisqually January 16, 1850.[63]

Dear Sir,

I just drop'd you a line to say that the flour purchases here at $10.00 have been nullified so that it is not to be had now at that rate. I thought I had better let you know, lest counting upon my letter of yesterday you might be misled. Yours very respectfully,

Geo B. Roberts

[P.S.] If you can spare me a little onion seed, I should be happy to send you any of the finest that I have in return, say Parsnips, Turnips, &c.

Document 1.05: A letter from Peter S. Ogden, Vancouver, to William F. Tolmie, Nisqually, January 29, 1850.[64]

Dear Sir,

I have taken the measures you have suggested in regards to the affair of the late Mr. [Joseph T.] Heath and when I write a reply, will duly communicate the same to you. I cannot see with what propriety you can call on me to act in the affairs of the Puget's Sound Company and shall in future decline acting should I be called on. Gov [James] Douglas and yourself are the Puget's Sound Coy agents in this Country. On the 15th February I propose forwarding a Boat to Cowlitz to meet the Gov, where your ploughs will be forwarded [as] Mr. Douglas declined taking them. Yours Respectfully,

Peter Skene Ogden

Document 1.06: A Letter from George B. Roberts, Cowlitz Farm, to William F. Tolmie, Nisqually, February 14, 1850.[65]

63 Nisqually Papers/Miscellaneous Documents FN 1254, Soliday Collection of the Huntington Library of San Marino, California.

64 UW Library, Tolmie Papers Acc. 4577-001, Box #1, Folder #8.

65 BC Archives, MS-0557, Box 1, File 1, E/B/R54.

Dear Sir,

The Steilacoom Mail is sent by [James] Cook[66] who, accompanying Col [William] Loring & Staff, I have enclosed the Bill of expenses $70.00 to Lieut [John] Dement & hope all will be right. We have fitted out the party this season considered the best we are able. The horses will remain at Steilacoom until the return of the gentlemen. I expect your XP [plow] shares by the boat. They shall be sent as soon as rec[eive]d. In consequence of fitting out the party, I shall have no horse to send to meet Mr. [Eden] Colvile. In great haste, I am dear Sir, Respectfully Yours,

G. B. Roberts

Document 1.07: A letter from George B. Roberts, Cowlitz Farm, to William F. Tolmie, Nisqually, February 18, 1850.[67]

Dear Sir,

I have this moment rec[eive]d the accompanying letter from Vanc[ouve]r to be forwarded to Capt [Bennett H.] Hill [of the] US A[rmy] with utmost dispatch. I have much pleasure in informing you that Mrs. [Martha Crabbe] R[oberts][68] on Saturday Last presented me with another daughter [Emma Margaret][69] and that both are doing well thank God.

An Indian of the Fishing tribe was lately killed at Vanc[ouver] by some of the soldiers. In extreme haste, I am respectfully,

G. B. Roberts

Document 1.08: A letter from George B. Roberts, Cowlitz Farm, to William F. Tolmie, Nisqually, February 21, 1850.[70]

Dear Sir,

The Gov [James Douglas] & party arrived here with the assistance of the Cowelitz[71] horses found at [Sidney S.] Ford's[72] at the [Chehalis mud] mountains (where we had them recreating) on the evening of Tuesday. The boat from Van[couve]r arrived for them ½ an hour before so they started Wednesday bright & early for Ft Vancouver via Chinook & the Cape.

By [the] last arrivals from Van[couve]r, we learn[ed] that the [US Army] troops were running off in large bodies. Mr. [Peter S.] O[gden] says if pressured

---

66 Believed to be the James Cook identified in Watson, *Lives Lived*, 1:284.

67 Nisqually Papers/Miscellaneous Documents FN 1254, Soliday Collection of the Huntington Library, San Marino, California.

68 Martha Crabbe Roberts would succumb to this difficult childbirth, and pass away five months later on July 22, 1850.

69 Not much is known of Robert's youngest child, Emma Margaret, who died in 1870. For a short biography, see Watson, *Lives Lived*, 2:821.

70 UW Library, Tolmie Papers Acc. 4577-001, Box #2, Folder #1.

71 This spelling is correct for the period. Only later was the "e" dropped and the name standardized to "Cowlitz."

72 Sidney S. Ford Sr. was born in 1829, and came from Missouri to Oregon in 1845. The Ford family moved north to Puget Sound in the summer of 1846 with Joseph Borst, and settled at the confluence of the Skookumchuck and Chehalis Rivers, halfway between Cowlitz Landing and New Market, that became known as Ford's Prairie. The Ford home was a frequent stopping place for those traveling between forts Vancouver, Nisqually, and Steilacoom Barracks. On June 10, 1847, Ford's wife gave birth to a daughter (afterwards Mrs. John Shelton), the first American girl born north and west of the Columbia.

too close they intend to show fight; the main body is [now] at Champoeg. Mr O[gden] thinks the few men at Van[couve]r will also go. The Cowelitz men, I have every reason to believe, will make a move too. I have done my utmost to prevent desertions since the gold fever broke out. Those who go generally find some good excuse for their conduct. I am at this moment really uncomfortable in view of their running away. Once gone, there will be no replacing them. An Indian now is scarcely to be had here on any terms. Thus, I have not raised the price of labour so far. Many of them will now ask $2.00 p[e]r deim, & the settlers in some instances give $20.00 a month to inferior Indians.

As to the note for $150.00 I sent, please destroy it as it is now paid. Mr. Ogden has now sent the X.P. [plow] shares with a vengeance, i.e., that is with the whole appendage—14 X.P. Ploughs—no less. This, I hope, is to be transported on Nisqually horses & borne on your Inventory. There has been upwards of 100 for these last 6 years at Van[couve]r, an eye sore & an encumbrance which no doubt Mons[ie]r Peter [Ogden] is glad to be rid of. We have but 150 Bus[hels] of wheat sowed & here [it is] the 21st Feb. The Co will not get a bushel of last year's crop from the settlers. [Simon] Plamondon is under an exclusive engagement with M[isters Nathaniel] Crosby & [Jacob] Smith, &c., is buying up every bushel of grain he can get hold of. To facilitate his operations, he is supplied by the Co with [a] boat & 167 bags since [last] summer. Once in a while he goes to Portland with produce where he gets a load of liquor & other quick merchantable goods for this market. Of course, with the united currency of the farm & himself none [are] so blind as those who will not see. I have told Mr. Ogden of the state of things, but it is with difficulty it seems [that] he can look at [Simon] Plomonden in his true colors.

Pretol[73] came here the other day & made up matters with me so that I invited him to dinner.

Mrs. R[oberts] is, I am happy to say, doing well as also the *tenas* [little one]. But [I'm] sad to say that for a few weeks one of her arms (the whole right limb) has been paralyzed. We were in hopes that after delivering she would recover the use of it. But this is the 6th day & tho' I have continued to rub it well, kept it warm & supplied Camphorated mixtures, [there is] no sign of returning strength yet. This arm, when [she was] a child, was dislocated at the Elbow & has been always smaller & weaker than the other arm.

We have large parties always going & coming & under present circumstances they are a great inconvenience. Good God, what a state things will be in shortly, particularly at Van[couve]r?

Friday Morning

All the Owhyhees are gone, & [John] Johns[t]on[74] [is] to start with permission of Gov [Eden] Colvile on return of Col [William W.] Loring. Mrs. R[oberts] Sadly—with only one arm—no one to Cook—[two] girls to take charge [of]—Lewis[75] or others attend the children—this is too painful to dwell on. It is an old saying that it is always darkest before day, so hope, hope on.

We have our [John] Sutherland & two or three Indians left. I rather think the

---

73 "Pretol" is believed to have been Roberts' name for Jean Baptiste Proveau(a) who settled in the Cowlitz area in 1839. The "matter" which needed making up is undisclosed. See Watson, *Lives Lived*, 2:795.

74 For Johnston see Watson, *Lives Lived*, 2:491. This is believed to be this laborer from Fort Vancouver.

75 "Lewis" is likely an Indian working at Cowlitz Farm at this time.

Owhyees, who have wifes of this place [do] contemplate returning after executing a few things for M[ister] O[gden]. But then he may be in such a position as to require their serving at Vanc[ouve]r. With much respect & kind regard to the Gentlemen at Nisqually, I am, dear Sir, Yours very sincerely,

(S[igne]d) G. B. Roberts

[P.S.] [John] McLeod[76] & [Edward] Shearer[77] are reported to have died in California.

Document 1.09: A private letter from William F. Tolmie, Nisqually, to Archibald Barclay, London, March 2, 1850.[78]

My dear Sir,

I had the honor duly to receive your favor of June 1849, and [now] consider that the commencement of my reply ought to be an explanation of the circumstances that prevented my writing either yourself or the other Agents of the Puget's Sound Company by the Spring Express last year.

Early in March last, the late Mr. J[oseph] T. Heath departed this life after a protracted illness during which I was very frequently in attendance on him. I, having thus had much additional work to perform, I trusted to the after Express to forward Reports and letters by, but was much disappointed to find on reaching Vancouver that a second despatch of letters was not to be made.

As the Duplicates of Reports to the Agents in London now forwarded convey information on the state of the business during the past year, I need not say much more on that head.

I have had a difficult and harassing post to fill during the past year and cannot expect any improvement during the present as, what with abundance of money and abundance of liquor, the persons employed in looking after the livestock are becoming more and more disorganized; indeed it is difficult to get a good day's work out of anyone now. Mr. [James] Douglas is to send me three or four steady men from amongst the recruits expected by the Cowlitz and Norman Morison, and should they prove faithful, affairs will, I hope, prosper. There is likely to be a brisk demand for Beef and Mutton for the future and it shall be my endeavor to raise the price of these Commodities as much as possible.

From the importance of my charge and its being a distinct business from the

---

76 For McLeod see Watson, *Lives Lived*, 2:669. Also, Steve Anderson's "A Crofter's Tale: Adventurous John of the Clan MacLeod," *Columbia Magazine* (Summer 2010), 27–33.

77 From various entries in the fort's *Journal of Occurrences* and *Indian Shop Blotter*, Shearer, an English sheepherder/farmhand, arrived at Nisqually in late August 1847. At that time, he appears to have been engaged in the plains hunting cattle. By late November, he was stationed at Whyatchie Farm—located north of the fort in today's Lakewood, Washington. March 1848 found him at Muck Station. In late May 1848, Shearer was supplied "with a gun for his own protection" primarily because he was still working at Whyatchie Farm with John McLeod and the threat of Indian attack was mounting at this point. After the May 1849 attack on the fort, Shearer and others "came in from their Stations to have an understanding about getting higher wages and Bills for their balance up to last June, and if they failed to get them they would leave the service at once. Dr. William Tolmie gave them to understand that he had no authority to give more, and also dictated to them of their dishonorable like conduct, in leaving their posts, before the end of their contract."

78 BC Archives, MS-0557, Box 2. From a typescript copy.

Fur trade, I conceive myself, in justice, entitled to remuneration for my services to the Puget's Sound Company and I have written the Agents in London the subject on two occasions; once in April last, and again in October.

Expecting two maiden Aunts (Miss Tolmies formerly Boarding school Teachers in Dingwall and Inverness) to come out and settle on Vancouver's Island, I am anxious to have a furlough in 1851 in order to get a residence prepared for them. Should my Aunts not come out however, or should the Coy—by increasing my yearly income—enable me at a smaller pecuniary sacrifice to get them established on the island, I could remain on duty in 1851, if the interests of the concern required it. I would think it hard to have to remain on my present pay and to be obliged to employ people I could not overlook to carry on operations on the Island so, if my applications to the Agents of the P[uget's] S[ound Agricultural] Co should prove unsuccessful. I trust that I may not be disappointed in obtaining a furlough.

'Tis greatly to be regretted that the Coy have made their terms so vigorous in regard to the settlement of Vancouver's Island. I myself, when I retire from the service, would greatly prefer residing there to going elsewhere and I am still buoyed up with the hope that the terms may be greatly ameliorated—at least for the old servants of the Company.

The clause in the prospectus providing that laborers shall be brought out by each purchaser of 100 acres of land amounts in the present state of affairs to an obligation to bring so many settlers to American Oregon.

Requiring prepayment for the land sold is also, in my opinion, an injudicious arrangement. Indeed, nothing but an extremely liberal policy will induce intending settlers to select Vancouver's Island as their place of abode for in American Oregon every man occupies 640 acres of land which he confidently hopes to receive as a donation or, at the worst, to have to pay the Government price for at some distant day when the lands shall have been surveyed.

Having lately got married to Jane [Work], eldest daughter of C[hief] F[actor John] Work, I have ceased thinking of revisiting the Land o' Cakes [Scotland], and look forward to ending my days as a settler on Vancouver's Island.

(Signed William F. Tolmie)

Document 1.10. A letter from Peter S. Ogden, Vancouver, to William F. Tolmie, Nisqually, March 12, 1850.[79]

My dear Sir,

I have nearly time to return Mrs. [Jane Work] Tolmie and yourself our [belated] congratulations on your marriage and our thanks for the wedding Cake and you have my best wishes that you may long enjoy many happy years together.

Your Requisition has been duly enclosed in the official despatches with my wish it may be granted. I, however, apprehend some of us will be disappointed on where the lack of success will fall, it is difficult to say—my application is for '51 or '52 but not beyond. Gov [Eden] Colvile & [Archibald] McKinlay are at present on a trip of pleasure to the upper [Willamette] Settlements. The whole

79 UW Library, Tolmie Papers Acc. 4577-001, Box #1, Folder #8.

united forces of the F[ederal] troops started yesterday from Oregon City with their personnel in pursuit of the deserters.[80] Gov [Joseph] Lane had persuaded them to use the Matilda of the Company. All on both sides are abundantly supplied with the implements of War; if they should return to make use of these, time will tell. The Deserters number one hundred and Sixty one (161) encamped in a body and [Lieutenant] Lane regularly laid their plans and appointed one of their number as Commander with the title of General. The Farmers have liberally supplied them with food, taking orders on the Quarter Master Gen[era]l, which I, having severe doubts, will be [a] general nuisance to the [PSAC's] operation where they can [abscond with food, supplies, &c., they] will do that.

We expect to start the [easterly bound mail] Express by the 18th or 20th Instant [illegible] and as you may suffice it is busy times with me, and with my kind respects to Mrs. [Jane] Tolmie and friend [John] Tod if he be with you. I Remain Yours Truly,

Peter Skene Ogden

Document 1.11: A letter from James Douglas, Victoria, to William F. Tolmie, Nisqually, March 13, 1850.[81]

Dear Sir,

I have to acknowledge your letter of the 8th inst, with invoice, Bill of Lading and other documents per the Cadboro. With reference to these I have to remark that the price charged for beef is unreasonable and altogether beyond the value of the article, which is at best hardly fit for use and so poor and dry that the seamen of the Company's ships have repeatedly refused it, and the consumption is encreased by a half when used in the ships, in consequence of the pieces rejected, and the loss of weight in cooking. You will however please to leave the charge as it is, and we will arrange the matter hereafter.

I observe the payment to John Nisbet[82] and Andrew Crawford,[83] which you will please charge to Fort Victoria Sale Shop. I have to request that no advances may be hereafter made to Crawford as he is improvident and has rather overdrawn his account.

The Specie [gold and silver coin] was found correct as per accompanying account.

I have put up a small supply of woolen and cotton goods which will be forwarded by H[er] M[ajesty's Steam] Sloop Driver[84] proceeding at our requisition to Fort Nisqually for sheep and neat cattle in aid of the Colony. The handsome manner in which Captain [Charles R.] Johnson[85] tendered his services for our relief, is beyond all praise. He proposes to bring down a full cargo say about 200 head

80 This is a reference to 161 soldiers who deserted from Vancouver Barracks and headed south to the gold fields of California.

81 UW Library, Tolmie Papers Acc. 4577-001, Box #1, Folder #2.

82 For Nisbet see Watson, *Lives Lived*, 2:726.

83 For Crawford see Watson, *Lives Lived*, 1:298–99.

84 *Driver*, Her Majesty's steamer sloop. The *Driver*, Captain Charles Richardson Johnson, was a wooden, paddle-driven sloop, and credited with the first steam-powered circumnavigation of the globe. It had 6 guns, a complement of 149 sailors and marines and carried wool, cotton goods, neats (horned oxen), and sheep for the HBC/PSAC. For more information see en.wikipedia.org/wiki/HMS_Driver_%281840%29.

85 Johnson was the captain of the HMS Steamer *Driver* who was supporting the Company at this time.

of neats [cattle], and 4 or 500 sheep. I beg that every exertion may be made to get the cattle brought in as soon as possible, as he cannot spare more than 7 days for this service. Governor [Richard] Blanchard will probably accompany the Driver to Nisqually and I beg to recommend both these gentlemen to your special attentions.

I wrote you a hurried note by Mr. [John] Dement, who came here in search of deserters, informing you of our intention of dispatching the Driver, in order that you might be prepared for her arrival. Two deserters from the American Troops at Steilacoom secreted themselves in the Cadboro the night after she left Nisqually, having gone on board in the night, with or without the knowledge of the deck watch. They remained concealed in the forecastle during the voyage and landed on their arrival here. None of the officers had any knowledge of their being in the Cadboro, or they would have sent them back from some point on the way. Being now on British Territory they can be removed only [through] the action of the Civil courts, which I should be happy to see put in force against them. Pray explain this matter to Captain [Bennett] Hill, and tell him that I have refused to employ or have any dealings whatever with them. I have given them food, which they cannot procure elsewhere and we cannot allow them to die of hunger.

Please to forward the accompanying packet immediately to Vancouver as it contains important communications for the Express. With best wishes, Yours Truly,

James Douglas

[P.S.] Having received a larger supply of sugar than expected from the Sandwich Islands you may resume the sale at Nisqually. You may also dispose of 100 bushels of salt. J D

Document 1.12: A private letter from William F. Tolmie, Nisqually, to Archibald McKinlay, Oregon City, March 13, 1850.[86]

My dear Mackinlay,

Finding an Indian about to start for Cowlitz, I embrace the opportunity to address you a few lines and state how matters are progressing on board the [brig] Sacramento.[87]

[Captain William A.] Mouat[88] has taken 120 M [thousand] Shingles from the Coy and Contracted for about 300 spiles [pilings] of from 20 to 25 feet at $3.00 each delivered at high-water mark. He expects to be ready for sea in about a week or ten days hence. Should I not previously have advices from you, I will, when the brig is laden, open the box of specie and defray all charges, retaining the balance here until by you directed how to dispose of it.

If you are of opinion that it would pay to Ships [sic] cargoes of spiles [pilings] from Puget's Sound to San Francisco, I will be happy to go shares with you in any such undertaking and can get a cargo prepared beforehand.

Men are also offering to square Timber which they would deliver on the [Nis-

86 BC Archives, MS-0557, Box 2. From a typescript copy.

87 Captain William Alexander Mouat was the master of the American Brig *Sacramento* in 1850. This vessel is owned by Lafayette Balch of Port Steilacoom. Principle cargo was pilings, milled lumber, shingles, English cart wheels, and flax seed.

88 For Mouat see Watson, *Lives Lived*, 2:707.

qually] reach for from 20 to 25 cents a foot I presume. Please let me know by return or first opportunity what you think of our getting a cargo of squared Timber and spiles [pilings] ready for next trip of the Sacramento, and make a calculation of the probable expence.

I should like to get a side saddle from Portland, or Oregon City, unless the price is very high, (in which case I would declare off entirely) would take two others for friends at Victoria. Will you be kind enough to excuse this commission for me and to get such on a[ccount] Ft Nisqually, Vitz; 4 Brass Bottling Cocks.

(Signed William F. Tolmie)

Document 1.13: A private letter from William F. Tolmie, Her Majesty's Steam Sloop *Driver* at Nisqually Roads, to James Douglas, Victoria, March 22, 1850.[89]

Dear Sir,

Her Majesty's Steam Sloop "Driver", Captain [Charles R.] Johnson, announced herself here on the 20th Inst. Your letters by Mr. [John] Dement arriving the same afternoon and those by Indians accompanying a packet box for Vancouver Coming to hand only last night.

Notwithstanding the short notice we have succeeded in putting on board [85] head of Cattle and [800] Ewes—list of which is herewith enclosed. It was quite impossible [*rest of letter unreadable*]

Document 1.14: A letter from William F. Tolmie, Nisqually, to Peter S. Ogden, Vancouver, March 25, 1850.[90]

Sir,

I forward by the present courier packet in one case despatches received at different dates last week from Victoria, and the earlier of which I delayed forwarding being aware that another was to be expected.

H.M.S. Driver came here last week and [when leaving] conveyed 85 head of cattle, and 800 Sheep to Victoria. Richard Blanshard Esq, Governor of Vancouver's Island came in her as passenger.

I shall endeavor to send the Wedder [wether: castrated ram] sheep to Vancouver before the rivers rise, and would beg to suggest that [John] Sutherland should join the party from Cowlitz onwards, as during the lambing season [John] Macphail cannot be spared. In haste, I remain Sir, Your very Obedt Sert,

S[igne]d Wm Fraser Tolmie

Document 1.15: A letter from H. Bishop, Olympia, to William F. Tolmie,

---

89 BC Archives, MS-0557, Box 2. From a typescript copy.

90 Fort Nisqually Correspondence Outward, 1850–1852; Commencing March 25th, 1850, Ending August 12th, 1852, Hudson's Bay Company Archives, Archives of Manitoba, B.151/b/1, Folios 3–34. This marks the beginning of the first Fort Nisqually Letterbook used in this work. All successive documents not otherwise footnoted were taken from and transcribed using this one source.

Nisqually, April 1, 1850.[91]

Doctor Tolmie,

Dear Sir, I send the bearer, an Indian, for some spikes. The number required is sixty of the large kind. The young man in your store will recollect they were taken from a box in the corner of the ware-room. Please send me also a few pounds of nails, if you can spare them. I will pay you when I come down. Very Respectfully, Your obedient servant,

H. Bishop

Document 1.16: A letter from William F. Tolmie, Nisqually, to James Douglas, Victoria, April 2, 1850.

Sir,

As the Brig Sacramento is to touch at Victoria, I avail myself of Captain [William A.] Mouat's kindness to forward by him the Nisqually Requisitions for outfit 1850, and two spare Cart's [wheels] ~~which~~ which I have earnestly to request may be returned, shipped by the earliest opportunity. I do note in account of the wheels now sent with summary application for 2 pairs of the wheels expected from England, as I am fully persuaded that there will be full employment for all 'ere the Year is out.

[The Hawaiian] Niaupalu's[92] account is sent—his trunk and kettle will go by next opportunity.

S[igne]d W. F. Tolmie

Document 1.17: A private letter from William F. Tolmie, Nisqually, to George T. Allan,[93] Oregon City, April 2, 1850.[94]

My Dear sir,

The "Sacramento" is now ready for sea and in case you may have preceded her to California, I enclose a statement of your account with the Hudson's Bay Co. In re-landing the shingles from the "Sacramento" a number of Bales came to pieces and, as they unavoidably lay exposed for a couple of nights on the beach, 'tis possible that some may have been stolen by Indians, but this cannot be known until the broken ones are repacked, which shall be done as soon as possible.

'Tis much to be regretted that the "Sacramento" did not arrive earlier, as throughout the winter I had repeated offers of $10 p[e]r M [thousand] for all the shingles here, and relying on her coming about the expected time I purchased on the Coy's a[ccount] 100 M Shingles at 10 p[e]r M Cash in order to be certain of having the number contracted for—400 M—when the Brig [*Sacramento*] should arrive.

Please write me what you may wish done with the shingles stored here by [Captain William A.] Mouat. I am at present greatly occupied and cannot write more fully. Mouat will be able to give you every information regarding the pros-

---

91 BC Archives, MS-0557, Box 1, File 1, A/C/40/B54.

92 For information on the Hawaiian Niaupalu, see Bruce M. Watson and Jean Barman, *Leaving Paradise, Indigenous Hawaiians in the Pacific Northwest, 1787–1898* (Honolulu: University of Hawai'i Press, 2006), 367. Hereafter cited as Watson and Barman, *Leaving Paradise.*

93 For Allan see Watson, *Lives Lived,* 1:145–46.

94 BC Archives, MS-0557, Box 2. From a typescript copy; the letter's destination was not noted.

pects of getting Cargoes of Spiles [pilings] here. He has been very zealous and active in getting on with his work. I hope you may feel satisfied with all that has been done for you here and trusting that the shipment may find ready and remunerative sale. I remain, in haste, Dear Allan, Faithfully yours,

Wm F. Tolmie

Document 1.18: A private letter from William F. Tolmie, Nisqually, to Misters Probet, Smith & Company, San Francisco, April 2, 1850.[95]

Gentlemen,

Agreeably to the wishes of Mr. [George T.] Allan, I now forward herewith Invoice and bill Lading of Cargo of Lumber forwarded by the Brig Sacramento and consigned to your care. I am, Gentlemen, Your very obedt sert,

Wm F. Tolmie

Document 1.19: A letter from Peter S. Ogden, Vancouver, to William F. Tolmie, Nisqually, April 2, 1850.

Sir,

Yours of 25th Ult reached this on the 31st with the Victoria Packet all correct. Capt [Bennett H.] Hill has officially reported here that two of his Soldiers had deserted and were secreted and conveyed on Board the Hudson's Bay Coy Schooner Cadboro to Victoria and there, on demand, refused to deliver them to Am[erica]n Govt. This has caused a considerable excitement here and without any information from you on the subject I could merely deny that the HB Coy would commit such a disgraceful act and have only to express my regret, you had not communicated with me on the subject.

I shall give no instructions that [John] Sutherland should accompany the Sheep here [as] his visit here last Summer caused the desert[ion] of your men and those of Cowlitz also. Mr. [George B.] Roberts and yourself must clear ways and means of sending them without the assistance of Sutherland—and when it suits your will and pleasure.

In regard to Mr. [George T.] Allan, he declines having anything to do with the Shingles and I have no further Instructions to give you and I beg leave to refer you to my letter wherein I state that it is no longer my intention to interfere in any way either in regard to Puget's Sound or HB Coy affairs. James Douglas Esq[ui]re is the Gent[lema]n you must transmit your business with now. Yours Truly,

Peter Skene Ogden

Document 1.20: A letter from Archibald McKinlay, Oregon City, to William F. Tolmie, Nisqually, April 3, 1850.[96]

My Dear Tolmie,

Your welcome favor[97] of 13th ulto reached me on the 1st inst and many thanks

95 BC Archives, MS-0557, Box 2. From a typescript copy. Probet, Smith & Company has not been identified.

96 UW Library, Tolmie Papers Acc. 4577-001, Box 1 Folder 6.

97 This letter from Tolmie to McKinlay has not been found.

for the information therein contained.

I am glad to hear that the [schooner] Sacramento [Captain William A. Mouat] was getting on so well with her Cargo. I have not the slightest doubt but the spiles [pilings] put on board will pay well. With regard to shipping another cargo of such timber from Puget Sound, the market of San Francisco is so very fluctuating that I do not think it would be advisable to get either squared timber or spiles prepared beforehand. Mr. [George T.] Allan left this [place] about a week ago for California, but whether he has got over the [Columbia River] bar, or not, I cannot say. He will, on arrival at San Francisco, inform himself particularly regarding the prospects of continuing the log trade and will send me word by the earliest opportunity, which will enable me to give you the necessary information.

Mr. Allan informed me on his return from Nisqually last fall that you were going shares in such cargo as might be got for the Sacramento. If, therefore, you are willing to take a third of the present consignment, you can do so and we shall be most happy to accept your proposal. With respect to other adventures in Spiles &c., should such be considered a safe and profitable speculation, please let me know by the earliest opportunity whether you take a share in the cargo now sent.

I have this day drawn on you for ($7,586.09 ½) seven thousand five hundred and eighty six dollars & 9 & half cents in favor of Mr. [Peter S.] Ogden, which please pay and retain the Balance which may remain on hand after paying for the Spiles [pilings] and send me an account of the same as soon as convenient.[98]

In your letter you mention that Capt Mowat had taken 120 M [thousand] shingles on board [the *Sacramento*] which I am sorry to learn. Had Mr. Allan's letter reached you sooner, this would not have been the case. I hope Mr. Allan will get to San Francisco in time to dispose of the Sacramento's Cargo so as to ensure commission &c.

I do not know whether I informed you that I have sent in my resignation [from the HBC]. I get my furlough on the 1st June. Allan and [my]self have leased the house and store formerly occupied by the Hudson's Bay Company from D[octor John] McLoughlin [and] where we purpose making a hard push to get some of the Gold dust which is so abundantly pouring in to others.

I am just about starting for the [Oregon] City and if there are any side saddles in the country shall get one for you. Meantime, you must not grudge from $10 to $50. The [barrel/spigot] Cocks shall also be forwarded if [such are] to be had.

Young [William Seton] Ogden[99] is the bearer of this [letter]; he can give you much correct information regarding the state of affairs here.

My health has been very poor lately. I lost about 50 [pounds] in weight this winter.

Excuse this scribble, [my] wife joins me in best regards to Mrs. [Jane] Tolmie and yourself. And I remain, Yours faithfully,

---

98 At 2018 rates, this amount would equal approximately $209,300 in U.S. funds.

99 This Ogden, who often goes by "Seton," was not related to the famous HBC chief factor, but was an American citizen and partner with John M. Breck in a Portland general mercantile store in the early 1850s. On November 11, 1852, he married Mary E. Dryer, the daughter of the first editor of the *Oregonian*, Thomas J. Dryer. Marriage certificate at the Oregon Historical Society Research Library, and through WorldCat record id 710913201.

Arch McKinlay

P.S. I have also drawn on you for four hundred dollars in favor of Mr. William S. Ogden which please honor. S[igned, Archibald] McK[inlay]

Document 1.21: A letter from Peter S. Ogden, Vancouver, to William F. Tolmie, Nisqually, April 5, 1850.

Dear Sir,

I am confidentially informed by a Friend[100] that it is more than probable the next Trip of the Cadboro she will be seized for landing British Goods in the Am[erican] Territory without paying duties. There is but one Port of Entry for Oregon Territory and by the Laws of the U[nited] States you are bound to send your manifest and duly enter your Ship there—on this subject you had better without delay consult with Chief Factor [James] Douglas—all this has been caused by the unfortunate secret[in]g of the two Soldiers on board the Cadboro, a most unfortunate circumstance for our Interests and[101] I seriously apprehend will lead certainly to great trouble and expense and our standing here as respectable Men has been much lowered in the interrelations of the leading Men in consequence [of] it—all events, whatever may be the final result—as it shall get me ended by it. I sometimes since forwarded you a receipt from [the lawyer] Mr. [H.J.] Maury for legal advice in the Estate of the late Mr. [Joseph T.] Heath for Thirty dollars sum on Vancouver—if the said [H.J.] Maury has been paid please first apply your man the correct information as I have pledged myself for this payment.

Captain [Bennett H.] Hill, in his report, appears to be very violent on the subject of his Men being taken away by the Cadboro. I wish to God this unfortunate affair had not happen'd and shall here take Considerable Care in May's transactions by Her it. She will be committed and we must now do all we can to return his soldiers from it. William Ogden, who is well conversant in Custom House affairs, will give you any information you may require. Yrs Truly,

Peter Skene Ogden

Document 1.22: A letter from James Douglas, Victoria, to William F. Tolmie, Nisqually, April 11, 1850.

Dear Sir,

I have to acknowledge your several letters of the 22nd and 23rd March and of the 2nd and 3rd of April with the Nisqually Requisition for Outfit 1850. The [HMS] Driver arrived here the day following her departure from Nisqually and landed

100 Chief Factor Ogden's "friend" can only be one of two men: 1) Amory Holbrook, a lawyer who was working with the territorial government, or 2) Hugh Goldsborough, a leading American settler who was sympathetic to the HBC's situation. Both would be called upon to represent the HBC in the legal entanglements that soon arose. According to the fort's journal, this letter was delivered on April 13, 1850.

101 Within the original HBCA letterbook, Chief Factor Ogden's letter ends here. It is made complete through a copy of the original in the UW Library, Tolmie Papers, Acc. #4577, Box #1, Folder #8, and so continues as shown.

803 Sheep and 85 head of neat Cattle including the Cattle of both kind bought by Captain [Walter Colquhoun] Grant, [and] which have been delivered and ought to be deducted from the numbers.

I am sorry to hear that Captain [Bennett H.] Hill takes so serious a view of the Cadboro affair and trust after explanations given in a formal letter, he will not detain the vessel, a proceeding which would put us to very considerable inconvenience and lead to national questions of an unpleasant character. The seizure of the vessel would be, moreover, an unnecessary exertion of power, as the Cadboro is not about to leave the coast and you may assure Captain Hill that we will make every reparation in our power for the loss he has suffered.

Mr. [Lieutenant John B.] Gibson [Jr.],[102] the Purser, paid for the supplies Furnished for the [HMS] Driver at Nisqually, which may be charged on account with this station.

In reply to your question if we are likely to have much more shipping of cattle this Summer, I beg to inform you that we shall be under the necessity of making frequent demands upon Nisqually in that way, and I think it highly important as you have suggested that the road to the beach should be fenced in which I think will be found to be a great saving of expence in the end.

I am sorry to hear of the desertion of the three Sandwich Islanders[103] who have hitherto been so faithful to the service. I would strongly recommend measures being taken to recover them—the nominal high wages of the Country appearing to be the great inducement to desertion. I would recommend your adopting the rates of the country both in regards to wages and supplies, which would have the effect of satisfying the men while it would not come more expensive to the company.

The Hawaiians who we've lately engaged at the Sandwich Islands receive 20 dollars a month and we will charge their supplies at the current prices of the country. Something of the kind might be tried with the Puget's Sound Company's accounts, and I have no doubt with good effects. I shall be happy to hear your opinion on the subject, as I am otherwise not possessed of sufficient information as to the rate of labourer's pay at Nisqually to come to a determination.

Captain [William A.] Mouat delivered the Cart wheels and flax seed. The wheels will be returned when finished. A part of the Nisqually requisition is now forwarded consisting principally of Blankets and other entire packages. The remainder will follow as opportunities occur. The order for the Puget's Sound Company from England is Shipped. Four pairs of English Cart wheels are also sent, two of those being intended for the use of the Cowlitz farm if required.

I now send you a reinforcement for the Establishment of Nisqually, consisting of William [Edward] Huggins, a colonist, who lately arrived by the Norman Morison, [and who is] strongly recommended by Mr. [Benjamin] Harrison[104] for employment in the service, Louis Trudelle[105] and three of the trustiest Orkney Men.

The former [Huggins] is engaged for one year; Trudelle up to the first of June

102 A career soldier, Gibson was a lieutenant in the U.S. Army's Company M, 1st Artillery, stationed at Steilacoom Barracks at this time. Tolmie's designation of him as "purser" for the *Driver* is mistaken. No other information could be found regarding this individual.

103 Within the fort's journal these three are identified as Cowie, Kalama, and Keave'haccow, all of whom are noted later in this work.

104 Mr. Harrison was the HBC's Secretary and primary recruiter in the Company's London Office.

105 For Trudelle see Watson, *Lives Lived*, 3:942.

1851 at £20, and the other latter are on contracts for 5 years at £17 a year.

The three latter, in common with the newly arrived English servants, receive an allowance of 1/5 [pound] Tea and 1 [pound of] Brown Sugar a week which, though they cannot claim as a right, it would be good policy to continue. I would have sent a few more hands had I not supposed from your discharging [the Hawaiian] Niaupalu that they were not desired.

Please to send the [mutton?], Pork and Beef, by return of the Cadboro and as many cattle as can be shipped without retaining the vessel at Nisqually, as we want her here as soon as she can possibly get back. I beg that no shingles may be shipped as they are not required having a stock on hand.

I regret the loss of your riding horses and hope you will succeed in getting the stray cattle driven in.

The Company have agreed to make advances to [John] Lidgett's[106] ships, the concern [William] Brotchie[107] is connected with, to the amount of £400 St[erlin]g. If Brotchie applies for cattle at Nisqually you may sell to the amount of £100 taking his bills in Triplicate for the same, but do not exceed that sum. You may also make advances for Father [Pascal Ricard] Richard[108] to the amount of 600 Dollars at Nisqually, his friends in Europe having giving security for its repayment.

I now forward a packet for Vancouver containing letters and documents received from England per the Norman Morison, which I beg may be sent on as soon as possible. We are excessively busy at present with ships and accounts and I have not time to write you so fully as I wish but will do so at the earliest moment. Referring you to the Invoice and bill lading herewith, I remain, Dear Sir, Yours Truly,

James Douglas

Men's Names & Wages

[Edward Huggins]

Louis Trudelle	Time out	1st June 1851	£20 [per year]
George Edwards[109]	[Time out]	1st [June] 1854	£17 [per year]
Edward Hoare[110]	[Time out]	1st [June] 1854	£17 [per year]

106 Lidgett was the London-based owner of the doomed bottom ship *Albion*.

107 For Brotchie see Watson, *Lives Lived*, 1:228–29.

108 "Pere" or "father" Ricard was born in Allauch, near Marseilles, France, in 1805. He was ordained a Roman Catholic priest in 1831, joined the missionary group Oblates of Mary Immaculate, and came to the Oregon Country in 1847, where he founded St. Rose's Mission among the Yakamas. A year later, June 1848, he established St. Joseph's Mission four miles south of Newmarket (which became Tumwater) on Puget Sound. He returned to France in June 1857, where he died at Notre Dames des Lumieres, January 9, 1862. William N. Bischoff, S. J. *We Were Not Summer Soldiers: The Indian War Diary of Plympton J. Kelley, 1855–1856* (Tacoma: Washington State Historical Society, 1976), 167.

109 Within the fort's employment records, George Edwards, a general laborer and gardener, signed on with a four year contract at £17 per annum. However, in early November 1851, he deserted from the service, only to reappear in April 1856 as a new employee. In November of that same year, he drifted away again, only to be mentioned in the fort's journal for the last time in 1868 as an attendee at a funeral of one of his former co-workers at the fort. No other information about him is known at this point.

110 Edward Hoare [variation: Hoar, Hore] (fl. 1849–50) was a HBC-sponsored settler/PSAC agricultural laborer who came to Vancouver Island as an emigrant laborer in 1850. After his arrival, he went to Fort Nisqually, likely in July, where he worked mainly with raw hides, participating from the slaughtering to the rendering of the fat. After September 16, 1850, when he failed to appear for work because he was intoxicated, he worked only a few more days in the slaughterhouse before being given outside work. On October 14, 1850, he parted ways with the Company and may have hid himself aboard the brig *Orbit* at the landing. William Fraser Tolmie searched the brig but was content not

William Young[111] [Time out] 1st [June] 1854 £17 [per year]

Document 1.23: An "official" letter from William F. Tolmie, Nisqually, to Captain Bennett H. Hill, Steilacoom Barracks, April 16, 1850.

Dear Sir,

Will you be good enough to favor me in writing with your reasons for seizing the Hudson's Bay Co's Schooner Cadboro on the 14th Inst in order that I may report thereon in the proper quarter? Will you also be pleased to inform me why Mr. [George] Dixon,[112] First officer of the Cadboro and "Mahon" Sandwich Islander,[113] the cook of said Vessel, were sent ashore yesterday afternoon, and whether they were by you directed to come to me for board and lodging? I remain Dear Sir, Very respectfully Yours, S[igne]d

Wm F. Tolmie, Agent

Document 1.24: A private letter from William F. Tolmie, Nisqually, to Bennett H. Hill, Steilacoom Barracks, April 16, 1850.[114]

My Dear Sir,

Referring to my official note [above] for strictly business Matters, I would feel much obliged if you would give some information as to what will be the course of proceeding with regard to the Cadboro on Mr. [John A]dair's arrival—of which I would like much to be notified, and I have directed the Beef Carter to arrange with some Indian lad at Steilacoom to bring me notice if you would be kind enough to drop me a note when Mr. A[dair] reaches Steilacoom.

I trust that some arrangement may be arrived at admitting of the Cadboro's proceedings directly to Victoria as her prolonged detention here will cause serious derangement of the Company's business.

Vessels belonging to the Hudson's Bay Co, which has weighty interests at stake in Oregon, cannot be viewed in the same light as foreign ships would be owned by parties having no property in the country and which might never revisit this part of the world. I remain My dear sir, Very truly yours,

Wm F. Tolmie

---

to find the "worthless lazy fellow." He had communicated with his mother probably shortly after his arrival for, on July 8, 1851, his mother wrote back from St. Mary's Cray with news of the family and some motherly advice: "You must not do as you said you wood Marry a Black girl you must Come Back as sune as you can." Information courtesy of Bruce M. Watson.

111 Young (1830–1913), who was born in the Orkney Islands, came to the Northwest on the *Norman Morrison*. On the voyage out he contracted small pox and was on the sick list from November 21 to December 11, 1849. He died at Tacoma in 1913. See also the *Tacoma Daily Ledger*, October 31, 1948, and Jerry Eckrom's "Reconstructing Willie," *Occurrences*, 17:4 (1999).

112 For Dixon see Watson, *Lives Lived*, 1:335.

113 Mahoy, Charley. See Watson and Barman, *Leaving Paradise*, 338–39. We believe this is the "Mahon" of the Cadboro as mentioned in these letters, as Charley Mahoy was a cook later in life, and no other HBC-employed Hawaiians demonstrated a culinary aptitude in their work records.

114 BC Archives, MS-0557, Box 2. From a typescript copy.

Document 1.25: A letter from William F. Tolmie, Nisqually, to Peter S. Ogden, Vancouver, April 16, 1850.

Sir,

I have to acknowledge receipt of your letters of the 2nd, 5th, and 9th Instant.[115]

I am happy to inform you that the facts of the desertion case completely bear out the assertion you made when the matter was first mentioned at Vancouver, namely that the Hudson's Bay Company would never connive at such a disgraceful act as assisting the escape of deserters.

The following is a brief [expl]anation of the circumstances:

On the 9th March, after signing Bills of Lading, Captain [James] Sangster went on board the Cadboro, accompanied by Lieut [John B.] Gibson [Jr.], US A[rmy] and myself and having had a hint that some soldiers were secreted on board he informed Mr. Gibson thereof, and directed the first Officer to search the vessel thoroughly and report. Before Lt Gibson left, the first Officer stated to Captain Sangster that his search had been in vain. Captain Sangster after dropping anchor in Victoria's outer harbor ascertained that two US soldiers were concealed on board, and immediately sent them ashore. Governor [Richard] Blanshard, when here in H.M.S. [steamer] Driver replied in the negative to Captain [Bennett H.] Hill's application as to whether the deserters would be delivered up in the event of his sending an officer and party of men to Vancouver's Island. It has come to my Knowledge lately that the deserters started in a canoe, ahead of the Cadboro, got on board of her at anchor the first night and were concealed by some of the crew until the Schooner had reached her destination.

On the 13th Inst the Schooner Cadboro under command of Captain Sangster arrived here and discharged part of her cargo. The same evening, I received your letter of the 5th Inst stating that you had heard that the Cadboro was to be seized for non-payment of duties on her next trip to Nisqually and [the] next morning, Sunday, Captain Hill sent an Officer with some soldiers who seized the Cadboro and took her down to Steilacoom. On the 15th he ordered Mr. [George] Dixon, first Officer and Mahon, the Sandwich Island cook, to leave the vessel. Captain Sangster protested against the seizure of the Cadboro at the time she was taken and I did so soon after. Mr. [Eben May] Dorr, it appears, has been commissioned to seize the Cadboro and he is expected from Newmarket today. I have delayed writing Mr. C[hief] F[actor] Douglas for two days in the expectation of seeing Mr. Dorr.

Captain Hill informed me yesterday that he is to forward an Express to Vancouver in a day or two to make known the seizure of the Cadboro, and have legal proceedings instituted against that Vessel or her owners. I shall probably write you again by the Govt mail should Mr. Dorr have previously arrived. Would it not be well to look out for and retain the ablest lawyer in Oregon City to undertake the Company's cause?

With regards to the shingles charged against Messrs [George Traill] Allan and [Archibald] Mackinlay, I have acted conscientiously and as far as I can see,

115 This last letter was not found.

equitably to the parties concerned, due consideration being, as to the arrangements previously made I cannot therefore on my own responsibility make any alteration in the accounts.

Andrew Crawford, late carpenter on board the Cadboro, has been paid off here, and received his discharge. I have the honor to be Sir, Your very Obedt Sert,

S[igne]d William F. Tolmie

Document 1.26: A letter from William F. Tolmie, Nisqually, to Captain Bennett H. Hill, Steilacoom Barracks, April 17, 1850.

Sir,

Herewith is enclosed my protest against the proceedings of the Officers & Troops acting under your orders in the Capture of the Hudson's Bay Company's Schooner Cadboro, in the Roadstead of this place on the 14th Instant. I have the Honour to be Sir, Your Very Obedt St,

(Signed) William Fraser Tolmie

Document 1.27: A Declaration of Protest for the Seizure of the Hudson's Bay Company schooner Cadboro by United States Army forces. [116]

In the name of the Hudson's Bay and Puget's Sound Companies, I do hereby most solemnly protest against the Capture by Violence and force of arms of the Hudson's Bay Company's Schooner Cadboro with her stores, rigging, apparel, and cargo on the 14th day of this month, while lying at anchor in Nisqually Roads, by Lieut [John] Dement, with a detachment of United States Soldiers acting under the orders Captain [Bennett H.] Hill Commander of the United States troops Stationed at Steilacoom near Fort Nisqually. The said Vessel, having been engaged in no unlawful Calling, and employed solely for the Service of the said Companies in transporting supplies to and exports from the establishment maintained by the Hudson's Bay Company at Nisqually, according to the Provisions of a Treaty Concluded between the Plenipotentiaries of Great Britain and the United States at Washington the 15th day of June in the Year of our Lord, One Thousand and Eight Hundred and Forty Six, which secured to these Companies the right of Occupation of these Posts, and of Carrying on their trade within the United States Territory of Oregon, in the same manner as previous to the making of the said Treaty, and I hereby hold the said Parties and all by whom they were employed liable and responsible for all loss to the said Companies from the detention of said Vessel, the Capture of such goods and the stoppage and derangement of business thereby. Signed,

William Fraser Tolmie, Agent, Puget's Sound & Hudson's Bay Companies

---

Document 1.28: A letter from William F. Tolmie, Nisqually, to James Douglas, Victoria, April 19, 1850.

Sir,

116 Chronologically, this was written into the fort's letterbook on April 20, but is brought forward to this location for the sake of context, continuity, and relevance.

The present express is forwarded to convey the intelligence that the Schooner Cadboro, having arrived here on the 13th Instant, and discharged part of her cargo, was on the 14th (Sunday) seized for alledged infringement of the Revenue Laws, and taken to [Port] Steilacoom by Lieut [John] Dement and a party of armed soldiers acting under the orders of Captain [Bennett H.] Hill the Commanding Officer of the United States troops stationed at Steilacoom [Barracks]. On the 15th, Mr. [George] Dixon, Mate, and Mahon, S[andwich] I[slander], the cook, were ordered by Captain Hill to leave the Vessel and on the 17th Captain [James] Sangster left of his own accord, but with my approval, as I thought that under existing circumstances his health would suffer by his continuing on board. On the evening of the 17th, as I was informed by a note from Captain Hill, the US Inspector of Customs for Puget Sound, a Mr. [Eben May] Dorr, arrived at Steilacoom and made the Custom house seizure of the Cadboro for a violation of the Revenue Laws.[117] I called on Mr. Dorr yesterday and was informed that the Cadboro would be detained until a court should be held [at] Steilacoom, which will probably be in three weeks hence when Judge Pratt is expected to preside. Captain Hill forwarded an Express to Vancouver yesterday by which the District Attorney was requested to have legal proceedings instituted against the Cadboro or her owners.

I wrote Mr. C[hief] F[actor Peter S.] Ogden two days ago informing him of the seizure of the Cadboro and suggesting his retaining one of the leading Lawyers of Oregon City as counsel for the Company at the approaching trial. I trust that he will do what is necessary in the matter, although he has in two letters received within the last two Months informed me that he did not wish to have anything more to do with the business of Fort Nisqually.

Mr. Dorr is to be here today and intends to, I think, to seize that portion of the Cadboro's Cargo that was landed on the 13th. He affirms that he would have seized the Vessel, although no part of the cargo had been landed because she had formerly transgressed the Revenue Laws. In answer to my enquiry as to what arrangements for the future should be made with the Custom house Department, he referred me to the Attorney General of Oregon Mr. [Amory] Holbrook,[118] who, it appears, officiates as Collector during Genl [John] Adair's absence in California.

20th April

Mr. Dorr accompanied by Captain Hill arrived here about 1 p.m. yesterday and proceeded to the Beach Store, I and Mr. [George] Dixon of the Cadboro going down also. Mr. Dorr, calling to witness Mr. [Thomas] Glasgow,[119] the squat-

---

117 At this point in the letter, the following words are inserted between the lines: "The words within brackets are copies from Capt [Bennett H.] Hill: Note."

118 Amory Holbrook's role in the ongoing struggle between the Company and the settlers will grow in the coming chapters and so he will be fully introduced at that time.

119 Glasgow, a 34-year-old Pennsylvanian in 1850, was described by Edward Huggins as a southerner, "a large and powerful man, [with a] fiery temper . . . was rather intelligent, and had received some education." Glasgow had arrived in the Oregon Territory in 1847, tried his luck at farming on Whidbey Island in 1848, and eventually squatted near the fort in May 1849. He would later advise Tolmie on matters concerning the PSAC's sheep shearing operation. By early summer in 1850, Glasgow was "living in a cabin not far from the [abandoned] Richmond Mission house" on American Plain with his Indian wife. Before long, he moved to the waterfront and attempted to squat on a claim at the mouth of Sequalitchew Creek, as noted in chapter 2. Edward Huggins, "The Seizure of the Hudson's Bay Company Schooner *Cadboro*," *Portland Oregonian*, October 28, 1900.

ter on the Company's Lands at Sequalillitchew or the "Fort Creek" declared all the imported goods as seized by the Custom house department as likewise the Oahu [Hawaiian] salt and the wheat lately received from Victoria partly for our own consumption and partly to have ground into Flour at the Newmarket Mill and reshipped to Vancouver's Island. Mr. Dorr stated that he did not feel quite certain as to the property [propriety?] of his seizing the salt, but that he would hereafter instruct his Agent, Mr. Glasgow, how to act with regard to it. After comparing the packages in the store with the Invoice & Bill Lading of the Cadboro's cargo, which I had shown him, and breaking open a keg of nails, regarding the contents of which he entertained a doubt, Mr. Dorr committed the Store and goods therein to Mr. Glasgow's care, agreeing, however, that as we had some Columbia River Flour there, with some Hides, and Lumber which were not seizable, access to said store should be afforded as often as necessary. On returning to the Fort, I applied for the Invoice & Bill Lading, but Mr. Dorr stated that as the ship had no manifest he should retain the Invoice & Bill Lading instead, whereupon I had the Invoice copied.

On returning from the Beach Store to the Fort, Mr. Dorr, as a matter of courtesy, as he said, to the Officers of the Hudson's Bay Company and myself, read me his instructions from the Custom house Authorities. These required him to seize any vessel found violating or known to have violated the Revenue Laws, and the Schooner Cadboro [and Steamer Beaver][120] were particularly specified. The instructions also empowered him to enter and examine any building wherein he had reason to suppose goods were stored that had not been entered at the Custom House.

When Mr. Dorr had finished reading his Instructions, he demanded the keys of the Stores, and entering first one, and then the others, declared all the imported goods therein to be seized, entrusting the keys to [Thomas] Glasgow for the night. I remonstrated several times, but ineffectually, against the above detailed proceedings, Mr. Dorr maintaining that he was justified in seizing any imported goods that had been shipped to Nisqually since the ratification of the Boundary Treaty in 1846.

As a special favor, Mr. Dorr allowed me to retain some Blankets, Shirts, &c., for payment of Indian Labor and some Tea, Sugar, Rice, &c., as stores, but he holds me answerable for all goods thus excepted, should they be required when the court sits.

We have today been busily occupied from sunrise 'till sunset in inventorying, and making packing accounts of the goods seized. Glasgow was present, and, after everything was put into Store No. 2, he locked and sealed the Door of that building. In course of the day, Glasgow received a note from Mr. Dorr at Steilacoom directing that the Oahu salt in the Beach Store should be considered as seized.

Referring you to Captain [James] Sangster's letter for further particulars regarding the seizure of the Cadboro, I have the [honor] to be sir, Your very Obedt Sert,

S[igne]d W. F. Tolmie

---

120 This reference to the HBC steamship *Beaver* was not penned into the HBCA's letterbook manuscript, but is found in the original letter, a copy of which is found at the University of Washington Archives. At this point, the vessel was skippered by Captain Charles E. Stuart (Stewart), with its principal cargo being furs, trade goods, and livestock. Built in England in 1835, she was 101 feet long, 20 feet in the beam, and had an 11-foot deep hold. After sailing around the Horn and arriving at the Fort Vancouver via the Sandwich Islands, the *Beaver* was assigned the Fort Nisqually to Fort Simpson run. Thirty men, ten of whom were wood choppers, comprised the crew. For more information see Watson's *Lives Lived*, 3:1098–1100.

Document 1.29: A letter from William F. Tolmie, Nisqually, to Eben M. Dorr, Olympia, April 20, 1850.

Sir,

Herewith is enclosed My protest against your proceedings in taking possession of the property of the Hudson's Bay & Puget's Sound Companies at this establishment on the 19th Instant. I have the Honour to be Sir, Your Very Obedt St,

(Signed) William Fraser Tolmie

Document 1.30: A Declaration of Protest for the Seizure of the Hudson's Bay & Puget's Sound Agricultural Companies' property by Eben M. Dorr, Inspector of Customs, Puget Sound dated April 20, 1850.[121]

In the name of the Hudson's Bay and Puget's Sound Companies, I do hereby most solemnly protest against Eben M. Dorr, United States Inspector of Customs for Puget's Sound, who on the 19th day of April entered the Hudson's Bay Co's establishment at Nisqually accompanied by Captain [Bennett H.] Hill, Commanding the United States troops stationed at Steilacoom, and after demanding the keys proceeded to take possession of the Property of the Hudson's Bay and Puget's Sound Companies contained in there several storehouses, placing the Custom House Seal on a door of one of the same, wherein he had caused said property to be placed and denying access thereto to the Company's Officers or their necessary business, and to their Manifest loss and detriment, in violation of the provisions of a Treaty Concluded between the Plenipotentiaries of Great Britain and the United States at Washington the 15th day of June 1846, which secured to these Companies the right of occupation of their Posts, and of Carrying on their trade within the United States Territory of Oregon, in the same manner as previous to the making of said Treaty, and I hereby hold the said Eben M. Dorr and all under whose orders he was for the time, liable and responsible for all loss to the said Company thereby. Signed,

William Fraser Tolmie, Agent, Puget's Sound and Hudson's Bay Companies

Document 1.31: A letter from Peter S. Ogden, Vancouver, to William F. Tolmie, Nisqually, May 2, 1850.[122]

Dear Sir,

The enclosed letter[123] from General [John] Adair, Collector of the Customs, conveys instructions for the liberation of the Cadboro on your forwarding the necessary Invoices and Manifests of the Cadboro's Cargo. General Adair informs me she was seized by the Express orders of the Dep[ut]y Collector [Dorr] and not on the authority of Capt[ai]n Hill who merely acted on the occasion by orders of

121 This was written into the fort's letterbook at a latter point chronologically, but is brought forward to this location for the sake of context and continuity.

122 UW Library's Tolmie Papers Acc. 4577-001, Box #1, Folder #8.

123 This letter has yet to be located.

the Civil Government. I am not aware what measures Mr. C[hief] F[actor James] Douglas or Gov [Richard] Blanshard have taken in regard to the seizure. I am not authorized to give you Instructions nor do I intend to as it might cause a clashing of orders and be intricate. I shall therefore say no more. You will, I presume, forward this information to Victoria. The Mary Dare[124] arrived here in safety and has commenced unloading. Some of the Crew have already deserted and before three days [pass] not one will be remaining. To me it appears more than doubtful if I can attain another Crew. I shall at all events discharge and reload her and use my utmost endeavouring to procure another Crew. Seamen's Wages are now fifty dollars each per month. I have to request you forward this letter provided you consider it expedient to communicate with C[hief] F[actor James] Douglas as I am at present too much occupied to write. Yours truly,

Peter Skene Ogden

P.S. We are most anxious to have our Sheep, the sooner the better. A License has been granted to the Prince of Wales[125] and she has now full permission to sail. P. S. O.

Document 1.32: A letter from William F. Tolmie, Nisqually, to Peter S. Ogden, Vancouver, May 4, 1850.

Sir,

On returning from Victoria on the 2nd Instant, I received your communication of the 25th Ult in which you express regret that my report on the seizure of the Cadboro was so mixed up with irrelevant matter that you "could not lay it before a lawyer to obtain his service." Now, in this matter, I must respectfully take leave to differ from you. My letter of the 16th April to which you refer, certainly touches on various matters, but all relating to the seizure of the Cadboro is contained in the fourth paragraph which is the form of an extract [that] could have been submitted to a lawyer had you in other respects deemed it advisable to have employed counsel at once. I now forward a copy of my report to Mr. C[hief] F[actor] [James] Douglas on the capture of the Cadboro by a military force from Steilacoom and the seizure of the Company property at this establishment by Mr. Dorr US Inspector of Customs for Puget's Sound. Duplicates are also enclosed of my protest against the proceedings of the US Authorities in these, their violations of our rights as guaranteed by Treaty.

I have communicated with Mr. C[hief] F[actor James] Douglas as regards the 120 M [thousand] shingles shipped on board the Sacramento, [Captain William A. Mouat] on account of M[isters George T.] Allan and [Archibald] Mackinlay, and relanded here at their risk and Mr. D[ouglas] has instructed me to charge said Shingles to Ft Vancouver Depot at their cost price, *vizt.*; 100 M [thousand] at $10 per M, and 20 M at $4 per M. Please forward per first opp[ortuni]ty on account Ft Nisqually O[utfi]t 1850—2 Brass Bottling Cocks. Mr. [James] Douglas informs that there was lately a large stock of them on hand at Vancouver.

S[igne]d Wm F. Tolmie

---

124 *Mary Dare*, HBC brig. See Watson, *Lives Lived*, 3:1118

125 *Prince of Wales*, HBC schooner. See Watson, *Lives Lived*, 3:1126.

Document 1.33: A letter from William F. Tolmie, Nisqually, to Peter S. Ogden, Vancouver, May 8, 1850.

Dear Sir,

I had the pleasure to receive on the evening of the 7th your official communication of the 2nd Inst conveying the gratifying intelligence that the Cadboro would be restored to us on my forwarding the necessary Invoices and manifest of the Cadboro's cargo. My expectations were rather damped however yesterday when on calling on Captain [Bennett H.] Hill at Steilacoom [Barracks], I could learn nothing favorably from him. General [John] Adair's instructions regarding the Cadboro are, I suppose, contained in a letter for Mr. Dorr accompanying Captain Hill's packet but as Mr. D[orr] is absent, I cannot for a few days yet, when he is looked for back, ascertain what is to be expected from the Custom house Authorities. For my own part, I am not without apprehension that the strict letter of the law will be enforced against the Coy without regard to the rights and privileges secured to us by the Oregon Boundary Treaty. I delivered the Invoice & Bill Lading of the Cadboro's cargo to Mr. Inspector Dorr and cannot obtain them 'till his return, as he insisted on retaining possession. I shall then perhaps ascertain too, as you speak of Invoices, whether the Invoices of former cargoes will have to be forwarded, as well as that of the present ones. I have not despatched an express to Mr. [James] Douglas and expect him here today, or tomorrow, and have horses in readiness for his speedy progress towards Cowlitz. I hope that, as Genl [John] Adair seems inclined to compromise matters, he has stayed legal proceedings against the Cadboro.

Mr. [Michael T.] Simmons[126] of Newmarket is of opinion that when in 1848 he presented orders from Pere [Pascal] Ricard and Mr. G[eorge] B. Roberts for $100, and $20 respectively, he overpaid in Ft Vancouver Sale Shop to the amount of ($14) fourteen dollars, and he has requested me to make enquiry on the subject. Please to send when convenient a statements of J[ean] B[aptiste] Jollibois' account.[127]

William Fraser Tolmie

P.S. I hope to have your Wedders washed and shorn next week, and started for Cowlitz immediately thereafter. It would be necessary to have a few horses from Vancouver awaiting the party at Kaweeman.[128] T

Document 1.34: A letter from William F. Tolmie, Nisqually, to Archibald Barclay, London, May 10, 1850.

126 Simmons (1814–1867) was born in Kentucky. Moving westward, he married Elizabeth Kinder in 1836 in Iowa, and in 1840 settled in Missouri, where he built a grist mill. Joining the westward migration, Simmons was elected the wagon train's "colonel" by a majority of the train's members. They arrived at Washougal on the Columbia River in 1845. Simmons moved north of the Columbia River and settled on the Deschutes River in Washington, naming it New Market. Simmons served as an Indian Agent for the Puget Sound tribes, and was the first postmaster of Nisqually in 1850. He later moved to Big Skookum Bay, and built another mill. Simmons died in 1867 at Lewis County. Shanna B. Stevenson, *Lacey, Olympia, and Tumwater: A Pictorial History* (Norfolk, VA: The Donning Company, 1985), 17.

127 For Jollibois see Watson, *Lives Lived*, 2:495.

128 For Coweeman Post see Watson, *Lives Lived*, 3:1050.

Sir,

I take advantage of an opportunity from Puget's Sound to San Francisco, to write for the information of their Honours, the Governor, Dep[ut]y Governor, and Committee that the Schooner Cadboro was taken possession of at this place by the United States military authorities on the 14th Ulto and on the 19th all the goods in our warehouses, including wheat from Victoria, Vancouver Island, and Salt from Oahu were seized and placed under the Custom house seal by a Mr. Dorr, Inspector of Customs for Puget's Sound. After, on the 20th, making packing accounts, and Inventory of the goods seized, I hastened to Victoria to inform Mr. Chief Factor [James] Douglas of what had happened and consult with him as to future proceedings, and on my return the accompanying Protests were handed to Captain [Bennett H.] Hill, Commander of the US Troops stationed at Steilacoom in this neighborhood, and to Mr. Dorr respectively.

Since the establishment of a custom house in Oregon in Spring 1849, supplies forwarded from Victoria to Nisqually have always been invoiced at prime cost, and I have been instructed by the Board of Management to pay duties upon them, as soon as any Custom house Officer should be appointed on Puget's Sound. There was no person here commissioned to collect revenue when the Cadboro arrived for a very few days previously. I had put the question directly to Captain [Bennett H.] Hill and his answer was that he himself had no authority neither did he know of anyone who had.

The Cadboro is now lying at Steilacoom roadstead in possession of the US authorities and her case will be tried before a circuit court soon to be held in this county—a violation of the Revenue Laws is the charge to be advanced against us and I am inclined to think that such is the spirit of commercial and national jealously afloat, our long possessed rights of free navigation, and trade guaranteed by the Boundary Treaty of 1846 will be overlooked in the eagerness to obtain a conviction, and further trammel[129] and derange our business.

A feeling in disfavor of the Company was unfortunately occasioned by an occurrence which took place when the Cadboro last sailed from Nisqually in March 1850, for a couple of deserters from the US troops at Steilacoom getting secretly on board the Cadboro somewhere in Admiralty Inlet, managed during the short passage by exciting the sympathies of a white man on board and by bribing the Indian crew, to keep out of sight of Captain [James] Sangster and his mate 'till the Schooner was at anchor in Victoria harbour.

Captain [James] Sangster before leaving Nisqually had taken precautions to prevent anything of the sort by having the vessel carefully searched for deserters which Lieut [John B.] Gibson [Jr.], of the US A[rmy] Steilacoom, was on board—when, subsequently, Govr [Richard] Blanshard of Vancouver's Island visited Nisqually in H.M.S. Driver, Captain [Bennett H.] Hill enquired of him whether the deserters would be given up were he [Captain Hill] to send a party in quest of them to Victoria—and on the Governor replying in the negative, he, I believe, made such representations of the matter to the US authorities on the Columbia River as to have led to their subsequent proceedings against us.

I am daily looking for Mr. C[hief] F[actor James] Douglas here and had hoped to have seen him in time enough to have written the Govr and Committee by the

129 The term "trammel" means to limit or restrict.

present opportunity.

I have just learnt from Mr. C[hief] F[actor Peter S.] Ogden that the greater number of the Mary Dare's crew have deserted in the Columbia River. That vessel was to have taken a cargo of flour and salted provisions to Victoria, and 'tis to be hoped that Mr. [Chief Factor Peter S.] Ogden may soon succeed in getting her off.

Here, our business as merchants and Indian traders is quite at a stand [still].

The Puget's Sound Company business has as yet sustained no derangement. There has been a considerable loss of horned cattle and horses during the past very severe winter and backward Spring. Lambing has gone on favourably. Beef sells at from 4d to 5d per [pound] and Wedders at $5.00 or 2 of 10 each. Mr. [Chief Factor Peter S.] Ogden has applied for a thousand wedder [sheep] which he hopes to sell at from 20/ to 25/ each. The demand here will increase when the Mail steamers call at Puget's Sound, an arrangement soon to take place. The California market is now overstocked with Lumber and Provisions and cargoes of both purchased at San Francisco [are] being sold in Oregon at remunerative prices. Having nothing more of importance to communicate, I have the honor to remain Sir, Your very obt Sert,

(Signed) W. F. Tolmie

Document 1.35: A letter from William F. Tolmie, Nisqually, to Eben M. Dorr, Olympia, May 18, 1850.

Sir,

In making application, as per my letter to you of the 19th Ulto, that you should exempt from seizure articles of Stores essentially necessary for the use of this establishment, on the hurry of the moment, as you were pressed for time, I forgot to mention certain goods of which after your departure for New Dungeness, the want was immediately felt. Of other things, I asked for too small a supply expecting that in a very short time an equitable arrangement would have been made between the US Custom House authorities and the Hudson's Bay Company. I have therefore on the present occasion to request that you would allow me to have on such terms as you may deem just, the articles mentioned in the subjoined list[130] from amongst the goods seized upon by you, at this place on the 19th April 1850. I have the Honour to be Sir, Your Very Obet Servant,

(S[igne]d) William Fraser Tolmie

Document 1.36: A letter from Eben M. Dorr, Port Steilacoom, to William F. Tolmie, Nisqually, May 18, 1850.[131]

Sir,

Your letter of this date requesting to be allowed certain goods now under seizure for infractions of the U.S. Revenue Laws, and which you state as "essentially necessary" for the use of the Puget Sound Agricultural Company and Hudson's Bay Company, has been received, and with the full & distinct understanding that the permission will be entirely on act of courtesy & not of right, it will afford me

---

130 See the next letter in this chapter for a complete list of goods requested by Dr. Tolmie and allowed by Dorr.

131 UW Library's Tolmie Papers Acc. 4577-001, Box #1, Folder #2.

pleasure to grant you the privilege of taking the following articles as desired by you:

Two pairs Cart wheels
100 Bushels of Salt
500 [pounds of] Brown Sugar
1 Case Congo Tea
2 Cwt [hundred-weight] Mottled Soap
200 Wool Sheets & Bags &c., on ac[count] PS Agricultural Compy
2 doz Sheep Shears
2 pieces Baize
2 Nests Tin Kettles
50 3 point Blankets
28 [pounds of] shot
[50] Sheep & Cow bells
I am Sir, Resp[ectfull]y Your Obdt Sert,
Eben May Dorr, U.S. Insp[ecto]r [of] Customs

Document 1.37: A letter from William F. Tolmie, Nisqually, to Peter S. Ogden, Vancouver, May 20, 1850.

Sir,

I received on the 17th Instant your communication of the 10th conveying your views on the late proceedings of the US Customs house authorities in the seizure of the Cadboro and of the imported goods in the Company's stores at this place.

On the 18th I called on Captain [Bennett H.] Hill and on Mr. [Eben M.] Dorr who had just returned from an excursion to Possession Sound and Admiralty Inlet.

Captain Hill, with whom I first conversed, informed me that Mr. Dorr had received a letter from Genl [John] Adair advising him to stop proceedings against the Company, and release the Cadboro, but that Mr. D[orr], whose intent it is to have the property confiscated and sold, declined doing so unless on receipt of positive instructions to that effect from Genl Adair. Captain Hill added that that it was also his own desire that the Law should take its courses as a compromise now would, he thought, imply condemnation of his conduct in having seized the Cadboro in the past instance.

Mr. Dorr repeated in substance the communication made by Captain Hill and stated his intention of immediately writing by express to or visiting General Adair at Astoria.

I obtained, on the 18th from Mr. Dorr, an order for some goods and stores for the use of the establishment from amongst the articles seized on my becoming personally responsible to him for the full value of the things thus obtained.

I should like to have, in the event of a sale by auction of the Company's property, your opinion as to what articles it would be advisable to buy [and] whether it would pay to bid high for Cotton goods, and what you think, considering the value of goods in California and Oregon, ought to be our ultimate bid for Blankets, Baize and Strouds?

Signed W. F. Tolmie

CHAPTER TWO

June 1st, 1850–November 30th, 1850

"Business progresses here much as usual except that money is becoming rather scarce."
—William F. Tolmie to Peter S. Ogden, August 9, 1850

As the accounts of Outfit 1851 opened, seven company servants from Vancouver Island (deserters who had hoped to reach California) arrived at Nisqually. Stripped of their belongings by the S'Klallam Indians living near today's Port Townsend, all begged (save one) to be "forgiven for the present escapade" noted Tolmie in the *Nisqually Journal*.[1] The French Canadian Michel Lafleur,[2] a hold-out for higher wages, would later be joined by François Coté.[3] Their departure from the Company's employment, along with that of apprentice clerk Samuel Robertson,[4] further illustrates "gold fever's" impact on the region's labor market. Eventually, Coté would discard a dozen years of loyal Company service to begin working at a grist mill recently established at Deschutes River falls in today's Tumwater. Undoubtedly offered double or perhaps triple his former wages, how could he refuse?

With the *Cadboro* and the Nisqually's warehouses still under the customs officials' "watch and ward," James Douglas toured HBC/PSAC holdings on American soil. His itinerary included talks with leading customs officials. On June 12, a courier "arrived about [noon] with a letter from Mr. Chief Factor Douglas dated Fort George,[5] 5th June, and stating that the Cadboro & goods would be released [as] soon as General Adair should arrive [at Nisqually]."[6] That day John Adair, his subordinate Eben Dorr, and U.S. Navy Captain William P. McArthur[7] rode into the fort and officially announced the Company innocent of all smuggling charges. Now vindicated, Tolmie likely viewed the seizures as a one-off anomaly. Unfortunately, having one's vessels and warehouses under "the opposition's" control for two full months had already "deranged" Nisqually farm's business to a great extent.

1 Dickey, ed., *Nisqually Journal*, June 1, 1850.
2 For Lafleur see Watson, *Lives Lived*, 2:550.
3 For Coté see Watson, *Lives Lived*, 1:289.
4 For Robertson see Watson, *Lives Lived*, 2:824.
5 Fort George see Watson, *Lives Lived*, 3:1047–1050.
6 Dickey, ed., *Nisqually Journal*, June 12, 1850.
7 William Pope McArthur was actually a lieutenant commander when he visited Fort Nisqually in 1850. See en.wikipedia.org/wiki/William_Pope_McArthur.

Now mindful of the Company's precarious situation, Collector Adair warned Douglas and Tolmie that his successor might not be so equally, or fairly, disposed. Also, the practice of transporting supplies between Victoria and Nisqually via Indian canoe (which had successfully circumvented the Olympia customs officials) had become known to Adair. He now demanded that the practice be stopped.

As the *Cadboro*'s seizure ended, over 1,000 Nisqually sheep were herded southward towards Vancouver.[8] John McPhail, a lowly, illiterate Scottish herdsman who suffered from rheumatoid arthritis and alcoholism, assumed the responsibility of driving that massive flock southward. It was a significant boost in responsibility.

In contrast to McPhail's rising status, Captain Henderwell, a well-educated, no-nonsense gentleman of means had lost his command and his ship, the *Albion*. Most of his crew had deserted to California. With no immediate means of returning home, Henderwell's status became that of castaway. And though Secretary of the Treasury William M. Meredith[9] later agreed with Adair that the *Albion* should be returned unharmed "on payment of all costs attending to the seizure,"[10] by then the vessel had been auctioned off, renamed *Elizabeth*, loaded with spars, and sailed to San Francisco. There, she was unloaded and unceremoniously sunk as part of a breakwater project.

With John Adair's sympathy towards the Company publicly validated, the settlers sought a new champion. Oregon Territory's delegate to the U.S. Congress, the "Honorable" Samuel R. Thurston, fit the mold perfectly.[11] In the fall of 1849, he had gained a partner—the Oregon Territory's new Indian Agent Jesse Thornton.

On learning of the May 1849 murder of Leander Wallace during the melee at Fort Nisqually, Senator Thurston heard Thornton's version of the so-called "battle." Perhaps inadvertently, two parallel (but unrelated) "blankets as gifts to Indians" stories emerged. Both stories shared three elements: 1) Dr. Tolmie's role as a leading protagonist; 2) the purchase of HBC blankets from the fort's sales shop as a payout to Indians; and 3) the death of an American settler by Indians at the British fort.

The first story involved 80 blankets paid as a bounty to Indians who had delivered Wallace's supposed murderers to the authorities. These blankets had been purchased from the fort's sales shop, and thus from Dr. Tolmie, by the territory's United States Indian agency—but indirectly through the U.S. Army.

8 The sale and transport of Nisqually's sheep remained steady throughout the rest of the year, even after the blockade of trade routes which occurred in the fall.

9 A native Pennsylvanian, Meredith (1799–1873) was a Secretary of the Treasury under President Zachary Taylor. A strongly patriotic Whig, Meredith opposed free-trade legislation and worked to protect the American worker. His main contribution while in office was his Annual Report of 1849 in which he set forth an elaborate argument for a protective tariff. www.treasury.gov/about/history/Pages/wmmeredith.aspx.

10 William M. Meredith to John Adair, January 11, 1851. Edward Huggins Collection, Washington State Historical Society, Tacoma, WA, letter #11.

11 College educated, Thurston (1815–1851) arrived in the Pacific Northwest in 1847 via the Oregon Trail. He first practiced law in Hillsboro, Oregon. By 1848, however, he was elected to the Provisional Legislature from the Tualatin District. In 1849, he represented the Oregon Territory in the U.S. Congress. Smearing the Company's (and McLoughlin's) name had become a common tactic for Thurston. An example of this was his authorship of the Donation Land Claim Act, its principal purpose being to relieve McLoughlin of his Oregon City acreage to the benefit of territory's burgeoning state legislature. In addition, Thurston frequently perjured himself, making false accusations about McLoughlin (and in this case Tolmie) before the U.S. Congress in an effort to publicly discredit both men and the HBC.

The second story involved blankets purchased privately by Dr. Tolmie. Adhering to a long-standing Coast Salish tradition of respect and remembrance of the dead, the doctor's personal gift had been presented to the families of other friendly Indians who had also been killed during the same melee as Wallace.[12]

Senator Thurston, a politician who had built his reputation by opposing the HBC in general, and Dr. John McLoughlin in particular, used the stories to further his attacks on the Company. Merging the two stories, he stood on the floor of the U.S. Congress asserting that the blankets had been personally bought by Tolmie and gifted to the relatives of the Indians that had been hung for Wallace's murder, rather than those injured in the melee. This "foreigner" had done so, according to the congressman, to "conciliate the Indians of the Territory of Oregon, and to prejudice them against our people and Government."

On learning of Thurston's indictments, Tolmie roundly dismissed them as "contemptuous trickery . . . ridiculous" and an attempt to "stir the pot" in order to increase the settlers' dislike of him and his employer's concerns. Unfortunately for Nisqually's chief trader, Thurston's subterfuge worked. It alarmed citizens throughout the region, as well as politicians and cabinet members in Washington, D.C. As Thurston's lies wended their way through the halls of our nation's capital, Secretary of the Treasury William M. Meredith and Secretary of the Interior Thomas Ewing[13] reacted in outrage. Convinced that Thurston's claims were valid, they enacted a maritime blockade of the Company's ports south of the 49th parallel, effectively cutting off trade routes between Victoria, Nisqually, and Vancouver.

Company officials, stunned by this development, worked overtime to control the damage.

Chief Factor Ogden's letter to territorial Governor John Gaines maintained that the HBC had no control over the Indians nor did it prejudice them against the settlers. The HBC, Ogden reiterated, was "open to the strictest investigation and the conduct and active parts taken by their Agents in the unfortunate Massacre of American Citizens [at the Whitman Mission in 1847]. The Rescue and preservation of the Lives of Fifty-four Individuals, who, were chosen to die, should in itself be fully sufficient to convince all unprejudiced men that the accusations brought against those by the Hon[ora]ble S[amuel] R. Thurston are destitute of truth." In a letter to the HBC Secretary Barclay, dated October 5, 1850, Douglas again slighted the 1846 Treaty as "that loosely expressed, and vaguely defined instrument." He also noted that since 1846, the HBC had the right of free navigation between those ports, but that the American authorities were now acting "strictly in accordance" with the language of the treaty. Douglas continued, observing "that right [of navigation] is now denied to us, and our vessels are threatened with seizure and confiscation, if found within the waters of Puget's Sound."[14]

12 In a March 17, 1852, letter from Dr. Tolmie to Indian Agent Edmund Starling, the doctor remembered buying several blankets which he later presented to the relatives of the Indians shot dead during the melee, not the relatives of those hanged for Wallace's murder. For specifics, see letter 5.39 in chapter five of this work.

13 Thomas Ewing (1789–1871) was a Whig and later National Republican politician from Ohio. He served in the U.S. Senate, as the Secretary of the Treasury, and as the first Secretary of the Interior. en.wikipedia.org/wiki/Thomas_Ewing.

14 James Douglas to Archibald Barclay, October 5, 1850, James Douglas's *Victoria Letters*, 124–25.

With Thurston's "contemptuous trickery" supplanting reality, the Company's ability to conduct business had, once again, become far more difficult. When news of the blockade reached Tolmie's desk, he dispatched a canoe to Douglas with a message that "should the Cadboro arrive here prior to your receiving and replying to this, I shall, in earnest, discharge and despatch her immediately." By early October, the doctor had also sent a message to Ogden that recognized the new arrangement. Apparently, it did not impact the Company's sheep business south of the boundary line or its ability to move personnel by canoe to and from Victoria. Dr. Tolmie, his wife Jane, and her sister Sarah Work Finlayson,[15] took that trip on October 12 without Olympia's customs officials' objections (or notice).

General Adair's selection of a squatter named Thomas Glasgow as Port Nisqually customs agent only worsened the situation. Glasgow's short-lived term in office aside, Adair's choice seems to have been a matter of convenience rather than qualification or temperament. Glasgow had sited his squatter's shack just north of the Company's beachfront warehouse/dock at the mouth of Sequalitchew Creek. Straight away, the man's intractable disposition exasperated neighboring Indians, Company employees, and especially Tolmie.[16] The man's bad behavior would prove to be his undoing. Edward Huggins remembered that the man "could not get along with Dr. Tolmie, who disliked him more for his cruel treatment of the Indians than anything else."[17] This included quarreling and physically abusing his Indian neighbors. "On the land [Glasgow] claimed [for himself] were many Indian graves," Huggins stated. "I am of the opinion that [he] disturbed some of these Indian tombs, or did not treat them with the respect that usually white people paid to them."[18] "He one day got into a dispute . . . [and] from bad words, blows resulted, which ended by Glasgow . . . knocking [an Indian] prostrate, jumped on him, smashing his ribs, causing his death."[19] The death was accidental, according to Huggins, but Glasgow's actions put his own life in peril so he quit the customs job and fled his claim.[20]

Concurrently, a new source of gold was found, this time to the north of Vancouver Island. In an August 17 letter from Douglas to HBC Secretary Barclay, the chief factor noted that John Work was on his way to Queen Charlottes Island where Indians had "found Gold on the west coast of the island, as far as we can gather from their reports, about Cape Henry, Englefields Bay."[21] Douglas warned

---

15 Finlayson (1829–1906) was born at Fort Colvile to John Work and Josette Work. She married Roderick Finlayson and was mother to Mary, Sara Jane, Catherine, Anne Jane, John, and six others. www.geni.com/people/Sarah-Work/6000000014037056571 and wc.rootsweb.ancestry.com/cgi-bin/igm.cgi?op=GET&db=nisqually&id=I004.

16 In one of the letters of this chapter, Dr. Tolmie lamented about two pairs of undeclared socks in the "Victoria Bales" that alarmed Inspector Glasgow to the point of seizing the vessel's entire load. This small, but "troublesome" incident illustrates the two men's increasingly strained relationship and turbulent enmity that they shared for each other.

17 Huggins, "Seizure of the Schooner *Cadboro*."

18 Ibid.

19 Edward Huggins to Clarence B. Bagley, October 14, 1903, UW Library's Clarence B. Bagley Papers.

20 Huggins, "Seizure of the Schooner *Cadboro*."

21 James Douglas to Archibald Barclay, August 17, 1850. HBCA Correspondence Inward, A.11/72, fos. 290-293d. Although it is likely that James Douglas discussed this with Dr. Tolmie soon after, we do not see mention of the Queen Charlottes Island gold in these letters until August 1851.

that "[o]ur accounts of the discovery are in consequence derived from other Indians, who have not visited the District since the gold was discovered, and are somewhat conflicting in their details. Some say that the gold is found in rocks, while other assert that it is in the sand, in such small particles that it is difficult to pick up. It is probably found both *in situ* and travelled."[22] While such news was typically kept secret by Company officials, Puget Sound's settlers soon learned of the gold as well. The bellicose Haida tribe of Queen Charlotte Island was about to get a visit by gold hungry American settlers.

Squatters continued to harass Tolmie. Then, President Millard Fillmore exacerbated the issue by signing the Donation Act/Oregon Land Law.[23] Many settlers now firmly believed the Company's lands were open for the taking so their aggressiveness increased. In order to counter the encroachments, the Company privately deeded lands to a select group of officials—principally its gentlemen (ie., chief factors, chief traders, senior clerks). Huge tracks of land on the Columbia River, Cowlitz Farm, and at Nisqually where deeded over to officers like Tolmie with the hopes of securing title until the United States fulfilled the treaty's promise of a buy-out. Parcels of Nisqually's prairie lands were held in the names of Tolmie, Douglas, Work, et al.—but on paper only.

And while Tolmie understood the need for such contrivances, he also felt slighted—even overlooked—by the HBC's Board of Management in the area of advancement to a chief factor's position. Once again, he appealed for a raise in this chapter's documents. Tracts of land on Vancouver Island had also been offered to the HBC's upper management at bargain prices, a development that solidified the doctor's views about retiring on land north of Fort Victoria.

Land acquisition was not solely the domain of the Company's gentlemen. For those who had previously worked the PSAC's outstations at Nisqually, many squatted on some of the most fertile ground available. At the PSAC's Muck Farm, retired carpenter Charles Wren[24] claimed some of that outstation's most arable sections for himself. Still consumed with threading the Americans' naval blockade,

---

22 Ibid.

23 The Donation Land Claim Law entered the books on September 27, 1850, and allowed every 21-year-old citizen living in the Oregon Territory to select 320 acres of land, live upon it, and cultivate it for five full years. If married, the couple was entitled to an additional half section, equaling 640 acres. Individuals wishing to take advantage of this public "give-away" had to move to Oregon before December 1, 1853, to qualify. On February 14, 1853, the act was extended for two more years, though the amount of land allowed for the taking was reduced to half of that allowed by the original act. After 1854, the land was sold at $1.25 per acre.

24 Sometime early in Charles Wren's (c.1827–1873) life, his name was anglicized from Reine to Wren, obliterating the traces of his Swiss father, who died in the employ of the HBC, and mixed descent mother. Eleven years after his widowed mother married Horatio Nelson Calder, Charles joined his stepfather on the westward trek of Red River settlers to north of the Columbia. Wren began work with PSAC on September 20, 1843, doing mainly carpentry work ranging from making wheels for barrows and coopering beef casks to erecting houses. However, by the end of 1846 and beginning of 1847 he ran afoul of his employer. On May 1, 1849, he became the central figure in a rare slugging and shooting incident with a party of Snoqualmie and Skykomish natives who had rushed the fort to possibly kidnap some Indian women and children. At the end of that month he was ordered to Victoria and he became free on September 30, 1849; on November 15, 1849, he settled a claim of 641 acres in Pacific County. Charles Wren died in Victoria on February 24, 1873. Information provided courtesy of Bruce M. Watson, 4/27/2015.

Tolmie realized that Wren's squatting could set a dangerous precedent, so he had no choice but to discuss matters with an attorney.

With the onset of fall, two 1849 deserters, John Montgomery[25] and the supposedly "deceased" John McLeod, arrived at the fort's gates having traveled overland from California's gold fields. Montgomery had signed on with the PSAC in 1839, managed some of the earliest herds of horned cattle and horses in western Washington history—and possessed a butcher's skill-set. McLeod had arrived earlier than Montgomery, worked initially on the steamer *Beaver*, married an Indian wife, and herded sheep throughout present-day Lakewood and University Place, Washington. Hats in hand, both approached Tolmie in an attempt to regain forfeited wages, and perhaps a reposting. The chief trader needed men, but he was weary of further desertions. In this case, both men were awarded their past wages, but only John Montgomery was brought back on as the fort's head wrangler/butcher. John McLeod would have to fend for himself from this point forward.

Several new correspondents appear in this chapter. Hugh A. Goldsborough was a prominent settler in the territorial government, customs house activities, and an American "friend" to the Company.[26] He witnessed the signing of several Indian treaties and was connected through his business concern with Fort Steilacoom. Chief Trader Roderick Finlayson also appears for the first time in this chapter.[27] An Irishman, Finlayson had worked in the fur trade since 1837, but came west in 1839 to work as a clerk at Fort Vancouver. By 1850, he was second in charge at Fort Victoria under James Douglas—and a peer to Tolmie. The HBC's North American Governor Sir George Simpson's name is also mentioned in the following pages.[28] Simpson had held that position since the amalgamation of the HBC and Northwest Company in 1821. Though he rarely communicated directly with Dr. Tolmie, the two did correspond from time to time.

The blockade persisted throughout the winter of 1850–1851. And while Tolmie was absent on business matters, the aging former postmaster from Cowlitz Farm, Charles Forrest, was left in charge at Nisqually.

Here then are the letters for the first half of Outfit 1851.

Document 2.01: A letter from William F. Tolmie, Nisqually, to Roderick Finlayson, Victoria, June 1, 1850.

Dear Sir,

Yesterday evening, seven of the Victoria men, [Michel] Lafleur and six

25 For more information on John Montgomery, see Steve Anderson, "The Forgetting of John Montgomery: Spanaway's First White Settler, 1845–1885," *Pacific Northwest Quarterly* (2010), 71–86.

26 For more information on Goldsborough (1818–1890), see Reese, ed., *Journal of Kautz*, 417.

27 For Finlayson (1818–1892) see Watson, *Lives Lived*, 1:377–78.

28 For Simpson (c. 1786–1860) see Watson, *Lives Lived*, 3:870.

Englishmen, [George] Miller,[29] [Henry] Wain,[30] [Charles] Fish,[31] [William Walter] Sims,[32] [Joseph] Gray[33] and [George] Richardson,[34] arrived here. But, having been pillaged of all their property by the S'Klallam's encamped at Point Partridge[35]

---

29 Miller [variation: Millar] (fl. 1849–50) was an independent emigrant laborer, possibly from Dartford, England, associated with the barque *Norman Morison* (1849–50) as a passenger. He came to Vancouver Island on the *Norman Morison* working for Captain W. C. Grant, and thus is only peripherally attached to the fur trade. After he reached Vancouver Island on March 24, 1850, he began working for Grant but as early as May was charged with riotous conduct. On July 17, 1850, he deserted along with fellow Grant employee Samuel Robertson as well as with the *Mary Dare* steward, William Martindale. Two undelivered family 1850 letters to Miller, from Dartford, England, rest in the HBCA. *PS:* HBCA YFASA 29-30; YFDS 21; B.223/d/195; with Captain Grant, A.11/72, fo. 289; MisI 5; BCA Colonial Correspondence, extracts from police register [charged with "Riotous Conduct" May 20, 1850]????; *SS*: Mouat, "Notes on the *Norman Morison*," 213. Biographical information collected by and printed here courtesy of Bruce M. Watson

30 For Wain see Watson, *Lives Lived*, 3:964. In Watson's work there is no mention of this desertion on the basis that it would not be included in his personnel files because Wain returned to duty shortly thereafter.

31 Fish (c.1830–51) was a HBC sponsored settler/blacksmith, born in Sturminster, Dorset, England, He came to Victoria as a blacksmith at age 19 in 1850. Just prior to his brothers joining him, he and some others went off in high spirits to fire a cannon in salute from the Fort Victoria bastion. As Fish was ramming the cannon, it went off, blowing off his hand. Dr. J. S. Helmcken, who had come to Victoria with Fish, tried to stop the advancing gangrene by amputating the arm twice. It was to no avail and the 21-year-old died and was buried on November 16, 1851, at the old fort graveyard at the corner of Douglas and Johnson Streets. *PS*: HBCA YFASA 29-32; FtVicDS 1; BCA BCCR-CCCath; *PPS*: Helmcken, *The Reminiscences of…*, 140–41; *SS*: Mouat, "Notes on the *Norman Morison*," 213. Biographical information collected by and printed here courtesy of Bruce M. Watson.

32 Sims (c.1833–1916) was a HBC sponsored employee, born in Dorsetshire, England. He was 16 years old when he decided to come to Vancouver Island from Dorsetshire on the *Norman Morison*. He worked his first two seasons at Fort Victoria paying off his debts to the Company. In 1852, with rumors of gold in the Queen Charlotte Islands reaching Victoria, the HBC brig *Recovery* [William Mitchell] was outfitted to explore the area, the crew, of which Sims was a member, to share the profit after expenses. The venture was unsuccessful and he and two partners leased 800 acres in the James Bay area from the HBC, naming it Beckley Farm. When the lease ended in 1860, Sims became a butcher for a short time. He finally began a 40 year career with the City of Victoria, 30 years of which were with the Waterworks Department. William Walter Sims died at his resident on Rudlin Avenue on March 15, 1916. Sims had one wife, Ellen (c.1843–?), who came out on the *Norman Morison* in 1853 and whom he married in 1859, and eight or more children. *PS:* HBCA YFASA 29-32; FtVicASA 1; VPL *The Colonist*, March 21, 1915, p. 7; March 17, 1916, p. 7; *SS*: Mouat, "Notes on the *Norman Morison*," p. 213. Biographical information collected by and printed here courtesy of Bruce M. Watson.

33 Joseph Gray (fl. 1849–1854) arrived on Vancouver Island in 1850 and worked for the HBC for four years. It is uncertain when his wife Annie came out but they were likely together when they set up residence in Esquimalt by 1860. He died of cancer at his home in Esquimalt at the age of 66. *PS*: HBCA YFASA 29-32; YFDS 23; FtVicDS 1; FtVicASA 1-2; VPL *The Colonist*, Aug. 31, 1894, p. 5; *SS:* Mouat, "Notes on the *Norman Morison*," 213. Biographical information collected by and printed here courtesy of Bruce M. Watson.

34 George Richardson (c.1826–1922) came to Vancouver Island in March 1850 on the *Norman Morison*. After arriving, he worked for the HBC at Fort Simpson where he refused to do work on September 3, 1850. Shortly afterwards he returned to Victoria, went off the HBC records, and may have returned to England where he married, for a George Richardson and wife arrived back at Victoria in 1858 aboard the *Princess Royal*. That year he bought 300 acres in the South Saanich area. He was a voter in 1860 and, by 1871, had become the proprietor of the Victoria Hotel. He later became the proprietor of the Windsor Hotel until he retired around 1902. *PS:* HBCA YFASA 29-31; YFDS 21; Log of *Princess Royal* [2] 4; BCA BCGR-CrtR-AbstLnd; Mallandain, *First Victoria Directory, Victoria, 1960*, p. 67; *Victoria Times*, June 19, 1922; *PPS:* Helmcken, *The Reminiscences of…*p. 77; *SS* Mouat, "Notes on the *Norman Morison*," 213. Biographical information collected by and printed here courtesy of Bruce M. Watson.

35 Point Partridge is today's Port Townsend, Washington.

("King George"[36] and his gang), the six Englishmen have consented to return to Victoria and resume duty on condition that their offence in having deserted should be forgiven and their wages already earned secured to them, on which points I have given them a written assurance that it should be as they had stipulated. [Michel] Lafleur wishes to see Mr. [Chief Factor James] Douglas before returning as he positively objects to ever again working in the same shop with [Jean Bastiste] Beauchamp.[37] [The *Cadboro*'s first officer] Mr. [George] Dixon accompanies the party to Victoria whence he will return immediately. Please send by Return—24 Skenes Roping Twine, I remain Dear Sir, Respectfully Yours,

W.F. Tolmie

Document 2.02: A private letter from William F. Tolmie, Nisqually, to Roderick Finlayson, Victoria, June 13, 1850.[38]

My Dear Sir,

Having been much occupied of late finishing potato planting and with a staff of greenhorns getting the Wool harvest secured, I have not been able to get a long letter for you advanced, but hope that Jane [Work] and your Victoria correspondents may omit nothing in the way of news. Mr. [James] D[ouglas], who has just made a Grand Tour, ought to furnish a large quota of intelligence.

John [Work Jr.,][39] has been with us about six weeks and during that period has improved himself in writing, arithmetic, and the speaking of English.

I have ascertained that there are four strong working horses out of Mr. [John] Work's band still alive and serviceable at Cowlitz—this is from Mr. [Charles] Forrest. [George B.] Roberts, as usual procrastinates, says he should make enquiry regarding your horses but has not yet concluded his investigation.

Mr. [James] Douglas, to whom I spoke when last here, proposed that you should make a claim on the Company for so many horses and said that by so doing you would recover more than by tracing out the old stock. [Charles] F[orrest] tells of 4 Mares & Foals that perished during a severe winter ('42–'43); of a stout plough horse that dropped dead in harness; of a Blond 3 yr old marron lost with a cabress on his neck; of a mare shot by accident by [John] Sutherland; a bay horse given to

36 King George [var: K'Lows-ton, S'Hai-ak, Trots-tin, K'rot-ston, George] (c. 1807–c. 1870). The eldest son of S'Klallam headman Lach-ki-num and his wife Qua-tum-a'low, K'Lows-ton received his royal title from British sailors who perceived him as the "heir apparent" to the chieftainship of the S'Klallam tribe. Historically known for his easy-going manner, appetites for sloth, liquor, and spectacle, King George also exhibited impudence and heaped a "parade of grievances" on a series of Fort Nisqually traders. Furthermore, he did not get along well with his siblings and spouses, and during one rather heated argument, reportedly jumped in a canoe and paddled off into the fog, never to be seen or heard from again. Mary Ann Lambert Vincent, *The House of the Seven Brothers & Trees, Roots and Branches of The House of Ste-Tee-Thlum & A Genealogical Story of the Olympic Peninsula Clallam Indians*, (Port Townsend: Privately Published, circa 1951).

37 For Beauchamp see Watson, *Lives Lived*, 1:182.

38 Royal British Columbia Museum & Archives, William F. Tolmie Papers, Tolmie Letterbook, MS-0557. From a typescript copy to which no recipient is noted. Hereafter cited as BC Archives, with file, box, and volume noted.

39 John Work Jr. was the son of the famed chief factor, born August 1, 1839, at Fort Simpson. He would have been 12 at this point.

[Jean] B[aptis]te Proveau;[40] a bay lost at Nisqually but the value recoverable from the Indian who rode him to death; a grey crooked leg mare exchanged with Indians at Nisqually; [a] yearling colt of the said mare remaining at Nisqually, 1844; [a] white mare & colt sold to [John] Jackson for shingles in 1848; a big brown Stallion sent from Cowlitz to Victoria & strangled in the stable there; a grey gelding given by Dr. [John] Maclaughlin to P[ierre] Charles[41] and for which [Simon] Plomondon has since refused $100; a Brown gelding drowned in [the Des]Chutes River by [John] Johnson,[42] [a Red River] farmer at [Tualatin] Plains when coming to settle at Nisqually in 1842.[43]

Document 2.03: A letter from William F. Tolmie, Nisqually, to James Douglas, Vancouver, June 13, 1850.

Dear Sir,

I had the pleasure of receiving yesterday your communications of 5th and 11th Inst when I had also the satisfaction to obtain from Gen [John] Adair the keys of the Company's Warehouses, shut up nearly two months ago by Mr. [Eben] Dorr, Dep[ut]y Inspector of Customs for Puget Sound. Genl Adair has gone to Steilacoom today to release the Cadboro.

There being a fair wind today, the Scadgets [Skagit Indians] awaiting you here are anxious to leave, so I must defer writing more at length 'till the Cadboro sails. The Scadgets have behaved well while here and I have given to each of them a note stating the amount he is to receive at Victoria for labor performed at Nisqually.

I have not received the Invoice of Capt [David D.] Wishart's property you mentioned having forwarded in yours of the 11th, but Captain [James] S[angster] has made one out from a Document of the kind received along with the goods from Wishart.

Your saddle and Bridle is forwarded by the bearers. The case, basket and other bundling appurtenances will be forwarded per Cadboro. I have the honor to be Dear Sir, Your very obedt Sert,

Signed Wm F. Tolmie

Document 2.04: A letter from William F. Tolmie, Nisqually, to Peter S. Ogden, Vancouver, June 20, 1850.

Dear Sir,

I take advantage of an opportunity to Cowlitz to inform you that Gen [John] Adair, immediately on his arrival, released the Cadboro and goods and that I have since paid him duties on all our importation since April 3rd, 1849, which, with

---

40 For Proveau see Watson, *Lives Lived*, 2:795.

41 For Charles see Watson, *Lives Lived*, 1: 263–264.

42 John Johnson was one of Tualatin Plain's "Red River Boys" who at first attempted to settle at Nisqually in 1842, but, after receiving what they perceived as poor treatment by the Hudson Bay Company, left for free land in Oregon. For more see www.washingtoncountymuseum.org/wp-content/uploads/2013/01/Hillsboro-Background-for-Teachers-Final.pdf.

43 Tolmie's private letter, or rather his list of horses, abruptly ends here with no sign-off or the typical closure attendant with nearly all of these correspondences.

costs, amounts to $3,102.76. I have raised the price of 3 p[oin]t Blankets to $11 each and of green to $12.00 each but continue to sell Cottons as before. Being desirous of ascertaining Vancouver prices, I enclose a list which [you will] please return with the sale shop price to each article enumerated.

Having been sued for payment of the enclosed certificate[44] to the deserter [Robert] Dockery,[45] I acted on the advice of Genl Adair and settled it, the costs amounting to $3.00. John Macphail will start with a Thousand Wedders for Vancouver in about ten days hence.[46] I remain Dear Sir, Very Respectfully Yours,

(Signed) W. F. Tolmie

P.S. I have given Captain [Richard O.] Henderwell, late of the Albion, a letter of credit on you for $200, Two Hundred Dollars, he has credit on the Coy for £500 from the owner [John] Lidgett and has given Bills of Exchange to Mr. C[hief] F[actor James] Douglas for £300.

Document 2.05: A letter from William F. Tolmie, Nisqually, to James Douglas, Victoria, June 22, 1850.

Sir,

The Cadboro, having now a cargo of horned Cattle on board, is despatched for Victoria under command of Captain [James] Sangster and Mr. [George] Dixon, Mate, and a crew of six Indians—that number being deemed necessary owing to the nature of the cargo. The Indians, as will be seen by their contracts, have been engaged for a term of four months and, with the exception of a few necessaries to be received on reaching Victoria, they are not to receive pay until their period of service expires.

Your communications of 5th, 11th, and 18th June have come duly to hand.

Genl [John] Adair, having considered it best to have the Invoices valued here, we did so during the early part of this week, and on the 19th Instant I paid him Twenty six hundred and Thirty Four Dollars and Seventy Cents [$2,634.70]—duties, and Four Hundred and Sixty Eight Dollars [$468.00] for expenses consequently upon the seizure of the Cadboro and for Customhouse charges and fees—the total amounting to $3,102.70.

Genl Adair, being unable to find anyone else, appointed [Thomas] Glasgow Customhouse Agent or Landing Waiter, and it will be his duty when cargoes arrive to take account of the packages, compare them with the Ship's manifest, and to open as many as he may desire. The Genl having recommended that in case of his [Adair's] being superseded, we should import such goods as might be required for a year's consumption as speedily as possible. I have made up an additional requisition which is forwarded herewith. By the collector's desire, I am to keep all Invoices of Goods received until I hear from him.

I forward herewith Mr. [Captain Richard O.] Henderwell's second and third of exchange for £300 on John Lidgett. The Albion is to be taken to the Port of Entry, Astoria, and Mr. H[enderwell] has proceeded thither where he intends remaining 'till the Customhouse proceedings against the Albion are closed. I

44 This certificate was not found.

45 For Dockery see Watson, *Lives Lived*, 1:335.

46 For McPhail see Watson, *Lives Lived*, 2:678. Note: McPhail actually departed with the flock on July 5 according to the fort's journal entry of that date.

have supplied him on account with $200 cash, and given him a letter of credit on Mr. [Chief Factor Peter S.] Ogden for a similar amount.

[Signed William F. Tolmie]

P.S. I have been informed by the Collector [Adair] that goods cannot be imported in any Vessel of less than 30 Tons burthen.

Document 2.06: A letter from H. Bishop, Newmarket, to William F. Tolmie, Nisqually, June 26, 1850.[47]

Dear Sir,

Should you [happen to] send to mill in a few days, [would you] please send me two hundred pounds of beef, if you have any good? The beef I got from you last is really too poor to eat. I never had so bad an article. I know you would not have had it put up if you had known the condition of it. Very Respectfully, Yours, &c.,

H. Bishop

Document 2.07: A private letter from William F. Tolmie, Nisqually, to David D. Wishart Victoria, July 9, 1850.[48]

Dear Sir,

I am happy to inform you that your consignment has escaped seizure but the duties were heavy, amounting to $125.36. Some of the articles have sold at higher prices than those given in your account, but the majority will not bring Invoice prices. I think you told me when at Victoria to make the best I could of the adventure, but in case I should be mistaken I shall await your instructions in writing before selling below Invoice prices. Our interests in the matter are identical as the more the goods bring, the better will be my commission. I am, dear sir, Yours,

Wm F. Tolmie

Document 2.08: A letter from William F. Tolmie, Nisqually, to James Douglas, Victoria, July 9, 1850.

Sir,

I had the honor to receive Yours of the 1st Inst by the arrival of the Cadboro on the evening of Saturday, the 6th. The Cadboro's cargo was discharged yesterday. She is being laden with sheep today and will sail this afternoon, the wind being propitious [favorable]. I regret my inability to attend at present to your requisition for Cheviot Rams, as the rams are this season of the year at Tenalquot [Farm].

I have not yet been able to obtain horses suitable for Gov [Richard] Blanshard, but hope in the course of a month to procure two good riding nags, such as he desires. I fell in [with] one young stallion today which I have purchased for Mr. [Roderick] Finlayson. Having nothing further of importance to communicate and, being unwilling to delay the schooner's departure a moment, I remain Sir, Your very obedt Sert,

47 UW Library's Tolmie Papers Acc. 4577-001, Box 1 Folder 1, letter #11. No information was found regarding this settler.

48 Royal British Columbia Museum & Archives, William F. Tolmie Papers, Tolmie Letterbook, MS-0557. From a typescript copy.

William Fraser Tolmie

P.S. [François] Coté and Mr. [Samuel] Robertson, late App[rentice] Clerk at Victoria, arrived here on the 6th having, by their own acknowledgement, deserted from Victoria. I offered each a passage back in the Cadboro on condition of his returning to duty, but neither would accept. [François] Coté informs me that he has been engaged to work the sawmill at Newmarket. W. F. Tolmie

[P.S.S.] It will be necessary hereafter to have two copies of the Ship's manifest, and to have every article in the Invoice copied into the manifest, of course without the prices. The Inspector [Glasgow], having found today in one of the Victoria Bales, 4 p[iece]s Gartering not entered in the manifest—was rather troublesome about the mistake.

Document 2.09: A letter from William F. Tolmie, Nisqually, to Charles Wren, Muck Plain, July 22, 1850.[49]

Sir,

I hereby give you notice in writing, as I have already done verbally, that in building or otherwise improving at Muck [Farm],[50] or Douglas River, you are trespassing on the lands of the Puget's Sound Agricultural Company secured to said Company by the Boundary Treaty, ratified at Washington, by the plenipotentiaries of Great Britain and the United States of America on the 14th June 1846.

As you resided at Nisqually in 1846 and for some years previously, you must be fully aware that the prairie land on both sides of Douglas River[51] from where it issues from the timberlands to its confluence with the Nisqually [River] was occupied by the flocks and herds of the Puget's Sound Company long prior to the settlement of the Boundary question in 1846. I remain Sir, Your very obedt Sert,

William F. Tolmie, Agent, Puget's S[oun]d Agric[ultura]l Comp[an]y

Document 2.10: A letter from William F. Tolmie, Nisqually, to Peter S. Ogden, Vancouver, August 3, 1850.

Dear Sir,

I received on the 31st Ulto your communication of the 26th July, accompanying sundry letters and a packet of Newspapers for Victoria, and regret that you did not mention whether said letters were to be forwarded by express or not. The packet for Kahannui[52] must have been left at Cowlitz.

I hope that the sheep party [of John McPhail's] have 'ere now reached their destination, and that you may obtain handsome prices for the Wedders. Sold fifty

49 Royal British Columbia Museum & Archives, William F. Tolmie Papers, MS-0557, File A/E/RB/V5B.

50 Old Muck was a farm located near the marshlands east of the fort developed in the 1840s. New Muck, located east of Old Muck along the Muck Creek, was developed in 1852. For more see George Dickey's "The Outstations," *Occurrences*, 12:1 (1994), 3–7.

51 The Douglas River was a feeder tributary of the Muck River. It is often referred to as the Upper Muck River, the general vicinity being called the Douglas Burn.

52 Kahannui, Sandwich Islander. See Bruce M. Watson and Jean Barman, *Leaving Paradise: Indigenous Hawaiians in the Pacific Northwest, 1787–1898* (Honolulu: University of Hawai'i Press, 2006), 266-67.

a short time ago at five dollars each, but here beef sells at 8 cents p[er] lb., which at Vancouver and Oregon City, the price is much higher. I hope, if it can be spared, that you will send the thread lately applied for, and beg you to keep in remembrance that Nisq[uall]y is a Hudson's Bay establishment.

S[igne]d Wm F. Tolmie

Ref[erenced]: In mine of 8th May occurred the following paragraph to which being, as yet unreplied to, I beg again to drew your attention: "Mr. [Michael T.] Simmons of Newmarket is of opinion that when in 1848, he presented orders from Pere [Pascal] Ricard and Mr. G[eorge] B. Roberts for $100 and $20 respectively, he overpaid in Ft Vancouver's Sale Shop to the amount of ($14) fourteen dollars, and he has requested me to make enquiry on the subject." Simmons owes a balance here of about $150, and wishes to deduct $14 from that amount for the reason assigned above. He mentioned his mistake to me in 1848.

W. F. Tolmie

Document 2.11: A letter from William F. Tolmie, Nisqually, to James Douglas, Victoria, August 9, 1850.

Sir,

I have the honor to forward by return of the Indians conveying Govr [Richard] Blanshard's express, some letters as p[e]r Packet List, received from Vancouver a few days ago.

I trust that by next trip of the Cadboro you will send our requisition as complete as possible and have particularly to request that the supply of Ploughshares, Mule Collars, Cod lines and other agricultural necessaries may be ample.

Herewith forwarded [is] a small additional requisition for Nisqually O[utfi]t 1850 which I hope may be attended to p[e]r first opportunity. We are, now about half finished with harvest, our grain store[53] is up and roofed.

S[igne]d W. F. Tolmie

Document 2.12: A letter from William F. Tolmie, Nisqually, to Peter S. Ogden, Vancouver, August 9, 1850.

Sir,

The present express from Cowlitz is forwarded to convey some despatches from Gov [Richard] Blanshard, Vancouver's Island, to Earl Grey[54] of the British Colonial Office and I take advantage of the opportunity to send some letters &c., as per packet list received a few days ago from Victoria by the arrival of Captain [William] Brotchie.

Please prepay the postage on the letters for Earl Grey Esquire and Henry

53 The "grain store" noted here is none other than the "New Granary" as constructed by Jean Baptiste Chaulifoux. Portions of this original structure exist today at the restored fort in Tacoma's Point Defiance Park.

54 Grey (1802–1894) was the 3rd Earl Grey, who presided as a minister in the British Government and was, in 1850, the Secretary of State for War and the Colonies, an office he held from July 1846 through February 1852. en.wikipedia.org/wiki/Henry_Grey,_3rd_Earl_Grey.

Blanshard Esquire[55] and charges either against Ft Victoria or Fort Nisqually, advising me if against the latter. Any expenses connected with the forwarding of the present express, will also have to be transmitted to Victoria where Mr. Blanshard will settle for all charges incurred. Business progresses here much as usual except that money is becoming rather scarce.

S[igne]d W. F. Tolmie

Document 2.13: A private letter from William F. Tolmie, Nisqually, to David D. Wishart, Victoria, August 28, 1850.[56]

Dear Sir,

Yours of the 18th Instant accompanying two letters for England, came to hand two days ago and the letters shall be forwarded p[e]r first mail.

In case the Cadboro should not return to Nisqually prior to your departure for England, I forward now the cash collected and remaining after the payment of Custom house duties to the amount of $125.36 as already advised.

Cash remaining &c.,	$223.96
Less Commission 5 p[e]r cent	11.20
	212.76
[Less] Postage on two letters	
To be paid at Vancouver	1
	211.76

Forwarded in a case addressed to James Douglas Esquire. Expecting you to inform me 'ere leaving Victoria how the proceeds of future sales are to be disposed of during your absence I remain, Dear Sir, Respectfully yours,

Wm F. Tolmie

Document 2.14: A letter from William F. Tolmie, Nisqually, to James Douglas, Victoria, August 29, 1850.

Sir,

The Cadboro arrived here on the 26th, discharged on the 27th, and took in her cargo on the 28th Inst. She is now ready to sail having all the wool on board. I received per Cadboro your three letters[57] of from 15th to 19th August and shall pay due attention to their contents.

The furs and cash on hand are now sent and in the box containing the money is a bag to Captain [David D.] Wishart's address containing money which please deliver. Some shutter hinges and Shingle nails for fort use, and stock locks for sale are now indented for. I hope you will complete the various requisitions for O[utfi]t 1850 as fully as possible by ensuing trip of Cadboro and please to have the manifest made out at Victoria, as the Customhouse officer [Thomas Glasgow] is rather

55 This is believed to be the Colonial Governor's brother.

56 Royal British Columbia Museum & Archives, William F. Tolmie Papers, Tolmie Letterbook, MS-0557. From a typescript copy.

57 These three letters were not found.

disposed to be troublesome when any informality in the papers gives him occasion to speak. I [now] send a scroll of the PS Co's charges ag[ains]t the HBC for your revision and correction.

The 190 Sheep last sent were Gimmers [young females] and amongst them were, as I have lately ascertained, some purebreds. I cannot say how many until after comparing notes with Walter Ross. Herewith is sent a statement of the marks of our purebreads, which will enable you to ascertain the number of full-blooded Gimmers at Victoria. I rem[ai]n Sir,

[Signed William F. Tolmie]

Document 2.15: A letter from William F. Tolmie, Nisqually, to James Douglas, Victoria, August 31, 1850.

Sir,

Having had a letter yesterday from Captain [Richard O.] Henderwell, late of the Albion, requesting me to forward his effects left here to Victoria whence he wishes them conveyed in the Mary Dare to Columbia River. I despatched Charles Ross [Jr.] with Indians in the Company's canoe to put said property on board the Cadboro should he overtake her, or therein to proceed with it to Victoria. The expense of the trip will of course be charged to [Captain] Henderwell's account.

[Captain] Henderwell writes that he wishes the whole of the Balance of his £300 after defrayal of expenses here, made payable at Vancouver. He has already rec[eive]d $400 and I shall request Mr. [Chief Factor Peter S.] O[gden] p[e]r first opportunity to advance him $400 more.

I forward for your perusal, the enclosed received from Mr. Ogden by return of [John] Macphail yesterday. I shall inform Mr. O[gden] that the sheep have been already charged at $5.00 but that I have forwarded his letter to you.

[Signed William F. Tolmie]

Document 2.16: A letter from William F. Tolmie, Nisqually, to Peter S. Ogden, Vancouver, September 2, 1850.

Sir,

I beg to advize that I have this day drawn upon you for Four Hundred Dollars payable on demand in favor of R[ichard] O. Henderwell, who on obtaining the same will have received eight hundred dollars of the Fourteen and Forty credited to him here in April last. Please charge the $400 against Fort Nisqually O[utfi]t 1850.

Being at a loss to reply to some parts of your communication of the 19th August regarding the price of sheep &c., I have, agreeably to suggestion, forwarded the letter to Mr. C[hief] F[actor James] Douglas.

The Govr & Committee having sent out instructions last year that all supplies furnished by the Puget's S[oun]d Co to the Hudson's Bay Co should be charged at the market price the sheep sent at your request to Vancouver by [John] Macphail's party, have been charged as follows: 1,021 Wedders at 20/10 each & 20 old Ewes (for the use of the party as food in voyage) at 12/16 each. It is not for me to say anything as to the justice of this arrangement.

I shall comply with your directions regarding the account of John Macphail,

PS Coy's Shepherd, and have the honor to be Sir,
S[igne]d W. F. Tolmie

Document 2.17: An official letter from William F. Tolmie, Nisqually, to James Douglas, Victoria, September 9, 1850.

Please let me know as soon as convenient what quantity of salted beef you will require from Nisqually this autumn, and send Bbls [barrels] and Terces wherein to pack it.
[Signed William F. Tolmie]

Document 2.18: A letter from Peter S. Ogden, Vancouver, to William F. Tolmie, Nisqually, September 5, 1850.[58]

Dear Sir,

I herewith enclose you a copy of a letter from S[amuel Royal] Thurston,[59] to the Hon T[homas] Ewing,[60] Sec[retar]y of the Interior, from Cha[rle]s H. Engles[61] conveying direct charges against you as the Agent of the Hudson's Bay Coy.

My reply to Govr [John P.] Gaines[62] is also forwarded to you and it will be necessary [that] you forward without delay affidavits taken before a Justice of Peace or C[aptain Bennett H.] Hill refuting the Ch[arge]s so that they may be here by the 18th at the latest date. Yours Sincerely,
(Signed) Peter Skene Ogden

[P.S.] You are at liberty to forward my letter to C[hief] F[actor James] Douglas.

[P.S.S.] By first opportunity, inform C[hief] F[actor James] Douglas that I, last evening, purchased on or about 80 Barrels Pork at 20$ per Barrel, half paid in goods.

Document 2.19: A copy of a letter from Samuel R. Thurston, Oregon City, to Thomas Ewing, Sr., Washington, D.C., May 25, 1850.

Sir,

We take the liberty to make to you the following Representation and make the following Request. The HB Company make it their study to conciliate the Indians of the Territory of Oregon, and to prejudice them against our people and Govern-

58 This letter appeared several pages later in the actual Fort Nisqually letterbook, but is brought forward to this position for the sake of context and continuity as many of the following letters refer to it.

59 Thurston was an antagonist to the HBC/PSAC's interests. "Thurston County was created by an act of the Oregon Territorial Legislatures January 12, 1852. The intent at first was to name the area Simmons County for Michael T. Simmons, but upon the news of the sudden death of Thurston, first Territorial Representative to Congress from Oregon, the name was changed to Thurston "to perpetuate his memory." www.co.thurston.wa.us/permitting/historic/docs/TC-Commissioners-1852-present.pdf.

60 Ewing (1789–1871) was a National Republican and Whig politician from Ohio who served in the U.S. Senate, as the Secretary of the Treasury, and as the first Secretary of the Interior. en.wikipedia.org/wiki/Thomas_Ewing.

61 Nothing could be found that identified this person.

62 Gaines (1795–1857) was a U.S. military and political figure. He was a Whig member of the United States House of Representatives, representing Kentucky from 1847 to 1849, and he served as Governor of the Oregon Territory from 1850 to 1853. en.wikipedia.org/wiki/John_P._Gaines.

ment. To show you what we mean, allow us to say that an Award of 80 blankets was offered for the surrender of the Indians who murdered [Leander C.] Wallace,[63] as you have learned from Governor [Joseph] Lane's Report. Those blankets were bought of the HB Company and when they were delivered by the Agents of the Company to the Indians, as per Governor Lane's order, these agents of the Company represented to the Indians & made them believe that those Blankets were presents from the HB Coy. Such is their constant effort.

We have, therefore, to request you that you give instructions to the Governor and to all officers there having anything to do with Indian matters, to guard against this evil and to take care that all presents and goods given or paid to the Indians pass through the hands of Americans and be purchased of American traders. This Company have so Managed that the Indians exact Cash for everything, refusing to take goods from Americans & American traders, and as soon as they get the money they go direct to the HB Co's stores and buy of them, and we desire, moreover, that in treating with these Indians, that the Consideration paid should be in those useful articles which the Indians need and not in Cash in whole or in part. I have the honour to be Your Sert,

(Signed) Samuel R. Thurston

[Endorsement:] The facts stated above are known to me in part on information derived from Reliable sources as to the Residue. Wm P. Bryant,[64] Ch[ief] Jus[tice], Oregon Territory[65]

Document 2.20: A copy of a letter from John P. Gaines, Oregon City, to Peter S. Ogden, Vancouver, September 4, 1850.[66]

Sir,

I have the Honour to enclose herewith a copy of a letter from the Hon S[amuel] R. Thurston, delegate from this territory to the Congress of the US, to the Secretary of the Interior of the 25th May last, upon which is an endorsement Requiring one to take measures to Remedy the evils complained of.

I send you this communication in the confident hope that such explanations may be made as well be satisfactory to the Government & people of the US and assure that I am instructed to cultivate friendly feelings with the Company over

63 In early May 1849, Snoqualmie Indians attacked Fort Nisqually, killed American settler Wallace, wounded two other settlers, and injured a friendly Indian and a boy, both who later died. Wallace's death and the wounded settlers have been historically portrayed as mere "collateral damage" that occurred during that fracas. Two of the six Indians tried for the murder—Kussas and Quallahwort, both chiefs of the Snoqualmie tribe—were convicted and executed for Wallace's death. William P. Bonney, "The Murder of Leander Wallace," in *History of Pierce County, Washington* (Chicago: Pioneer Historical Publishing Company, 1927), 54–61. Keyed for the internet by Gary Reese and found at www.usgennet.org/usa/wa/state/leanderwallace.html.

64 Bryant (1806–1860) was an American jurist from Kentucky who eventually served as the first Chief Justice of the Oregon Supreme Court in the Oregon Territory. en.wikipedia.org/wiki/William_P._Bryant.

65 At this point Peter Ogden adds this side note: "Referred to the Com[mission] of Indian affairs. Set the necessary directions be given to the Governor of Oregon with a View to correct the evil complaint of/by Mr. Thurston. Dep[artmen]t of the Interior—May 25th 1850."

66 This "copy" of the letter to Chief Factor Ogden from Oregon Territorial Governor Gaines appeared several pages later in the fort's actual letterbook, but is brought to this position for the sake of context as many of the letters that follow relate to this document.

which you preside. I am Sir, Very Respectfully, Your Obt Servant,
Hon J[ohn] P. Gaines, Govr of Oregon Territory

Document 2.21: A letter from William F. Tolmie, Nisqually, to Bennett H. Hill, Steilacoom Barracks, September 12, 1850.

Sir,

Referring to the documents herewith enclosed and enumerated in the subjoined list,[67] I beg you to favor me with a statement of what took place here in September 1849 when the Indians charged with the Murder of [Leander C.] Wallace were surrendered to you. I ask for this as the Hon[ora]ble S[amuel] R. Thurston charges me in his letter of May 25th, 1850 to the Hon[oura]ble T[homas] Ewing, Sec[retar]y of the Interior, copy of which is now submitted to you, with having caused the Indians of this quarter to believe that the present of Eighty Blankets made to the relatives of those given up, came not from the US Authorities, but from the Hudson's Bay Company. I have the honor to be Sir, With respect, Your very obedt Sert,
(S[igne]d) Wm F. Tolmie

Document 2.22: A letter from Bennett H. Hill, Steilacoom Barracks, to William F. Tolmie, Nisqually, September 12, 1850.

Sir,

I have to acknowledge the receipt of your letter of this date enclosing a copy of a Communication for me, the Hon[ora]ble S[amuel] R. Thurston & Chief Justice Bryant of this territory, addressed to the Secretary of the Interior under date of 25th May 1850, together with a copy of a letter from His Excellency Gov [John] Gaines to Mr. [Chief Factor Peter S.] Ogden dated 4th Inst and Mr. Ogden's letter to yourself, and requesting me to furnish you with a Statement of what took place in September 1849 when the Indians guilty of the Murder of [Leander C.] Wallace were surrendered to me.

A few days after my arrival in the Sound in August 1849, I received a letter from J[essie] Q. Thornton Esqu[ire], Sub Indian Agent, informing me that he had offered to the Snoqualmie Tribe of Indians Eighty Blankets if, within a certain time, the Indians whom he named as those principally concerned in the Murder were brought in and delivered up to me.

In the early part of the following Month [of] September, the Indians charged with Wallace's murder were brought to this place by this Tribe and Judge Thornton, having in the meantime returned to Oregon City, I purchased on his account as Sub Indian Agent at your Post, then the only store in the Sound, the number of Blankets promised the Indians which were brought to this place and distributed by myself.

At my request, both with a view to identify the guilty Indians and assist me as Interpreter, You were Kind enough to ride down and be present on the occasion, but no question has ever been entertained here, or, to my Knowledge by any Citizen in the Sound, but that the matter was properly understood by the Indians and I have not even heard a rumour that any such representations were made to them,

67 The list is not included as it identifies the letters herein presented.

as you are charged with in the letters to the Secretary of the Interior of 25th May 1850. I am Sir, Very respectfully, Yr Obt Sert

(S[igne]d) B. H. Hill, Capt Art[iller]y, Comm[andin]g Post

Document 2.23: A letter from Bennett H. Hill, Steilacoom Barracks, to William F. Tolmie, Nisqually, September 12, 1850.[68]

My dear Doctor,

I send you a letter in reply to yours of today. The 2nd par[agraph] of your letter (I think on reflection) had better be omitted as these charges refer without doubt to your establishment on [the] Columbia River and Mr. [Peter S.] Ogden can fight his own battles. I therefore run a pencil over it & change in pencil 1850 to 1849. In the hope that this will be Satisfactory to you I remain, In haste, Truly yours,

[Captain] B. H. Hill

P.S. I have ret[aine]d copies of Mr. Thurston's letter, Gov Gaines' & Mr. Ogden's, and I send your letter [back] to you, which please return [to] me if you make the alteration I suggest.

Document 2.24: A letter from William F. Tolmie, Nisqually, to Peter S. Ogden, Vancouver, September 13, 1850.

Sir,

I had the honor to receive on the evening of the 11th Inst your Communication of the 4th accompanying Copy of a letter dated May 25th, 1850 from the Hon[ora]ble S[amuel] R. Thurston, Delegate to the US Congress from Oregon Territory, to the Hon[ora]ble Tho[ma]s Ewing, Sec[retar]y of the Interior, with a Copy of Governor [John P.] Gaines' letter to you under date Septr 4, [18]50 and your reply dated the 5th Inst.

Having been directed, in yours of the 4th Inst above acknowledged, to make affidavit before Captain [Bennett H.] Hill as a Justice of the peace, in denial of the Charges professed against me by Mr. J[essie] Q. Thornton[69] in his letter to the Sec[retar]y of the Interior of date May 25th, [18]50, I waited on Captain [Bennett H.] Hill yesterday and, informing him of the Circumstances of the Case, professed my reactions to letters in hand, that I never represented to the Indians that the Eighty Blankets given to the [Snoqualmie] Snowqualimie Tribe on the surrender of the Indians accused of the murder of Wallace were a present from the Hudson's Bay Company. But Captain [Bennett H.] Hill declined receiving my affidavit on the plea that he was not a Justice of the peace.

My reply to your [having our rebuttal] being present at Vancouver by the 18th Inst at latest time did not permit of my going in quest of a Magistrate, and I, therefore, addressed a letter to Captain [Bennett H.] Hill, enclosing for his perusal Copies of items of the [correspondence] above referred to viz.:

---

68 UW Library's Tolmie Papers Acc. 4577-001, Box 1 Folder 4.

69 Here, Tolmie mistakenly wrote Jessie Q. Thornton's name in for Samuel Thurston, but perhaps revealing that the territory's Indian Agent Thornton was the originator of the lie that was subsequently elevated to the heights of the U.S. Congress by Thurston.

Mr. Thurston's Communication to the Secretary of the Interior, bearing date May 25th, 1850;

Governor [John P.] Gaines' letter to you of the 4th Inst;

and yours to me of the 5th.

A Copy of my letter to Captain [Bennett H.] Hill is enclosed.

From Captain Hill's letter to me, which I now forward, it will be seen that the [sic] such reports as that [called] out by Mr. Thornton was ever heard of on Puget's Sound. For if anything of the sort had transpired, no person residing in the Neighbourhood would have had earlier intimation of it than Captain [Bennett H.] Hill himself.

From the 1st May, when the unfortunate [Leander C.] Wallace was Murdered, 'till the 4th October, when his Murderers were executed, I incurred a great deal of trouble and some risk in negotiating between the United States Authorities and the three hostile tribes of Indians. And I can honestly and without assumption attest that it was mostly through my exertions and influence with the Natives, that the horrors of an Indian War were, in [the] Summer [of] 1849, averted from the Puget's Sound Settlements, defenseless as they then were.

Such actions, having been my share in the transactions of Indian affairs on Puget's Sound during the Year 1849, it is at best annoying to be Called upon to relent [yield to] such a ridiculous charge as I must take leave to Call that made against me by the Hon S[amuel] R. Thurston. Setting aside/apart the obvious dishonesty of this Prosecution, he imparts to me that impolicy and shortsightedness are equally appropriate for speedy detection. On this parting, both Whites and Indians would Certainly have followed any such attempt. By far, other's misdeeds than such Contemptible trickery as Mr. Thornton's imputations [accusations] would imply that the Hudson's Bay Company obtained and kept up their influence amongst the Aborigines of North America.

Should my Affidavit still be required in negation of Mr. Thornton's charges, please inform me by return of the bearers & I shall forward it with the least possible delay. I have the honor to be Sir, Your Very obet Sert,

William F. Tolmie, C[hief] T[rader], Hudson's Bay Comp[an]y

Document 2.25: A letter from Peter S. Ogden, Vancouver, to John P. Gaines, Oregon City, September 15, 1850.

Sir,

I have the honour to acknowledge the receipt of your communication of 4th Inst enclosing a copy of a letter from the Hon[ora]ble S[amuel] R. Thurston, Con[gressional] Delegate to/from this territory to the Congress of the United States, to the Secretary of the Interior dated 25th May last, and I now beg leave to make a few remarks on reply.

The HB Coy have made and do make at their study to conciliate the Indians of the Territory of Oregon and elsewhere in the Vicinity of their trading Posts, but without prejudice to the American people or Government which, as Indian Traders, they may properly do. The HB Comp[an]y did sell to Govr [Joseph] Lane, or to his Agents or, to the Agents of the Government, the eighty Blankets mentioned, and delivered them to Govr Lane or his agents aforesaid. They surely are not responsible for the use made of the Blankets after their sale and they deny emphatically the implications of the Hon[ora]ble Mr. Thurston's letter, that is to say they represented to the Indians that these Blankets were presented to them from the HB Company; but they assent and will prove by the affidavit of their trader Wm F. Tolmie Esq that the direction of Govr Lane, or of the Indian Agent [Thornton], was Minutely and correctly obeyed, in Regard to the Blankets.

The HB Comp[an]y do not presume or does not pretend to interfere with the American Govt, its Agents or people in their choice or discretion of Merchant from whom Indian goods may be purchased, or the means they may see proper to take as prescribed in the distribution of Indian presents. Nor, on the other hand, can the HB Company compel the Indians of Oregon to trade with any trader in any particular Manner as the consideration exacted by the Indians from Americans or others should be useful or useless . . . Cash or Goods. HBC Traders or Agents of the HB Coy are acting for the Coy only, and not for any Government or people, and let me here remark before I close this, that acts of the HB Company are open to the strictest investigation and the conduct and active parts taken by their Agents in the unfortunate Massacre of American Citizens. The Rescue and preservation of the Lives of Fifty-four Individuals, who, were chosen to die, should in itself be fully sufficient to convince all unprejudiced men that the accusations brought against those by the Hon[ora]ble S[amuel] R. Thurston are destitute of truth. As the supposed transaction took place at Fort Nisqually, I shall Report the same without loss of time to William F. Tolmie Esq[ui]re, and Request him to forward affidavits which I am confident, Knowing his upright and honourable character, will fully Refute. I have the Honor to Remain, Yours most Respectfully,

(Signed) Peter Skene Ogden

Document 2.26: A letter from William F. Tolmie, Nisqually, to James Douglas, Victoria, September 18, 1850.

Sir,

By Return of Mr. R[oderick] Finlayson, I forward some copies of letters by which you will be made acquainted with certain accusations lately made against the Agents of the Hudson's Bay Coy in Oregon by Mr. Thurston, the Oregon Delegate to the US Congress and with the means adopted by Mr. Chief Factor [Peter S.] Ogden and myself in disproof and denial of Mr. Thurston's Charges. Business progresses here much at usual and referring you to Mr. Finlayson for the news. I have the Honor to be Sir, Your Very Obt Servant

(Signed) William Fraser Tolmie

P.S. Should the Cadboro have been despatched prior to Mr. F[inlayson's] reaching Victoria and the Shingling Nails have been forwarded, please send a Keg by Return of Canoe. Yours T[rul]y,

(S[igne]d) W. F. T.

Document 2.27: A letter from John Adair, Astoria, to Peter S. Ogden, Vancouver, September 18, 1850.

Dear Sir,

Enclosed you have a Copy of a letter[70] from the Secretary of the Treasury [Meredith] relative to the admission of Goods imported by the Hudson's Bay Company into the Territory. You will perceive by the Instructions contained in the letter that Said Company are prohibited from further trade between the points Victoria & Nisqually.

Will you be Kind enough to inform Governor [James] Douglas & Dr. Tolmie of the fact? And should any Goods have been received since the last Entry cause them to be entered by Mr. [Edward] Edwards[71] forthwith. Very truly Yours &c.,

(Signed) John Adair, Collector

Document 2.28: A letter from Peter S. Ogden, Vancouver, to William M. Meredith, Washington, D.C., September 18, 1850.

Sir,

I have now the honor to acknowledge the receipt of a copy of your letter to the Collector of the Customs in Oregon dated Treasury Department, May 30th, 1850. Also, a letter from the Collector dated 8th Sep from Collector Office, Astoria, the latter a copy of which I now enclose, prohibiting any further trade between Victoria & Nisqually. I now beg leave to make a few remarks and to call your most serious attention to this prohibition.

Some time previous to the receipt of your letter, the US Govt had made Nisqually a port of Delivery, also Portland in Oregon. In consequence, an arrangement was effected between the Collector & Myself in regard to the Duties on all goods landed at Nisqually by the Hudson's Bay Company, the former having appointed an agent to receive the same which were duly paid.

From the tenor of your letter, by which the Collector has without doubt been actuated in prohibiting any intercourse between Victoria and Nisqually, I am confident you cannot then have been aware of the understanding existing between us. This Prohibition could act Most decidedly against our Interests in so far as furnishing supplies to the Puget's Sound Coy's Servants and in Preventing us from obtaining supplies for the use of Victoria. I trust that on a careful perusal of the Treaty [of 1846] it will be ascertained that it was never understood by the high concerning Parties that such a Prohibition should exist and, probably, you may not be aware of the following circumstances: a ship leaving Victoria for Nisqually by proceeding to Astoria as the Port of Entry must go out of her route 358 miles, cross & re-cross the Columbia Bar attended with some danger & very great expense from the high wages given to Seamen & the high rates of Postage.

The present Individual appointed by the Collector at Nisqually as Deputy since it has been made a port of Delivery has, I am confident, not the slightest cause of complaint against the Offices of the Puget Sound Coy in not strictly complying with the Laws of the US, and I trust that the Collector at Astoria can faithfully report the

70 John Adair to Peter S. Ogden, September 8, 1850, HBCA Copy, A.11/70, fo. 515, is not included in this work.

71 Edward Edwards. This is likely one of the "Edwards" listed in Watson, *Lives Lived*, 1:357–58, who was residing at Fort Vancouver at this point, although it is difficult to determine which one it was by this entry.

same in regard to the HB Coy's Officers here. The Collector has also, consistent with his duty to his Govt, afforded us every facility in his power. Since last April, we have paid Duties to the amount of Seventy-eight thousand Dollars [$78,000].

I have not seen the Copy of Sir George [Simpson]'s on Mr. Thurston's letter to which you refer. Consequently, I can make no comments on either.

It would be most desireable if you could, consistent with your high official duty to your Govt, forward Instruction that Nisqually be made a Port of Entry. I have the honor to be, Sir, Your Obedient Servant,

(Signed) Peter Skene Ogden, HB Coy

Document 2.29: A letter from William F. Tolmie, Nisqually, to James Douglas, Victoria, September 27, 1850.

Sir,

By the present express are forwarded: an open letter to you from C[hief] F[actor Peter S.] Ogden dated 20th September [18]50; and a copy of his letter to Sir George Simpson under date Septr 18th, [18]50; also a copy of Collector General [John] Adair's letter to Mr. Ogden of Septr 8th, [18]50; and of a letter bearing date May 30th, [18]50 to the Collector of Customs Astoria, Oregon from W[illiam] M. Meredith Secretary of the Treasury (Washington, US); with copy of a letter from Mr. C[hief] F[actor] Ogden to the Hon[ora]ble W[illia]m M. Meredith Secretary of the Treasury dated 18th Septr [18]50.

From the tenor of the above mentioned letters it appears that there is again a prohibition on our trade between Nisqually and Victoria, but should the Cadboro arrive here prior to your receiving and replying to this, I shall, in earnest, discharge and despatch her immediately, getting Mr. [Charles Kinney] Kenny[72]—Customs House guardian of the Ship Albion to act as Customhouse Officer as [Thomas] Glasgow has resigned [from] that office. It appears to me that the prohibition cannot justly be enforced prior to your receiving notice thereof, the [sic] which I use all despatch to convey.

[Michael T.] Simmons, whom I have seen since last writing you, does not seem willing to state the demand of Four Hundred Dollars (400$) p[er] month for the hire of the Orbit,[73] maintaining that after being a year in our possession, the Vessel would require many repairs. He appeared more desirous to have the Brig chartered or to take livestock to Victoria at so much per head rather than let out the Vessel without a crew. Should you feel disposed to contract with Simmons for the transport of livestock to Victoria, please inform me how much to offer him per head for

72 Kinney [var: Kenny] was an American settler and ship's captain living in Port Steilacoom at this time. He was the one who took control of the doomed British bottom ship *Albion* when it was seized by U.S. Army troops. No other information could be found on this individual.

73 *Orbit*, American brigantine [var: *Recovery*]. For an overview of the *Orbit*'s owners, skippers, and various exploits, see "Brigantine *Recovery*—Revenue Vessel of the Fraser River," August 24, 2010, queenboroughrevenuestation.wordpress.com/2010/08/24/brig-recovery-revenue-vessel-of-the-fraser-river. See also James A. Gibbs Jr., *Pacific Graveyard: A Narrative of the Ships Lost Where the Columbia River Meets the Pacific Ocean* (Portland, OR: Binfords and Mort, 1950), 153–90; Murray C. Morgan, *Puget's Sound: A Narrative of Early Tacoma and the Southern Sound* (Seattle: University of Washington Press, 1981), 78–79.

sheep, horned cattle and horses, and whether payment would be made in goods, or cash. I have the honor to be Sir, Your very obet Sert,

(Signed) W. F. Tolmie

Document 2.30: A private letter from William F. Tolmie, Nisqually, to a Trusted Party, Inverness, October 1, 1850.[74]

[To Unidentified Recipient:]

Of the £35 now remitted, please forward £10 to [my aunt] Miss Catherine Fraser,[75] 25 Rose Street, Inv[erne]ss and £5 to Provost William Simpson,[76] Cattle Street, Inverness as a contribution to the fund of Ragged School, established or about to be so in Inv[erne]ss from W[illiam] F. T[olmie] of the HB Co, N[orth] W[est] A[merica].

Mr. S[impson] and I were school-fellows altho' he is considerably my senior and we are but slightly acquainted. He is a very charitable person, and I think a prime mover in the ragged school establishment. I do not know the proper address for a provost or Ex-provost, but give that designation to make sure of the right person.

Hold the £20 St[erlin]g at the dispo[s]al of the Rev[eren]d Mr. Lynch,[77] P[arish] P[riest], Frankford, King's Country, Ireland. It is remitted by an Irish soldier named Tam Flinn[78] to his Mother, who must personally appear before Father Lynch 'ere pays her the money. Should she be alive, his reverence will apply to you for the amount and should she be no more, he will request you to advize me in order that I may refund to Flinn. [I remain, Dear Sir, Respectfully yours],

Wm F. Tolmie

Document 2.31: A letter from William F. Tolmie, Nisqually, to Peter S. Ogden, Vancouver, October 2, 1850.

Sir,

I duly received your open letter to Mr. C[hief] F[actor James] Douglas, accompanying copy of yours to Sir. G[eorge] Simpson date Septr 18th, [18]50, with copy of Collector General [John] Adair's letters to you of Septr 8th, [18]50 and of a letter bearing date May 5th, [18]50 to the Collector of Customs Astoria, Oregon from W[illiam] M., Meredith, Secretary of the Treasury (Washington, US), also a copy of your letter dated Sept 8th, [18]50 to the Hon[ora]ble W[illiam] M Meredith, Secretary of the Treasury; all which have been forwarded to Victoria by an express canoe.

'Tis satisfactory to think, in view of the prohibition now re-imposed on the trade between Ft Nisqually and Victoria, that the post is well stocked in the most essential articles of trade. The embargo being unjustly applied will not, I trust, be of long duration, and its evil effects will, for the present, chiefly be felt in the check given to our exportation of livestock to Fort Victoria.

---

74 BC Archives, (William F. Tolmie Letterbook), MS-0557, Box 2. From a typescript copy.
75 No information could be found on Dr. Tolmie's aunt who was then living in Scotland.
76 No information could be found on this provost who was then living in Inverness, Scotland.
77 No information could be found on this priest who was living in Ireland at the time.
78 No information could be found on this soldier who was living in Ireland at the time.

With regard to your proposal to Mr. [James] Douglas to send some supplies for Nisqually by way of the Cowlitz Portage, I Subjoin a short list of some articles greatly needed for the trade and which if they can be spared, please forward to Cowlitz as soon as possible in order that we may get the bales across 'ere the rivers become swollen.

Herewith are forwarded invoice of the goods received at Ft Nisqually since the last Customhouse entry made when General [John] Adair was here in June.

I was directed to forward the accompanying packet for the HB Coy, London by express to Vancouver, in order to get it there in time for the Mail of the 1st October; but as it was not received here 'till the 27th Ulto I thought the expense of an Express would be incurred in vain, and it, as well as the other papers, are now sent by the Steilacoom Mail. Please inform me in your next when the monthly mail leaves Oregon. I have the honor to be Sir, Your very obedient Sert,

(Signed) Wm F. Tolmie

Articles required at Ft Nisqually
on ac[count] Outfit 1850

60 p[ai]rs Trousers—Corduroy, Moleskin & Com[mon] Cloth
30 p[ai]rs Men's shoes
1 M [1,000] B.T. Needles
20 [pounds of] Thread, Colored

Document 2.32: A letter from Hugh A. Goldsborough, Olympia, to William F. Tolmie, Nisqually, October 6, 1850.[79]

My Dear Sir,

I send you some letters rec[eived] by the last mail. Postage on those for J[oseph] S. Heath ... $2.33 ½. If you should not wish to receive them, be so good as to return them by bearer. The one for yourself was given to me by Mr. P[eter] S. Odgen & relates, I apprehend, to the [seizure of the] Cadboro &c.

Have you Sir George Simpson's work[80] in this Country? If so, can you conveniently loan it to me for perusal. Be happy to reciprocate. Yours Very Respectfully,

H. A. Goldsborough

Document 2.33: A letter from William F. Tolmie, Nisqually, to Peter S. Ogden, Vancouver, October 11, 1850.

Sir,

Having received your letter of the 24th September requiring a list of the Indian tribes on Puget's Sound for Colonel [William W.] Loring US A[rmy], I have much pleasure in now forwarding a statement of the names and places of residence of the various tribes (of Indians) from Cape Flattery along the Coast to Point Roberts as

79 UW Library's Tolmie Papers Acc. 4577-001, Box #1, Folder #3.

80 This is a reference to Sir George Simpson, *Narrative of a Journey Round the World, During the Years 1841 and 1842* (London: Henry Colburn, 1847).

correct in orthography and other respects as it has been in my power to make it.[81]

Herewith are forwarded letters received two days ago from Victoria which Mr. [George B.] Roberts will forward by first opportunity from Cowlitz. I have the honor to be Sir, Your very obedient Sert,

(Signed) W. F. Tolmie

[P.S.] In case you should have to settle with Collector [John] Adair for the late entries of goods at Nisqually and of which invoices were lately forwarded to you, please deduct $106 from the amount to be paid. I, having deducted that sum on Genl Adair's Account, to the man who had charge of the Cadboro, and whose Receipt I hold. T.

Document 2.34: A letter from William F. Tolmie, Nisqually, to George B. Roberts, Cowlitz Farm, October 11, 1850.

Dear Sir,

Please forward the accompanying letters for Vancouver by the first opportunity.

You spoke, I think, some time ago of sending some of the cattle Returned by Settlers across to Nisqually. And if such is your intention, and [it is] your wish to get clear of the Cattle, let me know by Return of bearer and I will send [Jean Baptiste] Lapoitrie[82] and a party for them.

My reason for applying to you is that I owe [Thomas] Glasgow 7 Cows with Calves of 1850 and 7 Yearling heifers, which we have just failed in endeavoring to get across the Squally River for him. And to save horseflesh, I would sooner at once drive him the required heifers from Cowlitz, he being, in that case, bound to aid himself and to be accompanied by at least one mounted Indian. If at [the] same time three or four Cows could be driven across for Tho[ma]s Linklater[83] [at Tenalquot Farm], it would [be] doing him a great service and exempting us from delivering him Cattle next Spring. I enclose a copy of my last agreement with [Thomas] Glasgow by which you will perceive that he is bound to take one Cow and Calf for two Yearling Heifers in case the full number of the Cattle cannot be turned over to him. [In the process of] going across [the portage] for Cattle, can take you some old Ewes from Tenalquot? But, unless it would suit your purpose at Cowlitz and not conflict with any disposition of your Cattle, you may be aware Mr.

81 This statement was not found.

82 This farm laborer came to Nisqually in July 1847, and was a steady laborer throughout the 1850s. Nicknamed "Puss," because of his apparent "likeness to a cat, and the trick he possessed of imitating the mewing of a cat" according to Edward Huggins, "A Trip from Fort Nisqually to Cowlitz in 1850," *Portland Oregonian*, September 9, 1900. According to the *Federal Census of Lewis County, Oregon Territory*, this French Canadian was 48 years old and married to 18-year-old Philoma in 1850. files.usgwarchives.net/wa/lewis/census/50lc.txt.

83 Linklater (c. 1815–1890) was an Orkney Islander who worked as a laborer earning £17 annually for his first five years. He served at Fort Vancouver from 1834 to 1836, and then seven years at Fort McLoughlin, on Millbank Sound. From 1843 to 1846 he worked on the Steamer *Beaver*. In 1846 he came to Nisqually, and worked as a laborer/carpenter at £22 a year until 1849. In the autumn of 1849 he took the job of head shepherd at Tenalquot Farm, located in today's Thurston County. He retired in 1851 and took a donation claim on Tenalquot Farm. On February 20, 1890, he died in Olympia's St. Peter Hospital. Drew Crooks, "The Life of Thomas Linklater," *Occurrences* 10:3 (1991), 10–12.

D[ouglas] intends to make, I would not wish you to send Cattle across as proposed.

Please to send by return of bearer your acc[oun]ts Ch[ar]g[e]d Ft Nisqually for Out[fit] [18]50. I have paid Mr. M[ichael] T. Simmons on his presenting your order $228.90 for the Taxes at Cowlitz for the Current year. Please inform me whether he gave you a Receipt for said amount as he told me he had done so.

[Signed—William F. Tolmie]

Document 2.35: An invoice from William F. Tolmie, Nisqually, to Archibald MacKinlay, Oregon City, October 12, 1850.[84]

Ordered from Mackinlay & Allan:

2 good & complete Cooking Stoves if to be had at from $30 to 40 each
2 Steelyards to weigh 200 lbs.
5 Corn or Flour Sieves

Document 2.36: A letter from Robert C. Fay,[85] Brigantine *Orbit* at Station in Olympia, to William F. Tolmie, Nisqually, October 19th, 1850.[86]

Sir,

I shall leave this place with the Brig Orbit tomorrow or Saturday and will touch at Nesqualy on my way down the Sound. Very respectfully Yours,

[Captain] R. C. Fay

Document 2.37: A letter from William F. Tolmie, Nisqually, to Peter S. Ogden, Vancouver, October 29, 1850.

Sir,

On returning from Victoria on the 27th Inst, I received your letters of the 1st, 3rd & 9th, also by [Rocque] Duchenay yesterday, those of the 18th and 21st Inst, accompanying the supplies to this post from Vancouver which were found correct according to invoice.

Along with yours of the 21st, Copies have been received of the Entries of Goods lately made in the Cadboro from Victoria as to Nisqually, and, as required by Genl [John] Adair, the original invoices of said goods are now forwarded.

Having paid in June last to Genl Adair, copy of whose receipt in subjoined, the sum $468 for expenses consequent in the seizure of the Cadboro and of the

---

84 BC Archives, MS-0557, Box 2. From a typescript copy.

85 Fay (1820–1872) was born in Cuttingsville, Vermont, and at age 25 sailed as mate on the American whaler *Harvest* with Captain Coffin, master. They left Tarpaulin Cove, February 1845, bound on a whaling voyage to the Pacific Ocean. On Wednesday, July 5, 1848, they came to anchor back in Nantucket Bay. In 1849, Fay found himself in San Francisco having sailed there in the schooner *Exact*. At the time this letter was written, he was the skipper of the *Orbit*. From that point until his death in 1872, Captain Fay remained on Puget Sound taking an active interest in the arrival of all newcomers, helping different families in building their homes, and averting serious trouble among the Indians during the uprising of 1855–1856. He was appointed as the Indian Agent for the Puget Sound Country. On September 12, 1860, Captain Fay married the widow of John Alexander and spent the remainder of his life in Coupeville. freepages.genealogy.rootsweb.ancestry.com/~fayfamily/winslow1787.html.

86 UW Library's Tolmie Papers Acc. 4577-001, Box 1, Folder 3.

goods at this post, and for customhouse charges and fees, I am surprised at his having called upon you to pay the $213 disbursed by him to [Thomas] Glasgow, as my impression was that the aforementioned payments of $468 repayed all charges against us which Genl Adair informed me had been made [as quickly] as possible and a confirmation of this view of the case is afforded by the fact that Genl Adair requested me to pay, after his departure, the Soldiers who had had charge of the Cadboro, the sum of $106 which he distinctly stated would be deducted at my next settlement with him for goods entered. Genl Adair paid [Thomas] Glasgow at this place and why, if the Coy had been still liable for this charge, did he not call upon me for the amount at once?

I now forward the Soldier's receipt for the $106, which please have deducted from your next payment to Genl Adair and credited to Fort Nisqually thereafter.

With regard to obtaining goods p[er] the Orbit, we do not, I am happy to say, stand in need of anything of consequence.

I shall, according to your instructions, supply to Lieut [John] Dement the sum of one Thousand, or Fifteen Hundred Dollars as soon as the means are at my disposal of it.

[Signed—William F. Tolmie]

Document 2.38: A letter from William F. Tolmie, Nisqually, to James Douglas, Victoria, October 30, 1850.

Sir,

Rocque Ducheny,[87] having arrived here two days ago bound for Victoria, I despatch the present canoe to convey him thither and at same time forward in his charge six choice Rams for the Victoria Ewes. I have not been able to induce any of our working Indians to whom wages are due, to go to Victoria for Payment by the present conveyance.

We have about 4,500 Ewes to put to the Rams. Having Nothing further to communicate, [I remain, &c., &c.]

W. F. Tolmie

P.S. Please let [François] Coté have 12 [pounds of] Sugar on ac[count] Nisqually O[utfi]t [18]51, he having made himself very useful while here. Tolmie

Document 2.39: A private letter from William F. Tolmie, Nisqually, to James Douglas, Victoria, October 30, 1850.[88]

Sir,

Being desirous of settling on Vancouver's Island I hereby make applications to you for the purchase of 200 acres of land on the Hudson's Bay Company's reserve there. The place of my selection is that known at Victoria as the "Grand Basfond",

87 For Ducheny see Watson, *Lives Lived*, 1:345.

88 BC Archives MS-0557, Box 2. From a typescript copy.

and with your permission, I shall commence getting improvements mad[e] there forthwith on this understanding, that should the Coy decline selling land on their reserve I shall in that case have full remuneration for all improvements made. I have the honor to be Sir, Yours

W. F. Tolmie

Document 2.40: A letter from Alonzo M. Poe,[89] Olympia, to William F. Tolmie, Nisqually, November 8, 1850.

Sir,

The Bill left by Bowen [?] for [Joachim] LeFleur I passed to his Credit on the Books of [Michael T.] Simmons & [Charles H.] Smith.[90]

A. M. Poe

Document 2.41: A letter from William F. Tolmie, Nisqually, to James Douglas, Victoria, November 9, 1850.

[Sir,]

Since I last addressed you on the 30th Ulto by Duchinais [Rocque Ducheny], several letters and newspapers to your address have come to hand which, along with other mail matter, are now forwarded by Mr. James Tod, who is supplied with a canoe and Indians, and bears half the expenses of the trip.

Mr. C[hief] F[actor Peter S.] Ogden, in a letter dated the 28th Ulto, informs me that some gentlemen have proposed to him to send a ship to Nisqually for a load of Sheep to be taken to California. He has stated that our prices would be at least /$5/ five dollars apiece for sheep, and he wishes me to acquaint him without delay as to our terms and conditions, as some of the parties desirous of entering into the speculation reside in California and will have to be made acquainted with our prices &c., 'ere any arrangement can be entered into. Mr. O[gden] mentions that from 500 to 1,000 will be taken.

---

89 Poe (1826–1866) was born in Clinton, Missouri, and arrived in the Oregon Territory in 1845, settling in Tumwater one year later. He was elected sheriff of Lewis County in 1847. He attended the Cowlitz Convention, the organization beginning of Washington Territory, and represented Olympia. In 1851 he attended the rescue of the failed gold hunting expedition to the Queen Charlotte Islands. The following year he was elected as clerk of Thurston County and appointed Deputy U.S. Marshall. He moved to Bellingham Bay and obtained a donation land claim of 303 acres in 1854. That same year he was admitted to the bar as a lawyer and appointed notary public in Thurston County. In 1854–55 he was a member of the territorial legislature—representing Whatcom County—and appointed county auditor for Whatcom County. In 1855 he was a lieutenant in the Rangers in the Indians war in Thurston County. In 1858 he surveyed and platted the Town of Whatcom. In 1861 he founded and was editor of the *Overland Press*, later to be the *Pacific Tribune*, the first daily newspaper in Washington Territory. This same year he moved to California for his health and he died in 1866 in Napa Valley of "inflamation of the lungs." www.portofbellingham.com/DocumentCenter/View/3145.

90 Smith was an American settler and early Tumwater/Olympia area resident. He was also the trusted business partner of Michael T. Simmons—that is until he absconded with $60,000 in cash and credit in 1851 during a California business trip. Simmons and other settlers of Puget Sound were economically devastated by Smith's deception.

I have deferred replying to Mr. Ogden regarding the sale of sheep as above proposed until I can ascertain from you whether the requirements of Victoria considered it would be advisable [sic] to dispose of so many Wedders, as he speaks of, Wedders being, I presume, the kind of sheep wanted. There were on Inventory Novr 1st 1850, 1,584 Dinmonts or Wedders rising two years, and 1,055 Wedders lambs. And instead of 4,500 as mentioned in my last, 5,200 Ewes have this season been put to the Rams.

I had a visit yesterday from [John] Montgomery and [John] Macleod, formerly stock keepers for the Coy here. They made application for payment of their c[urren]t Balance in the Coy's books and, in being told that through desertion they had forfeited the same, offered to return and serve out their time left on the terms of their broken contracts, provided their balances would be thereafter paid them. [John] Montgomery's services are worth securing, he being better acquainted with the cattle and their haunts than anyone now in the employ. [John] Macleod can very well be dispensed with here, [John] Macphail, whom I have just seen, [being now] uncertain about remaining after the 1st March, when his contract expires.

Father [Pascal] Ricard has given Bills of Exchange in triplicate for £190.10 St[erlin]g, having overdrawn by upwards of one hundred dollars, the amount ($800) to which you limited him. He has applied for a fresh credit in a letter here enclosed.

Charles Wren, having squatted on the Company's lands at Douglas burn and recorded a claim there, has taken possession of two potato fields cultivated by the Coy since 1848, and has just been asking me to sell him the fence poles, which I have declined doing. I am in doubt whether the fence poles ought to be removed or left on the ground for Wren to appropriate as well as the land. There may be about 2 or 2,500 fence poles.

The monthly mail is despatched from Newmarket about the 20th of each Month & should the present canoe return speedily from Victoria, I may be able to reply to Mr. [Chief Factor Peter S.] Ogden regarding the sheep by the November Mail.

S[igne]d Wm F. Tolmie

Document 2.42: A letter from William F. Tolmie, Nisqually, to Peter S. Ogden, Vancouver, November 17, 1850.

Sir,

Having received a sudden summons to proceed to Victoria, where Governor Blanshard is reported dangerously ill, I must study brevity in the present communication.

I beg to advize having this day drawn upon you in favor of Capt [Richard O.] Henderwell for the sum of Four Hundred and Thirty Two Dollars Fifty Cents ($432.50) which, please pay on demand.

I have consulted Mr. [James] Douglas regarding the sale of sheep, as proposed in yours of the 29th Ulto and, as he will expect me at Victoria, presume that he will communicate directly with you on the subject. I regret you having had cause of complaint with regard to the Invoice lately sent, the present is forwarded in charge of [Rocque] Ducheny who returns to Vancouver.

S[igne]d W. F. Tolmie

CHAPTER THREE

December 1st, 1850–May 31st, 1851

"Having understood that you are the Hudson's Bay Coy's Legal Advizer in this country, I beg to submit to your consideration the accompanying statement of facts regarding the encroachment by Messrs Wren and Chambers on the Puget's Sound Coy lands at Nisqually."
—William F. Tolmie to Amory Holbrook, February 15, 1851

Gloomy, overcast skies and a sharp frost welcomed the fort's denizens in December 1850.[1] The Tolmies were once again at Fort Victoria where the doctor and James Douglas exchanged views on a number of issues; the Americans' increased aggressiveness being their main concern. Proof of this is voiced in Douglas's letter to HBC Secretary Barclay: "It is difficult to account for the conduct of the United States authorities in imposing these harassing restrictions, unless we suppose that they are acting under the influence of a rooted hostility to the Company, and a determination to drive them by these oppressive acts, from their possessions South of 49°. We trust Her Majesty's Government may do something for our relief otherwise our position is full of danger."[2]

Tolmie's anticipated retirement to Vancouver Island in 1851 was also discussed. As proposed, the doctor's elderly aunts were to be brought from Scotland after he had established his own private farm near Fort Victoria. By mid-March, his relatives' refusal to leave Scotland and an honest appraisal of his replacement (by Douglas), forced a change of plans.

1 Dickey, ed. *Nisqually Journal*, December 1–10, 1850.
2 James Douglas to Archibald Barclay, December 3, 1850, Bowsfield, ed., *Victoria Letters*, 137.

Arriving at Nisqually aboard the American brig *Orbit* was a group of farm laborers including "the bailiff" Thomas Dean[3] and his wife Emily "Grace,"[4] their son George,[5] Richard Thornhill[6] and his wife Emma,[7] Richard Fiander/Fiandre,[8]

3 Dean (1802–1874) failed at several kinds of businesses in England. On November 4, 1850, PSAC offered him the position of bailiff or foreman at their Nisqually sheep farm. He accepted and shortly after he and his wife and two grown sons, Thomas Aubrey and George, left London for Victoria, Vancouver Island, where they arrived on May 9, 1851. Son Aubrey stayed at Fort Victoria while Thomas, his wife, and son George continued on to Fort Nisqually. Disembarking from the *Orbit* at Fort Nisqually on May 24, 1851, Dean performed various agricultural duties around the fort until June 21 when he went off to the nearby Tlithlow farm on the plains to commence his bailiff duties. Not only did he oversee the sheep operations, he also thrashed oats, slaughtered animals, and helped with the planting. During all of this, a seemingly insignificant September 7, 1853, was to pass like any other day except, in order to protect the Tlithlow farm on PSAC claims on what was then U.S. territory, he recorded the farm (320 acres) under his own name at the same time signing an agreement with PSAC stating that it was, in fact, their property. This agreement was later to haunt both Dean and PSAC. Between 1853 and 1856, he appeared regularly in the Nisqually journals doing a variety of tasks. On November 17, 1856, when Thomas Dean was about to retire, he produced a letter from Mr. Smith, HBC secretary in London, to the effect that if Dean were able to make the Company more profitable by the end of his term, the Company would present him a gratuity of £300 sterling. Tolmie, when presented with the letter, disagreed with the substance and, feeling that Dean had not increased the profit of the Company, offered Dean a reduced "gift" of £100 with the proviso that Dean was to give up Tlithlow and all PSAC property contained therein. At first Dean agreed but within a couple of hours changed his mind because he felt that Tolmie was cheating him out of $1,000. As a result, Dean claimed all of Tlithlow for himself. What followed for the next three months was a sad series of altercations of comedic opera proportions. Twice Dean threatened to shoot PSAC employees on his property, "Flithlane." PSAC eventually took Dean to court and lost. Dean sued PSAC for back wages and in the week of March 8, 1858, a jury could not agree on a verdict, leaving Dean without the money he felt owed him. He eventually sold his farm, "Flithland," for $1500 in 1862 and on March 2, 1866, his wife, Emily, was committed to an insane asylum from San Francisco Co.; six years later, on November 22, 1872, she died there of consumption. Thomas Dean died two years later in Tillamook Co., Oregon. Thomas Dean had one or more successive wives and two recorded children. Dickey, ed., *The Journal of Occurrences at Fort Nisqually*; *Washington Territory Land Claims*, 154; Huggins, "Reminiscences of Puget Sound," 131–32; biography courtesy of Bruce M. Watson.

4 Not much is known of Thomas Dean's wife, Emily (c. 1805–1872). She did not fit in well with Nisqually denizens. Removed from the upper crust of London Society, the 50-year-old Mrs. Dean retreated into herself, and her mental health undoubtedly suffered. The relationship between Dr. Tolmie and Thomas Dean no doubt suffered through Mrs. Dean's impudence towards Mrs. Tolmie and the other women of the fort. She eventually abandoned her husband for the richer high life of San Francisco. Towards her end, she was committed to a mental hospital. Author's notes.

5 Eighteen-year-old George Dean was likely living with his father and mother in London when he signed on with HBC for his journey to Vancouver Island. His relationship with the Company, however, was to last only a year. On May 11, 1852, the company was relieved when they saw the last of George. Dean then appears to have changed his ways for he settled on a claim of 160 acres in South Muck, Pierce County, on December 1, 1853. That same year he was given a warning for squatting on PSAC land. He became a citizen in 1857 but Huggins claimed that he left the country for good after that. In 1860, he was the co-owner, with James Dean, of the Vale Villa Farm of 150 acres in the Lake District of Vancouver Island. Courtesy of Bruce M. Watson.

6 Thornhill first worked at Nisqually as a laborer and cook from 1851 to 1853. From 1854 to 1855, he served as steward to the gentlemen of the fort. In 1856 he was sent out as a shepherd at one of the farm's outstations, which would have been considered a demotion from his previous jobs, and was eventually discharged in September of that same year. See Anderson's *Physical Structure of Fort Nisqually*, Appendix A, Servant's Lists, MPD, 1988.

7 For a full discussion on Mrs. Thornhill, see Emma Milliken, "The Thornhill Story," *Occurrences*, FNLHM, Metro Parks, 20:1 (2002), 8–11, and Emma Milliken, "Choosing between Corsets and Freedom: Native, Mixed-Blood, and White Wives of Laborers at Fort Nisqually, 1833–1860," *Pacific Northwest Quarterly* 96, No. 2 (2005), 95–101.

8 Richard Fiander [var: Dick Fiandre] (1832–1916), was an English farm hand from Dorset initially

William Cross,[9] William Northover,[10] Henry Barnes,[11] and George Hayward.[12]

Dean—Tolmie's supposed successor—was found to be, by Douglas's assessment, lacking in every sense of the word. Eventually, Dean and his family were moved out to Tlithlow Farm, and from there managed the Company's business in the plains. Considering these and other developments, Tolmie believed that "absenting himself" would jeopardize the fort's operation, and so he decided to reengage for several more years.

As previously illustrated, the customs officials' obstinate behavior had increased tension among the Company's managers. Expressed financially, James Douglas estimated that "[t]he present account [of $12,669.25 in damages] ... represents the direct pecuniary loss sustained by the Company through those arbitrary proceedings [vessel and warehouse seizures], but does not attempt, as that indeed would be next to impossible, to represent the more indirect consequences of that measure, and its effects on our social position and the fatal blow intended at our political influence over the native Tribes of Oregon."[13] In spite of this, the Company's business with the U.S. Army at Steilacoom Barracks had begun to flourish. There are even hints that Tolmie had begun acting as a lending bank for the barracks' quartermaster Lieutenant John Dement. This mutually beneficial relationship would grow and solidify in the coming years.

---

listed on the fort's employee list from May 1851 to November 1855. That May, he arrived at Victoria on the *Troy*, and within a week was brought to Nisqually on the *Orbit*. His immediate posting appears to have been manager of Muck Farm at £22 per year. In the letters ahead, you will see his attempt to file a claim on Muck Farm for himself. Abandoning his post during the Indian Wars, he worked sporadically—sometimes for the Company, other times as an independent for American settlers—as a "cattle killer." He was also caught stealing PSAC calves. Despite these shortcomings, Fiandre was considered a "good hand" as he was again hired by the Company in October 1859 at a rate of £37.15.6 per year. He married an Indian wife "Betsy" by 1853, but was later noted as marrying "Kate," the wife of deceased Scottish immigrant Lyman "Sandy" Smith, who had settled on the lower Squally Plain. For general employment records see Anderson, *Physical Structure of Fort Nisqually*, 173–80.

9 Cross, who had arrived at Fort Victoria on the *Tory*, May 14, 1851, as a laborer employed by the PSAC, was an English servant who worked around Fort Nisqually with livestock and crops, eventually being transferred to Tlithlow Station in November 1855.

10 Northover (?–1874) was an English farm laborer. During his time at the fort he was largely engaged in manual labor and routine duties. He worked variously at several outstations, including Tlithlow and Sastuc Stations. On February 6, 1870, he was shot by John Calder, but survived for another four years. He passed away in 1874.

11 Barnes was an Englishman who entered a five year contract with the PSAC at this time. Over the next two years, he served as a laborer/gardener, likely working in the fort's gardens. It appears that he deserted late in 1853, only to become one of the squatters/trespassers on Company land. See Anderson, *Physical Structure of Fort Nisqually*, 174–76.

12 Hayward was an English laborer. He worked at the fort, but within a month he was transferred to Tlithlow Station and appointed "dairy man." By 1852 he had "taken his place in the plains" and was herding sheep—at one point driving a flock of them to Vancouver. In late September 1852, he deserted his post and by 1856 had aligned himself with Thomas Dean—who ran against grain and was now claiming Tlithlow Station as his own. By November 1856, both Hayward and Dean were "warned off" for trespassing at Tlithlow. Hayward appears to fall back into the Company's graces for a time, working for Edward Huggins and William Grieg on PSAC projects. By December 1856, he was released from their employment. The last mention of him doing anything in the Tlithlow Farm neighborhood is in January 1857.

13 James Douglas to Archibald Barclay, December 27, 1850, Bowsfield, ed., *Victoria Letters*, 145. Douglas's assessment broke down as follows: the *Cadboro*'s seizure amounting to $6,988.25; while the seizure of Fort Nisqually's storehouse amounted to $5,681.00.

New Year's Day, 1851, was greeted with "a slight frost . . . a grand ball at Rossville" (present day Fort Lewis Golf Course) and the arrival of George Roberts. As magistrate for the Cowlitz settlement, Roberts had been "called upon to perform the marriage ceremony between Miss A[lice] McAllister and Mr. John Chambers which was this day celebrated" noted Tolmie.[14] Elsewhere, men and women drank ale and brandy, dined on mutton and beef, and danced the night away. The next day, as might be guessed, "little work was done."

With the festivities concluded, Tolmie prepared to file lawsuits against the squatters. On the eastern edge of the Company's land claim were some of the most fertile prairie lands east of Puget Sound. There, Charles Wren had been observed staking off land on Muck Creek. Tolmie's "statement of facts" detailing Wren and Thomas Chambers' encroachments was mailed off to the Company's attorney in Oregon Territory, Amory Holbrook.[15] Holbrook had traveled west in 1848 from Massachusetts after being appointed the Attorney General for Oregon Territory by President Zachary Taylor. Retained by the HBC in 1850, he later served as Oregon City's mayor and in the Oregon Legislative Assembly. "Pray not that you are annoyed by so frequent efforts on the part of new emigrants to disregard and violate your rights," Holbook would write. "But, I presume, that after our Courts are fully established, these troubles and trespasses will cease. I hope to have the pleasure to see you at your place during the Month of May, at which time I will be happy to render you any assistance in my power, and, if previously there is any other matter in regard to which I can be of service to you."

While publicly sympathetic to the doctor's situation, the counselor was also aware of the Company's precarious legal standing in the territory. The *fait accompli* trial and fate of the *Albion* had revealed to all that any suit would ultimately end up before a jury composed of the Company's adversaries—peers of the very squatters that Tolmie targeted for expulsion. Under such circumstances, winning any suit against them decreased exponentially regardless of the treaty's language, real or circumstantial evidence, or the court's opinion.[16]

The HBC's Clerk James A. Grahame, a correspondent of Tolmie's who appears frequently in this work, is first mentioned in this chapter.[17] He joined the Company in 1843, and moved to Fort Vancouver in 1844 where he remained throughout the 1850s, attaining the rank of chief trader in 1854 and chief factor in 1867.

---

14 Dickey, ed., *Nisqually Journal*, January 1, 1851.

15 Holbrook (1820–1866) was a college educated attorney and politician who came to the Oregon Territory in 1848 and was the first United States Attorney for the territory. He was a leading proponent of the HBC/PSAC and the Company's attorney for several years. See en.wikipedia.org/wiki/Amory_Holbrook.

16 Holbrook would later point out that the loss of just one precedent-setting case could insure the rights of all past, present, and future squatters. Correspondingly, it would sweep aside the Company's possessory rights from the territory as well as any chance of remuneration by the U.S. Government. This being the case, the lawyer advocated the documentation of all efforts to eject the squatters, largely through the issuance of trespass notices; the presence of witnesses being critical in backing the legal battles that were sure to come.

17 James Allan Grahame (1825–1905). See Watson, *Lives Lived*, 2:415.

A new squatter, Captain Lafayette Balch, also joins Tolmie's list of correspondents.[18] Captain Balch, a native of Trescott, Maine, sailed his brig *Sacramento* to California in 1848 and then either sold it or leased it to others. His later cargoes consisted largely of pilings which his other ship, the brig *George Emery*,[19] hauled between Puget Sound and San Francisco. Balch made the first of three voyages to Puget Sound in February 1850. Previous attempts to build in Olympia were thwarted by established competitors, so he set up shop near Steilacoom Bay—today's Chambers Bay. He christened it "Port Steilacoom," which at the time included only his store (built by July of 1850). Following Holbrook's advice, Tolmie issued Captain Balch a trespass notice in January 1851.

One of Balch's rivals was Olympia merchant Michael Simmons. Tolmie had utilized Simmons' vessel, the brig *Orbit*, to make runs to Victoria with livestock since before the blockade, thereby assuaging concerns of customs officials. Other American vessels, such as the brig *George Wilkins Kendall*,[20] skippered by Albion Butler Gove,[21] were similarly employed.

By the end of March it was reported that "Mrs. Tolmie safety delivered of a son this morning." She had just given birth to the couple's first born: Alexander John Tolmie.[22]

---

18 Balch, Lafayette (1825–1862). For more see Lucile McDonald, "Brush-off at Olympia Led to Founding of Steilacoom," *Seattle Times*, June 25, 1950; and Carol Neufeld, "Lafayette Balch, Founder of Steilacoom," *Steilacoom Historical Museum Quarterly* 14 (Fall 1985), 1, 4–6.

19 *George Emery*, American brig. Captain and owner Lafayette Balch and over time skippered by captains James M. Bachelder, Enoch S. Fowler, John W. Wilson, and W. H. Diggs. Primary cargo hauled was dry goods and merchandise.

20 *George Wilkins Kendall*, American brig, Captain Albion Butler Gove. Named after a famous war correspondent and owned by Samuel Merritt, the 183 ton brig was built at Booth Bay, Maine. After sailing to the Pacific Northwest in 1852, she was loaded at the port of Olympia with 6,700 feet of sawed lumber, 5,000 feet of hewn lumber, 10,000 shingles, and 100 barrels of oil, bound for San Francisco. Roland Carey, *The Sound of Steamers* (Seattle: Alderbrook Publishing, 1965). See also en.wikipedia.org/wiki/George_Wilkins_Kendall and www.maritimeheritage.org/vips/merrittSamuel.html.

21 It is at this point that we get introduced to one of three ship's captains from Maine: brothers Albion, Warren, and David Gove. They are easily mistaken one for the other, especially when a letter's author merely refers to them as "Captain Gove." I have attempted to clarify each person within the letters as he is noted in his place and time. Albion Butler Gove was born in Maine in 1826 and first went to sea on the *Atlantic* serving until 1848. The following season he joined a company of forty-niners who purchased the brig *George Wilkins Kendell* for a voyage to California, Gove coming out as mate. On arrival at San Francisco in 1850, he bought an interest in the *G. W. Kendell* with Dr. Samuel Merritt. After making two trips to the Columbia River he finally ran her to Puget Sound in 1852, trading there for eight years. Wright, *Lewis & Dryden's Marine History of the Pacific Northwest*, 63. See William Henry Gove, *The Gove Book: History and Genealogy of the American Family of Gove and Notes of European Goves* (Salem, MA: Sidney Perley, 1922), 272n. archive.org/stream/govebookhistoryg00gove/govebookhistoryg00gove_djvu.txt.

22 Alexander (1851–1903) was born on March 31, 1851, at the fort, and was the eldest of the Tolmie children. R. G. Large, ed., *The Journals of William Fraser Tolmie: Physician and Fur Trader* (Vancouver, BC: Mitchell Press, 1963), 400. See also Watson, *Lives Lived*, 3:932–33.

In April, the fort experienced the normal passage of visitors and news. The Reverend Robert J. Staines,[23] attended by Letitia Work,[24] canoed down from Victoria under the guidance of seasoned Company servant Jean Baptiste Jollibois.[25] Henry E. Hetling, an apprentice clerk from Vancouver, passed through heading in the opposite direction with a mail packet. Newspapers of the day brought various forms of intelligence to the doctor. And while it was reported that Congressman Thurston had died, the politician's deception lived on, gaining additional traction and patronage in Washington, D.C. Rumors now spread that the federal government was contemplating additional restrictions on the Company's Indian trade—and in the worst-case scenario, the wholesale termination of the Company's business with all aboriginals.[26]

Tolmie was also provided with an eye-witness account of San Francisco's destruction by fire, courtesy of Peter Ogden. He also learned of the appointment of Hugh Goldsborough to a leading position within Olympia's customs house.

Here then are the letters from second half of Outfit 1851.

---

23 Staines was "the first Anglican Clergyman, of Cambridge, who conducted services in the Mess Hall in the Hudson's Bay Co's Fort in Victoria. This gentleman reached Victoria sometime in the late forties, remaining in that position until his disagreement with the Company, when in company with the late James Yates, an opposition party to the rule of the Hudson's Bay Co was formed and Mr. Staines was deputed to proceed to England for the purpose of bringing the grievances of the dissatisfied settlement before Parliament. He took passage on a sailing ship on the 5th Feb., 1854. This ship foundered at sea and Mr. Staines with all others lost his life." James Robert Anderson Papers, "Notes and Comments on Early Days and Events in British Columbia, Washington, and Oregon," ch. 15. Add. Mss. 1912. Box 8/18, Archives, Victoria. Huntsman's note: "On the 1 March 1854 Staines boarded the *Duchess of San Lorenzo* at Sooke Harbor and which was bound for San Francisco with a heavy load of timber. It foundered in Juan Fuca Straits and all were lost." Halpenny, ed., *Dictionary of Canadian Biography* (Toronto: University of Toronto Press, 1985), 8:835–36. See also www.biographi.ca/en/bio/staines_robert_john_8E.html.

24 Born in present-day Idaho's Snake River region, Letitia Work Huggins (1831–1910) was the third of twelve children born to HBC Chief Factor John Work and Josette Legace. Throughout the 1830s, her father worked in posts all along the Pacific Northwest Coast. Educated by her father until 1842, "Lettie" began formal instruction while at Fort Simpson. Living at Fort Victoria through the middle 1850s, Letitia was hired on to teach needle skills. During this time, she traveled back and forth to Fort Nisqually—attending to her sister Jane (who had married Dr. Tolmie) and helping with her sister's growing family. While there, two suitors, Edward Huggins, a British HBC clerk, and William W. Miller, an American customs official, vied for Letitia's attentions. In the end, Edward and Letitia married October 21, 1857, at her sister's Fort Nisqually home. Letitia stayed with the Tolmies for six months while her husband finished building their new home at Muck Creek in eastern Pierce County. After the Tolmie's move to Victoria in 1859, the Huggins family moved into the Factor's House at the fort. When the HBC/PSAC closed up shop on U.S. soil in 1870, the Huggins homesteaded the property as American citizens and acquired an additional 1,000 acres of farmland around the old fort site. They raised nine children and remained there until 1906 when they sold the property and moved to Tacoma. Edward died in 1907 and Letitia in 1910. Biographical information gathered by Dana Repp at the editor's request. Sources include Oregon Historical Society, Eva Emery Dye Collection, Edward Huggins Correspondence; UW Library, Clarence B. Bagley Collection, Correspondence Outward; death records, Tacoma Cemetery.

25 Dickey, ed., *Nisqually Journal*, April 13, 1851.

26 Rumors of this nature persisted, but would not be substantiated or enforced until individuals with more political and military clout arrived in the region.

Document 3.01: An extract of a private letter from William F. Tolmie, Nisqually, to James Douglas, Victoria, December 16, 1850.[27]

[Sir,]

On more mature consideration, I think that the Mitchousin [Metchosin] Waterfall claim [on Vancouver Island] will suit me better than the "Grand Basfond" [Grand Bas Fond] with its present uncertainty of tenure I would take 200 acres to include the waterfall, and the fern clad slope on the seashore, where the Indian fortification now stands, and would like [Jean Baptiste] Jollibois to have his lot adjoining. Please inform me in your next whether this arrangement can be entered into.

[William F. Tolmie]

Document 3.02: A letter from William F. Tolmie, Nisqually, to James Douglas, Victoria, December 17, 1850.

Sir,

In charge of J[ean] B[aptiste] Brulé[28] are forwarded sundry letters and papers received from Vancouver at different dates. Please let Brulé have, on account of Ft Nisqually O[utfi]t [18]51, Thirty Shillings Sterling at the 50 P[e]r cent Tariff for labor performed here. Please to inform me per first opportunity how many of the Indians sent to Victoria along with James Tod[29] were paid there for the trip. I have the honor to be Sir, &c., &c.,

S[igne]d W. F. Tolmie

Document 3.03: A letter from William F. Tolmie, Nisqually, to Peter S. Ogden, Vancouver, December 19, 1850.

Sir,

On returning from Victoria [on the evening of December 12], I had the honor to receive your communication of the 3rd Inst,[30] in which you express surprise at not having received a decisive reply from me regarding the price of Sheep. I deferred answering your letter on that subject until I could ascertain what number of Wedders had to be retained here to meet the wants of the Hudson's Bay Company at Victoria.

I have now to inform you that Sheep, both Wedders and Ewes, are for sale here at the price of five dollars each, but I cannot bind myself to hold any given number ready for delivery here, unless the party wishing to purchase became bound, under an adequate penalty, to take the sheep off my hands at the time appointed.

S[igne]d W. F. Tolmie

27 BC Archives, MS-0557, Box 2. From a typescript copy.

28 For Brulé see Watson, *Lives Lived*, 1:234–35.

29 For Tod (1818–1904) see Watson, *Lives Lived*, 3:929.

30 This letter has yet to be located.

Document 3.04: A letter from James Douglas, Victoria, to William F. Tolmie, Nisqually, December 29, 1850.[31]

Dear Sir,

The canoe and packet in charge of Jean Bapt[iste] Brulé arrived here safely and I had the pleasure of your letter of the 17th Decr with enclosures. The sum due Brulé (30 ft of Steel bar) will be paid and charged to Fort Nisqually according to your request. Three blankets were paid to the Indians who accompanied James Tod to this place being one each to so many Indians.

I do not consider it necessary that the Inventory or charges connected with the Nisqually accounts of Out[fit] 1850 should be valued, excepting the Livestock, say horses, sheep and neat cattle, furnished to the Hudson's Bay Company, which you will value at the rate fixed at our last meeting here.

An estimate of the loss and expenses incurred through the seizure and detention of the Company's property at Nesqually on the 14th April last is herewith forwarded under course to Mr. [Peter S.] Ogden to whom you will forward it after examination.

As it appears that a Bailiff [Thomas Dean] is expected by the first ship from England to be stationed at Fort Nesqually, you will please to get a house erected for his accommodation, either in the plains or near the Fort as you may consider most convenient for the discharge of the duties required of him.

I herewith forward a packet for Vancouver containing our District Accounts, which we beg may be forwarded by an early and safe conveyance, to their destination. With best wishes, Your's truly,

James Douglas

Document 3.05: A letter from William F. Tolmie, Nisqually, to Michael T. Simmons & Charles H. Smith, Newmarket, January 9, 1851.

Gentlemen,

Please give the bearer four of your best Chopping axes if the price does not exceed Three dollars p[e]r axe, and charge the same to your account against the Hudson's Bay Company.

Mr. [Thomas] Glasgow[32] delivers today his first load of potatoes for Mr. Simmons. I shall do my best to secure the potatoes ag[ains]t cold while stored here, but, as I cannot be responsible for their preservation, it would be well if Mr. Simmons came here soon to see them, and as this is our season for closing accounts, it would be agreeable, if convenient to Mr. Simmons were he come prepared to settle the account standing against him in the Coy's books.

S[igne]d W. F. Tolmie

31 UW Library's Tolmie Papers Acc. 4577-001 Box #1, Folder #2.

32 By this point, Thomas Glasgow was living south of the Nisqually River, farming land of his own.

Document 3.06: A letter from William F. Tolmie, Nisqually, to James Douglas, Victoria, January 13, 1851.

Sir,

I have to acknowledge your communication of the 29th Ulto and shall forward the packet for Vancouver, accompanying it on the 15th Inst. I think [Thomas Dean] the Bailiff for Nisqually, expected from England this spring, can be most usefully employed in the plains. Shall I get a log house built for him such as the American settlers live in, or a squared log building similar to those in the fort?

Herewith is forwarded George Borabora's[33] account, he being sent to Victoria by the present canoe. The Indian Chief Ayohoh [Â'yoáhoh],[34] bearer of the despatches, has been supplied with 1 C[otton] S[triped] Shirt here on ac[count] Gen[eral]l Charges O[utfi]t 1851. I have the honor to be Sir, Your very Obedt Sert,

(S[igne]d) Wm F. Tolmie

Document 3.07: A letter from William F. Tolmie, Nisqually, to George B. Roberts, Cowlitz Farm, January 15, 1851.

Dear Sir,

[Jean Baptiste] Lapoitrie is despatched to Cowelitz with the accounts of Forts Victoria, Langley & Nisqually in a packet box, which please forward to Ft Vancouver without delay, as it contains letters for the Mail Steamer of this Month.

I observe, in your account against Nisqually O[utfi]t 1850, that the expenses incurred at Cowlitz farm by [John] Macphail's Sheep Party have been charged against this post. Now, as the Wedders were sent to Vancouver at the particular and repeated request of Mr. C[hief] F[actor Peter S.] Ogden, it is self-evident that Vancouver ought to bear all the expense of their conveyance thither, & I beg you to forward to Mr. [Peter S.] Ogden an account of your charges for Sheep transport, distinct from the Farm account against Nisqually.

With respect to the Frying Pan entered in the sheep account as lost or retained by Macphail, he asserts that he took no frying pan from Cowelitz farm, but that he saw one in [John] Sutherland's possession for the first time at the Forks of Cowlitz and for the last at [Antoine] Gobin's,[35] when Sutherland left the party and proceeded to Vancouver ahead of them. I wish Lapoitrie to rest his horses for a couple of days at Cowlitz and remain Dear Sir,

S[igne]d W. F. Tolmie

---

33 For Borabora see Watson, *Lives Lived*, 1:210.

34 No other information was found regarding this tribal headman from Victoria.

35 For Antoine Petit (Gobin) see Watson, *Lives Lived*, 2:773. Also going by the last name Gobar, Antoine was a PSAC horse herder who occupied the lands near the confluence of the Cowlitz and Columbia Rivers, in the area of today's Kelso/Longview, Washington.

Document 3.08: A letter from William F. Tolmie, Nisqually, to Peter S. Ogden, Vancouver, January 19, 1851.

Sir,

By the present express conveying the Victoria and Langley accounts, I have the honor to forward the accounts from Nisqually which I trust may be found correct and satisfactory; also, the First & Second of a Bill of Exchange for £115.2/2 drawn first March 1850. There is likewise a letter from Father [Pascal] Ricard to his Agent in France on which please prepay the postage to New York, charging the amount thereof to Nisqually O[utfi]t 1850.

By reference to the account of Supplies from the HBC to the PS Coy, you will perceive that a charge of 20 p[e]r Cent is to be made on the gross amounts to cover the duties paid by the HBC on their importations into American Oregon. Now as duties have been paid on all goods Received at Nisqually since the 3rd April 1849, I submit to your consideration whether it would not be just and equitable to charge the Puget's Sound Company with 20 p[e]r Cent on two thirds of the supplies had during O[utfi]t 1849, to protect the Hudson's Bay Company from loss, consequent on the [res]pective operation of the Collector's proceedings when levying duties here in June 1850.

A Copy is now forwarded of Genl [John] Adair's letter to me of June 19th, 1850, which shows that he is bound to refund the Money ($106) paid at his Request to the soldiers placed in Charge of the Cadboro during her detention at Steilacoom.

Requisition is forwarded for some Axes and Scalping Knives & which [you should] please proceed [send] to Cowelitz P[e]r first opp[ortunit]y.

I have requested Mr. [George B.] Roberts to charge against Ft Vancouver the expenses incurred at Cowlitz for the transport of Sheep to Vancouver last Summer. A Copy of Mr. R[obert]'s Account as made out against Nisqually is herewith sent with some notes upon it on [John] McPhail's participation. I have the honor to be Sir, Your Very Obedt Sert,

(Signed) W. F. Tolmie

Document 3.09: A letter from William F. Tolmie, Nisqually, to Lafayette Balch, Near Steilacoom Bay, January 23, 1851.

Sir,

Having recently learnt that you have taken land and commenced improvements between Kittson's Island and Steilacoom Inlet or Bay, it becomes my duty to warn you that if such be the case, you are trespassing on the lands claimed by the Puget Sound Agricultural Company under the fourth article of the Boundary Treaty conducted at Washington, June 15th, 1846 between the plenipotentiaries of Great Britain and the United States of America. As you may not be in possession of a copy of the Boundary Treaty I subjoin a copy of the fourth article[36] above referred to and remain Very Respectfully, Yours Very Truly,

(Signed) Wm F. Tolmie

36 A whole copy of the treaty is included in the appendix.

Document 3.10: A letter from William F. Tolmie, Nisqually, to John Adair, Astoria, February 3, 1851.

Dear Sir,

Mr. [Michael T.] Simmons of Newmarket, having lately informed me that the Hudson's Bay Company and others could import goods in the Orbit, provided the cost of collecting the duties was defrayed by the parties importing, and that you would come across to enter the goods if your expenses from Astoria and back, were defrayed, May I enquire whether I have rightly understood Mr. Simmons and if so, when it would be most convenient for you to come across, and what the probable expense would be? Thanks to the friendly caution you gave me last June, we have an ample supply of woolens and most other essentials.

As Mr. Simmons proposes employing the Orbit 'till May next in transporting our livestock to Vancouver's Island, will you please inform me whether we could, without entering at Astoria, import on her Oregon Flour and Leaf Tobacco, both products of the United States?

S[igne]d Wm F. Tolmie

Document 3.11: A letter from William F. Tolmie, Nisqually, to Peter S. Ogden, Vancouver, February 3, 1851.

Sir,

I received yesterday evening your communication of Decr 28th, 1850, and in reply to your comments therein regarding the sale of Sheep I beg to observe that if mine of Novr 17th, [18]50 reached you, you must have been aware that I did not go to Victoria for instructions on that point, and in further proof thereof take the following extract from my letter to Mr. [James] Douglas of Novr 9th, [18]50.

I shall attend to your instructions as to forwarding money to Lieut [John] Dement A[djutant] A[rmy] Q[uarter] M[aster] 1st Artillery, Steilacoom. Enclosed is his rec[eip]t for Fifteen Hundred Dollars [$1,500] already supplied.

S[igne]d W. F. Tolmie

Document 3.12: A letter from William F. Tolmie, Nisqually, to James A. Grahame, Vancouver, February 3, 1851.

Dear Sir,

Being informed by Mr. [George B.] Roberts that you are to close the accounts of O[utfi]t 1850, I have to request you, if it be not too late, to make the subjoined corrections in the accounts of Ft Nisqually. And please advise me, by return of the Steilacoom [Barracks] courier, whether this shall have reached you in time for your making the desired alterations or not.

S[igne]d Faithfully Yours,
W. F. T.

To make the charge to Cash paid for Labor & provisions £34.2/11 instead of £21.2/11.

To add 23 Bl[an]k[e]ts, 2½ P[oin]ts B[est Blue] to Nisq[uall]y Inven[tor]y, Novr 2nd, [18]50.

Document 3.13: A letter from William F. Tolmie, Nisqually, to James Douglas, Victoria, February 11, 1851.

Sir,

I duly received your communication[37] of the 3rd Inst forwarded by [Augustin] Willings[38] and shall not fail to do what the Land Bill requires in the 6th & 7th sections referred to, in your letter.

Having agreed with Mr. [Michael T.] Simmons on the terms lately fixed by you, the Orbit is now despatched with [*space left blank*] head of horses and [*space left blank*] sheep for Victoria. Two year old horses are taken at $6.00 each, and yearlings of which only some half-bred American are sent at $5.00 each; Foals at $2 each. I shall, if possible, enclose a lot of the horses 'ere the Orbit sails.

John MacPhail, accompanied by the Indians, goes to assist in looking after the stock.

I have understood from Mr. Simmons that he does not wish to settle for each trip, but to have a final settlement when the cattle transport is over. He owes here an old balance of about $75 or 80, besides some recent supplies, nevertheless please let him have supplies at Victoria to pay his Indian crew, &c., &c.,

S[igne]d W. F. Tolmie

Document 3.14: A Statement of Facts by William F. Tolmie Relative to the Encroachment by Charles Wren on the Lands Occupied Prior to the Settlement of the North West Boundary Question by the Puget's Sound Agricultural Company at Nisqually, Puget's Sound, Oregon Territory. February 11, 1851.

Charles Wren, a half-breed from Red River Settlement, and formerly in the Coy's service, has taken a mile square of the Coy's most valuable pasture land and one of the best lambing stations on which the Coy, previous to Wren's squatting, had made the following improvements:

They had sheepfolds on the land as early as 1844 or '45, since which period the tract in question has been traversed daily by their shepherds and stockmen in performance of [their] duty.

A claim hut was built there soon after M[isters John] MacLoughlin and [James] Douglas, as representatives of the Hudson's Bay and Puget's Sound Companies, had given in their qualified adherence to the Provisional Government formed in Oregon in 1845. Another and larger house was built in 1847, and a patch of land cultivated to protect the place against claims seekers, many of whom knew little of the Treaty stipulations and regarded the Organic Law, framed by the Provisional Government, as the Alpha and Omega of legislation on Land claims.

---

37 This letter has yet to be located.

38 For Willings see Watson, *Lives Lived*, 3:985.

In 1847 also, 400 fence rails were split in a hummock of Pines close to where Wren's house now stands. In 1849, two potato fields were cultivated—the yield of which in 1850 amounted to 600 Bushels.

Wren took possession in 1850 and offered to purchase the fence rails, which I [William F. Tolmie] declined selling. He has since ploughed in and around the potato fields and he prevents the Coy's Shepherds from pasturing their flocks on what he designates his claim.

The tract squatted upon by Wren is the best adopted for agricultural purposes of any on the Company's lands and it has been visited by several American citizens in quest of claims, but it would seem that they were too intelligent to have meddled with a claim, however attractive, which presented such obvious sign of previous occupancy. To do this, a combination of ignorance, impudence and unscrupulousness was required, such as Wren prominently possesses.

Mr. T[homas] M. Chambers has claimed since Autumn 1849 some land at Steilacoom within the district occupied by the PS Ag Company prior to the settlement of the Boundary question.

On the Steilacoom prairie, the Coy has four experimental arable farms, as early as the year 1841, but when the capabilities of the soil were ascertained, the cultivation of grain at Steilacoom was found less profitable than stock farming, and from 1843 'till 1845, the land remained undisturbed by the plough. In that year, two of the farms were taken by a Mr. Heath who continued to occupy them, farming on shares 'till he died in 1849.

Mr. Chambers's claim includes a valuable mill stream and the most northern of the farms opened in 1841 from which however, the fence rails and buildings had been removed by the late Mr. Heath save one small building which Mr. Chambers reroofed and represented as his claim hut, prior to commencing permanent improvements on the land.

Mr. C[hambers] also prevents the Coy's sheep from pasturing on his claim and is incessant in his endeavors to persuade other parties to squat on the Coy's land in which, since the publication of the Land Bill, he has been but too successful.

(S[igne]d) Wm F. Tolmie

Document 3.15: A letter from William F. Tolmie, Nisqually, to Peter S. Ogden, Vancouver, February 15, 1851.

Sir,

I now forward the enclosed which was too late for the last Steilacoom Mail. The accompanying from Victoria I shall request Mr. [George B.] Roberts to forward by Express in order that the letters for Europe may be in time for the next Mail.

I should like to have Mr. [Amory] Holbrook's opinion on the statement [of facts] here enclosed by return of the Express if possible.

Mr. [Lieutenant John] Dement informed me the other day that in the event of their shifting quarters, they would require ($5 or 6,000) five or six thousand dollars, and he seemed under an impression that such an amount could readily be obtained from Victoria. I stated that Ft Vancouver alone could, to the best of my knowledge, furnish the desired amounts.

Please send to Cowlitz p[e]r first opportunity the articles mentioned in the enclosed list,[39] on account of Ft Nisqually O[utfi]t 1851.

(Signed) W. F. Tolmie

Document 3.16: A letter from William F. Tolmie, Nisqually, to Amory Holbrook, Oregon City, February 15, 1851.

Sir,

Having understood that you are the Hudson's Bay Coy's Legal Advizer in this country, I beg to submit to your consideration the accompanying statement of facts regarding the encroachment by Messrs [Charles] Wren and [Thomas M.] Chambers on the Puget's Sound Coy lands at Nisqually. And I have to request your opinion, at your earliest convenience, as to whether a decision could be obtained in the courts of Oregon on the points in question, and again, whether you think such decisions would be one favorable to the Coy. As items of information that may be useful, I may mention that the boundaries of the district occupied by the Coy prior to the date of the Treaty of July 17th, 1846 are well defined and have invariably been made known from the first to all persons seeking information on the subject. The tract is supposed to contain about 144 square miles and on that extent I paid the land claim tax levied in Lewis County last summer. Since the publication of the Land bill, the disposition to squat on the Coy's land seems to increase and, unless it can soon be checked, our interests will suffer very materially. M[isters] Chambers and Wren were duly warned that in settling where they have they were trespassing on the lands claimed by the PSC.

(Signed) W. F. Tolmie

Document 3.17: A letter from William F. Tolmie, Nisqually, to James Hall,[40] Steilacoom Barracks, February 16, 1851.

Sir,

You would oblige me much by getting a load or two of the spare fence poles at Steilacoom [Farm] taken to our wheat patch there in order that it may be thoroughly fenced in and made cattle proof next summer.

Adam [Beinston of Sastuc Farm] informs me that you are getting fence rails carried from Steilacoom [Barracks] out to one of the places in the plains we spoke of the other day [Army Gardens], from which I apprehend that we had not then an explicit understanding on the subject. I do not think it advisable to have any rails removed from Steilacoom plain as they may at some future period be required there. Hoping to see you soon again,

(Signed) Wm F. Tolmie

---

39 This list was not found.

40 Hall was the 1st sergeant of Company M. 1st Artillery, U.S. Army. He later established a homestead on the southern shore of American Lake. Dickey, ed., *Journal of Occurrences at Fort Nisqually* states that Hall eventually returned east with the officers to reorganize the Company. George Dickey, *Company M. 1st Artillery in Oregon Territory, 1849–53*. np. nd.

Document 3.18: A letter from William F. Tolmie, Nisqually, to James Douglas, Victoria, February 22, 1851.

Sir,

By Louis Trudelle whose time expires on the 1st June [18]51, and who purposes either settling or re-engaging at Victoria, are forwarded some letters and papers received lately by the Steilacoom Mails. Trudelle is accompanied by two Indian lads, formerly on board the Cadboro who, having wives from V[ancouver's] I[sland], desire to return to Victoria. His [Trudelle's] account at this post is now forwarded along with a statement of the amount due one of the Indians.

The enclosed copy of a letter[41] from A[rchibald] Barclay Esq[ui]re was received some time ago, but without instructions that it should be forwarded to Victoria. It appears, from an account received from Vancouver, too late to have had the mistake rectified that Mr. [Chief Factor Peter S.] Ogden by paying [Captain Richard O.] Henderwell $100 for which no order had been sent from this post, has overpaid him to that amount. The Coy however can still be saved from loss by advancing [William] Brotchie only $100 instead of the $211 reserved from him.

(Signed) William F. Tolmie

Document 3.19: A letter from Amory Holbrook, Oregon City, to William F. Tolmie, Nisqually, February 25, 1851.

Sir,

I acknowledge the receipt of your Communication dated 15th Feby [1851], with the accompanying statement of facts [regarding the squatters Wren and Chambers] in regard to which my opinion is desired.

I have examined the fourth Article of the Treaty upon which is based the claim of the PSA Company to the land in question. The language of that Article seems, in my judgment, to be as explicit and full as words can be: "The farms, lands, and other property of Every description belonging to the Puget Sound Agricultural Company, on the North side of the Columbia River, Shall be confirmed to said Company." The only question then, it seems to me, will be in regard to the facts which the Co are able to prove in order to having the lands in question within the descriptive clause of the Treaty.

In regard to the case of [Charles] Wren, there seems to be hardly a reasonable doubt that the right of the Co to the land now occupied by him is perfectly Valid, and will be fully recognized by the Courts of the United States. If the Company has the evidence to prove on occupation in the manner you state, I do not see how their right can be resisted.

As to the right of [Thomas M.] Chambers, there can be no doubt also, that he will be regarded, in law, as a trespasser if the Company can prove that prior to the date of the Treaty, the land upon which he is now located was openly and notoriously used and occupied by them for their legitimate purposes and pursuits.

---

41 This letter has yet to be located.

The Company, in order to perfect their rights in both these cases, and to prevent further encroachment, have only to employ the means placed within their reach by the Territorial Statutes to effect the ejectment of the trespassers. In Lewis County, it may be difficult to enforce your rights for want of proper and sufficient officers. But probably after the Election in June next, that difficulty will be removed. In the meantime, it may be well, as that must be preliminary to any legal proceedings, to give these men notice to quit in writing, taking care to preserve the original notice and proof of it service, as it may be served by attested Copy. It may also be that an intimation to them that, while they are remaining on the Co's lands to which they, of course, can never acquire a title, they are resisting the taxes, which under the "Oregon Land Bill" they will be obliged to spend in residence and occupancy of the land to which they ask for a patent from [the] Government. The improvements also, which they are foolish enough to put upon the Company's land, cannot by any means increase to their own benefit, but will only be productive of advantage to the Company.

I presume from your description of Wren, moreover, that he is not as yet under the Land Bill qualified as a naturalized Citizen [and is unable] to reap the benefits of that act.

Pray not that you are annoyed by so frequent efforts on the part of new emigrants to disregard and violate your rights. But, I presume, that after our Courts are fully established, these troubles and trespasses will cease. I hope to have the pleasure to see you at your place during the Month of May, at which time I will be happy to render you any assistance in my power, and, if previously there is any other matter in regard to which I can be of service to you, I trust you will give me the opportunity. I am &c., &c., &c.,

(Signed) Amory Holbrook

Document 3.20: A letter from William F. Tolmie, Nisqually, to James Douglas, Victoria, March 7, 1851.

Sir,

I have now the honor to acknowledge receipt of your letters of the 17th and 26th Ulto.

The Orbit as you have probably learnt 'ere's now, is fast aground near Admiralty Head, on Whidbey's Island, and will not be afloat 'till the next spring tides, if then. [Michael T.] Simmons having received $340 in cash at Victoria has at Balance for the Cattle Transport of about $225, but then he owes $213 for Salt beef and pork recently supplied his Ship, the Elizabeth,[42] formerly the Albion, besides an old balance of about $80. I mention the state of his account at Nisqually in case he may be visiting Victoria for more cash while the Orbit lies at Whidbey's Island. I promised to settle up when the Elizabeth should be ready for sea. I forward a copy of [Captain Richard O.] Henderwell's account at Nisqually also an account against him at Vancouver from a comparison of which it will be seen that he has been overpaid $100 at Vancouver.

42 *Elizabeth* (see *Albion*, British bottom ship).

With regard to the $9 paid to Sandy,[43] the Indian employed in looking after the horses on board the Orbit, it ought, I think, to be charged against Ft Victoria, as I agreed with Simmons to furnish an Indian for that purpose the first trip.

Jonas Pike[44] did not make his appearance here by the late canoe. Yahoh [Â'yoá-hoh], the Indian Chief, says that no white man accompanied him from Victoria. I have detained the Indian 'till now in expectation of letters from Vancouver which have arrived today. Having nothing further of importance to communicate [I remain,]

(Signed) Wm F. Tolmie

Document 3.21: An extract from a private letter from William F. Tolmie, Nisqually, to George Simpson, Fort Garry, March 12, 1851.[45]

[Sir,]

Subjoined to my report to the Agents of the Puget's Sound Agricultural Company is a copy of the valuation of the Puget's Sound Company's property made by the Assessor of Taxes last summer.

The taxes for 1850 have been very heavy amount[ing] on PSC property to $956. The taxing of Land claims was a measure of [Samuel R.] Thurston's getting up in the legislature of 1849 with the especial view, I have been informed, of exacting money from the HB and PS Coys.

I was advised by Captain [Bennett H.] Hill and some other Americans to refuse paying the tax on Land claims, on the plea that our claim to a tract of 144 square miles had not yet been recognized by the US Gov't. I thought it best, however, to pay for once without demur, and Mr. [James] Douglas, whom I consulted on the subject, was of the same opinion.

And now for a few words on my own concerns in which I make bold to believe you kindly take an interest. Having received intimation from my aunts last fall, that as the period of embarkation drew nigh, they could not muster courage to emigrate to Vancouver's Island, my desire to make an immediate commencement as settler there abated, and when Mr. Douglas again requested me to waive my right of furlough and remain in charge here, I at once consented, being unwilling, now that the necessity of absenting myself was removed to give up the charge I have so long held, and which would suffer at the outset under the management of a stranger, however talented he might be. Neither have I yet lost hope of making a favorable impression on Sir J[ohn] H. Pelly[46] regarding my claim for services rendered the PS Coy.

---

43 This trader (and laborer), an Indian nicknamed "Old Sandy," first entered the fort's written record on January 11, 1842, in the Huntington Library's Soliday Collection, Nisqually Papers, Fort Nisqually Indian Accounts FN 1242, when it was recorded that he "brought in several fine beaver and bear skins." His name frequently arises in the 1840s associated with day laborer's duties, as a letter-courier, and a trader in skins. He and his father were caught stealing Company beef in the late 1848 period—which may have led to his brief banishment as a laborer at the fort. Though he appears to have gained employment (and a second chance) in the current situation, he is not listed as an employee in the Indian account books of the 1850s.

44 For Pike see Watson, *Lives Lived*, 2:778.

45 BC Archives, MS-0557, Box 2. From a typescript copy.

46 John Henry Pelly (1777–1852). "Sir John was an English businessman and 1st Baronet, DL. During most of his career, he was an employee of the Hudson's Bay Company (HBC), serving as Governor

I would now address yourself more fully on this subject were it probable that this would find you at Norway H[ouse], but I say no more at present, intending to write you fully on business as well as private matters by an early mail. [I remain, your most obedient servant,]

[Signed William F. Tolmie]

Document 3.22: An extract from a letter from William F. Tolmie, Nisqually, to James Douglas, Victoria, March 16, 1851.[47]

[Sir,]

Should you consider it advisable to adopt Mr. [Amory] H[olbrook]'s suggestion and serve [Charles] Wren and [Thomas M.] Chambers and indeed all the squatters, with notices to quit [their claims], please to draft out a form for me, which, with minute alterations to suit particular cases, may answer for one and all who now, or may hereafter, encroach on the Company's lands.

The "original notice" ought, I presume, to be written in a book set apart for the purpose, and a copy thereof, attested by two persons, handed to the trespasser by two or more individuals from whom a certificate or affidavit should be taken to the effect that at such a time & place they had served "So and So" with a notice to quit [claim].

The obtaining an affidavit will be tedious, necessitating a trip to Judge [Hugh A.] Goldsborough's at Newmarket, but the parties employed might proceed thither after having made the round of the Squatters, which they could do easily in a couple of days. Please to instruct me fully in your next on all matters touched on in this paragraph.

[William F. Tolmie]

Document 3.23: A letter from William F. Tolmie, Nisqually, to Peter S. Ogden, Vancouver, March 12, 1851.

Sir,

I now forward the accompanying for the Y[ork] F[actory] Express which, if not in time for the first despatch, may, I hope, be forwarded by the second. I Duly received your communication of the 27th Ulto with its accompaniments for Victoria which were sent on immediately.

Cash Sales have been pretty brisk here of late and we, I believe, get nearly all the money put in circulation. I expect about the 1st April to have about $1,500 at Mr. [Lieutenant John] Dement's disposal.

If you can possibly spare any money, please send at first opportunity per Cowlitz—6 X.P. Plough Shares for this post. I would be very thankful for a smaller number, but cannot get through the Spring work with less than six. [John] Kalama, S[andwich] I[slander],[48] was here lately in quest of his wife and child. When he

---

of the HBC for three decades. He held other noteworthy offices, including Governor of the Bank of England. The title of Baronet Pelly was created for him." en.wikipedia.org/wiki/John_Pelly.

47 BC Archives, M-0557, Box 2. From a typescript copy.

48 For Kalama see Watson, *Lives Lived*, 2:505; and Watson & Barman, *Leaving Paradise*, 278–79.

left, he was accompanied by a poor,[49] helpless Kan[a]ka named [Alick] Napahay,[50] suffering under partial paralysis of the left side, who I have since understood has gone to Vancouver in the hope of being employed there as a watchman. He was perfectly useless at this place and if he can gain his livelihood at Vancouver as a watchman, so much the better. If not, he ought, I presume, to be sent back to Nisqually where it will probably cost less to support him, and where having contracted his infirmity, he has the best claim for assistance. I have the honor to be

(Signed) Wm F. Tolmie

Document 3:24: A letter from William F. Tolmie, Nisqually, to William P. Dougherty,[51] Round Plain/Palielah, March 15, 1851.[52]

Sir,

Having been informed that you are getting a house built and other improvements made at "Palielah" on the "round plain" near Steilacoom, I hereby warn you that in taking a claim on said plain, you are trespassing on land possessed by the Puget's Sound Agricultural Company prior to the year 1846, and therefore guaranteed to them by the Boundary Treaty ratified in July 1846 by the plenipotentiaries of Great Britain and the United States of America.

(Signed) Wm F. Tolmie

Document 3.25: A letter from William F. Tolmie, Nisqually, to James Douglas, Victoria, March 22, 1851.

Sir,

By the present canoe is forwarded a packet of letters &c., received from Cowlitz a few days ago. I beg your attention to the accompanying memo regarding the Indians taking the Express.

Being very much in want of X.P. Plough Shares, I beg that six or more may be sent by return of the present canoe, as without a speedy supply our farming operations will long 'ere be arrested.

(Signed) Wm F. Tolmie

49 The use of the word "poor" during this period refers to the Hawaiian laborer's "poor health"—a standard Victorian use of that term when referring to an individual. Napahay had been paralyzed by a stroke that rendered his entire left side useless.

50 For Napahay see Watson, *Lives Lived*, 2:716–17; and Watson and Barman, *Leaving Paradise*, 361–62.

51 Little is known of Daugherty's (c. 1816–?) early life. A lifelong Mason, he arrived in Oregon Territory by 1843, where he kept a hotel in Portland. After trying his luck in California's gold fields, he moved in 1851 to an area three miles east of Steilacoom Barracks and squatted in an area called "Round Plain/Paleilah," where he established a farm. In 1852 he was one of three settler/squatters appointed as commissioners of the new Pierce County, Washington Territory. In the 1860s, he was appointed as a probate judge. He held the position of Master Mason at Steilacoom Lodge #2. Hubert Howe Bancroft, *History of Washington, Idaho, and Montana 1845–1889* (San Francisco: The History Company (1890), 4, 58–59, 78, 367.

52 The place name "Palielah" is believed to have come through the PSAC's use of Hawaiian shepherds running sheep north of today's Lakewood in 1844–45. The "Palila" bird (*loxioides bailleui*), is a finch-billed species of honeycreeper that is found exclusively on the upper slopes of Mauna Kea on the big island of Hawai'i. It is theorized that that these Hawaiian shepherd boys glimpsed the similarly colored willow goldfinch (*carduelis tristis*) in the area. Thus, the term "Palielah," or in several cases "Round Plain," demarked that general area from the 1840s through the early 1860s.

Document 3.26: A letter from William F. Tolmie, Nisqually, to Peter S. Ogden, Vancouver, April 2, 1851.

Sir,

I have just received your communication of the 17th Ulto accompanying letters and papers for Victoria, which I am preparing to despatch tomorrow morning. I now send by the Steilacoom Mail, which starts tomorrow m[ornin]g, some letters received from ~~Steilacoom~~ Victoria yesterday afternoon. The Una[53] is to be here in a few days, housed with a supply of goods entered at Astoria. I would take it as a particular favor if you would send me a copy of the Ft Nisqually, HBC and PS [Agricultural Company's] Balance Sheets for Outfit 1850. By so doing you will greatly oblige Sir, Your Very Obedt Sert,

S[igne]d W. F. T.

Document 3.27: A letter from William F. Tolmie, Nisqually, to James Douglas, Victoria, April 3, 1851.

Sir,

Your communication of the 29th March with the accompanying letters for Vancouver was carried here on the 1st Inst and the letters are forwarded today by the Steilacoom Mail.

The present express which is in charge of [Jean Baptiste] Jol[l]ibois, conveys letters received yesterday from Vancouver which Mr. [Peter S.] Ogden desired should be sent on without delay.

Jonas Pike will start for Cowlitz tomorrow or next day.

Gratified as I am to learn that the Una is soon to be here with a supply of goods, I regret much not having had earlier intimation that a vessel was to have been sent at this time, as a supply of Leaf Tobacco for sheep washing might, in that case, have been obtained as well as several articles for trade.

Every endeavor shall be made to give the Una a speedy despatch. Her cargo will consist of Cattle, Wedder and Gimmer Sheep, it being now too late to send breeding Ewes. Lambing is going on favorably and grass is abundant. I have the Honor to be Sir, Your Very Obedt Sert,

(Signed) Wm Fraser Tolmie

Document 3.28: A letter from William F. Tolmie, Nisqually, to James Douglas, Victoria, April 10, 1851.

Sir,

The present express is forwarded to convey despatches from Vancouver received here yesterday evening, and four of the runaway miners have been allowed a passage in the canoe on prepayment of each. Nothing strange has occurred here since I last wrote. We have nearly completed grain sowing and are making preparations to plant potatoes extensively in the swamp which will 'ere long be thoroughly drained.

53 *Una*, HBC brigantine. See Watson, *Lives Lived*, 3:1131.

Lambing has so far gone on favorably. Cash Sales have been rather dull of late. I have the honor to be Sir, &c., &c., &c.,

S[igne]d Wm Fraser Tolmie

P.S. The Miners, having no money, I have taken a promissory note from Andrew [Hunter][54] for £2 St[erlin]g which is here enclosed, and the amount will be charged against Ft Victoria O[utfi]t 1851 as soon as you notify its payment. T.

Document 3.29: A letter from Peter S. Ogden, Vancouver, to William F. Tolmie, Nisqually, April 10, 1851.[55]

Dear Sir,

I have to acknowledge the receipt of your letter of 2nd Inst, with the Packet all safe. Your request for Statement of acc[oun]ts to be forwarded is at present unaddressable Mr. [Joseph W.] Hardisty[56] has more than he can possibly attend to. Mr. [Henry] Hetling[57] accompanys the Packet and I have to request you will forward him on to Victoria. Yours Respectfully,

Peter S. Ogden

[P.S.:] I have just received information that my Friend [Hugh A.] Goldsborough has been appointed Customs House Officer at Olympia—that place [having] Long been made a Port of Entry. If this be correct, and [sic] it might be desirable [that] you should ascertain [the truth of it] and communicate the same to Mr. Douglas. I am certain a Bill has passed in Congress but I have not heard it has passed the Senate. Yours Truly, Peter S. Ogden

[P.S.S.] [D]octor McLoughlin is elected Mayor of Oregon [City].

Document 3.30: A letter from John Dement, Steilacoom Barracks, to William F. Tolmie, Nisqually, April 12, 1851.[58]

Dear Doct[or],

Any day that you may feel like riding down will suit my purpose. The am[oun]t remitted to Mr. Brook was $294.80.

You have probably heard before this of the removal of the Rifle Reg[i]m[en]t from Vanc[ouve]r to New Mexico. They are by this [date], I suppose, en route. They go by way of Panama. Sixteen men from our Company left this morning for Ft Vanc[ouve]r to forward public property until further arrangements are made.

I left with your little Boy[59] yesterday a letter for Mr. [George B.] Roberts, with a request that you would have the kindness to forward it as early as possible, it being important that Mr. R[oberts] should get it by tomorrow in order to have

54 For Hunter see Watson, *Lives Lived*, 2: 474–75.
55 UW Library, Tolmie Papers Acc. 4577-001, Box #1, Folder #9.
56 For Hardisty see Watson, *Lives Lived*, 2:438.
57 For Hetling see Watson, *Lives Lived*, 2:457.
58 UW Library, Tolmie Papers Acc. 4577-001, Box #1, Folder #2.
59 While this may be a reference to the Tolmie's newborn, it is more likely reference to an Indian youth of the fort who carried the letter to the doctor.

transportation in readiness on the arrival of the detachment above mentioned. If it has not yet started, please hand it off without delay and charge any expense that may be incurred to [the United States] Govt. Very Respectfully Yrs,

Jn Dement, A[ssistant] A[djutant] Q[uarter] M[aster]

P.S.: I will be at home on Friday. J. D.

☙ Document 3.31: A letter from William F. Tolmie, Nisqually, to James Douglas, Victoria, April 21, 1851.

Sir,

I have to acknowledge receipt of your communication of the 10th Inst and, as therein directed, shall ship by the Una 10 unbroke Geldings rising three years.

Enclosed in an order from the Rev[ren]d R[obert] J. Staines in favor of this post for Sixty Dollars and forty six cents, that being the amount of his purchases at Olympia chiefly out of the store of [Michael T.] Simmons who owes the Com[pan]y.

By the present canoe Mr. [Henry E.] Hetling from Vancouver takes passage, a vessel containing 120 [pounds of] dried apples is forwarded, of which Mr. Staines is to have 70 [pounds] already paid for. I have the honor, &c., &c.,

S[igne]d W. F. Tolmie

P.S. I observe in an American paper which I regret it is not in my power to send you that Senator Ewing, in animadverting [commenting critically] on Genl [Joseph] Lane's conduct while Governor of Oregon, censured him for having permitted the British Hudson's Bay still to trade with the Indians, and denies that the Boundary Treaty grants them any such right, a right, he adds which no foreigner can exercise under any circumstances, nor a citizen of the US, without first obtaining a license. I abstain from comment on the above. W. F. T.

Memo: Enquired about canoe despatched on the 10th.

☙ Document 3.32: A letter from James Douglas, Victoria, to William F. Tolmie, Nisqually, April 21, 1851.[60]

Dear Sir,

The Indians arrived here safely with your letters and the packet from Vancouver, which contains Donald's [?] dates up to the 1st of Jany. The most important intelligence from the Hudson's Bay House is stated in a brief note of Mr. [Archibald] Barclay's—referring to the Dec fur sales, which were remarkably good—the following being the comparative prices of the two years:

Average prices	Jan. 1850	Jan. 1851
Beaver	5/8 per skin	9/5p skin
Musquash	5 d " "	8 ½ d "
Rabbit	9/1 p. doz	6/2 p. doz

60 UW Library, Tolmie Papers Acc. 4577-001, Box #2, Folder #3 – N.979.514, D74 1 #106.

The price of beaver is gradually on the rise, and maintains itself as formerly in the market, an almost to inspire hopes of a return of better times.

I am rejoiced to hear that the lambing is going on prosperously, and that farm work is so far advanced—the spring work has been remarkably favourable for field work in this quarter.

I have received payment of the two pounds due by [John and Annie] Muir,[61] which we have placed to the credit of "General charges account."

We have just heard from the interior; general welfare there; returns improving in New Caledonia and Thompson's River.

I am anxious about the Una and trust she is, before this, at Fort Nisqually, though we have neither seen nor heard of her as yet.

Pray forward the accompanying packets to Vancouver—corresponding—with the Governor and Committee, Governor and Council, Prospectors of Vancouver Island, Puget's Sound Company, and Sir George Simpson. Once a month in duplicate is rather more than should fall to my share of extra work—I am getting tired of it. With best wishes, Yours truly,

James Douglas

[P.S.] We are all delighted to hear that Mrs. [Jane] Tolmie was on the mend [after delivering baby Alexander], and trust she is before now in a fair way of rapid recovery. [Our daughter] Cecelia[62] is still confined to bed [with consumption/tuberculosis], and I fear her case will be protracted at the best. God bless you all. Sincerely yours, J. D.

P.S.S.: The present mail is forwarded by our regular postman, "Aseohemo"[63] [Aseohome], who will return with any letters that may have arrived in the interval from Vancouver. Your own canoe and the Indians all leave today. They have, as you requested, not been paid here—and retain possession of the axe and kettle.J. D.

Document 3.33: A private letter from Peter S. Ogden, Vancouver, to William F. Tolmie, Nisqually, April 24, 1851.[64]

[Dear Sir,]

We are all in health here—business [is] rather dull. The Troops [are] gone.

61 Muir (1799–1883), a native of Ayrshire (now part of Strathclyde), Scotland, was Nanaimo's first coal-master. He arrived at Fort Victoria, Vancouver Island, with wife Annie (Miller), and five children in June 1849. After leaving the Company's employ, he was a farmer, sawmill operator, and politician. He died at his home in Sooke, British Columbia. See www.biographi.ca/en/bio/muir_john_11E.html.

62 Cecelia (1834–1865), the eldest daughter of Chief Factor James and Amelia Douglas, was born at Fort Vancouver and privately educated in Oregon City. In 1849, she moved with her parents to Fort Victoria, Vancouver Island. At this point in the letterbook (April 1851) she was critically ill, possibly from tuberculosis. She would linger thus stricken, cared for by the HBC's Dr. John Helmcken, who eventually nursed her back to health and then married her in December 1852. She died in 1865 at the age of 30 of pneumonia soon after the birth of her son—who also passed away. www.royalbcmuseum.bc.ca/exhibits/tbird-park/html/pre/cecelia.htm.

63 No further information found on this individual.

64 UW Library, Tolmie Papers Acc. 4577-001, Box #1, Folder #9. Ogden's "private" note to Tolmie is essentially two different letters, which in the original document come to us as one. The first letter, acknowledged by Tolmie for the date noted, is followed the second letter, which had "P.S.O., May 21, 1851" inscribed on the letter's side panel. That second communication has been moved by the editor to its correct chronological and contextual setting within this work.

Major [John S.] Hathaway's[65] [Columbia Barracks] command is scattered and the Posts [are] occupied by the [Mounted] Rifles. [Samuel R.] Thurston [is] dead. [Joseph] Lane (Gov) [is] in the field purportedly about to be [politically] opposed by Sam[uel] Parker[66] who will be supported by [Samuel R.] Thurston's Friends the Missionarys. Now if you can, without making it appear so, give your influence in supporting [Joseph] Lane [as] it would be of service to the Fur trade. Mrs. [Mary McDermot] Lane [wife of HBC clerk Richard Lane][67] still continues alive but her days are fast drawing to a close.

Since two Months, we employed in the Mess House a young Nisqually Indian by name Charly[68] [and] he started [in] June. Was rather suddenly in company with the Chief, having been smitten by a young Girl and also three Gold Rings, one rather massive, they are [my] family relics, and all three con[tain] hair belonging to my Parents. If you could trace any of these rings and secure them for me you would indeed oblige me. One of them, the heaviest, Large quartz [. . . .] taken one and what is more, the original cost was Ten pounds St[erlin]g.

[George T.] Allan, our old friend, has just come in. He is on his way to [James] Birnie's[69] [at Cathlamet]; he appears in good health—it is probable I will accompany him. No Packet so far and we are very much in want of a supply—our [merchandise] is now very much reduced. The Indians have a large amount of money in their hands and are working to purchase Guns, Blankets and Shot.

[If] Mr. Douglas sends back [Henry E.] Hetling after asking for assistance, it would little do him good when finding another. I hear you had a visit from the Rev[eren]d Mr. [Robert J.] Staines and I was truly glad to find he did not extend his travels to this quarter. I do not wish to see him here.

[British Prime Minister] Lord [John] Russel[70] by the last dates had resigned. Neither Sir James Graham[71] or Lord [Edward] Stanley[72] could form a minority

---

65 On May 13, 1849, Brevet Major Hatheway (1813–1853) was Columbia Barrack's first commander. Like Dr. Haden, he was with the 1st Field Artillery, and his post became the first officially recognized U.S. Army post in the Northwest at that time. He commanded troops from Massachusetts in 1849. He lived in the post commander's house, now known as the Grant House. Hatheway attempted suicide while in the Northwest, and was finally successful taking his own life in May 1853 at Astoria, New York. See Donna L. Sinclair, *"Our Manifest Destiny Bids Fair for Fulfillment": A Historical Overview of Vancouver Barracks, 1846–1898, With Suggestions For Further Research* (Vancouver: Center for Columbia River History, U.S. National Park Service, 2004), 167.

66 Parker (1806–1886) was an Oregon Trail settler who settled in the Willamette Valley. Though Dr. Tolmie describes him as a "Californian" in June 1852, Parker was a farmer and livestock handler, who would later become a political rival of Governor Lane and participate in the legislatures of the provisional, territorial, and state governments of Oregon. See en.wikipedia.org/wiki/Samuel_Parker_%28Oregon_politician%29.

67 For a full biographical sketch see Watson, *Lives Lived*, 2:563, and www.biographi.ca/en/bio/lane_richard_10E.html.

68 There were several Indians given this name at this time, but with no other information on this person other than a name, nothing can be guessed about his tribal affiliation or home.

69 For Birnie (c. 1799–1864), see Watson, *Lives Lived*, 1: 201–202.

70 British Lord John Russell (1792–1878) was a leading Whig and Liberal politician serving as Prime Minister from 1846 to 1852. His leadership was contentious and led to the failure of his party. See en.wikipedia.org/wiki/John_Russell,_1st_Earl_Russell.

71 James George Graham (1792–1861), British baronet by title, was a statesman who served in parliament until his death. en.wikipedia.org/wiki/Sir_James_Graham,_2nd_Baronet.

72 Edward George Geoffrey Smith-Stanley (1799–1869), an English Lord, was a Conservative Party statesman and three time Prime Minister of the United Kingdom. en.wikipedia.org/wiki/Edward_Smith-Stanley,_14th_Earl_of_Derby.

[in parliament] and it is supposed Russel would continue in office. The French are trying to patch up a Treaty at the Lolands.[73] The negotiators by last accounts are a'waiting for further orders from France. It is reported the Americans will soon have the Lolands. I have my doubts John Bull [England] will allow it.

[Signed Peter S. Ogden]

Document 3.34: A letter from William F. Tolmie, Nisqually, to James Douglas, Victoria, April 28, 1851.

Sir,

Your communication of the 21st April came to hand on the 26th and the accompanying letters for Vancouver were forwarded yesterday by two officers of the [Mounted] Rifles who, having been in this quarter on a tour, were returning direct to Vancouver.

Intending to write by the Una, which arrived here yesterday, I despatch Aseohom[e] at once and, provisions being scarce here and his own supply ample according to John Ross,[74] I am less liberal than usual with him in that way.

Lambing is nearly over and potato planting commenced. Cash Sales have been dull of late, B[an]k[e]ts 3 p[oin]ts are now priced at $6.00, 2 ½ p[oin]ts at 4.50, and Baize 1.12/2 per yard.

I am very happy to learn that beaver is rising in price at home, and from the frequent advertisement and puffs of Fur cloth in the English and American papers, it may be hoped that the novel uses of our staple product may be permanently profitable to the furriers.

(Signed) Wm F. Tolmie

Document 3.35: A private letter from William F. Tolmie, Nisqually, to Robert J. Staines, Victoria, April 28, 1851.[75]

My dear Sir,

I did not expect to have written you so soon after having had the pleasure of seeing you here [on April 11], but not having been able to find the five volumes of [author Thomas] Arnold's Rome[76] [that] I laid on the table when delivering to you the volumes of Masheim[77] and Chaucer, I am under the impression that, misunderstanding my intention, you have taken them to Victoria.

73 This is probably the "lowlands" having to do with the proposed Anglo-Franco-American Treaty of 1852 with Spain concerning the ownership of Cuba. See www.latinamericanstudies.org/filibusters/treaty-1852-cuba.pdf.

74 For Ross see Watson, *Lives Lived*, 2:836–37.

75 BC Archives, MS-0557, Box 2. From a typescript copy. There is no recipient listed in the original typescript copy—but based on the fort's journal entries, the recipient was Reverend Robert Staines of Victoria, who had been at Nisqually on April 11. He was most likely the "representative of Walter C. Grant of Sooke Harbor," who was often referred to as "captain." Reverend Staines left Nisqually for Victoria on April 21, 1851.

76 Thomas Arnold, *History of Rome,* 3 volumes, and *History of the Later Roman Commonwealth, From the End of the Second Punic War to the Death of Julius Caesar; And of the Reign of Augustus: With a Life of Trajan*, 2 volumes, T. Fellowes, London, 1838, 1845.

77 Dr. Tolmie's personal library was extensive and wide-ranging. Here, he is likely referencing a book by Johann Lorenz von Mosheim (1693–1755) titled *The Institutionum Historiae Ecclesiasticae Libri IV*, which first appeared in 1726. Mosheim was a German Lutheran church historian, and Tolmie's copy was most likely the English translation done by James Murdock in 1832. See en.wikipedia.org/wiki/Johann_Lorenz_von_Mosheim.

My object in producing the volumes in question was that, as Captain [Walter C.] Grant's representative here, and while on book custodies, you might see the price marked on the first volume and add it to the money amount of books already in my possession as security for the sum lent by me to Captain Grant.

From the memoranda and calculations you made along with me adding £4.12/, the price of Arnold, to £19.8/, the amount of books I had taken at Victoria, &c., it must have been clear and evident to you that I included Arnold amongst the works taken by me, and I have now to beg of you to keep it for me until a safe opportunity offers, of sending it to Nisqually, or 'till I go to Victoria.

As a matter of courtesy, I gave up the Lays of the Deer Forest to Captain Grant, but as he made no reservations in empowering others and myself to take books as above stated, he has, I conceive, no right to resume possession of any work unless on payment of the sum it stands security for and in the present case, I would sooner have the books than the money, which please mention to Captain Grant should he talk of redeeming Arnold.

[William F. Tolmie]

Document 3.36: A letter from William F. Tolmie, Nisqually, to Peter S. Ogden, Vancouver, May 2, 1851.

Sir,

Herewith are forwarded a receipt for Seventeen Hundred Dollars [$1,700.00] from John Dement Esq[ui]re A[ssistant] A[djutant] Q[uarter] M[aster] 2nd Lieut, 1st Artillery, US A[rmy], and also some despatches received yesterday evening from Victoria by the arrival of Mr. [Henry E.] Hetling who is also bound for Vancouver but cannot get to Cowlitz in time enough to take passage thence in the Steilacoom Mail canoe. He will proceed in a day or two hence and will have from Cowlitz a crew of saltwater Indians bound for V[ancouver] who will be got for less than the regular hire.

I have to request, as a particular favor, your getting 3 C[ast] M[etal] Plough Shares made for this post to be sent by Mr. [Henry E.] Hetling's returning canoe.

The Una is now waiting the turn of the tide to proceed to Victoria with a cargo of horses and Sheep. Cash Sales are comparatively dull here at present.

(Signed) W. F. Tolmie

Document 3.37: A letter from William F. Tolmie, Nisqually, to James Douglas, Victoria, May 2, 1851.

Sir,

By the arrival of Mr. [Henry E.] Hetling yesterday afternoon, I received your communication of the 24th and 28th Ulto, and am happy to say that the oversight regarding Major [Hugh A.] Goldsboro's letter did not delay the Una a moment. In fact, it rather expedited business than otherwise, as Captain [James] Sangster will inform you.

Herewith are forwarded Invoice and Bill Lading of Livestock &c., &c., shipped p[e]r Una for Victoria, Jean B[aptis]te Lapoitrie, accompanied by four Indians, goes in the Una to look after livestock, and I have particularly to request that he may be sent back with as little delay as possible, as his services are much needed here at present. The four Indians are willing to engage for the Cadboro if needed, and three of them served on board last summer. No agreement as yet been made with them for the present trip.

Enclosed is Copy of a letter received yesterday from one of the three Squatters on the "Round Plain." Mr. [Walter] Ross saw [Joseph Smith] Broshears[78] on the 30th Ult, when B[roshears] threatened to shoot the Stud horse spoken of in his letter to me.[79] The [trespass] notices have not yet been handed 'round. I am still of opinion that, unless we soon take legal proceedings against some of these Squatters, the business will become much disorganized, and now, while yet they have but a slight hold on the Coy's lands, as the time for action. Mr. [Walter] Ross informs me that the "Round Plain" people employ dogs to drive the Cattle off the plain they have s[quatte]d upon. I hope for strict Justice from the American Government but nothing beyond, save that a reaction in our favor may to some extent take place at Washington [D.C.] when the calumnies [slanderous misrepresentations] of the infamous Thurston have been fully exposed.

I should like much to have by return of Lapoitrie: 2 Plough shares C[ast] M[etal], with a dull cutting edge at the point. Such are used in England for earthing up potatoes. Dalnall[80] or some other of the Englishmen at Victoria could probably describe the article meant. I have [the honor to be your most obedient servant,]

S[igne]d W. F. Tolmie

P.S. Govr Blanshard's horse cost $30, which and when paid please credit to Ft Nisq[uall]y. [Jean Baptiste] Jollibois understands that he is to pay freight for his horse. Finding [the horse] "Siskyo" a bargain, I purchased him and, as the number of Geldings was short, have shipped him. The fool's pair will be charged ag[ains]t Ft Victoria.[81]

Document 3.38: A letter from William F. Tolmie, Nisqually, to Joseph S. Broshears, Round Plain, May 3, 1851.

Dear Sir,

I only, on the 1st Inst[ant], rec'd your note of the 23rd Ultimo, stating that you would feel very much obliged by my removing from the Round Plain the horses and cattle belonging to the Puget's Sound Company, and complaining of the annoyances occasioned you by a Stud horse belonging to the Coy.

In the regular prosecution of our business, the Stud horse referred to will be removed, I hope, in the course of next week. But with every desire to oblige you in any reasonable or practicable way, I cannot think of attempting to remove the Company's cattle from the Round Plain which, beyond all question, forms part of the lands secured to the PS [Agricultural] Coy by the sacred and inviolable guaran-

78 Broshears (1828–1904) was a native Indianan who arrived in the Oregon Territory in 1846 and was prominent in the public affairs of the community. He died in Winlock, Lewis County, Washington. www.findagrave.com/cgi-bin/fg.cgi?page=gr&GSvcid=323025&GRid=93419438&; Alice Millner Wallace, 1986.

79 Dickey, ed., *Nisqually Journal*, September 21, 1851. The entry reads: "Fine all day, evening signs of rain. Mr. Ross [has come] in [from Tlithlow Farm]. Reports death of stud horse "Turk"—supposed to have been shot. He was found near William Daugherty's house at Steilacoom.

80 Nothing was found that helped identify this laborer, or blacksmith.

81 While this insulting quip contradicts Tolmie's usual, and predictably reticent commentary, it does reflect many Company officials' opinion of Governor Blanchard. To those officials, the governor was more the fool than a good politician or gentleman.

tee of the Boundary Treaty formed in 1846 between Great Britain and the United States of America.

In conclusion, I have to express my regret that you should be wasting your time and means in improving land to which you cannot obtain a title under the provisions of the "Oregon Land Bill" as it is therein expressly stated that Treaty rights shall be respected. Very Truly Yours,

S[igne]d W. F. Tolmie

Document 3.39: A second warning letter from William F. Tolmie, Nisqually, to all American squatters, Nisqually Plains, May 5, 1851.[82]

Sir,

Under advice Received from the United States District Attorney for this Territory, I again give you a warning that you are now occupying land belonging to the Puget's Sound Agricultural Company, under the fourth Section of the Treaty of 5th August 1846, which section is in the following words, viz; "The farms, lands and other property of every description belonging to the Puget's Sound Agricultural Company, on the North side of the Columbia river, shall be confirmed to the said company."

And I hereby give you formal notice to Remove from the premises now occupied by you, without any necessary delay, or otherwise I shall deem it my duty to take such legal measures as are provided by the Statutes of the United States and of this Territory against trespassers.

xx Mr. T. M. Chambers—Steilacoom
xx [Mr.] W[illia]m Dougherty—Round Plain, by Steilacoom
xx [Mr.] J[ohn] S. Broshears—[Round Plain, by Steilacoom]
xx [Mr.] John Bradley—[Round Plain, by Steilacoom][83]
xx [Mr.] [Henry] Murray—[Round Plain, by Steilacoom][84]
xx [Mr.] Joseph Lowrie—Salatal's Plain, [by Steilacoom][85]
xx [Mr.] [Daniel Fawber] Brownsfield—Salatal's Plain, [by Steilacoom]
xx [Mr.] John Macleod—Douglas [Muck] River, by Nisqually
xx [Mr.] Lyman A. Smith—[Douglas/Muck River, by Nisqually][86]

---

82 Huntington Library, Nisqually Papers, Misc., Documents, microfilm roll 9, viewed at the Oregon Historical Society by the editor, 1982.

83 Bradley, a native-born Irishman, came to the Oregon Territory around 1845. He squatted on Round Plain in the early 1850s and was a delegate to the Cowlitz Convention held in August 1851. Bradley was the first sheriff of Pierce County. He was appointed by the Oregon Legislature when the country was established in 1853. William P. Bonney, *History of Pierce County, Washington*, 3 vols. (Chicago: Pioneer Historical Publishing Company, 1927). 1: 71.

84 Murray came to the Pacific Northwest via the American brig *Orbit* and squatted on HBC/PSAC lands just east of Steilacoom Barracks in the area early maps denote as Round Plain (or Paleilah) shortly thereafter.

85 Lowry [var. Lowrie/Lowrey] was an early squatter/settler on lands along Clover Creek in today's unincorporated Pierce County, Washington. No other information could be found on him or his descendants.

86 Lyman A. "Sandy" Smith (c. 1815–1858) should not be confused with the "Indian Sandy" referred to in other fort records. Smith, whose name was also referred to variously as Lyman, Lion or Lyon, was a low country Scotsman who, according to Edward Huggins, also went by "Sandy"—perhaps in references to reddish-blond hair—and arrived on Puget Sound sometime between 1845 and 1848. He took up a small squatter's claim on Sahagalie or "high" Muck Creek about two miles from the PSAC's

xx [Mr.] Charles Wren—[Douglas/Muck River, by Nisqually]

I am, Sir, Your obedient Servant,
W. F. Tolmie, Agent, Puget's Sound Agricult[ural] Co

Document 3.40: A letter from William F. Tolmie, Nisqually, to Peter S. Ogden, Vancouver, May 7, 1851.

Sir,

I received yesterday your communication ("private") of the 24th Ult and was happy to learn that, with the exception of poor Mrs. [Mary McDermot] Lane, all were well at Vancouver.

On the 20th Ulto, by Captains [James Stuart] Stewart[87] and [Lieutenant Robert S.] Williamson[88] Esquire of the [Mounted] Rifles, and on the 2nd Instant by the Steilacoom mail, I forward despatches for you from Victoria, all of which have, I trusted, reached [you] in safety. In mine of the May 2nd was enclosed a receipt from Mr. [John] Dement A[djutant] A[ssistant] Q[uarter] M[aster] of the troops at the Steilacoom [Barracks] for Seventeen Hundred Dollars [$1,700.00].

Mr. [Henry E. Hetling] Heetling now proceeds to Cowlitz en route from Vancouver and takes some letters from Victoria which were, I regret to say, omitted by last opportunity. Hoping that you can send by return of the present canoe the C[ast] M[etal] Ploughshares applied for in my last, [I remain, &c., &c.,]

(Signed) William F. Tolmie

Document 3.41: A letter from James Douglas, Victoria, to William F. Tolmie, Nisqually, May 7, 1851.[89]

Dear Sir,

The Una arrived off Port on the 4th inst[ant], entered Esquimalt on the 5th, and her cargo of live steers was safely landed before night, with the loss of one steer, which died on the passage.

The total number of sheep landed here was 301 gimmers and 100 wedders, making with the gimmers which died on the passage 493 in all, or three head short of the number invoiced.

You will please charge the whole of that cargo of livestock to the PS Co's farm at Esquimalt, where they are now kept.

Muck Station. Huggins notes that "at one time Smith was a Free Mason, but, it was rumored [he had] been expelled for misconduct—drunkenness I suppose." Referring to him as "a big, raw boned, red headed low down Scotchman" and a "loud-mouthed vulgar fellow," Huggins also observed that "he was the first man to take a claim, 640 acres, land upon the Muck Creek." He also took an Indian wife of the Nisqually Tribe, was arrested by Governor Stevens for alleged collaboration with the Indians during the war in 1855–56, and apparently was a wife beater. His life ended on Friday, December 10, 1858, in an apparent gun cleaning accident.

87 The only information found on the Mounted Rifles' Captain Stuart (?–1851) was a congressional report that stated: "On the 18th of June, 1851, the said [Brevet] Captain [James] Stuart was slain in a skirmish with the Indians in Oregon, on the Rogue river." *The Reports of Committees 1852-United States Congress*. Senate: 30th Congress, 1st Session–48th Congress, 2nd Session, p. 313.

88 Lieutenant Williamson (1825–1882) was with the U.S. Army Topographical Engineers. See wikivisually.com/wiki/Robert_S._Williamson.

89 UW Library, Tolmie Papers Acc. 4577-001, Box #2, Folder #3 – N.979.514, D74 1 #106.

I have to acknowledge per Una your letter of 3rd May, with enclosures.

The four Indians who accompanied [Jean Baptiste] Lapoitrie to this place will return with him to Nisqually, as we are not in immediate want of their services on board the Cadboro, which will not be put into active service before the month of June. I have, however, agreed with these youth that they are to come here about that time, either in a canoe of their own or in the return mail canoe, and have paid them one blanket each for the present trip to and from Nisqually.

[Jean Baptiste] Lapoitrie has received his advances for the year, and will send no private order for the present season; he applied on your part for some Reaping sickles, but there are none at present on hand.

The two country plough-shares requested in your letter are not quite ready, and will be forwarded by next conveyance.

I shall credit Nesqually with the price paid for Governor [Richard] Blanchard's horse, when the account is settled. Pray send me Adam [Beinston]'s letter which you have inadvertently retained.

I am at a loss what to advise in reference to the squatters on the Company's lands at Nisqually; no doubt the proper course is to enter suits at law against them as soon as we possibly can, but since the Company are adverse to that and of proceeding, both on account of the expense and the uncertain issue of that test of right, I do not feel at liberty to act with the decision the case required. It is very evident, however, that something should be done to check those encroachments, or the Company's lands will soon be overrun with squatters. Suppose then we take one of the most glaring cases of trespass, say, Charles Wren; and enter suit on it at the approaching circuit court; the expense of our suit cannot be overwhelming, and the decision of the court in that instance will serve as a guide to future proceedings.

In the meantime pray let all the squatters be duly warned that they are trespassing in the Company's lands. I remain, dear Sir, Yours truly,

James Douglas

P.S.: Pray forward the letters to Vancouver by the earliest conveyance. J. D.

[P.S.S.:] The amount of Lapoitrie's book debts on advances here is 16 pounds and 4 pence.

Document 3.42: A letter from Peter S. Ogden, Vancouver, to William F. Tolmie, Nisqually, May 12, 1851.[90]

Dear Sir,

I have to acknowledge the receipt of your letter of 2nd Inst, including a receipt on the A[djutant] Q[uarter] Master [Rufus] Ingalls[91] for Seventeen Hundred dollars [$1,700.00] which has been forwarded. Altho' at all times [I am] most anxious to meet your wishes, it is at present impossible to do so as I have no Blacksmith now. [Concerning] Iron suitable for Plough Shares, if you cannot possibly do without,

90 UW Library, Tolmie Papers Acc. 4577-001, Box #1, Folder #8.

91 Captain Ingalls (1818–1893) served as quartermaster while stationed briefly at Steilacoom Barracks. A native of New England, he was reared in a prominent, well-to-do family setting. Attending West

your only claim is to apply to Vancouver's Island where Tradesmen of all descriptions are in superabundance. As for this place we have neither Carpenter [nor barrel] Cooper as Servants; in fact not one solitary Tradesman. Yours Respectfully,

P. S. O.

Le Lelay wawhau.[92]

❧ Document 3.43: A letter from William F. Tolmie, Nisqually, to Peter S. Ogden, Vancouver, May 15, 1851.

Sir,

I forward letters to Cowlitz as p[e]r accompanying packet list, to be conveyed thence to Vancouver by the first safe opportunity.

Nothing [is] new in this quarter except that we are now loading the Orbit with horned Cattle and sheep for Victoria.

On the 11th Inst a packet from Vancouver was received by the Steilacoom Mail containing several more letters &c., than were entered in the accompanying list bearing date May 6th.

(Signed) W. F. Tolmie

❧ Document 3.44: A letter from William F. Tolmie, Nisqually, to James Douglas, Victoria, May 16, 1851.

Sir,

Herewith are forwarded letters & papers from V[ancouver] & Invoice and bill Lading of Horned Cattle and Sheep shipped for Victoria p[e]r Am[erica]n Brig Orbit, Captain [David Swinson] Maynard.[93] The terms for freight are the same as you agreed upon with Mr. [Michael T.] Simmons when at Victoria and payment is to be made when the Orbit returns to Nisqually. Please, however, do let Captain Maynard have any supplies he may require for the Vessel at Victoria and forward a statement of their amount to this place as also of (Simmon's) former account at Victoria when adjusted after return of the articles borrowed.

Point, he graduated in 1843 along with Ulysses S. Grant. As a lieutenant, he served in the 1st U.S. Dragoons during the Mexican-American War in the New Mexico Territory in the Army of the West under Col. Stephen W. Kearny. His duty as quartermaster began in 1848, and he served in that capacity for the whole of his remaining career in the army. He served as a captain in the Union Army during the Civil War, and was reassigned as chief army quartermaster of the Pacific and Missouri Divisions for the following two decades. Retiring as a brigadier general, he moved at Oregon in 1883, then back to the east coast less than ten years later. He died at the age of 74. en.wikipedia.org/wiki/Rufus_Ingalls.

92 In searching for the definition of "Le Lelay wawhau" online, I found that "Le le" is Spanish for "loyal and faithful worker" while "wawha" is the Ojibwe word for the iconic Canada goose. So Ogden's sign off could be loosely interpreted as "Your loyal and faithful goose"!

93 In 1851, Hugh Goldsborough was the master of the *Orbit*. By December the brig's skipper was S.P. Moug. More than likely, "Doc" Maynard was supercargo (1808–1873). A native of Vermont, Maynard gained his physician's education at Castleton Medical School and, following his apprenticeship, married Lydia A. Rickey, whom he deserted. He then married the widow Catherine Troutman Broshears (1816–1906), the two falling in love during their journey across the Oregon Trail. He, being the "captain" of that wagon train, helped settle Seattle. See en.wikipedia.org/wiki/David_Swinson_Maynard.

I shall see Mr. [Amory] Holbrook regarding [Charles] Wren when court meets at Cowlitz.

Adam Beinston goes to Victoria in the Orbit to look after the livestock assisted by an Indian "Jim"[94] who goes partly on his own business, wishing to be landed at Whidbey's Island when the Orbit returns. Please to pay him according to the services he may render, as reported by [Adam] Beinston, either a f[atho]m Baise or [fathom of baise] and shirt, or a 2 ½ p[oin]t Blanket according to the duration of the trip.

Crops look well here, and the grass is unusually good. Your letters were forwarded yesterday by a chance Indian to Cowlitz. Should [Adam] Beinston not return in the Orbit, he can await the mail canoe.

(Signed) Wm F. Tolmie

[P.S.:] The Brown Sugar invoiced to us at 2,000 [pounds] net only weighs 1,889 gross. There was a deficiency of one bag in the number invoiced. Please return our Packet Box now sent full of Newspapers & letters. The latter are enumerated in a packet list.

Document 3.45: A letter from James Douglas, Victoria, to William F. Tolmie, Nisqually, to May 21, 1851.[95]

Dear Sir,

I have barely time to recommend the accompanying packet for Vancouver, to your special care—requesting it may be forwarded with dispatch. The Norman Morison arrived safely in London on the 20th. Feby. The Gold dust sent by her averaged $23.10 an ounce.

The Company have sent out Mr. [Joseph D.] Pemberton[96] as Surveyor and Engineer by Panama and he may be daily expected at Nisqually, Salary £460 per an[num].

I am now at liberty to dispose of such parts of the Reserve as the Company may not require, so you had better claim the Grand Bas Fond which I have reserved for you. With respects to Mrs. [Jane] Tolmie, With best wishes, Yours sincerely,

James Douglas

[P.S.:] Can you spare any Blankets or medicines from your private order? J. D. (A.L.S.).[97]

---

94 There are a number of indigenous laborers nicknamed "Jim" at Fort Nisqually. In reviewing all known candidates at this point in May 1851, the editor could not find a single "Jim" who fit this one's profile, job experiences, or tenure of service.

95 UW Library's Tolmie Papers Acc. 4577-001, Box #2, Folder #3.

96 Pemberton (1821–1893) "was a surveyor for the Hudson's Bay Company, Surveyor General for the Colony of Vancouver Island, a pre-Confederation politician, a businessman and a farmer. He was born in 1821 in Dublin, Ireland and died in 1893 in Oak Bay, British Columbia. Joseph Pemberton laid out Victoria's town site, southern Vancouver Island and townsites along the Fraser River. He married Teresa Jane Grautoff and they are the parents of Canadian painter Sophie Pemberton. The town of Pemberton was named after him." See en.wikipedia.org/wiki/Joseph_Despard_Pemberton.

97 At the end of this letter is this: "Endorsement: James Douglas, Esq, 21st May 1851."

❧ Document 3.46: A letter from Hugh A. Goldsborough, Olympia, to William F. Tolmie, Nisqually, May 18, 1851.[98]

Dear Sir,

I enclose [for] you a copy of the Law I had Reference to yesterday. To suit your case, you might omit all between brackets, and in lieu insert the following or something like it—"belonging to the Hudson's Bay Company to lade or unlade all articles, belonging to or intended for the use of the Puget Sound Agricultural Company at Nesqually, a Port of Delivery ~~in Puget S~~ in the Puget Sound Collection District, said authority to continue in force, unless previously revoked by Congress, so long as said PS [Agricultural] Co shall own & possess any Territory South of [the] 49th [parallel] in the immediate vicinity of said Port of Delivery."

The part over the brackets would require a trifling alteration, viz: instead of "Colonies" say, "the Island of Vancouver and the HB Co['s] possessions on the N[orth] W[est] coast of America," and of course change the "Enacting Clause."

I send you the letters on "Her Majesty's Service," 4 for [Michael T.] Simmons, & 2 for [John R.] Jackson—also a letter for Capt [William] Brotchie, 40 c[ents] & one for Pierre Bibian [Bibeau][99] 12 ½ c[ents].

If you have any late papers from the Eastern United States or Europe, I w[oul]d be obliged to you for their perusal—to be carefully Returned. Yours Very Respectfully,

II. A. Goldsborough

❧ Document 3.47: A letter from Peter S. Ogden, Vancouver, to William F. Tolmie, Nisqually, May 21, 1851.[100]

[Dear Sir,]

[Today, 15th May,] I have just ret[urne]d from [James] Birnie's [at Cathlamet]—was absent one night and settled my business without going on shore and by so doing gave offense—next visit all will come right.

By the Same Monthly Mail we have another great fire [on May 4th] in San Francisco, their fourth of the Town in which I was Housed Twice—Fire proof Safes even, caught there were melted down by heat. The Custom House saved 1½ Million dollars by throwing it in a Tub. The fire began in a Painter's Shop at 10 at night and continued until 2 p.m. Three Steam Ships were burned. Mr. Stainus got up Steam and escaped loss [and] extricated all his Millions. All the Ships would have gone [up] had the wind proved favourable. The 4th May will be a gloomy day in the remembrance of my hundreds and [of] strange coincidences. On the same day last year was the great fire but never before equal to this. All the Public

---

98 UW Library's Tolmie Papers Acc. 4577-001, Box #1, Folder #3.

99 For Bibeau see Watson, *Lives Lived*, 1:198.

100 UW Library's Tolmie Papers Acc. 4577-001, Box #1, Folder #9. This "private" note from Ogden is somewhat confusing chronologically for it contains two parts, the first sent off on April 24, and the second part sent off on May 21, after learning of the San Francisco fire—and the latter part has a "P.S.O., May 21, 1851" endorsement on the side panel of the letter.

buildings are gone and the Planks in the Streets now turned to ashes. I do not recollect one-half the names of the Merchants who lost all their property—Burgoynes [Bank], Baubury House, Starkey, Janion & Co, Smiths & Brothers, Hoot Brothers, Daws & Coy. Their names are alone familiar to me. I have no time to add more.

The Deputation of last week has not yet reached me. I have at present here [Archibald] McKinlay's family. They came here to follow Mrs. [Mary McDermott] Lane to the Grave.[101] Kind regards from all and me to Mrs. [Jane] Tolmie and congratulations on the birth of her Son [Alexander] and Your Marriage.

[Signed] P. S. O.

Document 3.48: A letter from William F. Tolmie, Nisqually, to Hugh A. Goldsborough, Olympia, May 22, 1851.[102]

Sir,

Mr. Lewis,[103] Second officer of the British barque Tory[104] and Michel Lafleur,[105] constable of Victoria, V[ancouver's] I[sland], arrived here last night with warrants for the apprehension of three seamen who stole a boat belonging to the barque Tory in Victoria harbor on the 18th Inst.

I now recommend M[isters] Lewis and [Michel] Lafleur to proceed with all despatch to your office feeling assured that you will promptly put in force the laws of the United States of America bearing on the case.

(Signed) W. F. Tolmie

Document 3.49: A letter from William F. Tolmie, Nisqually, to James Douglas, Victoria, May 23, 1851.

Sir,

I received on the night of the 21st your communication of the 19th Inst and Mr. Lewis who has since been at Olympia and seen Justice [Hugh A.] Goldsboro[ugh] & will report to you that gentleman's opinion as to the impossibility of apprehending the three seamen on a simple warrant from Victoria.

Major [John F.] Reynolds,[106] Paymaster of the troops in Oregon, who is, I

101 The comment "She died on the 10th" was written here in the original transcript, but is out of synch chronologically with the rest of this letter. Mary McDermot Lane, wife of HBC clerk Richard Lane, died at Oregon City after a long and painful illness on May 10, 1851. It is believed that Edward Huggins may have entered this comment later and the original transcriber, not understanding the paradox, just included it as Ogden's original text.

102 UW Library's Tolmie Papers Acc. 4577-001, Box #1, Folder #3.

103 Lewis, 2nd officer of the British barque *Tory*. No information on this officer could be found.

104 *Tory*, British barque. See Watson, *Lives Lived*, 3:1130–31.

105 For Lafleur see Watson, *Lives Lived*, 2:550.

106 Reynolds (1820–1863), a native Pennsylvanian, attended West Point and graduated from that institution in 1841. Commissioned as an artillery officer (2nd lieutenant), he served in a number of posts and took part in the war with Mexico. Though pro-slavery, he remained a loyal Unionist. He married Catherine Mary Hewitt. From September 1860 to June 1861, he was the Commandant of Cadets at West Point, where he also served as an instructor. "On the morning of July 1, 1863, as he was leading his forces towards Gettysburg, Pennsylvania, Reynolds received a message that Confederate forces were almost there as well. Reynolds led his First Corps to McPherson Ridge, when he received a bullet through the neck. Reynolds died instantly. He was the highest ranking soldier on either side killed

believe, a lawyer, informed me yesterday that in the United States 'ere a foreign fugitive or one from a neighboring state can be apprehended, his indictment must be produced and full proof afforded that he is the person meant therein. In the US the indictment must be signed by the Governor of the State in which the felony has been committed.

Your letters by the Orbit have not yet come to hand, [Adam] Beinston asserting that when 'ere taking passage with Mr. Lewis he asked Captain [David S.] Maynard for the letters the reply was that there were none. M[aynard] has been telling Mr. Lewis that he was to take [on] another Cargo here but without information from you on that point I cannot let him have one.

Herewith are forwarded two letters on which postage (52 ½ Cents) has been paid and charged against Ft Victoria Sale Shop. Your letters to Mr. Sec[retar]y [Archibald] Barclay will be forwarded very soon.

(Signed) W. F. Tolmie

P.S.: regarding Ten Dollars adv[ance]d Mr. Lewis, ch[arge]d ag[ains]t & payable at F[ort] V[ictoria] Sale Shop. T.

Document 3.50: A letter from William F. Tolmie, Nisqually, to Amory Holbrook, Cowlitz Farm, May 26, 1851.

Sir,

I duly received your valued communication bearing date 25th February in which you state your intention of visiting this quarter during the present month and, in the hope that you are still like-minded, I look forward to the pleasure of seeing you here in the course of a very few days.

Meantime, if after the subjoined explanation of my views you should deem it proper, I have to request you to enter at the District Court now in session, a suit in my name as Agent for the Puget Sound Agricult Co against Charles Wren for trespassing on the lands of said Company, and, should you think it of importance as strengthening the Coy's cause for damages for the loss of the use of the two fields unlawfully taken possession of by him, and of the pasture by sheep of the square mile of land he claims.

It was my intention and hope 'till the last hour, to have met you at Cowlitz, and had a consultation before commencing proceedings against Wren, but I find it impossible to absent myself from home at present.

Although as far as my own opinion goes, fully persuaded of the Company's right under the Treaty to the lands they claim, and equally confident that strict justice will ultimately be awarded them by the US government, I am yet doubtful as to how a jury composed probably of the friends and neighbors of the squatters might view the matter, and unless our rights could be made sufficiently demonstrable to such a jury, to render a successful issue on the part of the Coy as nearly certain as in the nature of such cases can be expected, I would be loath to run the risk of a trial at present, as a defeat before the District Court would probably do us much temporary injury.

---

at Gettysburg." www.battlefields.org/learn/biographies/john-f-reynolds.

By the enclosed rough plan of the country around [Charles] Wren's you will perceive that the 4,000 fence rails mentioned in my statement to you regarding Wren were split not in the hummock of pines nearest his house, but in one-half a mile distant from it. The statement is in other respects correct and can be substantiated by many witnesses, some of whose names I subjoin in case they may have to be summoned before the court adjourns. Expecting soon to have the pleasure of making your acquaintance . . . [I remain, &c., &c.,]

(Signed) W. F. Tolmie

Names of Witnesses
John Montgomery—Nisqually
Adam Beinston—[Nisqually]
Walter Ross—[Nisqually]
John Edgar[107]—Yelm Plain
Louis Latour—Cowlitz
Also if desirable:
Ch[arle]s. Wren—[Squatter]
John MacLeod—[Squatter]

They being both cognizant to most if not all the facts stated. T[olmie]

Document 3.51: A letter from William F. Tolmie, Nisqually, to James Douglas, Victoria, May 27, 1851.

Sir,

I have just this moment received your communications of 20th and 21st Instant, the former enclosing Copy of Mr. Thomas Dean's agreement with the Puget Sound Agricultural Company. I despatch "Asishowe [Aseohome]" & party forthwith with letters and papers received here on 25th and which I was to have sent on tomorrow by the Indians engaged for the Cadboro, who will then start with the Tory's boat and appurtenances which were delivered up to Captain [David S.] Maynard of the Orbit before that vessel reached this place.

Having heard nothing from you regarding a second cargo by the Orbit, I have declined giving in any on the former terms, although I offered wedders at 80 cents a head provided the voyage down occupied only two days, and 5 cents a head extra for each additional day until the original freight of one dollar each should be attained. Maynard did not feel himself authorized to accept and I did not at all regret this, as interruptions to sheep shearing during the present variable weather, when every fair day has to be made the most of, are anything but advantageous.

The newly arrived laborers have gone to work, and Mr. [Thomas] Dean will be in his new house 'ere long. I will write again tomorrow and meantime have the honor to be,

(Signed) W. F. Tolmie

---

107 Edgar (1814–1855), a native of Essex, England, enlisted for five years in 1840 as a PSAC stock handler at £35 per year. In 1842 he began working near Fort Nisqually. There, he managed the Steilacoom Farm at a salary of £40 yearly. In the autumn of 1847 Edgar left the PSAC's employment and moved to Yelm Prairie. He assisted the U.S. Army during the early part of the Indian War. In November 1855 he was seriously wounded in a skirmish on South Prairie, in Pierce County. He died at Fort Steilacoom, November 19, 1855. Drew Crooks, "The Story of John Edgar," *Occurrences*, 11, No. 1 (1993), 3–5.

☙ Document 3.52: A letter from William F. Tolmie, Nisqually, to Peter S. Ogden, Vancouver, May 28, 1851.

Sir,

By a Victoria express received yesterday, and to be today forwarded to Cowlitz, I have an opportunity of again writing, and I am commissioned to enquire by Sergt [James] Hall of the [1st] Artillery Company [M], Steilacoom [Barracks], what reduction you would make on the retail price of Prints, Domestics and Shawls, were he to purchase about two hundred dollars' worth once a month, which he would do through the agency of the mailman, should the prices suit.

(Signed) W. F. Tolmie

P.S.: Will there be any demand for Wedder Sheep at Vancouver this Season? T.

☙ Document 3.53: A letter from William F. Tolmie, Nisqually, to James Douglas, Victoria, May 29, 1851.

Sir,

The mail from Vancouver was forwarded on the evening of the 27th Inst by "Aseohome" and this morning's despatch the Indians engaged for the Cadboro, with the Tory's boat and compass. A list is sent of some advances made the Indians without which they were unwilling to start. They may consider said advances as payment for taking the boat down, although no definite understanding has been had with them on that score further than my saying that they would be remunerated. They agree to serve four months on board the Cadboro, and expect some advances before going to sea.

Will you please inform me by first opportunity of the quantity and kinds of lumber you spoke to Dr. [David S.] Maynard to furnish and say whether said lumber is to be taken from Mr. [Michael T.] Simmons or from any other party who may offer it cheaper. Mr. [William P.] Wells[108] offered to fill a Bill for 15 M [thousand board] feet at $25 per [thousand] so has hitherto asked $30, but he might make up the difference on the freight.

Please also to state for my own and Mr. Simmons guidance, what quantity of livestock you will have transported by the Orbit after she has been sold. The sale will take place about the 10th June. Some large packages were recd here by last mail for Simpson [P.] Moses Esq Collector, Olympia, from which it may be inferred that he will soon arrive.

(Signed) W. F. Tolmie

108 Not much is known of William P. Wells, a Nisqually Bottoms millwright. However, in 1903 Edward Huggins remembered: "I suppose you recollect the McAllister old mill. It was erected in 1851, I think, on the McAllister Creek, by [James] McAllister and [William P.] Wells. The latter was a Yankee, a decent man, who came to our fort with clocks for sale. We bought one, and a very good clock it was, and is, I think, running now in the country. That mill has now entirely disappeared." Edward Huggins to Clarence Bagley, November 10, 1903. Clarence Bagley Papers, Special Collections Division, University of Washington Libraries, Box 2, folders 4–17. Wells was a Democrat, and House of Representatives delegate from Thurston County in the second session of the Washington Territorial legislature.

CHAPTER FOUR

June 1st, 1851–November 30th, 1851

"I shall take the earliest opportunity of presenting the PSAC's claim to Mr. Preston, and have a map of our lands in readiness for him."
—William F. Tolmie to James Douglas, August 18, 1851

The U.S. Government's blockade did not destroy the company's business in the Oregon Territory. However, it did intensify Douglas's and Tolmie's need to avoid further complications by learning what they could of the new customs regulations. Gradually, they began outmaneuvering the customs officials' legal snares by 1) employing U.S. flagged vessels to carry the bulk of their produce, livestock, and lumber, and 2) continuing the clandestine practice of employing sea-going canoes to transport smaller shipments of goods and personnel between Victoria and Nisqually.

In what had become June's rite of passage, Tolmie's laborers were once again engaged in the seasonal washing and shearing of sheep, the wool being readied for shipment. Also, in July, John McPhail made his second trek across the portage south to Vancouver—this time with over 800 sheep.

Fort Nisqually's local business actually gained traction throughout the first half of this outfit. In a noticeable shift of customer base, orders of farming implements and merchandise appear heavily weighted towards the needs of settlers, mostly farmers, including a large order of plowshares. An increase in the U.S. Army's involvement in the Company's business was also evident, with hard cash for credit becoming routine. A budding financial relationship with the Catholic Church's Oblate Mission at Priest's Point (in today's Tumwater) was also on the rise. Demand for dimensional lumber to satisfy San Francisco's building boom gave rise to the thought of harnessing Sequlitchew Creek's power for an operational sawmill.

Tolmie's clientele were, in several cases, the very squatters he wished to eject. Unfazed by his "Notice of Trespass" leaflets, the settlers' shared employment included appropriating the Company's fence rails, occupying its open ground, shooting or running its livestock into the woods, and/or being a general nuisance. In 1892, Edward Huggins named them all: at Steilacoom Bay/Plain & vicinity, 1) Lafayette Balch—1850, 2) John B. Chapman—1851, and 3) Thomas M. Chambers—1850; at Pelailah/Round Plain/Puyallup Swamp (Leach Creek) & vicinity, 4) Henry

Murray—1851, 5) Daniel F. Brownfield[1]—1851, 6) Joseph Lowry—1851, 7) William P. Dougherty—1851, 8) John Rigney[2]—1851, 9) John Bradley—1851, and 10) Joseph Broshears—1851; at Sohagalie/High Muck Creek Plain & vicinity: 11) Charles Wren—1851, 12) John McLeod—1851, 13), Lyman A. Smith—1848, and 14) Henry Murray—1850.[3] Amory Holbrook, the Company's American lawyer, was convinced that the squatters' claims, though invalid, should be recorded by Tolmie, and handed a leaflet (with witnesses) as they occurred.

In 1851 the Company's claim at Nisqually was wholly defined by natural features: Puget Sound to the west; the Nisqually River to the south; and the Puyallup River to the east. Boundary lines to the north, northeast, and southeast remained a matter of conjecture. Attorney Holbrook wanted a lock on every square inch. He suggested that an accurately surveyed and detailed map be made, one that could withstand the scrutiny of Surveyor General John Preston and be successfully defended in a court of law. Pressing Tolmie, Holbrook requested "as complete a description [of the PSAC Claim on Puget Sound] as you may choose, with a Topographical outline." The suggestion was well worth the price of his retainer. True, maps of Nisqually already existed. But, these were a series of amateur sketches that Tolmie had likely executed in 1847[4] with illustrated hammocks of trees and grassland in the immediate vicinity of the Company's largest farms and outstations. Though interesting sketches, they proved nothing. Douglas agreed with Holbrook, and so Tolmie began his search for a professional surveyor. He found one in his newest squatter: John Butler Chapman.[5]

An educated Virginian, Chapman arrived on the Pacific Northwest coast in the late 1840s seeking fame, fortune, and land. A gifted orator, he was a self-taught

---

1 Daniel Farber Brownfield, a Lewis County settler/politician, served in the first Oregon Legislature. Soon after, the minority legislature had closed its brief session at Oregon City (1851–1852). He also became the first white settler at New Dungeness.

2 A native of Thomastown, Ireland, John Rigney immigrated to the United States in the spring of 1847 and enlisted in the U.S. Army, joining Company M, 1st Regiment of the U.S. Artillery. After time in the Mexican War, he married Elizabeth Lowry in 1848. In 1849 Rigney came to Steilacoom Barracks aboard the steamship *Massachusetts* and to Steilacoom by the sloop *Harpooner* (see Watson, *Lives Lived*, 3:1114.) There, Rigney finished out his enlistment in 1852. He then squatted on PSAC lands near present-day 64th and Orchard Streets in Tacoma. For more information see "John Rigney," *Steilacoom Historical Museum Quarterly* 22 (Summer 1993), 1, 6–9. See also George Dickey, "Company M. 1st Artillery in Oregon Territory," unpublished manuscript in the collection of the Fort Nisqually Living History Museum, Tacoma, WA; and "John and Elizabeth Rigney," historicfortsteilacoom.org/research/#toggle-id-24 .

3 Huggins, Edward. "Donation Land Claims in Pierce County," *Tacoma Sunday Ledger*, February 17, 1892 and *Tacoma Weekly Ledger*, March 4, 1892. See also Huggins, *Reminiscences of Puget Sound*, 1:17–24. Huggins knew them all well, for one of his jobs was to hand them Tolmie's infamous notice.

4 Dr. Tolmie's maps probably included F. 25/1: fo. 31, "Ground Plan of Puget's Sound Co's principal establishment at Nisqually," F.25/1, fo. 32, "Map of Lands Claimed by Puget Sound Agricultural Company at Nisqually," F. 25/1: fo. 33, "Map of some of the Pasture Land adjoining Shepherd's Station at Tlithlow, Nisqually," F. 25/1: fo. 34, "Map of some of the Pasture Land adjoining Shepherd's Station at 'Muck', Douglas Burn, Nisqually," F. 25/1: fo. 35, "Map of some of the Pasture Land adjoining Shepherd's Station at 'Sastuk' Nisqually, W. Tolmie, 1847," and F. 25/1: fo. 36, "Map of Pasture land adjoining Cattleherd's Station at Spanueh, Nisqually," Provincial Archives of Manitoba, Hudson's Bay Company Archives, Winnipeg, Canada.

5 For a full biography of Chapman (1797–1877), see Steve A. Anderson, "A New Look at an Old Map: Deconstructing Chapman," *Columbia Magazine* (Winter 2011–12), 22–27.

lawyer, physician, land speculator, and surveyor. Opposing the Company, as well as Lafayette Balch's Port Steilacoom, Chapman plotted his own "Steilacoom City" streets at odds with Balch's grid.[6] Apparently, Tolmie did not warm to the Virginian straight away, for he was not immediately engaged to survey the Nisqually claim.

Sickness took hold of Fort Nisqually. Perhaps it was the cold, wet Puget Sound climate, or the proximity of large groups of workers during the fall harvest. The lack of clean water certainly did not help. Whatever the cause, dysentery, head colds, and influenza carved their infectious paths through the fort's white and Indian populations in the fall of 1851. As with past epidemics, this outbreak laid waste indiscriminately, sickening and killing many with high fevers and dysentery.[7] Among the "grievously ill" were John McPhail and Thomas Linklater, manager of Tenalquot Farm.[8] By late October, Dr. Tolmie observed that "three Indians have died since yesterday forenoon & several more are lying sick in the camp suffering from dysentery."[9] This "prevailing complaint" attacked Edward Huggins, diagnosed with "le grippe" in late November. The fall plague of 1851 had all but subsided by early December.

When this chapter's letters were written, banking establishments did not exist on Puget Sound. The Company's banking practices—if they could even be called that—were, unfortunately, vulnerable to abuse. Illustrating this fact is the financial fiasco created by a North Carolinian named George W. Hawkins.[10]

In May 1851, Hawkins (a first lieutenant in Colonel William Loring's Mounted Rifle Regiment) generated a promissory note (aka check) for around $1,500.00.[11] Loans of cash were then based on one's reputation, personal associations, co-signees, or collateral—reasonable, but imperfect securities at best. Hawkins' transaction was personal (land speculation in Oregon City) so the army's quartermaster at Vancouver Barracks was not involved. As co-signer of the note, Dr. John Haden of Steilacoom Barracks, was involved. After Hawkins cashed the note through the Company's officials at Vancouver, he was transferred and reassigned to Arizona or

---

6 These two grid systems meet at "Union Street" in present day Steilacoom, Washington.

7 Dickey, ed., *Nisqually Journal*, September 1–11, 1851.

8 Tenalquot was a large, well-stocked sheep farm located south of the Nisqually River near present day Lacey, Washington. It too would be placed "under siege" by settlers who made unidentified "arbitrary demands" on Linklater, according to Douglas. These were, undoubtedly, references to squatters violating the Company's rights in that quarter as well. Ultimately, Douglas's proposal "not to send any sheep to that part of the country, if you can possibly find a sufficient range north of the Nisqually River" foreshadows that farm's abandonment by 1853. For more on the Company's outstations, see George Dickey, "The Outstations," *Occurrences: A Journal of Activities at Fort Nisqually Historic Site* 12, no. 1 (Spring 1994): 3–8.

9 Dickey, ed., *Nisqually Journal*, October 22, 1851.

10 Tolmie never communicated with Hawkins (1820–1854) directly, but this officer did impact the chief trader's life. Lieutenant Hawkins was born in North Carolina, attended West Point and, upon graduation, was promoted in the Army to Bvt. 2nd Lieutenant, 1st Infantry, July 1, 1844. He served first in the Midwest then in the War with Mexico, 1846–48. He escorted Governor Joseph Lane to Oregon, 1848–51. After being dismissed, he became a farmer in Warren County, NC, 1853–54, and died in 1854 at the age of 34. George W. Callum, *Officers and Graduates of the U.S. Military Academy at West Point, N.Y. from its Establishment in 1802 to 1890 with the Early History of the United States Military Academy*, 3rd ed., rev. and extended, Vol. 2, Nos. 1001 to 2000 (Boston and New York: Houghton, Mifflin and Company, The Riverside Press, Cambridge, 1891), 112.

11 The 2017 equivalent of the Hawkins' 1851 loan is about $46,600.

Texas. When the note came due for payment, and after an extensive search for the lieutenant, he tenaciously "protested" saying he would not pay it back. Hawkins' land deal had fallen through (thus his collateral), which brought Dr. Tolmie into the swindle. As co-signer of the note, Tolmie's colleague Dr. Haden found himself "on the hook" for his brother-in-arms' financial transgression. It would take the Hawkins affair over a year to play out, the letters illustrating its effect on Haden's relationship with Tolmie, whose job as collections agent was to badger the army's physician until the bill was paid.

William Winlock Miller,[12] a new customs inspector in Olympia, made his first appearance on Puget Sound in October 1851. An Illinois school teacher turned customs official, Miller eventually became a constant fixture at the Nisqually roadstead and in these letters as both a topic of discussion and correspondent with Tolmie.

The letters also speak of the long-anticipated arrival of a new customs collector for Puget Sound. Chief Factor Ogden had recently noted to the HBC's Secretary Archibald Barclay: "It is now some time since Nisqually was made a Port of Entry and a Collector appointed .... This Gent[leman] has not yet made his appearance & in a communication from the Collector of this Port [Vancouver], I am informed that he cannot grant permission to any ship to enter at Nisqually until the Collector duly appointed had arrived."[13] Some held a guarded optimism that the new collector would be fair and just. Others, especially Douglas and Tolmie, knew nothing of his temperament and so held their judgement.

Collector of Customs Simpson P. Moses (1823–c. 1890)[14] made his appearance in early November. Moses has been described as a "fiery young lawyer" who was primed to aggressively enforce the new revenue laws. Regrettably, Thurston, Thornton, Dorr, and lesser customs officials had already set the tone, one that matched Moses's conviction. In less than a month, the new collector's vigorous "letter of the law" interpretation of the territory's customs regulations went into action. In due time, U.S. Army Brigadier General E.A. Hitchcock, then Commander of the Pacific Division, received a letter from Moses requesting a half dozen rifles and ammunition. He insisted such was needed for his defense as customs collector.[15]

---

12 Miller, an Illinois school teacher, was appointed surveyor of customs for Port Nisqually in 1851 and traveled overland to Oregon arriving at Puget Sound that October. While there he held many posts including surveyor and inspector of revenue for Port of Nisqually, 1851; quartermaster general of Washington Territory Militia, 1857–61; director and commissioner for Olympia of the North Pacific Railroad Co., 1857; District Court Notary Public, 1857, 1861; superintendent of Indian Affairs for Washington Territory, 1861; treasurer of the Territory Fund for the Relief of Sick and Disabled Soldiers, 1862; and mayor of Olympia, 1872. For more information see William L. Lang, *Confederacy of Ambition: William Winlock Miller and the Making of Washington Territory* (Seattle: University of Washington Press, 1997).

13 Peter S. Ogden to Archibald Barclay July 16, 1851, HBCA, folio B. 223/b/39, 109.

14 An Act of Congress, approved February 14, 1851, created the first collection district on Puget Sound. Hailing from Ohio, Simpson P. Moses's commission as the region's first U.S. Surveyor of Customs was approved the following May by President Millard Fillmore. It would not be until mid-November that Moses, his family, and brother Benton, arrived in the Sound via the Isthmus of Panama route. Once there, he proclaimed Olympia as the port of entry, even though mile wide shallows and mud flats surrounded the burgeoning community at low tide. History would not remember him kindly. As Hugh Goldsborough so honestly foreshadowed in these letters, Moses's nitpicking approach was "pitiful trifling and utterly unworthy of official action." Lang, *Confederacy of Ambition*, 34–37.

15 Harvey Steele, "Fort Nisqually Besieged," *Occurrences* 12, no. 2 (1994), Fort Nisqually Historic Site,

For a lightly staffed customs office, it was an absurd amount of fire power. Coast Salish Indians had no real business with customs officials and Moses had little reason to fear them.

Then, on November 27, the brig *Mary Dare*, Captain William A. Mouat, and the steamer *Beaver*, Captain Charles E. Stuart,[16] dropped anchor at the Nisqually roadstead. Edward Huggins remembered: "The following persons, passengers, arrived in the steamer and landed at Nisqually [that] evening . . . namely Mr. Chief Factor John Work and his wife Mrs. [Josette] Work,[17] Miss[es] Margaret Work,[18] [Suzette Work],[19] Master John Work,[20] Miss Rose Birnie,[21] a middle aged maiden lady and sister of Mr. [James] Birnie [who was] a retired Hudson's Bay Company's officer at this time living at Cathlamet on the Columbia River."[22] Observing the new customs regulations, no goods were landed. However, the *Beaver*'s engineer and fire-stokers spent several hours ferrying cordwood from shore to ship in preparation for a quick trip to Olympia's customs house the next morning.

Passengers had been landed at Nisqually prior to entry at Olympia—a customs infraction.

Several pairs of socks and some trade goods were listed within the Company's books aboard the *Beaver*—a customs infraction.

Claiming these "alleged infractions of the Revenue Law," Moses seized both vessels and thereafter held them in bond. The contraventions placed Tolmie and ship captains once more in "the lion's den." James Douglas later blamed the ships' captains for the seizures, grousing that they should have known better.

By October news of Queen Charlottes Island gold had reached Puget Sound settlers' ears. Thirty enthusiastic Olympians[23] chartered Captain William Rowland's sloop *Georgianna* on November 3 and sailed northward.[24] The Argonauts' dream of riches perished within three weeks as their vessel foundered, they being

---

Metropolitan Park District of Tacoma, WA, 8–13.

16 For Charles Edward Stuart, see Watson, *Lives Lived*, 3:895.

17 For Josette Lagace Work see Watson, *Lives Lived*, 3:989–90.

18 For Margaret Work see Ibid.

19 For Suzette Work see Ibid.

20 For John Work Jr. see Ibid.

21 James Birnie's 50-year-old sister Rose eventually married George Roberts in 1855 in Cathlamet. For more information on this event and the seizure of the *Beaver* and the brig *Mary Dare* because of the landing of these people, see Edward Huggins to Eva Emery Dye, May 27, 1904. Eva Emery Dye Papers, MSS 1089, Oregon Historical Society Research Library, Incoming Correspondence from Edward Huggins, 1899–1905, Box 1, Folios 16-17; and Edward Huggins to Frank Cole, October 12, 1904. E. Huggins Manuscript Collection T-145, Box 1/fo. 16A, Washington State Historical Society, Tacoma, Washington.

22 Huggins, "Reminiscences of Puget Sound," unpublished manuscript July 11, 1901, edited by Gary Fuller Reese, 1984. Section #2, 26–42. Original typescripts at UW Library's Edward Huggins Collection.

23 All those involved included William Rowland (captain of the *Georgiana*), Duncan McCune, Asher Sargent, Wilson Sargent, Nelson Sargent, Ambrose Jewell, Charles Weed, Daniel Shaw, Samuel Adams, Samuel Williams, James McAllister, John Thornton, Charles Hendricks, George A. Page, John Remby, Jesse Ferguson, Ignatius Calvin, Jared Hurd, William Mahard, Solomon S. Gideon, Sidney S. Ford Sr., Isaac Brown, Benjamin McDonald, George A. More, Alexander Wilson, Samuel B. Howe, Benjamin Gibbs, Roland Gibbs, William Billings, and Tamarae, a Hawaiian.

24 The following wording is paraphrased from J. C. Rathbun, *History of Thurston County, Washington from 1845 to 1895* (Olympia, Washington, 1895), 16–17.

"cast ashore on the east side of the island, [with all] plundered by the Indians." Now prisoners of the Haida, the *Georgianna*'s crew and passengers were held for ransom.[25] Another month would pass before this news reached Nisqually and Olympia. Ultimately, Dr. Tolmie and the HBC would become economically and politically entangled in this troubling situation as well.

Following are the letters from the first half of Outfit 1852.

Document 4.01: A letter from William F. Tolmie, Nisqually, to Amory Holbrook, Oregon City, June 6, 1851.

Sir,

I beg your attention to the enclosed communication addressed to you on the 26th May, and which, as it reached Cowlitz too late to overtake you there, Mr. [George B.] Roberts returned.

Mr. Roberts has informed me of what you said to him regarding the presentation of the Co[mpan]y's claims to the Surveyor General [John B. Preston];[26] & to [avoid] present[ing a] mistake or misapprehension [to the surveyor general,] it would be well if you wrote me a few lines on the subject on receipt of which I shall endeavor to do what may be necessary with the least possible delay. I am sir, Very Respectfully Yours,

Wm Fraser Tolmie

P.S.: I hope that the [law]suit against [Charles] Wren may be made to come on at the November Court. T.

Document 4.02: A letter from William F. Tolmie, the brig *Orbit*—Nisqually Roads, to James Douglas, Victoria, June 6, 1851.

Sir,

Mr. [Michael T.] Simmons, having agreed to the terms offered when I wrote you last, now proceeds with the Orbit to Victoria with a cargo of Sheep as per Bill Lading here with. I have heard that Mr. [Joseph D.] Pemberton, the Surveyor, has arrived in Oregon. The Nisqually Requisition will be sent by first opportunity.

Two men, William Cross and Joe Tapou,[27] go in charge of the sheep. Should Mr. Simmons want $200 or $300 at Victoria for the Sheep freight, please advance him to that amount.

(Wm F. Tolmie)

---

25 The "*Georgiana* Affair" has been widely covered in other publications. For a more complete review of this misadventure, and its handling by the U.S. Congress, see Lucile McDonald, "Early Custom Houses," at themossback.tripod.com/pioneers/spmoses.htm.

26 Preston was the first Surveyor General of the Oregon Territory in 1851. He was appointed by President Fillmore to create a system for surveying land in the territory, but lost his position in 1853 and "drifted into obscurity." Source and for more information see en.wikipedia.org/wiki/John_B._Preston.

27 For Tapou see Watson, *Lives Lived*, 3:905–906.

Document 4.03: A letter from William F. Tolmie, Nisqually, to James Douglas, Victoria, June 11, 1851.

Sir,

François Rabasca [Satakarata] has just handed me your communication of the 3rd Instant accompanying the original map of Nisqually with letters for Vancouver which will be speedily forwarded.[28] Please to inform me by next opportunity whether you still want the Deals [boards] mentioned in your letter of the 3rd.

From the tenor of that letter, I regret having sent a second cargo of livestock by the Orbit. I did so on the supposition that some months might yet lapse 'ere the Collector, who is said to coming via Cape Horn, will assume office at Olympia. [Michael T.] Simmons took lumber down on the strength of what passed between yourself and Captain [David S.] Maynard when the Orbit was formerly at Victoria. [François Rabasca/Satakarata] takes a packet of letters and papers received a few days [ago] from Vancouver.

(Signed) W. F. Tolmie

Document 4.04: A letter from William F. Tolmie, Nisqually, to Peter S. Ogden, Vancouver, June 14, 1851.

Sir,

In reply to yours of the 3rd Inst, I have to inform you that about 600 Wedders will be sent to Vancouver in a fortnight hence.[29] Will you please inform me by the earliest opportunity whether you can spare any Rams for Nisqually this season, and if so, how many and, should you have none to spare, have the goodness to say whether it would suit to you to exchange forty or fifty rams—which would be advantageous to both places as tending to improve the breed of sheep.

Signed Wm Fraser Tolmie

Document 4.05: A letter from William F. Tolmie, Nisqually, to James Douglas, Victoria, June 20, 1851.

Sir,

In fulfillment of your agreement with Mr. [Michael T.] Simmons, [a] Copy of which was handed me by Captain Butler, the Orbit has received a cargo of shingles and sheep, bill of Lading of which is enclosed. The wool will be ready in a week or ten days hence, and will amount to about forty bales. M[iste]rs [Robert] Clouston[30] and [Joseph D.] Pemberton will start for Victoria in cannot [canoe] this afternoon or early tomorrow morning. Please to inform me by the earliest opportunity, whether a good stock of X.P. Ploughshares have been received from England as if I can depend on a sufficient supply, I will get some more of that description of plough fitted up in course of the summer.

(Signed) Wm F. Tolmie

---

28 Neither the map nor Douglas's letter has been located.

29 Dickey, ed., *Nisqually Journal*, July 2, 1851. John McPhail left Nisqually for Vancouver in charge of 882 sheep on this date.

30 For Clouston see Watson, *Lives Lived*, 1:275.

P.S.: M[iste]rs [Robert] C[louston] & [Joseph] P[emberton] would have taken passage in the Orbit had the terms been more reasonable—$40 was asked for their passages. T.

Document 4.06: A letter from William F. Tolmie, Nisqually, to Peter S. Ogden, Vancouver, July 2, 1851.

Sir,

Herewith are enclosed a receipt from Mr. Q[uarter] M[aster John] Dement for One Thousand Dollars and a bill with letter of advice from Father [Pascal] Ricard for £75 St[erlin]g. There is also a letter from Pere [Pascal] Ricard which he wishes posted & prepaid at Vancouver & for which .30 cents postage are enclosed.

John Macphail starts today with 882 prime Wedders for you. Having no authority to price them at less than $5 each, I have never-the-less sent more than the number you asked for at that price, having recently learnt from good authority that mutton sold at 50 Cents p[e]r [pound] one month ago in [the] San Francisco market. Should that report have been correct, there ought to be a brisk demand for Sheep in the Columbia.

In the hope that the Pekin[31] may have arrived I have particularly to request your sending by return of Macphail 50 X.P. Ploughshares. Please advize me by return of the Steilacoom mail whether the ploughshares may be looked for as in that case measures will be taken to get them across from Cowlitz. Macphail promises to abstain from carousing [getting drunk] until he has delivered up his charge at V[ancouver] and I have to request, on condition of his dire observance of that pledge, that he may have [the] where with to enjoy himself thereafter. Enclosed is a list of the Indians [herders] & with a note of the terms on which they have been engaged. It has been agreed that they are to be paid at Vancouver, but should you send us any Rams, t'would be advisable not to pay more—more than half their earnings to those who are to return with Macphail, and they will get the remainder here and something to boot (on a[coun]t Ft Nisqually) as agreed upon. Squally [an Indian], however, may be paid in full.

(Signed) Wm F. Tolmie

Document 4.07: A letter from Amory Holbrook, Oregon City, to William F. Tolmie, Nisqually, July 21, 1851.

Dear Sir,

Your letters written in June were received by me just as I was starting for San Francisco, and I take the earliest opportunity offered since my return to answer them as far as they require immediate replies.

As to the trespassers spoken of, it seems to me hardly worth the trouble just at present to commence legal proceedings if you have given to them full and prompt notice of their occupancy of what is and has been for a long period notoriously

---

31 *Pekin*, British brigantine. See Watson, *Lives Lived*, 3:1125.

claimed by the Company. If a decision is now forced to be made in Court, I fear that in the present state of feeling in your Courts a greater risk than is advisable may be encountered. Beside this, it will not probably be long before the Surveyor General, after he learns the nature and Extent of the Company's claim, will be able to give such advice to trespassers as well [as] make them see the folly of wasting their time on land to which they can never obtain a legal title from their government.

In regard to my message sent to you by Mr. [George B.] Roberts, the object was to obtain from you such a statement of the Company's rights as would enable Mr. [John B.] Preston, the Surveyor General, finally to understand them. He is directed in his instructions from the Department of the Interior of Washington [D.C.], fully to investigate these claims, their character, boundaries, the time when made originally, &c., &c., and to report them at length. I think therefore it would be well for you to send to him at your earliest Convenience, as complete a description as you may choose, with a Topographical outline,[32] so that if possible, he may be able to send his report to Washington [D.C.], by the next session of Congress. You can send the statement to me and I will endeavor to assist him in any way in my power. I am very sincerely, Your obedient Servant,

Amory Holbrook

P.S.: If you will excuse me for troubling you, I am tempted to ask a favor of you at the suggestion of Mr. [Archibald] McKinlay, who tells me that you can more readily than anyone else, accommodate me. I am very anxious to obtain a good sea otter Skin, which I wish to send to my wife in Massachusetts and as it is almost impossible to find any in this part of Oregon, I will be very glad to have you secure one for me if you can do so at any reasonable price. It may be sent for me to Mr. Ogden, to whom I will pay its cost. Begging you to pardon me for the liberty I take, I am &c.,

A. Holbrook

☙ Document 4.08: A letter from William F. Tolmie, Nisqually, to Peter S. Ogden, Vancouver, July 31, 1851.

Sir,

I have to acknowledge receipt of your communications of the 8th and 18th Inst and now return the Bill of Exchange from P[ascal] Ricard with the required endorsements.

The accompanying letters &c., from Victoria, were brought here by myself a few days ago, and are now forwarded by express to Cowlitz whence I have requested Mr. [George B.] Roberts to send them, either by canoe or [overland] mail, as he may have been by you instructed. You do not acknowledge receipt of Mr. [Lieutenant John] Dement's receipt for $1,000 which was enclosed in mine of the 2nd Inst.

Signed W. F. Tolmie

---

32 Holbrook now suggests that Tolmie have a professional surveyed map drawn up of the Company's possessions on Puget Sound.

Document 4.09: A letter from William F. Tolmie, Nisqually, to James Douglas, Victoria, August 2, 1851.

Sir,

I forward by the present express some letters and papers received a few days ago, but whence from the difficulty of obtaining Indians could not have been forwarded sooner.

Enclosed is a letter[33] recently received from Mr. [Amory] Holbrook relative to the presentation of the PSAC Claim for land at Nisqually to the Surveyor General of Oregon, Document in the preparation of which I would be much benefitted by your advice and assistance.

Harvest has commenced early this season, and the crop ripening all at once. Cash sales have been dull of late.

Please to forward by return of the canoe—1 dozen Scythe Stones which are much needed at present; also 4 Scythes 48 In[che]s for Cradling. The Mary Dare sailed from Vancouver on the 17th Ulto.

(Signed) Wm F. Tomie

P.S.: Copies of my two letters to Mr. Holbrook referred to in his of July 21st are herewith sent. Please to inform me whether he can have a Sea Otter from Victoria, and at what price? Shall I send the Statement of claims to Mr. H[olbrook] or direct to the Surveyor General? Mr. [George B.] Roberts expects him soon at Cowlitz.

S[igned] W. F. T.

Document 4.10: A letter from James Douglas, Victoria, to William F. Tolmie, Nisqually, August 4, 1851.[34]

Dear Sir,

The [H.M.S.] Daphnae[35] returned to this port on Sunday morning, with the Governor [Richard Blanchard] on board. She sailed from Fort Rupert on the 30th ult and has had a fine run down.

The Neweete [Indian] affair[36] has not yet been finally disposed of, though they have been rather severely handled by a boat party of 60 men and officers from the Daphnae who surprised their village and carried it by assault in the midst of a severe fire from the natives, with very trifling loss—say two men slightly wounded, who have since recovered. The native position was very strong, and protected with a stockade, which they thought impregnable, and were consequently rather surprised when they saw it carried at one rush by a body of white faces. They however continued to make their escape by some secret passage with the exception of 5 or 6 killed [or] wounded, the chief, Nancy, being unfortunately among the former. All their property and provision were captured and destroyed together with about 20

33 Previously included: Amory Holbrook to William F. Tolmie, July 21, 1851.

34 UW Library's Tolmie Papers Acc. 4577-001, Box #2, Folder #3.

35 *Daphnae*, British, HMS corvette, Captain Edward Gennys Fanshawe. The *Daphnae* was an 18-gun sloop, launched in 1838, and patrolled in the Pacific until 1852. She attacked and destroyed the Neweete Indian village on Prince Rupert Island killing six. See next note.

36 For a thorough discussion on this tragic "incident," see Barry M. Gough, *Gunboat Frontier: British Maritime Authority and Northwest Coast Indians, 1846–1890* (Victoria, BC: UBC Press, 2011.

fine canoes—so that they have sustained a very severe loss. The tribe is now completely dispersed and are reported to be somewhere on the west side of the Island. [George] Blenkinsop[37] reports the Indians to be all quiet and civil, being greatly awed by the example made of the Neweetees. That feeling may however wear off, and mischief may yet be done to our people at Fort Rupert, even in the greatest possible care in preventing accidents.

The [miner named Andrew] Hunter had cleaned out the [mine] shaft and had the boring rods fixed [and] ready for work. He thinks well of the place and is sanguine as to the existence of coal, which he hopes soon to find. The Mary Dare had not arrived at Fort Rupert when the Daphnae left and indeed we have not yet heard of her departure from Fort Vancouver. Mr. Blenkinsop had received letters from Fort Simpson.[38] The steamer failed from some cause or other unexplained [circumstance] of reaching the gold district of Queen Charlotte's Island, but the Una was on the point of proceeding thither, with [John] Work and [William H.] McNeill[39] on board, so that, please God, there will be no failure in the second attempt.

Have the goodness to forward the letters for England as soon as possible to Fort Vancouver. Pray when will the Port of Nisqually be open to the Cadboro? With kind respects to Mrs. [Jane] Tolmie, Very truly yours,

James Douglas

Document 4.11: A letter from James Douglas, Victoria, to William F. Tolmie, Nisqually, August 7, 1851.[40]

Dear Sir,

The Nisqually mail canoe arrived last night, just in time to prevent the departure of a canoe, which we intended to despatch this morning with letters for the Columbia. I have now to acknowledge your communications of the 26th August [July 26th], with enclosures.

Though it is very unpleasant to yield obedience to the arbitrary demands of the people of Tanalquat [Tenalquot Farm],[41] I think it will be as well in the present state and circumstances of the country to avoid every cause of difficulty with them, and not to send any sheep to that part of the country, if you can possibly find a sufficient range north of the Nisqually River.

The letter of the Attorney General [Amory Holbrook] contains sound views lucidly expressed. I am, and have always been, of his opinion that it is not expedient at present to commence legal proceedings against trespassers. His meaning is obvious; it would be imprudent on our part, and dangerous to our interests to take such a course. The [quit claim] notice served upon trespassers is a sufficiently distinct assertion of our rights.

In reference to the Puget's Sound Company's land claim at Nisqually, the kind of Document wanted by the Attorney General is clearly described in his letters.

37 For Blenkinsop see Watson, *Lives Lived*, p. 1:205.
38 For Fort Simpson see Watson, *Lives Lived*, 3:1082–85.
39 For McNeill see Watson, *Lives Lived*, 2:676–677.
40 UW Library's Tolmie Papers Acc. 4577-001, Box #2, Folder #3.
41 Tenalquot Farm. See Dickey, "Outstations."

First, he requests a statement of the Company's rights to the land, as founded on occupation to the present extent since the year 1840.

Secondly, the extent and boundaries may be shown by the map in your possession which also exhibits the character of the country and many of its minuter features.

That map with an explanatory description in writing, strictly confined to the above points in all that I conceive necessary, according to the tenor of Holbrook's letter. Pray attend to that matter without loss of time.

I will select a fine sea otter for Mr. Holbrook and forward it by a safe conveyance. Many thanks for your private note, which will have my best attention. In great haste, Yours very truly,

James Douglas

Document 4.12: A letter from William F. Tolmie, Nisqually, to James Douglas, Victoria, August 18, 1851.

Sir,

Your communications of the 6th and 7th Inst came to hand on the 12th and the accompanying mail has been forwarded to Vancouver. There being now a weekly mail from Olympia to the Columbia River. Captain [Bennett H.] Hill has discontinued sending a monthly courier to Vancouver, and now posts his despatches at Olympia, his weekly messenger calling here in going and returning. Would it not be a considerable saving to post the Victoria mails at Olympia? Please instruct me how to act for the future in this matter.

Mr. [John] Preston, the Surveyor General, accompanied by Gov [John P.] Gaines, and Mr. [Nathaniel] Coe, Postal Agent,[42] are to be at Cowlitz tomorrow and will in all probability extend their excursion to Nisqually. I shall take the earliest opportunity of presenting the PSA Co's claim to Mr. Preston, and have a map of our lands in readiness for him. I am &c., &c.,

S[igned] W. F. Tolmie

Mem[oranda]: Gold dust bro[ugh]t by Mr. H[ill] to be sent p[e]r first safe opp[ortunit]y. 97 oz. 2 ___ 3 grs.

Document 4.13: A letter from William F. Tolmie, Nisqually, to John B. Chapman, near Port Steilacoom, August 24, 1851.

Sir,

Having recently been informed that you have taken land and commenced improvements at the Sandy Point near Kittson's Island on the seashore betwixt this place and Steilacoom, it becomes my duty to warn you that if such be the ~~question~~

42 Nathaniel Coe (1788–1868). "The postal agent appointed in 1851 was Nathaniel Coe, a man of high character and scholarly attainments, as well as religious habits. He was a native of Morristown, New Jersey, a Whig, and a member of the Baptist church. In his earlier years he represented Alleghany County, New York, in the state legislature. When his term of office in Oregon expired he remained in the country, settling on the Columbia River near the mouth of Hood River, on the eastern slope of the Cascade Mountains. His mental energy was such, that neither the rapid progress of the sciences of our time, nor his own great age of eighty, could check his habits of study. The ripened fruits of scholarship that resulted appeared as bright as ever even in the last weeks of his life." Hubert Howe Bancroft, *History of the Pacific States of North America* (San Francisco: A. L. Bancroft & Co., 1882–1890), 189.

case, you are trespassing on the lands claimed by the Puget's Sound Agricultural Co under the fourth article of the Boundary Treaty concluded at Washington June 15th, [18]46 between the plenipotentiaries of Great Britain and the United States of America. I am Sir, Your very obedt Sert,

W. F. Tolmie

Document 4.14: A letter from William F. Tolmie, Nisqually, to John B. Preston, Oregon City, August 25, 1851.

Sir,

Having learnt that you desire information regarding the nature and content of the Puget's Sound Agricultural Company's land claims at Nisqually, I beg to lay before you a colored map of the tract of Country occupied by the said Company for agricultural and stock farming purposes since the year 1840, and of which, as is well known in this quarter, they have claimed the exclusive right of possession, since the settlement of the Oregon Boundary question in the year 1846.[43]

Let me state, in addition to the information given in the map, that the spaces colored yellow and numbered "8" in the "explanations" show the situation of some experimental arable farms commenced by the Coy in 1840, and carried on 'till 1843, when the capabilities of the soil having been fully tested it was found advisable to abandon the endeavor to produce wheat for exportation and confine attention to sheep farming and the breeding of horned cattle and horses—pursuits the Nisqually plains are naturally best adapted for.[44]

The broad dark colored line number "9" on the map displays the direction in which the N[orthern] and E[astern] boundary [sic]lines would have to run through the forest land bordering Puyallip river in order to include all the land in that direction occupied by the Coy since 1840. To the Southward the same line shows the course of Nisqually River which forms our Southern boundary to where said line diverges toward the sea shore. The yellow line "10" points out the sea margin and the Western boundary of the Company's claim, the woodland there or elsewhere within the bounds affording much sustenance to the horned cattle especially during the winter months. In addition to the improvements shown on the map, roads have been opened through the belts of Timber in different directions, the small streams have been bridged, and artificial grasses sown in many parts of the plains. The farms marked J[ohn] Ross's, I[saac] Bastien's[45] and F[rançois] Gravelle's[46] were originally taken and improved with the Company's consent.

---

43 The map to which Tolmie is referring is not precisely identified, but it was not the one eventually sent to Preston for final review.

44 These were the "experimental" farm sites of the Red River Settlers, British subjects, who were brought out by the Company in 1840 to strengthen British claims north of the Columbia River. The experiment failed miserably, with all settlers quickly moving to the Willamette Valley and becoming American citizens.

45 By the early 1850s, Bastien [var: Bastion/Bastian] had retired from the HBC and taken a donation land claim near Roy, or Muck, east of Fort Nisqually. The French Canadian had arrived in the Oregon territory on April 8, 1839, at the age of sixteen, and then worked for the HBC from June 1840 to June of 1848 as a "middleman" or laborer. Then, from June 1848 to June 1849, he worked for the PSAC. Edna Price, "Isaac Bastian: A Link to Local History," *Nisqually River Notes: A Bimonthly Publication of the Nisqually River Council* 6, No. 5 (December 1993).

46 For Gravelle see Watson, *Lives Lived*, 2:417.

Any further information you may desire regarding the Company's land claim at Nisqually I shall have pleasure in furnishing when called upon, and meantime I have the honor to remain Sir, Your very obet Sert,

S[igne]d Wm F. Tolmie, Agent for the Puget's Sound Agricul Co
Nisqually, Puget's Sound, O[regon] T[erritory]

✕ P.S. The letter to Mr. [Amory] Holbrook on next page [and] with regard to the Sea Otter you wish to obtain, Mr. Douglas of Victoria, Vanc[ouve]r's Isl[an]d, is to select a prime one for you and send it to Mr. [Chief Factor Peter S.] Ogden by the first safe opportunity. W. F. T.

Document 4.15: A letter from William F. Tolmie, Nisqually, to Amory Holbrook, Oregon City, August 25, 1851.

Dear Sir,

I have now to acknowledge receipt of your letter of July 21, [18]51, to which I would have sooner replied had I not been led to expect the Surveyor General in this quarter, and to have had the opportunity of personally explaining to him the Company's claim for land at this place. As it appears that Mr. Preston does not at present intend visiting Puget's Sound, I herewith forward an open letter to him which after perusal please seal and deliver as likewise the accompanying Map or topographical outline of the PSA Co's ~~topograph~~ land claim at Nisqually.

In my letter to Mr. [John] Preston, you will observe I have said nothing regarding the squatters on the Coy's lands having considered that reference thereto would have been irrelevant in a communication setting forth the Coy's claims for land. Should Mr. Preston desire information on this or any other subject connected with the Coy's claim for land he will I hope write me and make enquiry.

The squatters are now twelve in number, mostly all of whom have taken possession this year, and I think it not unlikely that some of them may remove to more attractive quarters 'ere the year is out. The latest I have warned off is Mr. J[ohn] B. Chapman who has abandoned his town site on the Chehalis to commence another on Puget's Sound abreast of Kit[t]son's Island. I remain Dear Sir, &c., &c.,

S[igne]d W. F. Tolmie

Document 4.16: A letter from Joseph Hardisty, Vancouver, to William F. Tolmie, Nisqually, August 25, 1851.[47]

Dear Sir,

By return of the Canoe which landed me here on the evening of the 23rd Inst—Saturday, I forward you these few lines. The Balance Sheet for Fort Nisqually last Outfit that you asked for I herewith enclose. You will find it differs materially from your ac[count].

Dr. [Alfred R.] Benson[48] has no Ex[tractum] of Colocynth,[49] consequently there is none sent you.

---

47 BC Archives, A/C/20/H21; MS-0557. From a typescript and original copy.

48 Dr. Benson was the HBC's physician assigned to Fort Vancouver at this time. See Watson, *Lives Lived*, 1:193–94.

49 An extracted compound that was used to ease constipation, lethargy of the liver, headache, etc.

Seven-eighths of the people about here are down with the Influenza. The Indians who brought me here are so awfully scared of being attacked also, that they cannot be prevailed on to wait any longer. Hoping that you will, on this plea, excuse my brevity, I remain Dear Sir, Your Obedient Servant,

Joseph Hardisty

P.S. Please let me know what you think of the Balance sheet sent you. Hoping that Mrs. [Jane] Tolmie is again restored to perfect health, I remain, in haste, Yours truly, J. H.

Document 4.17: A letter from William F. Tolmie, Nisqually, to Peter S. Ogden, Vancouver, August 30, 1851.

Sir,

Please to remit to Mr. W[illia]m Dement,[50] Oregon City, brother to Mr. [Lieutenant John] Dement US A[rmy] Steilacoom [Barracks], the sum of Ninety One Dollars ($91.00) which charge against Fort Nisqually Outfit 1851. I have also to request you to send the accompanying packet by the earliest opportunity to Mr. [Amory] Holbrook at Oregon City. [John] Macphail has just arrived with the Rams, himself and Ind[ian]s sick. I am, &c.,

S[igne]d W. F. Tolmie

P.S.: I have received your packet by Mr. Wyhe.

Document 4.18: A letter from William F. Tolmie, Nisqually, to James Douglas, Victoria, September 6, 1851.

Sir,

The accompanying copy of a letter from Collector General [John] Adair of Astoria to P[eter] S. Ogden Esq[ui]re came to hand about a fortnight ago, and would then have been forwarded had Indians been obtainable, but it happened that I had just previously sent every disposable one to assist in getting in the harvest at Cowlitz.

For the last few days, I have been in daily expectation of seeing you here, Michel Langley[51] having positively informed me that you were to have started on the 4th Inst accompanied by Mr. [Henry N.] Peers[52] and [an apprentice clerk] Mr. [Richard] Galledge.[53]

I now despatch the Indian "Lecaille"[54] with the letters and papers accumulated

---

50 This younger brother of U.S. Army Lieutenant John Dement immigrated to Oregon City in 1843. He lived out his life in Clackamas County. He married Olive Johnson on July 4, 1846, and by 1850 he was not only a Mason, but also considered a merchant, having founded the Oregon City Woolen Mills and the Oregon City Railroad. The couple had seven children. http://wc.rootsweb.ancestry.com/cgi-bin/igm.cgi?op=GET&db=deharley&id=I30931.

51 Langley was a metis laborer and courier for the HBC who also worked for the PSAC at both Nisqually and Cowlitz Farm. No further information was found.

52 For Peers see Watson, *Lives Lived*, 2:764.

53 For Golledge see Watson, *Lives Lived*, 1:411–12.

54 Lecaillé (m) [var: L'caille, Caille' or Kaiyeh.] This Suquamish slave owner traded with the HBC and worked as a shepherd/laborer/courier for the PSAC from at least 1849 through 1853. Anderson, ed., "Fort Nisqually Indian Accounts Book; Commencing September 1849-Ending January 1851," Huntington Library, Soliday Collection, Nisqually Papers, FN 1242, vol. 2, San Marino, California.

here send last mail and direct him to be particularly watchful not to pass you on the way. I was at Cowlitz on the 1st Inst when the weather was showery as it has been since. The greater part of the crops there were still out and the farm was particularly behind, and the Indians having all either deserted or been laid up with the prevailing Catarrh[55] and Dysentery which latter complain has proved fatal to several.

Herewith are forwarded the Nisqually Servant's Orders for 1851 and a Tariff to which please have the prices at 33 1/3 and 100 p[e]r cent affixed.

(Signed) William Fraser Tolmie

Document 4.19: A letter from William F. Tolmie, Nisqually, to James Douglas, Victoria, September 25, 1851.

Sir,

Herewith are enclosed [the] account and bill lading for Sheep and Horses shipped per Georgiana[56] for Victoria. Please to send me a bill of the wood needed for the Sequallitchew Sawmill at your earliest convenience, and a statement of the terms on which the mill, after completion, will be let to the person constructing it &c., &c.,

S[igne]d Wm F. Tolmie

P.S.: An account against [William] Hudson,[57] seaman on board the Cadboro, is here enclosed. T.

Document 4.20: A letter from Peter S. Ogden, Vancouver, to William F. Tolmie, Nisqually, October 3, 1851.[58]

Sir,

I have to advise you of having this day drawn on you for the sum of Twenty Dollars ($20.00) in favor of John Ringley [Rigney] at Steelacoomb [Steilacoom]. We have received here the amount of the order & have passed the same to credit of Fort Nisqually Out[fit 18]51. I remain, Yours truly,

Peter Skene Ogden, HB Coy

Document 4.21: A letter from William F. Tolmie, Nisqually, to James Douglas, Victoria, October 13, 1851.

Sir,

Your courier, Michel, arrived here today, and the packet for London will be forwarded early tomorrow, in time to overtake the mail from Cowlitz to Astoria of this week.

---

55 An inflammation of a mucous membrane, especially in the nose or throat, causing an increase in the production of mucus, as happens in the common cold.

56 *Georgiana*, American sloop. Its primary cargo was passengers, mail, sheep, horses, oxen, furs, and gold dust. This ship was involved in an event which Lucile McDonald fully described in "Queen Charlotte Islanders Capture the *Georgiana* Gold Seekers," *Washington's Yesterdays* (Portland: Binfords and Mort, 1953), 166–67. See also: themossback.tripod.com/pioneers/spmoses.htm.

57 For Hudson see Watson, *Lives Lived*, 2:470–71.

58 UW Library's Tolmie Papers Acc. 4577-001, Box #1, Folder #9.

Robert Johnston[59] had brought some letters from Vancouver, a bale of Furs & also a bag [of] Gold Dust, and I have agreed to Captain [William] Rowland[60] [of the sloop *Georgiana*] for his passage at $1. p[e]r day, his provisions being supplied from the Fort.

I will write in full by the Indian tomorrow, and will then send the remainder of the Newspapers. Should cattle arrive in time, I may ship some oxen by the Georgiana at $6 p[e]r head. I expect to have four shipped for Mr. [Roderick] Finlayson. I am Sir, Your very obedt Sert,

W. F. Tolmie

P.S.: [Captain] Rowland charges $1 for freight of the bale of Furs. T.

Document 4.22: An "official" letter from William F. Tolmie, Nisqually, to Peter S. Ogden, Vancouver, October 14, 1851.

Sir,

A report having Circulated in this quarter during summer 1850 that Mathew Nelson,[61] who deserted from Nisqually in 1849, had died on his Return from California, and on his deathbed appointed You his executor, directing some of his fellow passengers to make known to you the address of his Relatives in Ireland, I have been Requested to enquire into the truth of this by a Mr. L[yman] A. Smith, lately appointed Administrator to Nelson['s estate], who, not having been heard of for upwards of a Year, is supposed by his friends in this Quarter to be dead. If you do have anything about Nelson's fate or Relatives, please inform me at your earliest Convenience. I have already addressed You on this Subject on the 8th Inst.

I duly Received Your Communication of the 1st Oct by R[obert] Johnston for whom I obtained a passage Yesterday on the Sloop Georgiana now traveling to Victoria & back. The Note you Request me to try & Collect, I could see Nothing of in Your enclosure. There was perhaps instead of it a letter from Mr. [Amory] Holbrook to you of Sept. 18, [18]51. I have not yet Received the letter he speaks [of]. Having nothing more, I have the honor to be Sir, Your Very Obt Servt, T.T.g[?]

(Signed) W. F. Tolmie

Document 4.23: A letter from William F. Tolmie, Nisqually, to James Douglas, Victoria, October 14, 1851.

Sir,

I addressed you briefly yesterday by Captain [William] Rowland of the Georgiana, on board which were shipped eight Oxen, 2 yrs old & upwards, the Horses sent belonging all to private persons.

---

59 For Johnston see Watson, *Lives Lived*, 2:494–95.

60 Rowland was the American skipper of the sloop *Georgiana* then at anchor at the roadstead. No other information on the captain was found.

61 Nelson is listed on the Servant's record for 1845 as a cook/laborer with a salary of £17 per annum. In 1846 he was listed as cook/laborer at Tenaqualt Farm. In 1847–1848 he was a cook/laborer at Whyatchie Farm, and in 1849 he was listed as a shepherd at Tenalquot Farm. Nelson was transferred to Fort Nisqually in March 1849. He deserted to the gold fields of California in 1849. He is not listed on the servants account in 1850. On the 1854 servant's accounts Nelson is listed as being deceased. Anderson, *The Physical Structure of Fort Nisqually*, 167–79.

I have been in Communication with a Millwright Regarding the Construction of a Sawmill here, and his offer was to engage for a year at $5.00 p[e]r day & board to put up the Mill & Work it. He proposes building a frame 40 feet x 20, and enclosed is a Copy of his estimate of the Timber Required[62] which Could be squared & delivered at high water mark, for about 16 Cents p[e]r running foot.

Herewith is sent a Copy of a letter from Am[or]y Holbrook to Mr. [Chief Factor Peter S.] Ogden Regarding the land claim here. The letter Mr. H[olbrook] speaks of having written to me, has not yet come to hand. We had the Meter or bounds to our possessions or, in other words, to the land we occupied prior to 1846, further than the Natural ones, we have since found it necessary to Make some artificial boundary lines.

The Collector of Customs for Olympia District is said to be in the Territory and is hourly expected at Olympia by Mr. [William W.] Miller the Inspector. The only reason they can assign for his non-arrival is the probability of his waiting for departure of the Steamer Sea Gull [63] which is expected to bring immigrants from Columbia River to Puget's Sound. I remain, &c.,

S[igne]d W. F. Tolmie

⁂ Document 4.24: A letter from William F. Tolmie, Nisqually, to Peter S. Ogden, Vancouver, October 18, 1851.

Sir,

Enclosed is an order on you for ($91) Ninety-one Dollars in favor of Mr. [William] Dement, Oregon City, and unless you should have already remitted him the Amount in Compliance with the Request Conveyed in Mine of Augt 30th, [18]51, I beg of You to do so now.

The present [mail packet] is forwarded by Three Sandwich Islanders, whose times are out. Cowie[64] & Koemie's[65] accounts are sent in order that should they want advances at Vancouver; you May know how they stand. Keave'haccow[66] has worked here 6⅛ Weeks, and has a Credit of £2.0.0 which, should he so desire, please pay him at Vancouver. It would not be safe to give any of them advances over their Credits. Should Cowie have no Credit, please let him have to the Amount of £2 St[erlin]g; he promises to Reengage on Arriving here, but if he asks for Credit it Might be well to engage him for 2 years at £25 per Annum.

Dr. [John M.] Haden has Requested me to ascertain of you whether a letter addressed to him for Lieut [George W.] Hawkins has been paid or Not? I Remain Sir, Your Very Obedt Servt,

(Signed) W. F. Tolmie

---

62 This estimate has not been found.

63 *Sea Gull*, American steamer. Captain Tichenor, master, ran passengers between Puget Sound, Portland, and San Francisco. It wrecked on the Humboldt Bar, California, on January 26, 1852.

64 For Cowie, (Hawaiian) see Watson, *Lives Lived*, 1:295.

65 For Koemi (Hawaiian) see Watson & Barman, *Leaving Paradise*, 323–24.

66 For Keave'haccow (Hawaiian) see Watson, *Lives Lived*, 2:524–25; and Watson and Barman, *Leaving Paradise*, 310–11.

Document 4.25: A letter from William F. Tolmie, Nisqually, to James Douglas, Victoria, October 25, 1851.

Sir,

As [James] Goudie[67] now returns to Victoria his account at this place is forwarded herewith.

There has been no mail from Vancouver since the last was forwarded on the 13th and 14th Inst.

We are now busy harvesting potatoes and have a good crop.

Mr. [William P.] Wells, who has just called, says that Mr. [William W.] Miller informed him that Collector [Simpson P.] Moses would arrive at Olympia by the first vessel from San Francisco.

(Signed) W. F. Tolmie

Document 4.26: A letter from William F. Tolmie, Nisqually, to Amory Holbrook, Cowlitz Farm, October 25, 1851.

Dear Sir,

Mr. [Chief Factor Peter S.] Ogden stated in a late letter that you intended writing me, subsequently to the receipt of mine of August 25th accompanying the Topographical sketch and letter for Mr. [John B.] Preston, but your intended letter has not come to hand.

I regret that, owing to the number of sick here, I cannot have the pleasure of seeing you at court, but hope, that as it has lately been reported in this quarter, you mean to ride as far as Nisqually when court business is over. In case, however, it should not be your intention to come farther than the County seat, please send me your Bill by return of bearer and I will by the earliest succeeding mail, request Mr. [Peter S.] Ogden to pay it. Had the long looked for Collector of Customs arrived at Olympia when expected, your sea otter would 'ere now have been at Vancouver, and I still have hopes that it may reach you prior to your departure for the States. I remain Dear Sir, Very Respectfully Yours,

William Fraser Tolmie

Document 4.27: A letter from Joseph Hardisty, Vancouver, to William F. Tolmie, Nisqually, October 31, 1851.[68]

Dear Sir,

Your favor of the 18th Inst reached me on the 29th. The Letters you enclosed will go by the Mail of the 8th Proxo and I shall take the necessary steps relative to the postage on them.

I enclose to you Cowie & Koemi's Ac[count]s with the HB Coy and hope they contain the necessary information. They have both renewed their Agreements for 1 year at a Salary of £25 p[er] an[num].

67 For Goudie see Watson, *Lives Lived*, 1:413–14.

68 UW Library's Tolmie Papers Acc. 4577-001, Box #1, Folder #4.

As to your Query whether Cowie has been placed on the Books for Outfit 1851, I have to reply in the negative and have merely to say that it will depend on the information contained in the Nisqually Books Outfit 1851—that will be sent here prior to the closing of the Ac[count]s—whether or not he came in the Abstract as a regular Servant for that Outfit.

Remember me Kindly to Mr. [Charles] Forrest. At all times (as long as I am able) ready for your Commands, I remain, My dear Sir, Your Obedient Servant,

Joseph Hardisty

P.S. I did not receive the amount of Advances in Vancouver Sale Shop to the 2 Kanakas whose Ac[count]s are herewith enclosed until the Ac[count]s were made out, which will account for the irregularity of their close. As they now stand Cowie is in debt to the amount of £3.1.5 & Koemi has a credit Balance of £14.14.11. Yours &c., J. Hardisty

Document 4.28: A letter from Joseph Hardisty, Vancouver, to William F. Tolmie, Nisqually, November 1, 1851.[69]

Dear Sir,

Since the Ac[count]s of the 2 Kanackas now on their way to Nisqually were made up, they have been advanced, at least Cowie has, 15. Dollars. This will have to be borne in mind in settling with them. Excuse haste, Yours truly,

(S[igne]d) Joseph Hardisty

Document 4.29: A second letter from Joseph Hardisty, Vancouver, to William F. Tolmie, Nisqually, November 1, 1851.[70]

Dear Sir,

Koemi has just been advanced $30.00 independent of the charges against him at this place—Outfit 1851—as contained in the ac[count] now sent you. Excuse haste, Yours truly,

(S[igne]d) Joseph Hardisty

Document 4.30: A letter from William F. Tolmie, Nisqually, to James Douglas, Victoria, November 11, 1851.

Sir,

Your communications of the 1st and 3rd Instant came to hand on the 8th Tuesday and I have also to acknowledge receipt of yours of the 21st October which Capt [William] Rowland delivered on his arrival about the end of that month.

Herewith is forwarded a statement of the amounts credited in the books of this post to M[ichael] T. Simmons for transport of livestock &c., to Victoria and which, in a total of $1,577.18, it was my intention to have debited against that post on supposition that the charges for transport would be made at Victoria. But as

69 BC Archives, A/C/20/H21. From a typescript copy.

70 Ibid.

you have decided that these are to be made from Nisqually, please inform me, what charge is to be made for the 1,616 Sheep to be debited against Victoria, and state also the Amount or amounts placed against Nisqually, as an offset to its charges for transport over and above the sum credited to Simmons.

A Copy is now sent of all the charges from Nisqually against Victoria the ship[pin]g &c., on account of Outfit 1851.

The absence of the article Flour from our Requisition for Outfit [18]52 was an omission which is now rectified in the additional requisition herewith.

In addition to the four Wool bales still here, we have 150 beaver and otter [skins] besides small furs ready for shipment.

I shall set about getting the N[orthern] and E[astern] boundary lines of the PS Coy land claim traced out as soon as possible. They cannot be satisfactorily effected without the assistance of a surveyor.[71]

We have this season put all the Ewes (4,100) to the Rams and will consequently have a large number of Sheep to dispose of in 1852. The Autumn had been remarkably favourable for the pastures there having been as yet no frost.

Geo[rge] Edwards deserted from the service about the 1st Instant, and has gone to work for an American at Tenalquot (Glasgow). A[dam] Beinston has expressed a wish to leave in Spring 1852 and although his verbal agreement bound him 'till 1853 his services can, at any time, be dispensed with.

I am sorry to inform you that Mr. [Edward] Huggins has been seriously ill with a dysentery affection for the last fortnight; he is now somewhat better although scarcely yet out of danger. John McPhail has recently been similarly affected. The disease had been very fatal amongst the Indians residing here and we have lost three Indian Shepherds by it.

There are no butt Hinges in any of the Stores in this neighborhood. If a supply has not arrived by the *[Norman]* Morison, I can send to the Columbia for them, but will await your instructions thereanent. Simmons has made no reply to my offer of 12 ½ Cents p[e]r [pound] for his Shingling Nails. Shall I offer more? I remain &c., &c.,

S[igne]d W. F. Tolmie

P.S.: I send in charge of Skuttal[72] a thoroughbred Collie, a female, for Viewfield [Farm], and a halfbred Dog called "Fred". The female has no name. T.

Document 4.31: A letter from David D. Wishart, Victoria, to William F. Tolmie, Nisqually, November 12, 1851.[73]

Dear Sir,

Capt [Charles E.] Stuart [of the steamer *Beaver*] is kind enough to take charge of some of my things at Nisqually, and I am presuming (in the absence of any letter from you) that you will not object to transact business for me again as last voyage.

71 On April 7, 1852, Dr. Tolmie would hire John B. Chapman of Steilacoom City to conduct the aforementioned survey. That agreement is included within this work and can be found in that time frame.

72 Skuttal (an Indian) [var: Skutalcoosim]. This man, a native trader, was from the Kuwachin area, near today's Okanagan, Washington.

73 UW Library's Tolmie Papers Acc. 4577-001, Box #2, Folder #2. The date cited here is different from the transcribed letter at the UW files as this letter was delivered to Dr. Tolmie by an Indian courier on Saturday, November 15, so it had to be written several days before then.

I have given Capt S[tuart] the invoices [and] they are made out at Prime Cost without any charges on them. If you think they will go with you, you will perhaps Kindly take charge of them on the same conditions that you did before, or If you felt inclined to take the whole at once off my hands, I won't take 50 p[er] Cent as the Comp[any] gave me.

Capn S[tuart] is kind enough to say if you do not take them yourself and you think these are things that won't sell, that he will bring them back again to me. Trusting we shall manage in some way to deal, I remain, Dear Sir, Yours Truly,

D. D. Wishart

P.S. I have left the retail Price entirely to yourself [to affix].

Document 4.32: A letter from William F. Tolmie, Nisqually, to John M. Haden, Steilacoom Barracks, November 14, 1851.

Dear Doctor,

I am at length enabled to communicate information regarding Lieut [George W.] Hawkins's Bill [endorsed] by you, and regret much that the tidings are not of a more agreeable nature. As you will learn from the Notice herewith, the Bill has been protested, and Mr. [Peter S.] Ogden has instructed me to apply to you for payment of the amount Fourteen Hundred and Fifty nine Dollars Thirty six Cents [$1,459.36], with interest thereon since date May 5th, [18]51 at 6 p[e]r C[en]t p[e]r annum amounting to Forty Six Dollars and three Cents which makes a Total of Fifteen Hundred and Five Dollars, Thirty Nine Cents ($1,505.39.)

As Mr. [Peter S.] Ogden is anxious to learn, previous to setting out for New York, whether you can meet the Bill or not, will you please inform me on that point by return of bearer. I despatch an Express for Vancouver tomorrow morning, and the necessity of preparing letter for it prevents my visiting you today, which the state of my patients I am happy to say, would now admit of. I am &c., &c., &c.,

(Signed) W. F. Tolmie

P.S.: Mr. Ogden desires to be respectfully remembered to Captain [Bennett H.] Hill and his brother officers.

Document 4.33: A letter from William F. Tolmie, Nisqually, to HBC Board of Management,[74] Vancouver, November 14, 1851.

Gentlemen,

I received yesterday evening Mr. P[eter] S. Ogden's letter of the 28th Ulto and also two from him dated the 31st. As instructed by Mr. Ogden, I today applied to Dr. [John M.] Haden of Steilacoom [Barracks] for payment of Lieut [George W.] Hawkins's promissory Note, endorsed by him, and protested at New York for non-payment on the 7th August.

Dr. Haden declared his inability at present to pay the Bill which, with Interest

74 At this time, the HBC's Board of Management was comprised of Peter S. Ogden, Dugald Mactavish, and John Ballenden, and it is to them that this letter was addressed.

amounted to $1,505.39. He stated that he held a mortgage on landed property in Oregon belonging to Lieut Hawkins which was valued at $5,000 in May last and seemed to think that by next mail intelligence would arrive of Lieut Hawkins readiness to meet his liabilities. He also spoke of the existence in Oregon of promissory notes from Genl [Joseph] Lane in L[ieutenant] Hawkins' favor to the amount of $15,000 but gave no definite information regarding them. I retain the Promissory Note and protest until further advised by you, and meantime remain, Gentlemen, &c., &c.,

S[igne]d Wm F. Tolmie

Document 4.34: A letter from William F. Tolmie, Nisqually, to James Douglas, Victoria, November 17, 1851.

Sir,

I forward the present [letter] to inform you of the arrival at Olympia of Mr. [Simpson P.] Moses, Collector of Customs for the Puget's Sound district of Oregon Territory, who has come, as was expected, in [Captain Lafayette] Balch's vessel from California.

I have just had an estimate made of the cattle belonging to M[ister John] Ross's Farm, and they amount to 55 head, mostly wild, of which you proposed taking half to Cowlitz in the course and I have offered to credit the Farm with the remainder as the rate they were originally charged at. The offspring of the cattle [originally] supplied the farm are scattered over all parts of the plains, and it's doubtful whether the number estimated is [accurate], only the ascertained deaths having been allowed for. On this account, I think the offer made a fair one and John and Walter [Ross] seem of the same opinion. Please let me know whether you approve of my taking the Stock off M[ister]s Ross's hands and if so whether you consider the terms above stated fair. I have the honor to be, &c., &c.,

S[igne]d Wm F. Tolmie

[P.S.:] The bearer arrived here on Saturday afternoon [November 15] with a letter from Capt [David] Wishart and a few letters for Vancouver & England chiefly from Gentlemen. He (the Indian) will be entitled to pay according to his dispatch. W. F. T., Fort Nis[qually]

P.S.[S.:] In addition to the Transfer forwarded by last opportunity, there is a charge for $393.30 Cash left by me at Victoria in July [18]51. Please remember to return our packet box now sent. T.

Document 4.35: A letter from John Bradley, Round Plain, to William F. Tolmie, Nisqually, November 29, 1851.[75]

Dear Sir,

A number of wild cattle came into my farm the other day and attacked a very fine animal of mine, and have injured him exceedingly. I am desirous to know what your mark [brand] is as I do not desire to injure any of your Stocks, as the damage

75 UW Library's Tolmie Papers Acc. 4577-001, VO250e, Box #1, Folder #1.

may be repaired without. But stock that I cannot ascertain whose it is I shall, of necessity, take summary a vengeance on for those ungovernable propensities. Very Respectfully yours,

John Bradley

N.B. An immediate answer is requested.

Document 4.36: A letter from William F. Tolmie, Nisqually, to John B. Chapman & Douglas Graines,[76] Port Steilacoom, November 29, 1851.[77]

Gentlemen,

As the road from Olympia to Steilacoom will, if Completed according to the New Route, pass diagonally through the Puget's Sound Agricultural Company's Farm at this place, to the great loss & detriment of said Company, I hereby Request you to appoint three disinterested householders of Lewis County to examine said Road, the whole distance the stream has been stabilized through the enclosed lands of the Company, and assess and determined how Much less Valuable the land or premises of said Company will be Valued by the opening of the said Road &c., &c., &c., according to section 6 of an Act on Roads and Highways of the Territorial Law of Oregon. I am Gentlemen, Very Respectably, Your Obedt Sert,

(Signed) W. F. Tolmie

P.S. It would suit as well if the viewers were directed to examine the road from the S[outh] E[ast] Bastion of Ft Nisqually along the lane to the N[orth] W[est] Corner of the enclosure through which the road would pass if carried out according to the first view.

W. F. Tolmie

---

76 Information on this individual was not found.

77 These two men comprised the Board of County Commissioners, Lewis County, Oregon Territory.

CHAPTER FIVE

December 1st, 1851–May 31st, 1852

"Captain Stuart, by the advice of Mr. Marge, started for Victoria on the eve of his intended arrest, so that the various suits to have been entered against him must be postponed until his reappearance at Olympia."
—William F. Tolmie to John Ballenden, January 23, 1852

The chief advocate of American interests, Simpson P. Moses, now held the office of collector of customs on Puget Sound. Employing his office's authority to match the agenda of many of the American settlers, he charged Captain Charles Stuart and the *Beaver* with landing "passengers before clearing at Olympia [and for possessing] a small remnant of the goods which were not entered in the steamer's manifest."[1] In addition, the *Mary Dare* was charged with smuggling. Writing to HBC Secretary Barclay on December 15, James Douglas noted: "One is at a loss to characterize such proceedings, or to believe that they could have existence in the Ports of a friendly power, or that they can have any other object than to drive the Company from Oregon, at the sacrifice of their property."[2]

Both seizures involved Moses's new lieutenant (and future correspondent), Deputy Collector of Customs Elwood Evans.[3] A native Philadelphian, Evans studied law and was eventually admitted to the Pennsylvania bar. An 1851 presidential appointment brought him to Olympia by November 15. The seizures of the *Beaver* and *Mary Dare* were his first acts as a public servant.[4] Tolmie's presence in Olympia at this time brought about a hand-delivered written protest[5] and also a note to Douglas which was immediately forwarded to the chief factor via courier.

1 Huggins, "Reminiscences of Puget Sound," unpublished manuscript July 11, 1901, edited by Gary Fuller Reese, 1984. Section #2, 26–42. Original typescripts at UW Library's Edward Huggins Collection.

2 Bowsfield, *Victoria Letters*, 243–44.

3 For a more complete biography on Evans (1828–1898) see John MacEachern, "Elwood Evans, Lawyer-Historian," *Pacific Northwest Quarterly* 52 (January 1961), 15–28.

4 Douglas later advised Tolmie to place a private bribe in Evan's pocket, something he felt might "rush the vessel through the Custom House without a word said." This proposal, and the chief factor's documented wish that Captain Stuart of the *Beaver* had thrown the customs officials overboard and sped away to Victoria, reveal Douglas's level of frustration.

5 Tolmie's formal protest letter was not found but was likely similar in form to those he wrote for the original seizure of the *Cadboro* in 1850.

As these events unfolded, Dr. Tolmie departed south to consult the Company's lawyers. This left Chief Factor John Work in charge at Nisqually. It is telling that both men applied the term "plunder" to their correspondences, underscoring a shared disgust each held for individuals the doctor refers to as "custom house land sharks." As the wheels of the territory's legal system ground slowly forward, the Company's new attorney, Simon B. Marge, advanced the notion that Collector Moses could be prosecuted for damages—specifically his contrived smuggling charges and disrupted commerce, both of which came at an expense to the Company.[6]

Tolmie also forewarned of Captain Stuart's culpability in the affair. "Early this morning Captain Stuart arrived from Olympia the bearer of a note from Dr. Tolmie," the fort's journal noted, "desiring that a canoe should be got ready immediately for [the captain] who had been advised by the Coy's lawyer, Mr. Marge, to fly and make the best of his way for Vancouver's Island as he would, in all probability, be [arrested and] liable for all the fines attached to the charges against the Steamer *Beaver*."[7] The very next day, U.S. Marshal Alonzo Poe appeared at the fort's main gate.[8] A futile search for Stuart gave rise to Poe's idle threat that he "intended detaining the Steamer until [Stuart] should make his reappearance."[9] However, the *Beaver* was soon released on payment of duties, while the *Mary Dare* was released on bond—the latter to eventually stand trial for smuggling in an "Admiralty Court." Both vessels were back in the Company's hands by January 25. Details of this incident and Moses's immoderate reaction for apparently minor infractions would, in due time, make their way to high-ranking government officials on both sides of the Atlantic Ocean.

As the business of the seizures was sorted out, news of the ill-fated *Georgiana* expedition involving gold seekers kidnapped on Queen Charlotte Island shocked Olympia's residents. Moses called on Steilacoom Barracks' Captain Bennett Hill for soldiers and Captain Lafayette Balch for the use of his schooner, the *Damariscove*.[10] On December 18, U.S. Army soldiers and heavily armed civilians sailed to Victoria. There, a $1,800 letter of credit (endorsed by Moses) was handed to Douglas who provided merchandise—enough to pay the Indians' ransom demands. The rescue party sailed on Christmas Day 1851 and by the end of January 1852, all of the *Georgiana*'s crew and passengers had been safely recovered.[11] Unfortunately, the gold expedition's misfortune did not impede others' pursuit of riches. Vancouver's John Ballenden later confirmed to HBC Secretary Barclay in London that not a few were moving north due to the "excitement in Nisqually and to the north owing

6 Simon Marge had no need to "proceed to adjudication" against Moses for the Steamer *Beaver* was soon exonerated by a judge and released. The *Mary Dare* remained charged with smuggling, but was allowed to leave on bond.

7 Dickey, ed., *Nisqually Journal*, January 21, 1852.

8 Poe arrived on January 22, 1852, at 1:30 p.m. with a large group of heavily armed men. Huggins, "Reminiscences of Puget Sound," unpublished manuscript July 11, 1901.

9 Dickey, ed., *Nisqually Journal*, January 22, 1852.

10 *Damariscove*. American schooner. Captain Eli Hathoway, skipper; Lafayette Balch, owner/captain; primary cargo—flour, mail, wool, furs, hides in salt, passengers, and dry goods.

11 Perhaps acknowledging the financial assistance afforded him by the Company in the retrieval of the *Georgiana*'s crew and passengers, Moses may have granted the Company some leniency in the case of the *Beaver* and *Mary Dare*, as both incidents occurred simultaneously.

to gold found in Queen Charlotte Island."[12]

Though Tolmie had returned from Vancouver, he had lost the use of his most able senior clerk, Walter P. Ross.[13] On December 22, Ross had ridden out "with the intention of killing cattle," according to the fort's journal. But his "horse (a spirited animal) fell with its whole weight on his leg, and broke it very severely."[14] The compound fractures proved problematic for doctors Tolmie and Haden who did what they could, but Ross would never fully recover from the accident.

Fort life, in many ways, remained unchanged. James Douglas wrote to Governor George Simpson noting that "the business of [Nisqually] is still conducted on the same plan as when it was transferred to the Puget's Sound Company [in 1839], the wages of five men and the Clerk in charge being paid by the Fur Trade, and all other expenses by the Puget's Sound Company."[15] The two companies were kept separate in the books, but in actuality shared personnel, buildings, and land. It was a complicated business arrangement; one that confounded Tolmie's bookkeeping and management skills on a daily basis.

"Of Nisqually I can say very little," remarked Vancouver's John Ballenden to Eden Colvile on March 22. "The fur trade returns are better than those of last year; but the amount of Cash sales there is a considerable reduction, arising from . . . the increased number of store-keepers, & the isolated situation of Nisqually from the settlement at Olympia."[16] The balance of Puget Sound's commercial trade with immigrants had begun to shift decidedly southward. In response, the HBC upscaled their importation of merchandise suitable to the settlers, and fewer items for the Indian trade. Dr. Tolmie juggled both the routine and fluctuating challenges as best he could, all the while pressing his superiors, both close and distant, for a promotion.

In April the doctor finally contracted John Chapman to survey the Company's Nisqually claim. Having laid out Steilacoom City, it remains plausible that Chapman presented himself as the only surveyor in the lower Puget Sound region with the equipment and knowledge capable of completing the enormous task. The contract between the two men (document 5.47 in this work) foreshadowed the possibility that Chapman's crew would not be welcomed by the squatters. On May 12 Tolmie informed Douglas that the surveyor had indeed been rudely cut off and sent packing by a heavily armed party comprised of Lyman A. "Sandy" Smith, Charles Wren, John McLeod, Henry Murray, Thomas Tallentire,[17] and Henry Schmidt/Smith.[18] The gun-toting mob had "made loud threats . . . to annihilate our

12 John Ballenden to Archibald Barclay, February 3, 1852. HBCA B. 225/b/39, 148.

13 Ross, who lived at Tlithlow Farm, was in charge of all the PSAC's outstations at Nisqually.

14 Dickey, ed., *Nisqually Journal*, December 22, 1851.

15 James Douglas to Sir George Simpson, May 8, 1852, HBCA, Correspondence Inwards, B.226/b/6, 71.

16 John Ballenden to Eden Colvile, March 22, 1852, HBCA, Correspondence Inwards, B. 223/b/39, 169.

17 "Tallentire was born in Cumberland County England in 1811. He came to the Oregon country in 1845. He married his wife Agnes in February 1850. Tallentire claimed an entire section of 640 acres in his donation claim. He located on it June 14, 1852. It lay north of Henry John's farm, and east of that of Peter Smith's, one of the earliest voting precincts of the country." Richard D. Osness, *From Wilderness to Suburbia* (Western Media Printing Inc., 1976), 4, 5, 7, 9, 11. Agnes Tallentire was born at Harrisburg, Pennsylvania, in 1820 and crossed the plains in 1847. She settled in the Puget Sound area in 1851. Mrs. Tallentire died at Olympia, April 13, 1876. *Olympia Transcript*, April 15, 1876.

18 A Prussian, Smith (1824–1888) immigrated to North America from the Baltic seaport of Danzig

party if we didn't stop" remembered Huggins.[19] The young clerk knew every one of the squatters, and believed their threats to be genuine, so "the surveying party came home."[20] Within the month, Chapman, Huggins, and the rest of the survey party quietly returned to the field and finished the work without further incident.[21]

Though out of place chronologically, the first letter in this chapter provides a full account of the Olympia customs house seizure of the *Beaver* and *Mary Dare* in early December 1851, thus providing ample context for the remaining documents throughout the latter half of this outfit.

Document 5.01: A letter from William F. Tolmie, Vancouver, to Archibald Barclay, London, December 25, 1851.

Sir,

I have in the present communication the honor to lay before you, for the information of the Govr & Committee, particulars of the seizure of the Steamer Beaver and Brigantine Mary Dare, which was effected at Olympia the Port of Entry for Puget's Sound, on the 1st Inst, by the newly arrived Collector of Customs, on [the] most trivial Grounds as will be shown below.

On the 27th Novr, while I was about in the plains on business, the Steamer Beaver and Brigantine Mary Dare arrived at Nisqually, and Mr. Chief Factor [John] Work, with part of this family and Miss [Rose] Birnie, passenger from England in the Norman Morison, landed and spent the night at the Fort.

Next day as soon as the Steamer was wooded, both vessels proceeded to the Port of Entry (Olympia), Mr. Work and Myself being on board the Steamer, and Miss [Rose] Birnie, Mrs. Work & the children remaining on shore [at the fort], they having merely landed from the Steamer for a Change of wearing apparel.

On Anchoring three Miles below Olympia on the evening of the 28th, the Beaver was boarded by a Mr. Crane who represented himself as Deputy Collector of Customs and, after sealing the hatches and leaving an Inspector on board, proceeded to perform the same duty on board the Mary Dare. Before Mr. Crane left the Steamer, Captain [Charles E.] Stuart distinctly informed him, that some of the Steamer's trade Goods were on board, but there would be nothing to land except Miss Birnie's luggage, and the few things belonging to Mr. Work's family. The Cap-

---

(today's Gdańsk, Poland). Apparently, he transformed from Herr Schmidt to Henry "Harry" Smith following his arrival in Texas circa 1846. Learning the vaquero's trade, he eventually saddled his way north with a herd of Texas longhorns over the Applegate Trail; the trek reportedly landed him on Puget Sound around 1851. Smith took up a donation land claim on Muck Creek in 1852, married Florence of the Nisqually tribe, and was one of those who opposed the HBC/PSAC surveying its claim. He was also arrested by Governor Stevens for alleged collaboration with the Indians during the war in 1855–56. After several more marriages to Indians or métis women, Smith died in 1888 and was buried on his family homestead on Muck Creek.

19 Edward Huggins to Clarence B. Bagley Jr., June 13, 1904, UW Library, Clarence B. Bagley Papers, Fo. 2/4-17, 1903–1907.

20 Dickey, ed., *Nisqually Journal*, May 1, 1852. Tolmie also noted that three-quarters of the work was done.

21 Chapman, John B. "[1852] Plan of the Puget's Sound Agricultural Company's Land Claim at Nisqually Washington Territory," (aka the Tilton Map of 1855); AR255-3-2: Puget Sound Agricultural Company, Map of Possessions at Fort Nisqually 1855–1855; Volume: 0.1.c.f., Archives of Washington State, Olympia.

tain also stated that the Steamer had been sent to Puget's Sound for the purpose of towing the Mary Dare up and down, and that both Vessels were to have a Return Cargo of Live Stock from Nisqually. Desirous of having the Vessels cleared with all possible dispatch, I went to Olympia on the night of the 28th and saw the Collector, Mr. S[impson] P. Moses, to whom I made known the landing of the passengers and other matters necessary for him to be made acquainted with.

On Saturday, the 29th Novr, along with Captains Stuart and [William A.] Mouat, I was early at the Custom House, but as there was then no prospect of Getting business done, Captain Mouat and myself proceeded to Newmarket Saw Mill to purchase deals [boards] Required for the purpose of fitting the Steamer and Brigantine for the transport of livestock, Captain Stuart remaining in the Custom house to assist in Copying out forms.

In the Evening, the Invoice of Mary Dare and other papers were looked over at the Custom house, when some conversation arose as to the Invoice price of our Goods, the Collector Maintaining that duties should be levied on the Goods Valued at the wholesale price of Ft Victoria, with all Charges added, save freight therein, to Nisqually and Insurance; whilst I contended that more than the Quantity of Good in Question had been purchased by the Company in London expressly for Nisqually, and that no fresh sale of said Goods had been made at Victoria, saying more to this same effect which it would be needless now to Repeat.

The conversation was interrupted by the presentation for signatures by the Dep[ut]y Collector of the affidavits preliminary to the Clearance of the Vessels, and it appeared to us that the discussion Respecting the Valuation of Goods had been dropped on the part of the Collector. No sooner however were the affidavits signed, than to our surprise he again broached the subject, which was argued on both sides more fully than ever, and I brought the matter to a Close by stating that desiring Greatly to have the Vessels cleared without further loss of time I would pay, under protest, duties at any Valuation of the Goods he might see fit to make.

In Course of the Evening, Captain Stuart, in making out from memory his manifest of Stores, Stated to Collector Moses, as he had done on the Evening of the 28th to the Dep[u]ty Collector [Mr. Crane], that there were some trade Goods on board the Steamer, and that if necessary, he could go down in his boat and bring back a Correct list of everything, to which the Collector made no Reply, being apparently satisfied that the list handed in fulfilled the Requirements of the law.

On Sunday the 30th Novr there was, of Course, no business transacted, but we indulged in the pleasing anticipation of getting cleared early on Monday and proceeding to Nisqually the same day. We never supposed that any part of our previous proceedings would have involved us with the Custom House authorities, having ourselves made known to Collector Moses at the Outset the Very informalities on account of which he afterwards seized the Beaver, and he when thus appraised, having appeared to Regard them as matters of little [consequence] and to be perfectly satisfied that all our infringements of the strict letter of the law, had arisen solely from ignorance and not in the slightest degree from any desire or endeavor to defraud the [U.S. Department of] Revenue.

On Monday, December 1, fresh causes of delay were started. I was informed that Ready Cash would be Required in payment of the duties, and Custom house officers were sent for Samples of the Crash Sugar forming part of the Mary Dare's Cargo; for Samples of the Steamer's Ballast, she having been Reported by Captain Stuart as in ballast trim, or Void of Cargo. In the afternoon, [we] were informed that Mary Dare was seized for having on board a package of Refined Sugar, weighing less than 600 lbs., under an Act of Congress of March 2nd, 1799, which, for such an offence, subjects both Vessel and Sugar to proper tare. The Beaver, we were told, was seized for having entered in ballast, and having no ballast on board. Mr. Work, Captains Stuart and Mouat & Myself immediately protested against the Collector's unlooked for proceedings and Requested a Statement in writing of his Reasons for the seizure of each Vessel, which he promised to furnish, and on the following day (the 2nd) he gave the necessary information Regarding the Mary Dare in a letter to Captain Mouat, but he deferred, although Repeatedly applied for, doing the same with Regard to the Beaver, until the 11th Decr when a letter to Capt Stuart—dated 2nd—was obtained from him in which he set forth at length the Various fines and penalties said to have been incurred by Captain Stuart. The following is an enumeration of them along with the Amounts of each

Failing to make entry of passengers &c.: $577.10
For proceeding to Nisqually port of delivery before Reporting at the port of Entry: $1,000.00
Delay of 15 hours at Nisqually &c.: $1,000.00
Forfeiture of Trading Goods on board the Steamer & Refusal to [supply] the amount of their Value Manifest of Stores presented by Captain Stuart & Cargo i.e., trade Goods on board: Steamer $577.17

For some days subsequent to the date of the seizure of the Vessels, we were in hopes that the Collector would have Released them as soon as he became satisfied of our ability to furnish the Necessary bond. On 11th Decr, I paid the fees under protest on part of the Mary Dare's Cargo, of which we stood in immediate want, and thereafter hastened with all expedition to this place [Vancouver] and delivered to Chief Factor [John] Ballenden[22] Copies of all the Correspondence Relative to the seizures. I Reported fully to Mr. C[hief] F[actor] Douglas before leaving Nisqually. Measures are now in progress for having the Vessels liberated on bond and [a] trial postponed until Communication shall have been had with the Treasury Department at Washington. I have the honor to be Sir, Your Very Obdt Servant,
(Signed) W. F. Tolmie

Document 5:02: A letter from Simpson P. Moses, Olympia, to William A. Mouat, Brig *Mary Dare*, Port of Olympia, December 2, 1851.[23]

Sir,

I respectfully communicate for your information the following "Statement of Reasons" for the seizure on yesterday, at about 4½ o'clock P.M., of the Brigantine "Mary Dare" commanded by you and now lying at anchor outside of the Bay or

22 For Ballenden see Watson, *Lives Lived*, 1:172.
23 Huntington Library, Soliday Collection, Nisqually Papers, Miscellaneous Documents, FN 1231.

harbor of this Port.

By the papers presented on Entry on the Evening of the 28th Ult of the cargo of the said Brigantine, there appears the following, to wit:

Marks: "N"
N[umbers]: 59
Packages: 1 Cash
Articles: Crashed Sugar
Quantities: 230 lbs.
In Foreign Currency: £2.17.6
30 [% LS.d.]: £2.17.6
Dutiable Value of goods in dollars: $13.92
Rate of Duty: 30 [%]
Amount of duty: $4.17

Crashed (or Crushed, both being the same Articles,) Sugar is regarded by the Government of the United States, as "Refined Sugar" as per Circular of the controller U.S. Treasury Department, Aug 17, 1838, which holds the following language: "Attempts are also made to elude the duty on refined sugar, by reducing it to powder, or crushing it, etc."

And, in further support of which I would state that, on noticing the above items, my suspicion of the character of the said sugar being aroused, I distinctly interrogated whether said sugar was "Refined Sugar," to which you and the consigner, Dr. W[illiam] F. Tolmie, both responded in the affirmative. I then ordered the same to be sampled, and upon examination it proved to be "Refined Sugar", which point being clearly established, and the quantity being distinctly set forth by said paper presented on Entry, on two hundred and thirty pounds of Crashed (or Crushed) Sugar, together with your vessel, became my positive and unquestionable duty [to seize both], as required by the 103 Sec[tion] of the Act of Congress, approved March 2, 1799, Entitled, "An Act to regulate the collection of duties on Imports and Tonnage", the applicable portion of which is as follows:

"Nor shall any refined lump or loaf sugars be imported into the United States, from any foreign port or place, by sea, except in ships or vessels of one hundred and twenty tons burthen, and upwards, and in casks or packages containing, each, not less than six hundred pounds weight; XXXX, on pain of forfeiture of the said refined lump and loaf Sugar, XXXX, imported contrary to the provisions herein described, together with the ship or vessel in which they shall be imported." I am very respectfully yours,

Simpson P. Moses, Collector, Puget's Sound

Document 5.03: A letter from Simpson P. Moses, Olympia, to William F. Tolmie, Nisqually, December 8, 1851.[24]

Sir,

24 UW Library's Tolmie Papers Acc. 4577-001, VO250e, Box #1, Folder #6.

Your expression of dissatisfaction with the Appraisement of your importation per Brigantine "Mary Dare" has been received and duly considered. I have to state that under the circumstances of your expecting that duties would be levied upon the London valuation, which accounts for the prices set forth in the Invoice, I deem it my duty to set aside both the Invoice and Appraisement, and give you an opportunity to avail yourself of the privilege extended by the 8th Section of the Tariff Act of 1840. I am with great respect, Yours,

Simpson P. Moses, Col[lector of Customs]

Document 5.04: A letter from William F. Tolmie, Nisqually, to James Douglas, Victoria, December 9, 1851.

Sir,

I am sorry to inform you that the Steamer Beaver and [brig] Mary Dare were seized by the Customs-house authorities at Olympia on the 28th November for alleged infractions of the Revenue Law. The Collector's reasons for the seizure of the Brig [*Mary Dare*] are given in a letter to Captain [William A.] Mouat, Copy of which is sent herewith but we have failed in obtaining any expression in wording of his reason for detaining the Steamer [*Beaver*] altho' he [Simpson P. Moses] has violated a promise in withholding such a document.

We have delayed informing you sooner of the seizure in the hope of previously ascertaining more satisfactorily in what way the Steamer had become liable and because I had been informed by a person whom the Collector frequently consulted on law matters that there was no hold on the vessel, which would probably be released about the end of last week.

Referring for further particulars regarding the seizures to my communication of Yesterday as well as the reports of Captains Stewart [Stuart] and Mouat[t] all forwarded herewith, I have the honor to be Sir,

(Signed) W. F. Tolmie

P.S.: I now propose proceeding with all despatch to Vancouver to prepare for the approaching trial of the vessels, the date of which is not yet known in this quarter. W. F. Tolmie.

Document 5.05: A declaration by Charles E. Stuart, Steamer Beaver, to U.S. Customs Authorities, Olympia, December 12, 1851.[25]

I, C[harles] E. Stuart, hereby declare in reference to the alleged violation of the United States Revenue laws, where, on the seizure of the Steamer Beaver, and the imposition of certain heavy fines, are grounded, as appears by letter[26] of Collector [Simpson P.] Moses of date 2nd Dec 1851, addressed to me and by me yesterday received, that any dereliction from the said laws has been though ignorance, and

---

25 Charles E. Stuart Declaration, Huntington Library, Soliday Collection, Nisqually Papers, Misc., Documents.

26 This letter has yet to be located.

that throughout my proceedings have been in good faith, without intention to defraud in any way, and without intention of concealment.

I claim indulgence for these alleged acts of omission and commission, upon the grounds of my ignorance, above stated, of the law or laws which I may unwittingly have violated; requesting special attention to the fact that I have fallen into them entirely through that ignorance arising from the absence of Broker, or Agents, properly qualified, as in larger Ports of Entry, to conduct the minutia of Customs House clearance and entry.

In support of this statement I beg reference to my official report of [James] Douglas, Esq, Chief Factor of the Hudson's Bay Co, connected with the matter in question.

Dated on board the Steam Vessel "Beaver" this 12th day of December, in the year of our Lord one thousand eight hundred and fifty one.

[Signed] C. E. Stuart

Document 5.06: A letter from James Douglas, Victoria, to William F. Tolmie, Nisqually, December 17, 1851.[27]

My dear Sir,

The tidings by [François] Coté arrived here in due time.

The detention of our two ships is a most serious affair to us, and will put the business to serious loss and derangement. It is much regretted that any handle was given to our enemies by the landing of passengers before entry, or by having the steamer's manifest of stores incomplete. These are irregularities but should not account to the forfeiture of a ship and cargo, though Mr. [Simpson P.] Moses appears determined to make the most of them. Such conduct in a public officer is scandalous, as he is invested with a dangerous power over the property of others, which it is supposed will be excercized in wisdom and moderation.

I long to hear the result of your journey to Oregon City, and trust it had terminated satisfactorily so far as the vessels are concerned. I regret that [Captain Charles E.] Stuart did not turn the Beaver's head towards Victoria, instead of running her nearer the lion's den after the seizure. That could have cut the Gordian Knot[28] and saved a world of trouble and expense: Jonathan doubtless smiles at our simplicity. A few dollars to [Deputy Collector Elwood] Evans for advice and correcting the papers might have enabled us to rush the vessel through the Custom House without a word said. Such people must be conciliated. I have written [Chief Trader John] Work by this conveyance, and leave you and him to arrange all matters for the best. I have addressed the Committee relative to the seizures, and sent home copies of your report just as it was written, as I saw nothing to amend; Stuart's [letter] has been slightly amended. I am well nigh worked off my legs. Referring you to friend [John] Work, Yours sincerely,

---

27 UW Library's Tolmie Papers Acc. 4577-001, Box #2, Folder #3—N.979.514, D74 1 #119.

28 This is a reference to a knot in Greek mythology—a knot which has no ends with which to untie it. Typically, the puzzle is solved by cheating—i.e., cutting it with a blade.

James Douglas

Document 5.07: A letter from John Work, Nisqually, to William F. Tolmie, Vancouver, December 23, 1851.[29]

Dear Sir,

The Indians who went to Victoria with the Express and papers relative to the seizure of the vessels returned this morning bringing dispatches from Mr. [James] Douglas for England and other letters which are now forwarded without delay.

Mr. Douglas recommends me to write home also giving an account of all that has taken place relative to the seizure of the vessels since the letters were sent off to him on the subject. This is unnecessary and would cause a needless expense, for by the arrangements before you left, you were to write home and give the Company a full account of everything that has occurred. This I would strongly recommend you by no means to omit, and also to send copies of all the transactions and correspondence, also even the opinion of your Counsel and any other information you may collect. I shall address a few lines to Mr. [Archibald] Barclay stating my reason for not attending to Mr. Douglas's suggestion.

Captain [Charles E.] Stuart is now here [at Nisqually] for a supply of provisions. In regard to the vessels, everything remains as when you left, no change has taken place whatever except frequent shifts of the officers kept on board the steamer who are mostly strangers, the old ones having nearly all gone off on the Expedition to Queen Charlotte's Island to relieve the shipwrecked people there.

Perhaps it would be necessary for you to engage two or even more able lawyers so that should one require to accompany you here, the other might watch affairs elsewhere, and perhaps both be needed to plead, but of this you must be the best judge.

A strict judge shall be kept here and should anything occur needful for you to know it shall be communicated without delay.

Pray endeavor to get the law books we talked of before you left, they may be useful on future occasions of vessels coming here and be a guide how to proceed and save much trouble.

Should you have occasion to make any communication to Capt Stuart or [William A.] Mowat it might be well for it to come direct here as if sent by post it might be sent here from Olympia for delay. A newspaper addressed to Mowat from England was brought here the other day [by] the postman from Olympia the other day when it might as well have been sent on board the ship to him. With best wishes, I am dear Sir, Yours very truly,

(S[igne]d) John Work

Document 5.08: A letter from John Work, Nisqually, to Archibald Barclay, London, December 23, 1851.[30]

Sir,

---

29 UW Library's John Work Papers, Accession #4981-001, Box #1, Folder—Outgoing Letters, 1848–1862.

30 HBCA: folio A11/49. Received in London, March 1, 1852.

Dispatches have first arrived from Fort Victoria from Mr. [James] Douglas to your address relative to the seizure of the "Mary Dare" and "Steamer Beaver" which I forward to Fort Vancouver without delay.

Mr. Douglas suggests to me to write for the information of the Hon[oura]ble Board of Directors on account of the occurrences since the letters on the subject were sent off to Victoria. This is unnecessary, as by arrangements with Mr. [William F.] Tolmie—who is now in the Columbia for the purpose of retaining lawyers and taking such steps as may seem necessary—is to send you a full account of the whole affair.[31] Everything remains as when Mr. Tolmie left waiting the decision of the US Judicial Authorities of the Territory.

In the meantime, a look out is being kept here and, should anything take place to require it, I will not fail to write without delay for the information of the Hon[oura]ble Board of Directors. I am Sir, Respectfully, Your Obedt Servant,

John Work.

[P.S.] Paper [is] very Scarce.

Document 5.09: A letter from James Douglas, Victoria, to William F. Tolmie, Nisqually, December 27, 1851.[32]

Dear Sir,

In my last communication, I omitted to acknowledge the receipt of your letter of the 17th Nov, to which I will now reply. The arrangement proposed with the [John] Ross family relative to the return of half the number of cattle they received from the Company, is satisfactory and judicious.

I am very sorry to hear that the Company's old and faithful servant, Charles Forrest, has departed this life, and I wish to be informed if he has made any testamentary disposition of his purport with reference to his daughter [Annie Forrest] at this place.

I am most anxious to hear what has been the result of your journey to the Columbia. The detention of our vessels at Nisqually will put the Company to a frightful expense and amount of inconvenience. The proceedings of Mr. [Simpson P.] Moses, in reference to the vessels, are vigourous in the extreme, in as much as there was no intention to defraud the revenue, but still it must be admitted that our own proceedings have not been so prudent and circumspect as they might have been, and have furnished the pretext of which he is now making so unmerciful a use. It was folly in [Captain Charles E.] Stuart to allow his passengers to land at Nisqually or even to stop there for the purpose of cutting wood, any other point on the communication would have been less objectionable.

Again, why did [Captain] Stuart keep any goods in the trade room of the steamer [*Beaver*], and why having such goods did he not make a correct post entry of them as return cargo, which may be done by a master at the cost of two dollars even after the entry of vessels in all cases when there are more goods found on board a vessel than the master thereof has reported? Explanations will not always answer to remove suspicion nor to establish rectitude of intention, it is always bet-

31 Tolmie's report is the first document of this chapter.

32 UW Library's Tolmie Papers Acc. 4577-001, Box #2, Folder #3.

ter to conform on all points of the law.

The Damariscove left this port for Queen Charlotte's Island on the 25th inst. Lieut [John] Dement was received with every attention here. He produced his instructions from Captain [Bennett H.] Hill and Mr. [Simpson P.] Moses's letter of credit, on which I thought it best to advance the goods necessary for the ransom of the Queen Charlotte's Island captives, which came to $1,838.91.

We took Mr. Dement's bill in triplicate on the collector, the first of which, with a certified invoice, are now forwarded for settlement. Seconds of the bill and invoice will be forwarded for better security by [an]other conveyance. That account should be presented to Mr. Moses for immediate settlement,[33] and you will please to advise us of the payment. With best wishes, My dear Sir, Yours truly,

James Douglas

Document 5.10: A letter from John Work, Nisqually, to Archibald Barclay, London, January 11, 1852.[34]

Sir,

Late last night, dispatches were received from Fort Victoria announcing the total loss of the Company's Brigantine "Una" which I now forward to Vancouver without delay.

In regard to the "Mary Dare" and Steamer "Beaver" under seizure here by the Custom house Officers, no change whatever has taken place since I had the honor of addressing you on the 23rd Ultimo. It seems the Whole matter is now Out of the hands of the Collector and transferred to the Judicial Authorities of the Territory. On the 29th Decr I received a letter from Dr. Tolmie dated on the 24th. He was then endeavoring to get the Judge ([William] Strong),[35] Lawyers, and Marshal assembled at the Judge's residence, and in hopes that the trial of the Vessels would be put off 'till the May term, and the vessels be released on bond, and that there would thus be time to have the matter referred to the Treasury Department at Washington [D.C.]. But no doubt Mr. Tolmie will have already informed you of all these particulars.

My not having heard from the Columbia since that date is probably owing to the almost impassable State of the Cowlitz Portage on account of the height of the rivers

---

33 James Douglas's demand for "immediate settlement" of the expedition's expenses illustrates his growing suspicion that the bill would not get paid quickly, or ever by Collector Moses—the letter of credit's issuer. Unfortunately, the chief factor's intuition would ultimately prove correct.

34 HBCA: folio A11/49. Received in London, March 1, 1852.

35 A native of St. Albans, Vermont, Strong (1817–1927) was educated at York College and became principal of an academy at Ithaca, New York. While following this occupation he studied law, moving to Cleveland, Ohio, in the meantime. In 1849 President Zachary Taylor offered Strong a three-year appointment to serve as one of the first three justices of the U.S. Supreme Court in the new Oregon Territory, a district that spread north from the lower Columbia River to the Canadian border, and from the Pacific Ocean east to the Rocky Mountains. He took passage on the United States Store ship *Supply* in November 1849, for San Francisco, and then proceeded to the Columbia by the sloop of war *Falmouth*. Judge Strong resided for a few years on the north side of the Columbia, but finally made his home in Portland. Additional reading: Harry McElroy Strong, *A Pioneer Judge & His Family in the Oregon/Washington Territories* ([Seattle?], 2001), and Hubert Howe Bancroft, *History of Oregon* (San Francisco, The History Company, 1888), 2:102.

caused by heavy rains. I have the honour to be, Sir, very respectfully, Your Obedt Servt,
John Work

Document 5.11: A notification from Simon B. Marge, Olympia, to Simpson P. Moses, Olympia, January 21, 1852.[36]

Sir,

You are hereby notified that at 10 O'c[lock] on the 22nd [of January] or as soon thereafter as I can be [notified], I shall move the Hon[orable] Dist[rict] Court of the United States for the District of Puget Sound, District of Oregon, to compel you to proceed to adjudication, or to abandon the seizure of the British Steamer Beaver, seized by you on the 1st Dec 1851, as Collector of said Port, which said Steamer of the Hudson's Bay Company as owner. [I remain, &c., &c.,]

Simon B. Marge, Attorney for Hudson's Bay Co

Document 5.12: A letter (extract) from William F. Tolmie, Nisqually, to John Ballenden, Vancouver, January 23, 1852.[37]

Sir,

I am happy to inform you that the Steamer Beaver with the [brig] Mary Dare in tow will proceed to Nisqually tomorrow, when the Admiralty Court held by Judge [William] Strong will adjourn.

The Beaver has been declared by the Judge in court not to be liable for the fine and penalties said to have been incurred by her Captain (Stuart), and Mr. Marge, the Company's attorney is clearly of opinion that Collector Moses can be prosecuted for damages for unlawfully seizure of the Steamer both personally and through his sureties in the United States who are pledged in his behalf to the amount it is supposed of one hundred thousand dollars. Captain [Charles E.] Stuart, by the advice of Mr. [Simon B.] Marge, started for Victoria on the eve of his intended arrest, so that the various suits to have been entered against him must be postponed until his reappearance at Olympia.

The trade goods found on board the Steamer have been seized by the Deputy Marshall and released in a bond for twice their appraised value, namely in the sum of Thirteen Hundred and Eighty Two 56/100 Dollars. Mr. Marge is of opinion in this matter that should said goods be forfeited the Coy will only be answerable for the amount of their appraised value as Six Hundred and ninety One 28/100 dollars and not for the penalties which, in case of condemnation, would have been imposed on the Captain, if within reach. The appraisement was, on most articles . . . [*rest of letter not entered in letterbook.*]

Document 5.13: A letter from William F. Tolmie, Nisqually, to James Douglas, Victoria, January 29, 1852.

36 Huntington Library, Soliday Collection, Nisqually Papers, Misc Documents.

37 For Ballenden see Watson, *Lives Lived*, 1:172.

Sir,

Mr. C[hief] F[actor John] Work having written you fully regarding the Coy's vessels here, and on matters relative to their seizure, I shall not at present address you thereanent.

I hope today or tomorrow to dispose of from two to three hundred Wedders for cash at $5. each to Captain [Albion Butler] Gove of the Brig "G[eorge] W[ilkins] Kendall."

We cannot hope to keep Squatters any longer off the Sequalitchew mill privilege unless by improving it ourselves. Yesterday, when at the entrance of the stream, I found two Americans just about to commence operations as settlers there. They said that various persons spoke of building a mill there, and that they wished to be first, but that of course, if I seriously intend building, they would desist.

I enclose duplicate of the late C[harles] Forrest's Will.[38] I have had my copy proved at the County Clerk's office, and have taken oaths as administrator.

An account against Capt [James] Cooper [of the schooner *Alice Douglas*][39] for Coy is sent herewith. Hoping to write more fully by next opportunity, I remain, Sir,

(Signed) W. F. Tolmie

P.S. [James] Goudie's horses are sent by [Captain] Cooper who charges 7 dollars for full grown ones and five dollars for yearlings, he wishes to class[ify] 2 year olds as large but ought to be satisfied with 4 dollars for such on account against Goudie for various expenses incurred for feeding, getting in, shipping, & foddering his horses on board the Alice, is sent P[uget] S[ound] A[ssociation] Herewith. T

Document 5.14: A private letter from William F. Tolmie, Nisqually, to George Simpson, Lachine, January 29, 1852.[40]

My dear Sir,

You will learn all that has transpired in the matter of the "seizures", since I had the honor to address you under private cover on the 31st Decr, from a copy of Mr. C[hief] F[actor John] Work's letter of this date to Mr. Sec[retar]y [Archibald] Barclay and the various documents accompanying it, all of which are forwarded herewith.

Owing to a continuance of the delays which, under one form or another, had so long hampered our endeavors to affect the release of the vessels, it was the 19th January before the parties concerned were all assembled at Olympia and on the 20th the Admiralty Court met. The Mary Dare's case was soon disposed of, the opposing parties agreeing regarding the "Crash Sugar" in every important particular, and Judge [William] Strong decided that the Steamer [*Beaver*] was in no manner liable for the penalties said to have been incurred by Captain [Charles E.] Stuart. This we had been prepared to expect, but its announcement from the bench proved very

38 Charles Forrest's will was not included in this work.

39 *Alice Douglas*, British schooner skippered by Captain James Cooper. Primary cargo: cattle and other livestock.

40 HBCA, Governor George Simpson Loose Inward Correspondence, Jan–Feb 1852, D.5/33 file 1. [After an inquiry regarding a missing page, on June 19, 2015, HBCA Archivist Holly McElrea emailed the editor: "I found the letter that you are looking for and you are, in fact, missing two pages." Those have been included in this transcription.]

satisfactory to us and as much the contrary to the landsharks of the Customhouse.

The Coy's attorney, Mr. S[imon] B. Marge, put a stop to further proceedings for the time being by a recommendation which Mr. [John] Work and myself, after some deliberation, sanctioned; namely that Captain [Charles E.] Stuart should immediately go beyond the jurisdiction of the Admiralty Court, an advice promptly acted upon and which spared us much additional expense, vexation and delay entailable by the investigation of each of the trifling and frivolous, yet undeniable, charges prepared against Stuart, and the consequent petitioning of the Treasury Department for a remission or mitigation of each of the penalties incurred.

I beg your particular attention to the copy herewith of Mr. Marge's letter to me of the 24th Inst wherein the legal proceedings &c., are stated in detail as well as Mr. Marge's opinion on various matters of interest connected with the Seizures.

Moses, I learn, is now apprehensive that his conduct towards us may be disapproved of at Washington [D.C.] and the Deputy Collector [Elwood] Evans has just started ostensibly for California, but with the intention, I am credibly informed, of going to Washington [D.C.] to justify as best he can, the outrageous conduct of his superior.[41] Elwood Evans is a young lawyer of considerable volubility [ability to talk endlessly], but not possessed of much discretion, nor is he over-scrupulous. Being better versed in legal matters than the Collector—also a soi-disant [self-professed] Attorney, [Evans] had great influence over the latter, I think, in urging him, reckless of remote consequences, to the extreme measures adopted against us. Tis not unlikely but that he may damage rather than benefit the cause he goes to advocate; still it would be well to have his proceedings at Washington [D.C.] noticed by someone in the Company's interest who might, if necessary, exercise a counteracting influence.

Simpson P. Moses is rather a weak and a very vain and ambitious man. Having ~~of late~~ been a resident in Washington [D.C.], while the late [Samuel] Thurston was there, he associated much with that defunct demagogue, and consequently became thoroughly indoctrinated with the belief that unmeasured hostility to the Hudson's Bay Company was the certain passport to Fame and popularity in Oregon. On arriving in the country, he therefore seized the first opportunity of recommending himself to the anti-Hudson's Bay party, and he reckoned on universal support when he seized our vessels in Decr last. Great, however, was his disappointment on finding that the more respectable and better informed citizens disapproved of his proceedings from the first. He was, and is still tho to a smaller extent, surrounded by a clique of hangers-on, Inspectors of Customs, &c., who, while enjoying his Brandy & cigars, buoy him up with hopes of being the next Delegate to Congress, and who hoped to have shared the plunder ~~with~~ had our vessels been condemned. Moses, soon after the seizures, bet so confident that the Mary Dare would soon be condemned and sold—as the Albion was—that he made overtures to [Captain William A.] Mouat to command her thereafter in an expedition to Queen Char-

41 In 1852 Evans made it to Washington, D.C., and there spoke in favor of dividing the Oregon Territory. On March 2, 1853, President Fillmore signed the bill creating the Territory of Washington. The newly appointed governor of the territory, Isaac I. Stevens, was commissioned to survey the country between St. Paul, Minnesota, to the Pacific Coast for the contemplated northern railroad route. He chose Evans as one of his civil aides for the expedition. Among Evans' duties was to keep notes of the activity of the survey party. MacEachern, "Elwood Evans, Lawyer-Historian."

lotte's Island. [Simpson P.] Moses will never prove, I fear, a man whose honorable intentions in office can be depended on and I shall be particularly on my guard in all future transactions with him. He attempted at the outset to levy duties on the Mary Dare's cargo valued at from 90 to over 100 p[e]r cent above prime cost, and I then paid, under protest, duties at this high valuation on a few articles we were immediately in want of. but, after the setting of the Admiralty Court, when Moses was dejected at the ill success of his machinations, and perhaps fearful of consequences, it was agreed, Mr. [John] Work and [Simon B.] Marge approving, that provided my protest should be withdrawn, the previous payment should be refunded and the whole Invoice entered at an advance of 50 p[e]r cent on prime cost.

It is still a great hardship having to pay fifty per cent of higher duties on importations here than is exacted at Astoria or elsewhere throughout the United States, and it is of importance to ascertain the easiest mode of avoiding this additional import. I would respectfully suggest therefore that enquiry be made at the Treasury Department Washington [D.C.], whether our object could not be gained by having the goods intended for Nisqually packed and marked separately in London and accompanied by a distinct invoice which should state their destination and bear the American Consul's certificate as to the correctness of its prices. The said goods might, if allowable, be landed at Victoria in a bonded warehouse or, otherwise, be transshipped on arrival into a vessel bound for Nisqually. I have not obtained any satisfactory information on this subject from Moses who would much prefer for his own convenience that a vessel came direct from England with our supplies, neither could I find in Gordon's Digest of the U.S. Revenue Laws[42] anything precisely applicable to our case. Perhaps, Mr. Sec[retar]y Corwin may have to write specially on this matter to the Collector of Customs here.

Olympia is the most inconvenient spot that could have been selected as the port of entry for the Puget's Sound (Custom's) district it being at the head of ship navigation and likewise, because ~~as~~ no vessel can be within two miles of the Customhouse without grounding at low water. There is no excuse now on the plea of want of protection and labor elsewhere, for the continuance of the port of entry there, as a settlement has recently been formed at Port Townsend the most suitable station on the Sound for a port of entry. Nisqually, being the only point where foreign importations are made will, I trust, remain a port of delivery, in fact a change in this respect would be grossly unjust towards the Coy, yet some people in this neighborhood are endeavoring, I understand, to bring it about.

I have invariably made it a rule here to avoid mixing myself up with any of the political squabbles or maneuvering of the neighboring citizens and, while firmly standing up on all occasions for the Puget's Sound Company's rights, I have had to restrain as much as possible personal ill-feeling even toward the most troublesome of the squatters, and many have been the proofs afforded of the beneficial effects of this mode of proceeding, which I shall, in an especial manner endeavor to carry through with regard to Moses who, from his situation, has the power either greatly to annoy or accommodate us as inclination may prompt. I have some hopes of yet persuading him to allow of our Captains to report from this instead of taking their vessels to Olympia, by which an average delay of six days would be saved. Still,

42 This is a reference to T. F. Gordon, *Gordon's Digest of the Revenue Laws of the United States* (Philadelphia, 1850).

as should Moses concede this favor, its continuance will depend on his good will and pleasure, t'would be advisable, I think, to endeavor to have the Port of Entry removed to Port Townsend forthwith, a change which must commend itself to every impartial person cognizant of the circumstances.

The Steamer and Mary Dare are now here and will proceed in a few days to Victoria with cargoes of Cattle and sheep.

The Puget's Sound Company's affairs go on much as usual, fresh encroachments are being made from time to time on the Company's lands and last summer we had a valuable stud horse shot by one of the Squatters whose horses he disturbed, but having no legal proof we could not obtain compensation for the loss. Another of the squatters branded a filly belonging to the Coy, but was obliged to return it and pay the costs of a suit before a J[ustice of the] P[eace] Court. When at Oregon City lately, I saw the Surveyor General Mr. [John B.] Preston, and by his advice, am to get the Company's boundary lines run out by a Surveyor in the course of the Spring. The citizens are now beginning to canvas the propriety of petitioning Congress to buy the PS [Agricultural] Coy out in this quarter. Many enquiries were made of me when at the Columbia as to the price of sheep here and the facilities of shipping them to California, and since returning home I have sold 250 Wedders and wedder lambs for five dollars each to the Captain of a brig bound for San Francisco. There will probably be further demand in course of the season and perhaps for brood Ewes as well as for Wedders.

In the Accounts of 1850, a D[ebenture] Balance of £1290 is made to appear against Ft Nisqually, but when at Vancouver lately I discovered that the place had been short credited £1014 on cash sent to Victoria during the outfit. Moreover, a charge of £400 was made against Nisqually at Vancouver for freight from Victoria P[e]r Cadboro, when under the circumstances a charge of £100 would have been amply sufficient. The Fur Returns of 1851 at this post far exceed those of the preceding year.

It would be advizable, I think, for the Company both on Puget's Sound and the Columbia River to aim at making their business a wholesale one, by which in present times they would have larger returns, and which, in the event of being purchased out by the US government they could carry on thereafter from a large depot at the most eligible point in each district. Since Oregon City and Portland have grown into importance, Vancouver seems very much out of the way. If an Agency were established in California which I think is very desirable, goods could be exchanged for such produce as generally commands a ready sale at San Francisco. Such an Agency should, in my opinion, be managed by one or more commissioned officers and it would, in time, prove very advantageous to our business North of Lat. 49°.

I have just been suggesting to my worthy father-in-law, Mr. [John] Work. to get a [barrel] Cooper for Ft Simpson, and employ him in making firkins and small kegs of different sizes wherein to salt the Nass River Oolahans[43] From the enqui-

43 Today Oolahan is commonly spelled "eulachon" in English and more commonly called the "candlefish." It had high trade value due to its natural oil (or grease). The Western Cree language does not have an 'L' sound, so the Cree substitute an 'R' making the word sound more like "oorichan" or "ourigan." It is interesting to speculate that this is the word that English speakers adopted as the name of the entire Oregon Country. Source: Mirjam Hirch, "The Canadian Studies International Interdisciplinary Conference Across Time and Space, Visions of Canada from Abroad," lecture given at the University College of the Cariboo, Kamloops, British Columbia, September 12–14, 2003. For more

ries made of me in the Columbia River, I am persuaded that Oolahans nicely put up would form a valuable article of export.

The Americans in this neighborhood seem very curious to Know whether the British Government will use measure to prevent their seeking gold on Queen Charlotte's Island, and my reply when asked usually is that Great Britain will not in that instance depart from the Free Trade policy so fully adopted in other matters. I may be wrong in this supposition yet it would probably fare ill with British subjects mining in California, were greater restrictions placed on Americans than on Britons digging gold on Queen Charlotte's Island. Neither, in such a case, would the position of HBC officers in Oregon be more agreeable and even as things are, most of them have trouble and vexation enough.

There is quite an excitement regarding Q[ueen] C[harlotte] I[sland] gold in this part of the country at present. To such a height has it got that some Americans, who were shipwrecked on the island in Novr [18]51, and have but recently returned from a two-month captivity amongst the Indians talk of returning thither by the first opportunity. Should gold prove abundant on the island, the Company will, I trust, reap a rich harvest.

With regard to my private affairs, in which I am pleased to think you take an interest, I am now the father of a stout boy who, along with this mother, enjoy good health. Master Alick is now ten months old. I have a farm in process of improvements on Vancouver's Island where, should the Colony prosper, I mean, when rich enough to retire some day. Meantime, while in the service, I hope to do some more good for the Company and myself and as promotion is about to reach some of my own standing as traders and my juniors as regards benefit of service, I trust that my own turn for the second step may be near at hand.

Desiring to be respectfully remembered to Lady Simpson, I remain My dear Sir George, Very faithfully Your's,

William Fraser Tolmie[44]

Document 5.15: A letter from John Work, Nisqually, to George Simpson, Lachine, January 29, 1852.

Sir,

Herewith I have the honor to forward to your address [a] Copy of a letter to Mr. Secretary [Archibald] Barclay and copies of the accompanying documents which contain all the proceedings relative to the seizure of the Company's Vessels the Mary Dare and Steamer Beaver and then liberated since Mr. [William] Tolmie's return from the Columbia. Doctor Tolmie's dispatches from the Columbia will have informed you of all the previous proceedings in this vexatious and unjustifiable transaction.

Doctor Tolmie, being the consignee and agent, has been the Acting man all through and everything was done in his name, I fully concurred with him in

---

see www.cwis.org/document/the-pacific-northwest-oolichan-oil-project.

44 At the end of this letter is noted the following: "Viz 1852, Nisqually 29 January, William F. Tolmie; Rec'd 2 April, Ans[were]d 29 May."

every step taken. I would beg leave to direct your attention to Mr. Marge's letter to Mr. Tolmie.[45]

(Signed) John Work

Document 5.16: A letter from John Work, Nisqually, to Archibald Barclay, London, January 29, 1852.[46]

Sir,

The dispatches forwarded to your address from the Columbia previous to Dr. [William F.] Tolmie's leaving that place will have informed you of the particulars relative to the seizure of the Company's two vessels the "Mary Dare" and "Steamer Beaver" by Mr. [Simpson P.] Moses, the Collector of Customs at this place, on the first of December last, and the reasons assigned for such seizure being made and other particulars relative to the transaction up to that time.

Mr. [William F.] Tolmie returned here from the Columbia late on Saturday 17th Inst. Judge Strong, Mr. [Simon B.] Marge—the Company's att[orne]y, and Mr. Sagun, the U.S. District Att[orne]y who accompanied him across the Cowlitz Portage having gone on direct to Olympia.

On Monday the 19th Mr. [William F.] Tolmie and I proceeded to that place. [During] the succeeding days, the Court sat and the Company's case relative to the seizure of the Vessels brought before it. The result of the proceedings are in regard to the "Mary Dare", against which no other charge was brought but that first preferred that of having a cask of Crash Sugar on board of less weight than that prescribed by law. She had already been bonded at the Columbia, a petition of facts was now presented to and accepted by the Hon[ora]ble Judge Strong, by him to be forwarded to the Secretary of the Treasury for his consideration, and the vessel is now released.

In respect to the "Steamer Beaver" it was sought to attach to her the penalties incurred by Captain [Charles E.] Stuart's inadvertent omission in regard to his Stores, passengers, &c. In this they were stopped short, there being no law for such a proceeding. Now, had they ever any right to seize or detain the Steamer, the proceedings towards her are illegal. As to the penalties charged against Captain [Charles E.] Stuart for his omissions, he would no doubt have been condemned in court. Appealing to the Treasury Department at Washington [D.C.] would have been a vexatious and tedious proceeding and attended with heavy law expenses in order to avoid which Mr. [Simon B.] Marge recommended Captain [Charles E.] Stuart's going beyond the jurisdiction of the Court which he did. He was pursued but they did not overtake him.

Thus, this part of the plunder which they were making themselves sure of, they have lost, as the Captain only is accountable for the penalties. Thus, after all their machinations and planning to plunder the Company of their property, the trade goods on board the Steamer—Amounting to about £130—are all that is left for them likely to succeed in. These are most likely to be condemned in court, but in

---

45 Mr. Marge's letter not found.

46 HBCA Correspondence Inwards, folio A11/49.

this case also there is an appeal to the Treasury at Washington [D.C.] should the Hon[oura]ble Board of directors deem such a step necessary. In order to avoid the heavy expense of Storage, these goods have been taken back and a bond given for them at the custom house appraised valuation which is not high.

Herewith are forwarded copies of all the papers relating to the proceedings which will give you the particulars in detail viz.,

U.S. vs. Mary Dare
U.S. vs. Cargo of Steamer Beaver
U.S. vs. Cargo of Steamer Beaver
U.S. vs. Charles Edward Stuart
U.S. vs. Cargo of Steamer Beaver—Petition of Claimant & affidavit
U.S. vs. Cargo of Steamer Beaver—Motion to Compel Collector to proceed
U.S. vs. The Cargo of Steamer Beaver—Bond
Invoice of goods pl[e]r Steamer Beaver, with Account of Articles missing
Notice to S[impson] P. Moses
Letter Simon B. Marge to W[illiam] F. Tolmie, Jany 24th, 1852
Mary Dare Sibel [sic]

I would beg have to direct attention to Mr. [Simon B.] Marge's letter. I have no means here to enable us to form an estimate of the damages sustained by the Company by the loss of time and great derangement of the business arising from the unwarrantable detention of the vessels—particularly the Steamer; but I have written to Mr. Douglas on the subject and have no doubt estimates will be prepared and transmitted to you by the earliest opportunity. Our firm belief is that all along from the commencement of this affair their object has been by the slightest infringement of the law or any pretext they could lay hold of to plunder the Company of their property. Witness the frivolity of most of the Charges against the Steamer. The passengers, for instance, who consisted of Myself, my Wife, a daughter 17 Years of age, two boys and a girl from 7 to 2 ½ years of age, I brought them here with the intention of returning immediately and expected to be absent from Victoria not over 8 or 10 days; and Miss [Rose] Bernie, who was going to [visit] her brother in the Columbia [at Cathlamet]. When they landed only a change of dress was taken. Everything else they had, even the bedding, was left on board so that there was not the slightest pretext for any intention of fraud on the Revenue. I sincerely hope the Honourable Board of directors will sanction their being prosecuted to the utmost extent for the damages sustained. So far as the Steamer is concerned, the case should be tried at the next District court which commences on the fourth Monday in May next.

The Collector [Simpson P. Moses] at first claimed to levy the duties on the Sale prices at Victoria the last port from which the goods were shipped. In order to avoid delay and get off the vessels, and also to avoid having the goods landed and appraised which would have incurred a heavy expense and much injury to the property, it has been deemed advisable to pay duties on 50 p[e]r Cent on the prime cost, which we consider most unjust. These goods were neither bought, sold, or made at Victoria and should have been considered as transshipment. Surely the Treasury Department at Washington [D.C.] would redress this injustice were they applied to by our Ministers.

Duplicates of this letter and of these papers are now forwarded addressed to Sir George Simpson lest he might see a pressing occasion to act upon them before receiving Advice from London.

It will be observed in Mr. [Simon B.] Marge's letter to Mr. [William F.] Tolmie that that Gentleman recommends the petition relative to the Mary Dare and other papers to be addressed directly to the Secretary of the Treasury and the British Minister at Washington [D.C.], but there being no means of attaining evidence or estimates of the damages here, We have deferred doing so for the present, but they will no doubt be forwarded from Victoria immediately after I return there, which I expect will be in a few days.

Mr. [William F.] Tolmie was the consignee of the Mary Dare's cargo and, being the Agent and everything transacted in his name through this tedious and vexatious affair, I have fully coincided with him in opinion in every step taken. I have the honour to be, Sir with much deference, Your Obedt Servant,

John Work

P.S. Since the above was written an estimate of the Mary Dare's Monthly expenses and damages and loss sustained by the detention of the vessel, has been received from Fort Victoria which is enclosed with the other papers. J.W.

Document 5.17: A Certificate of Imported Goods by William W. Miller, Port of Nisqually, February 5, 1852.[47]

I certify that W[illiam] F. Tolmie imported in to the District on the 28 November 1851 in the Brigantine Mary Dare of London, W[illiam] A. Mouat, Master, from Victoria, Vancouver's Island, to wit; [18]52

N#	31/33	3 Cases	ea[ch]	Congo	Tea
	34/36	3 do	do	Hyson	do
	37/39	3 do	do	Twankey	do

Which Cases have been marked as follows H.C.M. Containing Tea according to returns made to this Office [and] Given under my hand and Seal of office this 5th day February 1852.

William W. Miller, [Sincerely] &c., Nasqually

Document 5.18: A letter from William F. Tolmie, Nisqually, to Simpson P. Moses, Olympia, February 5, 1852.

Dear Sir,

As the Steamer [*Beaver*] and Mary Dare will, I hope, have their cargo on board tomorrow, Captains [Willliam A.] Mouat[t] and [John] Swanson now proceed to the Custom House for their clearances & which, I will feel greatly obliged by your processing as soon as convenient.

Having gone to considerable expense in fitting up the two vessels for the transport of Cattle &c., I would like that the vessels one, or both, should make another

47 BC Archives, MS-0557, Box 1, File 1, A/C/40/B54. Miller's header on this certificate reads: "District of Puget's Sound, Inspector's Office, Port Nasqually."

trip before clearing away the deck pens &c., prepare for the livestock. I have therefore to enquire whether in the event of one or both ships coming, you could allow of their reporting from this place. It being at the expense of bringing the proper officer down from Olympia to enter them—also whether it would make any difference provided the proposal made be admissible, whether the vessels came with cargo on board or in ballast trim. One or both Captains as the case might be, or as you might see fit to direct, would proceed with all despatch to Olympia to report &c., and, my word for it, nothing either animate or inanimate should land from the vessel 'till permitted by the officer appointed to enter them. I learn from experienced persons that the average trip of a sailing vessel from the Narrows to Olympia, and back is six days, and that loss of time, provided the *Mary Dare* came along, which is most probable, would at this season of the year be a serious consideration to us.

Hoping that the proposed arrangement may suit your views, and requesting an immediate reply in order that I may be enabled to write on the subject to Govr [James] Douglas forthwith. I am &c.,

(Signed) W. F. Tolmie

Document 5.19: A letter from William F. Tolmie, Nisqually, to James Douglas, Victoria, February 5, 1852.

Sir,

I had the honor to receive on the 31st Ulto your communication of the 8th accompanying Statement of the Mary Dare's monthly expenses &c., which will be forwarded forthwith to Mr. C[hief] F[actor John] Ballenden, to whom I will suggest the prospect of getting affidavits from disinterested persons as to the correctness of said statement, and estimates.

The Steamer [*Beaver*] and Mary Dare will leave tomorrow with full cargoes of Livestock, accounts of which will be forwarded herewith.

[February] 6th

If either or both vessels were sent back for cattle, I think we could in a short time put a good many on board. I have written Mr. [Simpson P.] Moses to ascertain whether he could not dispense with the vessels going to Olympia, either with Cargo, or in ballast trim, and expect his answer today.

Louis Clapp,[48] the cook & steward, who wishes to engage for Victoria in July [18]51 now goes thither in the hope of obtaining a situation. A permanent and comfortable place is a greater object with him than high wages.

I have also given a passage to Joseph Stafford,[49] who desires greatly to have his qualifications as a blacksmith tested and to get employment as such at some of the Posts, if found deserving.

Should you decide on sending back the Mary Dare, there will not, I am pretty sure, be any trouble with the Custom-house further. Mr. Moses would not give written directions, but the steps necessary on entering are sensible enough and now well-understood by Captain [William A.] Mouat[t]. Above all, the manifests should be complete and rather show an excess than otherwise. When at Vancouver,

48 No information on this individual could be found.

49 No information on this individual could be found.

I ascertained that Nisqually Out[fit 18]50 had been short-credited £1003.2.6 in the accounts on the amo[un]t of Cash & Gold Dust sent to Victoria during that Outfit. Please inform me how the mistake is to be rectified.

Five Indians go to Victoria as Cattle tenders whom please send back in a swift new midsized canoe for Expresses [and] to be purchased on account of General Charges, and if they brought a dozen spear paddles, it would be an advantage.

Mrs. [Isabella] Ross[50] and the younger brave [souls?] of her family go [as] passengers in the Mary Dare. I have informed the old lady that she will probably have to pay the usual freight for her stock but at the same time hope that she may, in this respect, be treated as an intending settler.

Mr. C[hief] F[actor John] Work having taken eight head of horses here, old and young, has return[ed] for part of his stock taken by the HB Co at Vancouver in 1836 or [18]37. Will you please inform me how to charge the said horses in the accounts of the current outfit?

Only sixteen ploughshares were received here instead of thirty as invoiced.

A copy of Mr. [Simpson P.] Moses' letter in reply to mine of Yesterday is sent herewith. Referring to Mr. C[hief] F[actor John] Work for further particulars.

(Signed) W. F. Tolmie

Document 5.20: A letter from Simpson P. Moses, Olympia, to William F. Tolmie, Nisqually, February 6, 1852.[51]

Sir,

Your note of today is received, and in reply I have to say that I have attended to the matter you have mentioned with as much expedition as circumstances would allow. I send down by Capt [William A.] Mouat[t] the Manifests and Clearances under seal to W[illiam] W. Miller Esq, who will hand them to you when properly prepared.

As you have not seen proper to comply with the requirement which it was my duty to make and which I duly notified to you when you were at this place, I have given direction to Mr. Miller to cause the "goods in the trade room" to be landed and warehoused under seal of the U.S. at Nasqually, the same not having been duly entered for exportation. The Law will not allow vessels [to] enter at and clear from any other than the Port of Entry. Very respectfully yours,

Simpson P. Moses, Collector

Document 5.21: A letter from William F. Tolmie, Nisqually, to John Ballenden, Vancouver, February 8, 1852.[52]

Sir,

By the present express are forwarded letters recently received from Victoria as well as a letter for you from Mr. C[hief] F[actor John] Work, and documents

50 For Isabella Mainville Ross see Watson, *Lives Lived*, 2:836.

51 UW Library's Tolmie Papers Acc. 4577-001, Box 1 Folder 6.

52 Within the original manuscript, this letter has a false start, some fill-in additions, a second start and completion plus two endings, which makes for a very confused read. For clarity, I have remixed the various pieces I found and assembled them into just one letter.

relative to the seizure and release of our vessels as per list accompanying.

With regard to the Statement of the Mary Dare's monthly expenses, and the estimate of damages sustained through her detention at Olympia, it will be necessary, if I understand Mr. [Simon] Marge aright, to attain affidavits from persons not interested, as to the reasonableness of said statement and estimates.

Mr. [Chief Factor Peter S.] Ogden last year, made an arrangement with Captain [Rufus] Ingalls that I should furnish all spare cash to the acting assistant [U.S. Army] Quartermaster here, take his receipt for the same in duplicate, and forward one copy thereof by first succeeding opportunity to Vancouver. Will you please inform me whether this understanding still subsists, as Mr. Q[uarter] M[aster Lieutenant John] Dement of the US A[rmy] Steilacoom will be accommodated by its continuance?

Flour (Oregon) sells readily here for $16 p[er barrel] retail, and will probably not fall much in price throughout the season. If you could send 100 b[arrel]s 'round by any sea-worthy ship, and trustworthy captain bound for Nisqually, or Puget's Sound, it would be advantageous; knowing the retail price of the article here, you will be able to judge of the profitableness of the speculation better than I can here. Should any vessel be bound for this quarter and not fully laden, the captain would without doubt agree to bring freight to Nisqually. Enclosed is a list of some other things required as well as Flour, in case an opportunity may present, also a note of wantages [sic] by [payment?] of the bearer of the present express.

Copy of the Nisqually Servant's account Book Outfit 1851 is now sent. The other accounts will be forwarded as soon as possible.

P.S. The Nisqually servants having had no advances from Victoria during the Outfit [18]51 are entitled, according to Mr. C[hief] F[actor James] Douglas, to have to the amount of £12 St[erlin]g each of their supplies here provided the 50 p[e]r Cent Tariff.

W. T.

Document 5.22: A letter from James Douglas, Victoria, to William F. Tolmie, Nisqually, February 10, 1852.[53]

Dear Sir,

The Steamer Beaver and Mary Dare arrived here on the 7th Inst and I had the pleasure of your communication by that conveyance. I have since decided on sending the Mary Dare back to Nesqually, for another load of cattle with which she will return as soon as possible.

You will send as many cattle as you can conveniently get on board and make up the cargo with sheep; as I do not wish her to be detained too long at Nesqually.

A further supply of goods for Nesqually consigned to you is now forwarded, and I beg that the utmost attention may be paid to the preparation of the Custom House Papers; that everything may be in proper form and no room left for cancel on the part of the Revenue Officers.

The Mary Dare will go direct to Olympia without calling at Nesqually, and Captain [William A.] Mouat[t] will advise you of his arrival from Olympia.

53 UW Library's Tolmie Papers Acc. 4577-001, Box #2, Folder #3, N. 979.413 D 741 #11.

I would strongly advise you to employ an agent at Olympia, to enter our vessels there until our Captains gain more experience in Custom House arrangements. Major [Hugh A.] Goldsborough while here lately, said he would gladly act as broker for the Company's vessels and I believe he is about the ablest man in that quarter. The expense of such an agent would not be great as he would simply be paid so much for the job, say perhaps twenty dollars [paid out] for each ship entered and that expense would be largely repaid by the saving of time effected.

The Steamer [*Beaver*] will leave in a few days on a voyage to Fort Rupert, and I will probably accompany her to that place with the intention of returning here in about 15 days. Refering you to Invoice and bill [of] lading herewith, I remain, Yours truly,

James Douglas

Document 5.23: A letter from James Douglas, Victoria, to William F. Tolmie, Nisqually, February 11, 1852.[54]

My dear Sir,

The Mary Dare sailed yesterday and has had a fair wind since. The canoe [that carries this letter] leaves this evening and I have still a word or two to say on business matters. In reference to the Mill stream at Nisqually—I would recommend your getting timber squared and hauled out to the Mill Site so as to give the public the impression that we intend to build on the spot, which will be sufficient to keep intruders off the land until we have the sanction of the Company, or at least their decision about the Mill. I hope the Mary Dare will come off scot free this voyage, and not get into further trouble. Pray get [Lieutenant John] Dement's Bill on the Collector settled as soon as possible; the Drawer being responsible for the sum—urge him that he may shame the Collector into honest habits.

I took copies of [Lieutenant John] Dement's instructions from his commanding officer, and letter of credit from [Simpson P.] Moses, and both are extant here.

Mr. [John] Work and [my]self have decided on entering suit against [Simpson P.] Moses for the detention of the Steamer [*Beaver*] and I will write [John] Ballenden covering that matter if space [allows], by next Post. Pray send [Jean Baptiste] Jollibois, cattle and axes, if possible by the Mary Dare. With best wishes sincerely yours,

James Douglas

[P.S.] Pray mail or forward the letter for London. J D

Document 5.24: A letter from William F. Tolmie, Nisqually, to Lafayette Balch & Cyrus Palmer, Port Steilacoom, February 20, 1852.[55]

54 This letter was sent by canoe after the *Mary Dare* had departed with Douglas's letter of the day before. Here again we see Douglas's anxious opinion on and request for the immediate repayment of the American's $1,800 letter of credit owed the HBC. His comment: "the Drawer being responsible for the sum—urge [Dement to pay] that he may shame the Collector into honest habits" may indicate that Douglas himself has privately covered the American's loan, or with his office's petty cash.

55 At this point in time, Balch and Palmer were business partners, "Merchants & Shipping Agents, Puget's Sound & San Francisco."

Gentlemen,

Herewith you will receive the articles ordered by Mr. [Cyrus] Palmer yesterday with the exception of the Salt Pork which will also be delivered today, if I can get it carted by Sergeant [James] Hall to Steilacoom landing. If that however cannot be managed I will request Mr. Hall to deliver you three barrels pork at the landing whenever it may suit your convenience to send there for it. Invoice of the goods sent is here enclosed.

(Signed) W. F. Tolmie

Document 5.25: A letter from William F. Tolmie, Nisqually, to Simpson P. Moses, Olympia, February 20, 1852.

Sir,

Having today ascertained that in case No. 2 of the Cargo recently imported by the Mary Dare there are one Dozen Iron Girth rings more than appeared on invoice, and in case No. 3 of Same Cargo, about two yards of Diaper are not entered on the Invoice. I hasten, as by law required, to inform you of these mistakes, which can be corrected when we adjust our business next week.

I would with equal promptitude have informed you of the overplus of two dozen Scythes in the previous importation by the Mary Dare had I not taken it for granted that Mr. Surveyor [William W.] Miller's representation of the matter would have proved perfectly satisfactory. As I think the Scythes are all getting rusted in the beach store, will you please inform me by return of the bearer whether you have any objection to my removing them to this Establishment?

When, in reply to your enquiry yesterday regarding the Flour, I stated that we would not at present require to use any of the stock in the Beach Store. I have just learnt from Mr. [Cyrus] Palmer of Port Steilacoom that Messrs [Lafayette] Balch and [Cyrus] Palmer had already contracted for a supply—today however, an order was received from them for twenty five barrels Flour to be supplied if possible by tomorrow, and I am furnishing said quantity from the Flour imported by the first trip of the Mary Dare. I remain Sir, Very Respectfully Yours,

(Signed) W. F. Tolmie

Document 5.26: A letter from Simpson P. Moses, Olympia, to William F. Tolmie, Nisqually, February 21, 1852.[56]

Sir,

The receipt of your communication of yesterday's date is respectfully acknowledged.

Since the little development made by an examination of the Cargo of the Mary Dare, it becomes my duty to require the Scythes to be brought forthwith to the United States Warehouse at this place to be subject to such action as the Law provides for cases of this kind (As approved April 2, 1844).

As regards the Case of Goods in which the piece of Linen &c., was found by Mr. Inspector Wylie, I have to inform you that W[illiam] W. Miller Esq, Surveyor &c., will be at your place (Nasqually) to make examination for his own better sat-

56 UW Library's Tolmie Papers Acc. 4577-001, Box #1, Folder #6.

isfaction. As yet, the question is not properly before me.

The Flour, I regret to say, will have to remain in charge of the U[nited] States until properly released by the production of the necessary documents, the forms of which I have particularly detailed to you. I am very respectfully Yours,

Simpson P. Moses, Collector

Document 5.27: A letter from William F. Tolmie, Nisqually, to James Douglas, Victoria, February 23, 1852.

Dear Sir,

Your communication of the 11th accompanying packet box for Vancouver has just been received, and the wind being fair and a letter marked "immediate" here to your address from Mr. C[hief] F[actor John] Ballenden, the Indians from Victoria are to return immediately.

We failed in an endeavor to drive cattle for the Mary Dare on Friday last and are to make a final attempt today. There is every probability that the Brigantine will be ready for Sea tomorrow.

I have had many applications from persons desirous of going to Queen Charlotte's Island and the enclosed is from a young man recently mate of the American schooner Franklin,[57] and now lodging in [James] Scarth's[58] [house] until informed of the Success of his present application.

The Customs House business has been managed without the assistance of a Broker or agent. There is no person at Olympia except Mr. [Simpson P.] Moses himself, whose services would be of value in that way. I am Sorry to inform you that in Case No. 2 of the Cargo of the Brigantine were found (11) eleven girth Rings more than on Invoice and in Case #3 in piece of diaper say about ten (10) yards not mentioned on the Invoice. As required by the Oath subscribed at the Custom house, I immediately wrote Mr. Moses informing him of these mistakes and enclose copy of my letter and his Reply. He seems disposed to make the most of everything, however trivial. He called on board the Mary Dare the other day and drew out forms of affidavits for the Olympia Customs House regarding the Flour and the X.P. Ploughs imported by the Mary Dare. Enclosed are Copies of the forms required and of a letter received from [Simpson P.] Moses thereanent prior to his visit to this place.[59] Please to return affidavits for the X.P. Ploughs and also for each shipment of flour by first opportunity as until these are presented at the Custom House it may be unsafe for me to dispose of any more Flour. The Flour sold [to] [Lafayette] Balch, 25 bbls [barrels] @ $16 [each] has been paid for.

Mr. [Thomas] Dean wishes to have three extra men sent to this place in view of our intended dairy operation. He has named the brothers Fish and a lad nicknamed "Grandfather" as suitable persons, and I hope that if convenient they may be sent up. The Captain and part owner (Hancock) of the Schooner Franklin have been doing their best to entice our men away to Queen Charlotte's Island, and may probably succeed with some of the Sandwich Islanders. I will write again by the

57 *Franklin*, American schooner. Captain Hancock master, and part owner, later skippered by G.W. Pinkham.

58 For Scarth see Watson, *Lives Lived*, 3:858.

59 These forms have not yet been found.

Mary Dare and meantime have the honour to be, Dear Sir, Your very Ob't Ser't,
William Fraser Tolmie

P.S. A packet of letters for you and another for Sundries received by Mail via Olympia are herewith forwarded. W. F. T.

Document 5.28: A letter from William F. Tolmie, Nisqually, to John Ballenden, Vancouver, February 24, 1852.

Dear Sir,

On arriving here [at Nisqually] yesterday evening, the past day, I had the pleasure to receive yours of Jan 20th, but was surprised to find that it bore the San Francisco post mark of Feby 4th from which it is evident that there is a new bias somewhere in the postal arrangements between Olympia & Columbia/Cowlitz. I wrote you on or about the 23rd Ult by Mr. [Peter S.] O[gden at Vancouver], and a few day ago dispatched some Express Indians with a large packet containing letters for you from Victoria, and also for England and Lachine (via New York) with copies of all the documents relative to the transactions regarding the Seizure and release of our vessels subsequent to my return to this place on the 19th Ult.

In mine of Feby 3, forwarded by said express, I requested you to send for Nisqually some Blankets, Baize and one hundred barrels flour, by any safe American Vessel bound for Puget's Sound from the Columbia River—since getting here however, I learn that the Mary Dare is close at hand and a second ship, and have moreover been informed that the Schooner now in the trade between Portland the Sound has a full cargo awaiting her at the former Place for a second trip. So, there will be no opportunity at present of shipping from Vancouver for Nisqually. Neither is it so very desirable to do so—while freight is $20 p[e]r ton—until it be ascertained what the prospects are of getting supplies when needed from Victoria and I will know more on that head after seeing how the Collector comports himself on the occasion of the Mary Dare's second Entry at the Custom House.

It would be decidedly advantageous if all letters from Victoria for Vancouver & foreign ports could be mailed at Olympia. But until greater regularity is established in the Post office Department of Oregon, I would lastly think it advisable to risk important dispatches through this Post office.

Please acknowledge receipt of this by return of post in order that I may know whether it shall have reached [you] in course. Meantime, I Remain, Dear Sir, Your Very Obt Servt,

Signed by W. F. Tolmie

P.S. The packet you state having forwarded to Mr. Douglas along with yours to me of Jany 20th has not come to hand.

Document 5.29: A letter from William F. Tolmie, Nisqually, to James Douglas, Victoria, February 24, 1852.

Sir,

The Mary Dare is now about to start with 781 Ewes on board, three Horses for Macaulay's farm, and one cow which [Jean Baptiste] Jollibois might take if he chooses as one of the two due him from Fort Nisqually.

I regret much that we have so completely failed in parking cattle at the beach. No precaution was spared to ensure success, in fact new devices were tried whereby to make it more certain.

Having written fully by the Indians yesterday, I shall not add more at present and have the honor to be, Sir

(Signed) W. F. Tolmie

P.S. Enclosed is an Invoice of goods from England now (with the exception of the Watch) at Victoria belonging to the estate of the late Charles Forrest. I am willing to take the Watch at cost £12.10/ which is more than it would fetch there. If you think it would sell higher at Victoria, please let me know & it will be sent down by first safe opp[ortunit]y. T

Document 5.30: A letter from William F. Tolmie, Nisqually, to James Douglas, Victoria, February 26, 1852.

Dear Sir,

Having sold to M[isters Lafayette] Balch & [Cyrus] Palmer 25 barrels of the Flour recently imported by the Mary Dare, part of which has turned out sour, Mr. Palmer has proposed, should the [American schooner] Damariscove, [Captain Eli Hathaway,][60] ~~touch at Victoria~~ call in going to Q[ueen] C[harlotte's] I[sland], to have the damaged flour exchanged at Victoria for a good article, an equitable arrangement which I have no doubt you will readily enter into. I have the honor to be, &c., &c., &c.,

S[igned] W. F. Tolmie

Document 5.31: A memoranda from William F. Tolmie, Nisqually, to Lafayette Balch & Cyrus Palmer, Port Steilacoom, February 26, 1852.[61]

Gentlemen,

As requested by your note of this date, I now send you from 6 to 800 [pounds of beef] which has been Killed since the order was received. A note of the weight and number of quarters will be forwarded with the beef.

Since Mr. Palmer called yesterday, I have been regretting that he did not, as I proposed, change the objectionable flour here, rather than take the chance of affecting an exchange at Victoria where they may now be scarce of the article having expeditions, &c., to fit out.

Should the [American schooner] Damariscove, [Captain Eli Hathaway,] call

60 An American sea captain, Hathaway [var: Hathiway/Hathoway] eventually landed at Penn's Cove on Whidbey Island and settled there, becoming sheriff in the early 1860s.

61 On the manuscript it states: "Mem[orand]a: Original handed to Mr. Palmer."

at Victoria, and Captain [Lafayette] Balch make use of the letter to Mr. Douglas I gave to Mr. Palmer Yesterday, it will be but fair to mention to Mr. D[ouglas] that I offered Mr. Palmer to exchange the barrels of sour flour here & that he objected on the score of the delay thence to arise. Wishing Captain Balch and his brother adventurers a successful trip, I am Gentlemen, &c., &c., &c.,

S[igne]d W. F. Tolmie

Document 5.32: A letter from William F. Tolmie, Nisqually, to John Ballenden, Vancouver, March 1, 1852.

Dear Sir,

I now forward a packet box Received a few days from Victoria and also the Nisqually Accounts for Outfit 1851 which, owing to the press of other business, Could not have been got Ready sooner. The account will, I trust, all be found Correct and explicit.

I have made a Charge against Ft Victoria of £1004.2.6 that being the Amount short-credited this post for Cash Remitted thither during Outfit 1850.

In further explanation touching the debit balance of £1294.1.10 appearing against Ft Nisqually Outfit [18]50, I have to state that the Charge of £600 St[erlin]g for freight ac[count of] Cadboro during last Outfit seems to me unreasonably high, say be £300 St[erlin]g, for the Vessel was sailed in 1850 at Very little Cost, having been Commanded most of the time by a Coxswain at £60 p[e]r Annum and manned Chiefly by Indians paid each about 12/ p[e]r Month. Moreover, the Schooner had always [carried] Cargoes to Victoria of Puget's Sound Co's produce and livestock. I have lastly to make mention of an omission of my own in not having charged against Outfit [18]49 its proportion about £200 St[erlin]g of the duties & charges paid Genl [John] Adair in June [18]50 on our importations at this place since April 3rd, 1849.

The price of the Sheep supplied Fort Vancouver during Outfit [18]50 has been fixed at 16/8 each by Mr. C[hief] F[actor James] Douglas of Victoria. The Sheep Supplied the HB Coy at Victoria and by his direction charged 10/ Cash were, I understood, to have been transferred to the PS Coy on Vancouver's Island.

Should this Reach [you] 'ere [François] Rabasca leaves Vancouver, please [do] not to send any Leaf Tobacco by him as we have, since [having] Requested some, been abundantly supplied from Victoria.

Subjoined, or Rather enclosed, is a fresh List of Articles wanted by Return of the express bearers.[62] Hoping that this may find you Completely Returned to health, I have the honor to be, Dear Sir, Your Very Obedt Servant,

(Signed) W. F. Tolmie

Document 5.33: A private letter (extract) from William F. Tolmie, Nisqually, to Eden Colvile, Lachine[?], March 1, 1852.[63]

[Sir,]

62 This list was not found.

63 BC Archives, MS-0557, Box 2. From a typescript copy.

For information regarding Puget's Sound Company's affairs I beg to refer you to my report to the Agents forwarded herewith. I also send a water color plan of the Puget's Sound Coy's lands similar to the one furnished the Surveyor Genl [Preston] which may interest yourself and gentlemen on the East side holding Shares in the PS [Agricultural] Co. I shall forward a copy to the Agents in London after the boundary lines have [been] run out.[64]

I hope my services to the P[uget's] S[ound] Association may be considered as entitling me to as early promotion to a Factorship as men of my own standing in the HB [Company] proper employ, [those] who have distinguished themselves by a faithful and effective performance of duty.

I have always considered my connexion with the PS [Agricultural] Co a turning point in my career, and sometimes as a trade which would not lead on to fortune. When at home on clerk's leave in [18]41-42, I had several conversations with your father [Andrew Colvile][65] and Sir H[enry] Pelly on the HB Coy's farming operations in the Columbia, and these interviews, I have always supposed, led to my appointment to Nisqually.

My own desire when at home was to be appointed to California on returning to the Columbia, and with that view I took lessons in Spanish while in London—for Dr. [John] Macloughlin in 1843 wished me to replace the deceased [William Glen] Rae at San Francisco and I was in daily expectation of starting for that p[l]ace overland, when in June 1843 a letter from the Govr and committee appointed me to Nisqually. Had I gone to California and enjoyed the same degree of health I have been blessed with here, the Coy would in all likelihood have had the best store in San Francisco in 1848 when the discovery of gold took place.

I hope you will excuse me for troubling you with the above little bit of personal history and, should you consider my claim just, I trust that you will bear me in remembrance when the next nominations are mad[e] for Chief Factorships.

[I remain, &c., &c., Yours, William F. Tolmie]

Document 5.34: A letter from William F. Tolmie, Nisqually, to John Ballenden, Vancouver, March 6, 1852.

Dear Sir,

I, last night, had the pleasure to Receive Your letter of the 26th Feby,[66] in which enquiry is made as to the price 3,000 Sheep Could be furnished at, here or at Ft Vancouver. Owing to the loss by deaths, and the number shipped to Victoria this Year, there are only 1,500 Sheep, Wedder lambs of 1851, Remaining for sale. These will be well-grown and in prime condition in September next, and can be delivered at Nisqually landing or beach for Five dollars and at Vancouver for Five 50/100 dollars each.

It would, I should think, be a great advantage to Sheep breeders in California, to have the inferior native Sheep of that Country Crossed with some of the Best

64 This "plan" is most likely one of Tolmie's making and has not yet been identified. The copy refers to the map that Tolmie will have Chapman create in 1852.

65 Andrew Colvile (1779–1856) was a London governor of the Hudson's Bay Company. See en.wikipedia.org/wiki/Andrew_Colville.

66 This letter has not been found.

European stock, and 4/5 bred Ram Lambs of the Cheviot, Leicester, Southdown and Merino breed Could be supplied here by the hundred if necessary, on the same terms as Wedders, provided notice were given me by the 1st May, of the number of each kind of Ram Required.

Should Mr. [Colonel William W.] Loring, or any other person design to purchase a large number of Sheep here in Summer [18]52, he would do well to give timely notice of his intentions, in order that hay for foddering said Sheep, on ship board may be secured at the most favorable season. It will be for you to decide whether a Certain sum should not be paid in advance by the intending purchaser, to be forfeited should he not come for the Sheep at, or about the appointed time, as besides the expense to be incurred in preparing fodder, the chance of selling the Sheep this season would probably be lost should the person for whom they would be set apart, fail to take them.

The Victoria Accounts Received here on the 23rd Feby were, along with those of this ~~place~~ post forwarded by special express on the 1st Inst. Owing to the interruption Caused by the second trip of the Mary Dare to this place, our accounts Could not be got Ready sooner.

The present is forwarded by mail from Olympia from which place I addressed you on the 14th and 16th Ulto and I am desirous to know when you received my letters of these dates.

Captain [James] Cooper on the Alice (Douglas) is now here for a Cargo of Cattle for Victoria. I have the honor to be, Sir, Your Very Obdt Servt,

(Signed) W. F. Tolmie

P.S. Should any X.P. Plough Shares have been Received by the Reliance,[67] please to lay aside 40 for this post, and to send them to Cowlitz by first opportunity. W. F. T.

Document 5.35: A letter from James A. Grahame, Vancouver, to William F. Tolmie, Nisqually, March 8, 1852.[68]

My dear Sir,

Can you inform me what became of the case of glass I sent by you to Portland when you went there in a boat with Mr. [Archibald] McKinlay. Mr. [W. Seaton] Ogden did not receive it. Mr. McKinlay, who is here at present, desires me to inform you that he sends you by this opportunity one pound of Onion seed [costing] $12.00. In haste, Yours sincerely,

Ja[me]s A. Grahame

Document 5.36: A letter from William F. Tolmie, Nisqually, to James Douglas, Victoria, March 11, 1852.

67 *Reliance*, British barque. Captain Harrower, master, sailed this chartered ship from London and arrived on the Pacific Northwest Coast in March 1852.

68 James A. Grahame to William F. Tolmie, March 8, 1852. BC Archives, A/C/20/G76.

Dear Sir,

I duly Received Your Communication of the 26th Feby making by or the arrangement you had entered into with Dr. [John F.] Kennedy[69] as to his being supplied here with Horses & Horned Cattle. Of the former we have none to spare except old or unsound Geldings [which we employ] only for occasional trips to Cowlitz with packs, so should the Dr. still desire Horses from this Quarter, I shall have to purchase for him from Indians as opportunities offer.

Having failed in two attempts to park Cattle at the Beach, I am unable at present to Comply with the Requisition for Cows & Oxen. In consequence of our Repeated failure of late with Cattle, I am forthwith going to have a strong park built on the North side of the Sequalitchew Creek with a fence leading into the American Plain. It will not be ready 'till the beginning of April, and it would therefore be unadvisable for You to order any Vessel for Cattle 'till that point. I have the honor to be, Sir, Your Very Obt Servt,

(Signed) W. F. Tolmie

P.S. Captain [James] Cooper takes 5 head of Cattle, and Completes his Cargo with Five Lambs for each of which delivered alive he is to have 62 2/3 Cents. The Cattle were Shipped before I had an opportunity of talking with him about their freight. W. T.

☙ Document 5.37: A letter from William F. Tolmie, Nisqually, to Cyrus Palmer, Port Steilacoom, March 11, 1852.

Dear Sir,

When at San Francisco, will you have the goodness to purchase for me one good cooking Stove complete and of the most approved pattern large enough to cook for a dozen persons? Also; 1 Set Buggy Harness including bridle & reins Strong & Substantial for my own use; 1 copy Gordon's Revenue Laws of the United States[70] latest Edition, the edition of 1844 not wanted; Some Indian rubber clasps or bands for holding letters together; letter envelopes of different sizes. Unless the above articles each and all can be had at San Francisco on reasonable terms, I would prefer waiting for a more favorable opportunity of getting them. Wishing you a pleasant, successful and speedy voyage, I am, Dear Sir,

William F. Tolmie

P.S. If desirable, Mr. [Edward] Huggins can today make over to you an amount of Cash equal to what it may be supposed the above mentioned articles would cost. T.

☙ Document 5.38: A letter from Joseph D. Pemberton, Victoria, to William F.

69 For Kennedy see Watson, *Lives Lived*, 2:530.

70 Thomas F. Gordon, *Revenue Laws, Regulations, Circulars, Reports, &c., (Customs.) A Collection of the Laws of the United States, Relating to Revenue, Navigation, Commerce, Light-Houses, &c., Including Treaties with Foreign Powers* (Philadelphia, PA: 1844).

Tolmie, Nisqually, March 15, 1852.[71]

My dear Sir:

I beg to thank you for the Ponderosor & Taxifolia[72] you kindly sent, the branches I received but, I regret to say, by some accident the timbers were thrown overboard.

It would be very desirable to experiment on specimens taken from trees full grown or nearly so, and I hope you will not, under the circumstances, think us too troublesome in applying to you for a second edition, 1 y[ar]d or so each, split 4" or so, and marked in pencil with "Pon" & "Tax" to prevent blunders. Capt [William A. Mouat] told me that the term "Bank-siah-na" took rise in the circumstances that the Bank whereon that wilde pine grows is "siah" which we much regret; but should any accidental opportunity occur—should the Yankees bring Birnham wood[73] a little near to your castle, or should the Indians bring the wood a little nearer to burn him, I'm sure you won't forget us. With my respects to Mrs. [Jane] Tolmie, I remain, my dear Sir, Yours very Truly,

[Joseph] D. Pemberton

Document 5.39: A letter from William F. Tolmie, Nisqually, to Edmund A. Starling, Port Steilacoom, March 17, 1852.[74]

Dear Sir,

In December 1851, Three Indians now living at "Kiawalamsam", or Port Steilacoom ([Lafayette] Balch & Co), drew their Knives on Mr. [Edward] Huggins in the trade Shop here without provocation, and as two if not all three of them came to trade to day, and were Rather Troublesome, I think it right to Complain to you of their Conduct.[75]

They probably entertain a grudge against the whites, as a Relative of theirs was shot here in 1849 in the affray, in which the late [Leander C.] Wallace fell. But, at the General pacification which took place, when Wallace's murderers were executed

---

71 UW Library's Tolmie Papers Acc. 4577-001, Box #2, Folder #1.

72 Pemberton is presumably referring to wood samples of ponderosa pine *(pinus ponderosa)* and the Pacific/Oregon yew, *(taxus brevifolia)* that Tolmie collected and forwarded to him.

73 Pemberton refers to Birnam, a town in Perthshire, Scotland, which was commonly known at that time because Birnam Wood is mentioned in William Shakespeare's tragedy *Macbeth.*

74 Starling was the first Indian agent in Puget Sound. In 1851 he was appointed Indian agent for Oregon Territory by President Fillmore, and assigned by Superintendent Anson Dart to the district of Puget Sound, the territory north of the Columbia with headquarters at Fort Steilacoom. He made an approximate census of the Indian tribes within his district based upon reports from the chiefs and head-men of tribes and bands. The returns of the tribes upon Puget Sound totaled 5,795; remaining bands west of the Cascade Mountains, 925. Those dwelling east of the Cascades, and west of the Columbia River, were estimated at three thousand. Evans, *History of the Pacific Northwest, Oregon and Washington 1889*, 1:343, as viewed at www.usgennet.org/usa/or/county/union1/1889vol1/1889volumeIpage333-349.htm.

75 Later in life, Edward Huggins recalled this day: "I got into an altercation with three down Sound Indians, notorious characters, which resulted in a serious quarrel. They threatened to seriously hurt me [with large knives], and [I] foolishly attempted to capture one ... when he suddenly turned and drew one of the fearful knives ... I was considering whether or not I should draw a small pocket pistol [I had with me, but to scare, and with] no intention of shooting ... when I heard Dr. Tolmie calling out 'Come back! Come back!'" Tolmie had seen the other two Indians level their guns and would have shot Huggins if he attacked their cohort. Edward Huggins to Clarence B. Bagley, April 19, 1906, UW Library, Clarence Bagley Papers, Box 2, folders 4–17.

at Steilacoom, the son of the slain Indian[76] had Blankets presented to him, and the matter was Considered as finally settled. I am dear Sir, Very Respectfully Yours,
(Signed) W. F. Tolmie

Names of Indian mentioned in foregoing letter: Sac-ewah, Chay-chah-chuck-tow principal, Nu-chaim.[77]

Document 5.40: A letter from William F. Tolmie, Nisqually, to James Douglas, Victoria, March 20, 1852.

Dear Sir,

Having Received by Mail Yesterday a packet to Your address under Cover from Mr. C[hief] F[actor John] Ballenden, who desired it to be forwarded with this packet, I now send an express Canoe with all the letters and papers accumulated here for Vancouver's Island since the departure of the Alice [Douglas] on the 10th Inst.

Since that date we have had severe weather here—frost and Snow—but winter, I trust, is at length over.

I have most particularly to Request by Return of the present Express the affidavits applied for in mine of the 23rd Ult Regarding the X.P. Ploughs and each Shipment of Flour imported by the Mary Dare, as Collector [Simpson P.] Moses will doubtless make a fuss shall they not soon be forthcoming, and in due form.

William Sales[78] is allowed a passage in order that he may get his we[a]rables back in the Canoe. His Cousin [William] Hudson has also been allowed a passage back to V[ancouver] I[sland]. I have the honor to be, Sir, Your Very Obedt Servt,
(Signed) W. F. Tolmie

[P.S.] Please to send, by Return of Canoe if possible, as many Hyquas (Copcops) [dentalium shells] as can be purchased at Victoria for eleven Blankets B.B. 3 p[oin]ts or equivalent, packed securely in a box, and addressed to George Gibbs Esqu[ire][79] or

---

76 Just two "friendly" Indians were killed during this brief melee. The first was an unnamed Skeywhamish or Skykomish medicine man who was killed outright by a gun shot that day, and these may have been his relatives. The other was Streass Steilacoom, a pre-teen who died in November 1849 from a sepsis infection after a bullet grazed his neck on May 1.

77 All three were known to the fort's managers. Sac-ewah is possibly referred to as Saqueakik in the fort's Indian Accounts book. Chay-chah-chucktow is possibly called "Chah" in that record. Nu-chaim is probably a variation of Nohsiatayoose, Nushiatayoos, Nuhsaiooss, or Nusheatayok as noted in the fort's Indian accounts.

78 William Sales, who appears here as a courier, eventually squatted on PSAC land near Spanueh in 1853. He also helped Nicholas DeLin establish a sawmill at the mouth of the Puyallup River, today's downtown Tacoma.

79 Gibbs (1815–1873) was born near Astoria, Long Island, the son of George Gibbs and Laura Walcott. He graduated from Harvard Law School in 1838, practiced law in New York, and spent 1842–46 as librarian of the New York Historical Society. He came to Oregon with the Mounted Rifle Regiment in 1849, and was appointed collector of customs at Astoria three different times: 1851, 1853, and 1858. In May 1854, Gibbs took a claim containing 318 acres, about a mile east of Gravelly Lake. He spent portions of 1855–57 exploring the Umpqua region, the Cascade Mountains, and Puget Sound. His major ethnological studies were incorporated in the Pacific Railroad study, 1853–55. His excursions in the Northwest were concluded by his three years on the International Boundary survey along the 49th parallel, 1857–60. In 1860 Gibbs returned to New York for what was intended to be

Walter Macdonald Esqu[ir]e, Care of A.H. Murdock, Esquire, Union Town, Humbolt Bay. Charge the Goods paid for, said Copcops, to Ft Nisqually, Outfit 1852.

❧ Document 5.41: A letter from William F. Tolmie, Nisqually, to John Ballenden, Vancouver, March 22, 1852.

Dear Sir,

Your Communications of the 4th & 8th Inst have been Received, the latter, by Return of our express, preceding by a day the former which came by mail. A Canoe was Yesterday dispatched to Victoria, with all the letters &c., for that Quarter.

By an early opportunity, I will send a full Requisition of Goods for Nisqually which might be sent to Cowlitz by the boats employed in Removing the produce of the farm there, and Could be got to this place in Course of the Summer when the Roads are Good, or then by Wagon or packhorses as may be found most expedient.

We have more Second Scarlet Cloth here than is required, and can supply Fort Vancouver with a few pieces if desirable.

Please to send ½ dozen Milk Pans to Cowlitz for Nisqually by the earliest Conveyance. They will be needed here soon.

In your letter of the 4th March, you say "With reference to the Sheep transferred to Fort Vancouver during O[utfi]t 1851, Mr. Douglas may fix their price at what sum he pleases but he said you must Recollect that there are always two to a bargain."

In Reply, permit me to inform you that in my Sheep transactions during Outfit 1851, I never lost sight of the self-evident proposition "that it needs two to make a bargain" and in proof thereof would beg you to refer to my Correspondence with Mr. [Chief Factor Peter S.] Ogden Regarding the price of Sheep.

On Septr 2nd 1850, I wrote Mr. O[gden] That in Consequence of instructions Received from the Govr & Committee, supplies to the Puget's S[ound] Comp[an]y to the Hudson's Bay Coy would hereafter have to be charged at the Market price, and that consequently, the Sheep sent to Vancouver in 1851 by Mr. O[gden]'s Request had been priced at 20/00 or Five dollars each.

On the 2nd June 1851, Mr. Ogden wrote me for five hundred Sheep provided the price still Continued at $5 each, the market price here. I had Yet sent him 832 instead of 500, having understood from Good authority that mutton about that time sold for 50 Cents, the $ in Sanfrancisco.

Thereafter, a letter from Mr. Ogden Came to hand dated Augt 25th/[18]51 making no further remark on the price of Sheep supplied Vancouver from Nisqually, but asking for Six Hundred More and stating that they sold Readily at

---

a temporary visit, but the outbreak of the Civil War changed his plans and he never returned to the Pacific Northwest. In 1871 he married his cousin, Mary Kane Gibbs, and after that lived at New Haven, Connecticut. He died there at the age of 58. William N Bischoff, *We Were Not Summer Soldiers: The Indian War Diary of Plympton J. Kelley, 1855–1856* (Tacoma: Washington State Historical Society, 1976), 150. George Gibbs, *Indian Tribes of Washington Territory* (Fairfield, WA: Ye Galleon Press, 1967), 1–4. See also William P. Bonney, *History of Pierce County, Washington* (Chicago: Pioneer Historical Publishing Company, 1927), 135.

Vancouver for Six dollars apiece.

I am surprised to learn that of the Nisqually Sheep sent to Vancouver, many when Killed, weighted only 21 [pounds] They must have greatly fallen off on the Rich pastures of Vancouver.

I wrote you on the 6th Inst by Mail stating in Reply to Your enquiry that 1,000 Sheep Could be supplied Mr. [Colonel William W.] Loring at Nisqually landing at $5 each or at Vancouver at $5.50, and would like to have his answer as soon as possible having had since the date of My last some offers for wholesale purchases here. I have the honor to be, Sir, with Respect, Your Very Obedient Servant,

(Signed) W. F. Tolmie

Document 5.42: A Letter from John Work, Victoria, to William F. Tolmie, Nisqually, March 29, 1852.[80]

My Dear Doctor,

The Schooner Honolulu,[81] Capt [William] Pattle, an Englishman (the Vessel though American-built is now under English papers), arrived here a few days ago and is chartered to bring Cattle from Your place. This will no doubt give you much trouble that you are ill-prepared to meet having so much other business on your hands. But the chance of getting Cattle here is favorable and terms moderate and I have no doubt you will be glad to get rid of some of your superfluous stock. And do your best to get them shipped. They are much wanted here as the heavy drain to feed the number of people here has much exhausted the stock, and the sheep, being all ewes, are not available. Besides, their number is greatly diminished by deaths, the Indians have Killed some of them even so late as yesterday notwithstanding the recent row with them. We live very poorly here now.

I have determined on purchasing the claim laying between you and [Robert] Clouston, the two claims will be a heavy outlay but I am induced to take both so that I may have some ground for pasturage and secure an outlet to the rocks and public land behind which I would otherwise be barred from by Mr. [Robert] Staines & the claim alongside of yours should anyone else get it. Without it, both myself and your brother Roderick [Finlayson] would be much limited for pasturage, until as we have not a great extent of clear land and it will require time and labour to get parks cleared of wood and yielding artificial grass in sufficient quantity fit for the purpose. Labour is so high I shall not likely live to see the day. In buildings at least for some time the expense for the two claims will be little more than for one. There will be altogether probably 56 less Acres should things not turn out prosperous. [If so] this outlay must go to the winds with the rest. I have my eye on Pottenger to commence operations & take charge of the property, perhaps Roderick [Finlayson] may find someone to begin before he can get here.

Tillage is greatly retarded here now on account of the poorness and weakness

---

80 BC Archives, MS-0557, Box 1, File 1, A/C/40/W89.

81 *Honolulu*, British schooner. Under contract, Captain William Pattle, hauled livestock, fresh beef, and cash for the Company.

of the small young oxen they have to work with. If in your power, endeavor to send me ten strong young oxen, branded with my name. Could one or two pair of them be broke in, it would be all the better to begin with and assist in breaking in the others. Perhaps you might find some handy Indian that could make 4 or 5 yokes. I have spoken to Mr. [James] Douglas about the oxen, and also about the remainder of my horses. Please endeavor to send down 8 or 10 more, as a horse and cow is the same price, it would be better to send six horses & mars and four quite good milk cows.

Mrs. [Josette] Work is shortly going to live in Mr. [Roderick] Finlayson's house at Rock Bay, without a particle of furniture. I intend trying to get a dozen of chairs & a couple of tables from the Islands. I don't think you would have any chance of getting anything of the kind about your quarter. Should you see any chance, I would feel much obliged [if you could] procure and send them? I don't mean to order anything of the kind from England till I see how matters are likely to turn out. I have still misgivings as to the straight forwardness of things, and have some time [been] suspicions that baits are laid to induce us to embark our money thus. But we must not respond, but try and make the most of it but not incur heavy expenses in erecting costly buildings & expensive furniture that will never yield any return. It will be time enough for these things when we see affairs prospering to our satisfaction and be an inducement to make it our final resting place. I am sorry to have to trouble both you and Mr. Finlayson so much as I do, tho' I am sure neither of you think any trouble of it. He has his hands full looking after almost everyone's affairs that are absent.

I have at last prevailed on Mr. D[ouglas] to give the whole of Staines' house for the School, and am in hopes it may now go on better. I must have a tackle with Mrs. S[taines] tomorrow, and see & bring her to a bearing in which I hope to succeed. I mean to leave Letitia and Margret with their Mother. Henry [Work][82] will only for a time at least be able to attend as a day scholar as I must have him under the doctor's charge, the exceptions on his limbs are getting worse. Mary has a swelling on her neck it is getting better. The rest are all well.

John [Work Jr.][83] saw his horse yesterday, but was much disappointed that he could not get ahold of him and mount at once. He says he wrote to you the last express and gave the letter to Mr. S[taines], who probably thinking it not as it ought to be suppressed it as it was not among those sent here. I trust you will have it in your power to send during the summer the cattle & horses asked for by poor Kennedy. If mine be sent the different voyages it will do but the sooner the better, but something might turn up to stop them. But I am troubling too long.

May God bless and preserve you, My Dear Children, Yours ever Most affectionately,

John Work

Document 5.43: A letter from William F. Tolmie, Nisqually, to John Ballenden, Vancouver, April 2, 1852.

Dear Sir,

82 Henry Work (1844–1856). One of John Work's twelve children.

83 For John Work Jr. see Watson, *Lives Lived*, 3:990.

By the present express is forwarded a packet box containing despatches for Vancouver, New York, and England with a large tin case addressed A[rchibald] Barclay Esq[ui]re &c.

Should two gentlemen, M[isters C. Samuel] Parker & [Stephen C.] Foster,[84] not accompany this to Vancouver, please address them a note at the post office, St. Helens, stating whether or not Mr. [Colonel William W.] Loring has agreed to purchase the Sheep mentioned in my letters to you of the 6th and 22nd Ulto.

Should the Sheep be still disposable, M[isters] P[arker] & F[oster] have agreed to take a thousand deliverable at the entrance of Cowlitz (Monticello) or on the N[orth] Side of the Columbia river, opposite St. Helens for Five 25/100 Dollars each in May or June next, as may hereafter be agreed on and they are to pay you in advance Five Hundred and Fifty Dollars, to be forfeited should they fail to take the sheep from this at or soon after the time to be appointed. Mr. Parker thinks it very probable that he will be across [the portage] to see the Sheep started from this place in which case he will make a further deposit with you of the amount they will probably come to. Should he be unable to come for the sheep, further arrangements will be settled by correspondence.

Please to send by return of the bearer "Taniah"[85] as many of the milk Pans and X.P. Plough shares asked for, as his canoe will contain a couple dozen children's Shoes [and] would find ready sale here.

(Signed) W. F. Tolmie

Document 5.44: A letter from William F. Tolmie, Nisqually, to Simpson P. Moses, Olympia, April 2, 1852.

Sir,

The Affidavits regarding the Flour and Ploughs imported in the Mary Dare are now sent, and will, I hope to learn, prove satisfactory. Having, owing to press of business, been unable to have the Invoices prepared this week, I shall not be at Olympia on Monday as agreed upon.

Will you please inform me whether the Monday following will suit you and you will oblige greatly by informing me by return of bearer, for first opportunity of the amount, and nature of the charges against the Mary Dare and Steamer Beaver you spoke of, when I was last at Olympia?

(Signed) Wm F. Tolmie

Document 5.45: A letter from William F. Tolmie, Nisqually, to James Douglas, Victoria, April 3, 1852.

Dear Sir,

I have to acknowledge Receipt of Your letters of the 28th Febry and 23rd & 27th

84 The editor could not find information that was conclusively linked to this partnership, of which Foster's side operated out of Sacramento, California, in 1852.

85 Tahniah (m) [var: Zahniah, Taniah, Tamah, Tzahniah, T'zniah.] Pronounced: tah'NAI-ah. Affiliations: Nisqually/Puyallup. Taniah was a shepherd boy, but here he was employed as a letter courier. Huntington Library, Soliday Collection, Nisqually Papers, FN 1242, Volume 2, Fos. 43 & 46.

of March, and have forwarded the packet Box & Tin Case to Vancouver in charge of a Careful Indian. The Nisqually express bearers got here seventeen hours before the Victoria Couriers.

I have to state in Reply to Your enquiry that 838 Wedders were sent to Ft Vancouver in July 1850. Mr. [Peter S.] Ogden had written me previously, offering to take 550 at ($5) five dollars each or 1,000 at five dollars. He subsequently applied for 600 more, stating that Sheep sold Readily at Vancouver for $6.00 a piece, but none were sent.

Mr. C[hief] F[actor John] Ballenden has been applied to at Vancouver Regarding the price of Sheep here &c., and I have informed him thereanent, and of the number for sale. I have since been visited by two drovers from California, who have seen the Sheep and are to take a thousand, deliverable at the entrance of Cowlitz, or opposite St. Helens, for 5.25/100 each. Should the parties first enquiring not have Concluded a bargain with Mr. C.F. Ballenden, I shall take Care to leave in other Case payment secured 'ere the Sheep leave Nisqually.

We are getting on well with the new Cattle park & fence, and will be Ready to Ship Cattle on board the Honolulu on or about the 12th Inst.

Should any goods be sent here by the Honolulu, they ought to be advanced 50/p[e]r Cent on London Cost in the Invoice accompanying. W[illia]m McNeill goes [as a] passenger in the canoe. I have detained it 'till post day but no letters have been received for you.

Signed Wm F. Tolmie

Document 5.46: A letter from William F. Tolmie, Nisqually, to Simpson P. Moses, Olympia, April 5, 1852.

Sir,

I have to acknowledge receipt of your communication of the 3rd Inst, and in reply to its concluding paragraph [I] have to say that my "business faith" as you therein term it, has hitherto, to the best of my knowledge, been unquestioned and will, I trust, remain unimpeachable.

When I made a deposit of two hundred Dollars with you to meet expenses connected with the seizures I did not surrender my right to be fully satisfied at a future period that each or any of said expenses had to be defrayed by me. I made the deposit in good faith expecting that all would be satisfactorily cleared up, at our final adjustments.

You will remember I did not conceal my surprise when last at Olympia, on hearing from you that the amount of expenses you expected me to pay more than trebled the sum deposited, and it was with a view to expedite business that I subsequently requested a written statement of the nature and amounts of the charge in question. May I request you to have such a statement ready on Monday the 12th Inst as it may become my duty before settling to consult the Coy's legal adviser at Portland, and if so it would be desirable to address him by the Mail of the 13th Inst. I hope D.V.,[86] to be at Olympia about noon on Monday the 12th Inst when, if nothing be required of me, save what is legally and justly due, a speedy settlement will be affected.

86 Here, Tolmie's use of the initials "D.V." stand for *Deo Volente*, the Latin term for "God willing."

(Signed) Wm F. Tolmie

Document 5.47: An Agreement between William F. Tolmie, Nisqually, and John B. Chapman, Steilacoom City, April 7, 1852.[87]

Article of an Agreement made and concluded this 7th day of April A.D. 1852 Between William F. Tolmie party of the First Part, and John B. Chapman party of the Second Part; Witness he,

That the said party of the First Part contracts and stipulates with the said party of the Second part to Survey, Mark, locate and plat The Land Claim of the Puget Sound Agricultural Company in pursuance of the following instructions given by the said party of the First Part to the said party of the Second Part __ to wit;

The said party of the Second Part [is] to repair to Fort Nisqually on the 17th day of April 1852 and there take the field of Survey.[88] He is to begin at a point below the Nisqually River on the Sound, ~~above the Yelm River~~ and along the Meander of said River to point above the Yelm Ford; Thence, run a line Eastwardly to the N.E. corner of Companies Claim East of the Walla Walla Road and the Plain through which it runs. Thence, to run a Westwardly direction so as to keep north of the Plains through which the Puyalup Road leads near to the Puyalup Bay and Thence, from the Puyalup Bay to Tide Water of the Shores of Puget Sound bay keeping on the north side of the small prairie lying North of Steilacoom Inlet. _ Thence along the Beach of Puget Sound Southernly to near about one Mile South of Nisqually Landing & Thence up the Meanders of said River to the place of Beginning. The said party of the Second Part is to keep a field Book with accurate notes of the several different courses He may necessarily run, and to note all natural Topographical Objects and the bearings of Mountain Rainier from some convenient corners if practiacable: And at some suitable points of said Survey to run random lines from the Main lines, at some Three or four places in the Prairie or plains and take practable observations of natural objects in view on the horizon: and immediately after closing the said Survey, the said party of the Second Part is to reduce the coarses & distance of those observations on the interior of said plat as the said Tolmie may require to be done; The said Field notes, plat and Topographical account of land to be the property of the said party of the First Part.

And In candid value of said Services and Labour to be performed by the said party of the Second Part, the said Party of the First Part Stipulates and agrees to pay to the said party of the Second Part as follows to wit; For the first day, the said party of the Second Part enters upon his duties: Ten Dollars, and Three Dollars per Mile for every Mile necessarily run in said Survey as per above Instructions, and for Plating the same, Maping & Noting Topographical observations so far as Doc Tolmie may desire to be done; The work to be performed [herewith?] at the House of said Tolmie or said Chapman, as the said Tolmie may desire. Ten Dollars per day to work the usual Office hours.

The said party of the First Part stipulates on his part further to furnish all necessary hands, provisions, pack horses & Camp equipment to consist of two

87 UW Library's Tolmie Papers Acc. 4577-001, Folio 2/5.

88 Chapman actually began work on Monday, April 19, 1852.

able Chain-carriers; Two Axmen; Cook & Packer all who are to be under the direction and control of the Surveyor. One Axman is to blaze and Mark the line of Survey, make Stakes and drive at Corners; The other to open the way ahead for Compass and Chains.

Should it be found necessary from lack of provisions, Sickness or other unavoidable causes to Stop Opperations for one to six days, it is hereby stipulated and agreed That all parties will wait at the place of Stoping in Three days Thereafter, and resume Opperations until finaly finished & completed all the work to be done in a workman like manner and the payment to be made on the completion of each of the several works required as done.

Should the said party of the Second Part become Sick or unable to work, He is to have the privilege of substituting a Competent hand in his place for whose acts and work his is to be responsible; or the work may be suspended for a time as Dr. Tolmie may desire.

It is hereby understood that should the Suveying Opperation be stoped by force & Strong hand, the the [sic] said party of the Second Part is to be paid for the time & work as far as remited until he returns.

[Signed] J. B. Chapman
W. F. Tolmie

Document 5.48: A note from William F. Tolmie, Nisqually, to Simpson P. Moses, Olympia, April 12, 1852.[89]

Sir,

I have to inform you that an error has been discovered in the Invoice of Molasses imported by me in the Mary Dare in Novr 1851 [and] by the correction of which are addition of Thirty two Dollars 18/100 has to be paid on the amount of duties leviable on said Molasses. V[er]y Resp[ectfull]y Yrs,

S[igne]d W. F. Tolmie

Document 5.49: A note from William F. Tolmie, Nisqually, to John Ballenden, Vancouver, April 14, 1852.

Sir,

I beg to advize having this time drawn on you for the sum of Two Hundred and Fourteen Dollars [and fifty cents] $214.50/100 in favor of Margareth Sternheirner,[90] Columbia Barracks; said sum to be charged against Ft Nisqually O[utfi]t [18]52. Your very Obedt Sert,

S[igned] W. F. Tolmie

Document 5.50: A notice of trespass from William F. Tolmie, Nisqually, to James Hall, South end of American Lake, April 15, 1852.[91]

89 This letter's last sentence was entirely stricken and unreadable in the original copy. The add-on sentence that followed appeared similar in content and is placed here instead.

90 Nothing could be found regarding this woman. Presumably she was the wife or daughter of one of the U.S. Army officers at Columbia Barracks.

91 Huntington Library, Soliday Collection, Nisqually Papers, Misc., Documents.

Sir,

I hereby warn you that in cultivating land and making other improvements where you now have Indians at work between Steilacoom and Mr. [Thomas] Dean's Tlithlow, you are Trespassing on land possessed by the Puget's Sound Agricultural Company prior to the year 1846, and therefore secured to them by the Boundary Treaty ratified in July 1846 between the plenipotentiaries of Great Britain and the United States of America. Very Respectfully Yours,

W. F. Tolmie, Agent, Puget's Sound Agricultural Company

We hereby Certify that the above is a true and Correct copy of the original filed in the Puget's Sound Agricultural company's Office at Nisqually.

[Signed] Edward Huggins; Charles Ross [Jr.]; F[rederick] W. Kennedy[92]

Document 5.51: A letter from William F. Tolmie, Nisqually, to John Ballenden, Vancouver, April 22, 1852.

Dear Sir,

I have to acknowledge receipt of your communication of the 2nd and 10th April and lose no time in forwarding in the form of an agreement, a statement of the terms on which M[isters C. Samuel] Parker and [Stephen C.] Foster may have a thousand Sheep at this place. Should they postpone taking the Sheep 'till September, the sum of Five Hundred Dollars should be deposited as a forfeit instead of Two Hundred and Fifty Dollars, as by such a postponement, the chance of selling Sheep to other parties would be greatly lessened.

As Mr. [Thomas] Carter[93] of Portland had been here recently enquiring about Sheep, and wishes to have the earliest notice, which please give him should M[isters] Parker and Foster decline accepting the terms offered.

The Cowlitz Portage road will bc in a very bad state for at least two months to come. Can you give me a correct idea of the expense if transporting a bale of goods from Vancouver to Cowlitz landing? I have the honor. &c.,

S[igned] W. F. Tolmie

[P.S.] Please to send by return of bearer 2 Screw augers ea[ch] ½ and ¾ Inch[es].

[P.S.S.] It would be greatly preferable if Parker and Foster, or any other persons purchasing Sheep, took them either here or at the entrance of Cowlitz rather than higher up the Columbia. T

Document 5.52: A letter from William F. Tolmie, Nisqually, to James Douglas, Victoria, April 29, 1852.

Dear Sir,

I received your letter of the 13th Inst on the Morning of the 20th, the Honolulu

92 For Kennedy see Watson, *Lives Lived*, 3:530–31. Within a year, this young clerk would be permanently reassigned to work at Fort Nisqually.

93 Not much is known of this person. His family (wife and two daughters) reached Portland in February 1848, and his daughter Elizabeth married a lawyer in Salem, and his other daughter became a teacher in Portland. Carter was active in Portland's city government in 1853 and 1854, and quite possibly in 1866, although with such a common name it may have been someone else.

having arrived from Olympia in course of the preceding night.

The log Park and lane having proved more difficult of completion than had been anticipated we did not commence driving cattle to the beach 'till the 26th and we finished today uncertain yet whether the Honolulu will be fully laden or not. The park answers the purpose admirably, but owing to rainy, boisterous weather, very few large herds of cattle could be found in the plains and we have not a sufficiency of horses to persist long in the effectual driving. I have hired Indians and others to drive at $2 per day (in goods), and shall do my best to have a cargo in readiness for the Honolulu against her next arrival.

Captain [William R.] Pattle[94] having objected yesterday to taking any more yearlings on board at $1 each, I agreed with him in consideration of his long delay &c., that he should this trip have $2.50/100 for Yearlings. If successful in our approaching drives, I hope to make up a cargo without yearlings, which are unprofitable for all parties.

I forward a statement of Livestock shipped this O[ufi]t on private account, and a description of a Yearling Bull which L[yman] A. Smith , one of the squatters here, says has been shipped to Victoria in one of the Coy's vessels. Should such have been the case, please send said bull back by the Honolulu, as Smith sets great value on it as a breed. I have proposed to Captain Pattle [to] postpone his fourth trip 'till a later season, by which [time] we will be enabled to get our dairies set agoing in due season. P[attle] is willing to put off his fourth trip.

Should there be any spare milk pans at Victoria, please set six dozen aside for Nisqually to be sent up by the Mary Dare.

The man [William] (Sales) sent to count the cattle, having been mistaken about the ages of those shipped, I am unable to send a correct Invoice of them, and some one or more efficient persons ought to be at the Honolulu's gangway when the Cattle are landed to take a correct account of them then.

A bag cont[ainin]g a packet of despatches to your address with letters and newspapers for various persons is sent per Captain Pattle. I have not settled with him for bringing the letters up.

S[igne]d W. F. Tolmie

Document 5.53: A letter (#1) from William F. Tolmie, Nisqually, to John Ballenden, Vancouver, May 3, 1852.

Dear Sir,

I wrote You on the 22nd Ulto a letter posted at Cowlitz, and accompanying a Contract for the sale of One Thousand Sheep to M[isters C. Samuel] Parker and [Stephen C.] Foster Sacramento City, California. I now forward a duplicate of said Contract in Case the first sent may have miscarried.

94 Captain Pattle, having arrived at the fort's landing on April 7, was upset about having to take on more livestock. Pattle was skipper and part owner of the British packet ship *Honolulu* and this occasion illustrates the kind of contract work he was doing for the HBC/PSAC. He also is credited with finding the coal deposits of Bellingham Bay.

Having nothing further of importance to Communicate, I have the honor to be, Sir, Your Very Obedt Servt,

(Signed) Wm Fraser Tolmie

Document 5.54: A letter (#2) from William F. Tolmie, Nisqually, to John Ballenden, Vancouver, May 3, 1852.

Dear Sir,

The accompanying packet to Your address from Victoria has just come to hand, and I forward it in the hope of its overtaking the Courier despatched [earlier] to day.

Mr. [James] D[ouglas] enquires of me whether the Mary Dare will be Required at Nisqually the 26th May. Now of this I have not hitherto entertained a doubt, but it might be well to make the enquiry of Judge [William] Strong or Mr. [Simon P.] Marge. She may not, in Reality, be Required unless Condemned by the Treasury Department, and although Condemned by Judge Strong for the technical Violation of the Revenue Laws, he will probably defer sentence until the answer of Mr. Convise[95] Comes to hand. Nevertheless, it would be provoking, in the event of the Condemnation and absence, to have to forfeit the Sum of Thirteen Thousand dollars. I have the honor to be Sir, Your Very Obedt Servt,

(Signed) W. F. Tolmie

Document 5.55: A letter from William F. Tolmie, Nisqually, to James Douglas, Victoria, May 12, 1852.

Dear Sir,

Your letter of the 8th Ulto, with accompanying packets forwarded by Sinahomish [Snohomish] Indians, came to hand about the 28th, and as the same men are now returning to Vancouver's Island, I send by them the Mail Matter accumulated here since the departure of the Honolulu.

I have to state in reply to the enquiry made in your last, that my understanding of the matter has been that the Mary Dare would be tried here on or after the 24th Inst when court meets. Judge [William] Strong informed me in January that although the Vessel might be found liable for the offences charged, he would defer sentence 'till the reply should arrive to our petition to Mr. Louden, Sec[retar]y of the Treasury at Washington, [D.C.]. I have learnt from Captain [Lafayette] Balch that the Mary Dare was seen in the Latitude of San Francisco about the 18th April, bound for the [Hawaiian] Islands.

(Signed) W. F. Tolmie

Document 5.56: A letter from William F. Tolmie, Nisqually, to Simpson P. Moses, Olympia, May 20, 1852.

Sir,

---

95 Nothing could be found that further helps identify Mr. Convise.

I hereby protest against the payment of Two Hundred and Fifty Two dollars, charged for Warehousing the Cargo of the Brigantine Mary Dare, claiming that, under the peculiar Circumstances of the present Case, as set forth in my [letter] to the Hon Judge [William] Strong, [a] Copy of which was handed to You at Olympia, Jany 22nd 1852, [that] the said expense should be paid out of the proceeds of the Sale of said Vessel, if Condemned, or if not, by the Government of the United States. Respectfully, Your Obedt Servt,

(Signed) Wm F. Tolmie

Document 5.57: A letter from James Douglas, Victoria, to William F. Tolmie, Nisqually, May 21, 1852.[96]

Dear Sir,

I forward this communication by [Scottish botanist and horticulturalist] John Jephreys [Jeffrey] Esq[ui]re[97] who is proceeding on his professional pursuits to Fort Vancouver, and will visit Fort Nesqually on his way thither.

The object of Mr. Jephrey's mission, is known to you by report, and also that he is travelling under the protection of the Hudson's Bay Company, and you are hereby authorized to furnish any supplies he may require in continuation of his journey to Fort Vancouver.

I feel assured that you will do everything in your power to promote his views by furnishing every necessary assistance and information respecting the country.

You will please to forward a valued and receipted copy of the account of supplies made to Mr. Jephrey's in your department when he leaves for Fort Vancouver and with these remarks I recommend him mostly warmly to your kind attention and hospitality.

I have just received your communication of the 18th inst, and have to thank you for the information it contains.

We expect the Mary Dare from the Sandwich Islands on or about the 10th inst, and if you ascertain that the [life] preserver is required at Nasqually, and will send her thither as soon as you communicate information of the same to us.

There have been no arrivals from any quarter since the date of my last communication, and nothing has occurred here worthy of particular notice. I remain, Dear Sir, Your ob't Serv't,

James Douglas

P.S. Antoine Gagnon[98] is travelling on board to Fort Vancouver, and will return from thence by way of Nasqually with Mr. [Alexander] McLean's[99] daughter and

96 UW Library, Tolmie Papers Acc. 4577-001, Box #2, Folder #3, N. 979.413 D 74 1 #116.

97 See Frank A. Lang, "John Jeffrey in the Wild West: Speculations on His Life and Times (1828–1854?)," *Kalmiopsis* 13 (2006): 1–12. According to the fort's journal, John Jeffrey arrived at Nisqually by canoe from Victoria on May 24, 1852.

98 For Gagnon see Watson, *Lives Lived*, 1:395–96.

99 McLean, Alexander. McLean was an American sea captain, master of the schooner *McAllen* in 1854.

his [Gagnon's] own two children. You will oblige me by supplying him with a horse to the Cowlitz and by sending them on to this place from Nesqually. J D

My dear Sir,[100]

I have received your private note[101] of the 12th [of May] and thank you for such intelligence. The attempt to arrest the progress of the surveyor [Chapman] was a very foolish thing and worthy of the men who made it. [Captain William R.] Pattle has no doubt long 'ere this made appearance at Nasqually, and I shall therefore say nothing about him. Large oxen are certainly much required here, and I think it would be advisable to employ men in driving them in as you have suggested. With Kind respects to Mrs. [Jane] Tolmie, Sincerely yours,

J. Douglas

Document 5.58: A letter from William F. Tolmie, Nisqually, to James Douglas, Victoria, May 28, 1852.

Dear Sir,

Your communication of the 6th and 21st Inst have been duly received.

I have been unable to purchase any gelding horses for you in this neighborhood as the Indians decline taking goods in payment and ask from fifty to eighty dollars cash each for their nags.

I have ordered 20 riding Saddles which will cost about 25 [pounds Sterling] a piece.

Captain [William R.] Pattle will, I hope, sail tomorrow evening with a full cargo of horned cattle, many of which are large oxen, and as much fresh beef as can possibly be obtained.

I have handed to Mr. C[hief] F[actor John] Ballenden [an] Invoice of cash ($4,572), forwarded in his charge also our Requisition for Outfit 1852 regarding which you will, I presume, soon decide whether it is to be supplied from Ft Vancouver or Victoria. I shall write again by the Honolulu and meantime have the honor to be,

(Signed) W. F. Tolmie

Document 5.59: A letter from William F. Tolmie, Nisqually, to James Douglas, Victoria, May 29, 1852.

Dear Sir,

Herewith is forwarded Bill Lading of shipment per Honolulu which sails today and is entitled to three days demurrage.[102]

He is associated with the settling of Bellingham Bay and the discovery of coal in that place.

100 This additional letter was written directly beneath the previous by Douglas, and appears to be his immediate response to a newly arrived correspondence from Tolmie, as it was written on the same piece of paper, but just under the postscript.

101 This private note was not found.

102 "Demurrage" is the detention or delay of a cargo carrier during its loading or unloading process,

In 1850, U.S. Army Captain Bennett H. Hill was the first commander of Fort Steilacoom, referred to here as Steilacoom Barracks. Hill was a regular correspondent with Dr. Tolmie. In early 1853 he was called back east and eventually fought for the Union during the Civil War. *Image by Mathew Brady. Courtesy of the U.S. National Archives (Public Domain #4222272352)*

One of Dr. Tolmie's principal correspondents, Chief Factor James Douglas was also the doctor's superior in PSAC business. In 1851, Douglas assumed the office of Governor of the Colony of Vancouver Island while continuing as one of the HBC's chief factors. This *carte de visite* image is circa 1860. *Courtesy of the Fort Nisqually Living History Museum, Tacoma, Washington*

Simpson P. Moses assumed the job of Puget Sound's first Collector of Customs in 1850. Moses was highly antagonistic toward Tolmie and HBC/PSAC operations at Fort Nisqually; by mid-1853, he was ordered back to Washington, D.C., to face disciplinary action involving allegations of widespread bribery and graft. *Courtesy of the author, original source unknown*

Samuel R. Thurston allied himself with the missionary Jason Lee in opposition to the Hudson's Bay Company. No friend to Tolmie, Thurston's widely proclaimed falsehoods had immediate and long-lasting effects on British and American relations in the Pacific Northwest. *From M. Colmer and C.E.S. Wood,* History of the Bench and Bar of Oregon *(Portland, OR: Historical Publishing Company, 1910), archive.org/details/historyofbenchba00histrich/page/278*

This *carte de visite* shows Chief Factor John Work, Tolmie's father-in-law. *Courtesy of the Magedanz Collection*

Jane Work, the daughter of Chief Factor John Work and Josette Legace, married William Tolmie in early 1850. This is the earliest known photograph of Jane, taken circa 1860. *Courtesy of the Magedanz Collection*

London-born Edward Huggins was 18 years old when he arrived at Fort Nisqually in the spring of 1850. The apprentice clerk quickly became Dr. Tolmie's right-hand man. This image, circa 1860, is one of the earliest known photographs of him. *Courtesy of the Magedanz Collection*

HBC Chief Factor Peter Skene Ogden was one of Dr. Tolmie's regular correspondents in the early 1850s. Stationed at Fort Vancouver on the Columbia River, Ogden was Tolmie's superior in all things related to the fur trade in the Oregon Territory. *Courtesy of the Oregon Historical Society, Portland (Image #OrHi 1707)*

The HBC's steamship *Beaver* was the first of its kind to ply the waters of the Pacific Northwest coast. Starting in 1836, the *Beaver*'s southern port of call was Fort Nisqually. This sketch by renowned maritime artist Hewitt Jackson shows the ship as it looked around 1850. *Courtesy of the Hewitt Jackson Estate and the Museum of History & Industry, Seattle*

"Jack-of-all-trades" John B. Chapman played a significant role in legitimatizing the claims of the HBC and PSAC in today's Pierce County. In 1851, he founded Steilacoom City. *Courtesy of the Steilacoom Historical Museum Association, Steilacoom, Washington (Image #088)*

Amory Holbrook, Oregon City attorney and friend to the HBC/PSAC's officers, including Tolmie. A consummate letter-writer, Holbrook was eventually hired to represent the HBC, consulting on issues involving its tenuous legal standing within the Oregon—and later Washington—Territories. *Wikipedia photo from Elwood Evans,* History of the Pacific Northwest, *Portland, OR: North Pacific History Company, 1889.*

CHAPTER SIX

June 1st, 1852–November 30th, 1852

"In any understanding you may have with Mr. Moses, I would place no confidence unless reduced to writing."
—John Ballenden to William F. Tolmie, November 1, 1852.

During June, Nisqually's labor force, including several dozen sheep handlers, endured unseasonably hot, wet weather. Their efforts resulted in 7,000 pounds of fully dressed wool, delivered to London's docks half a year later. Furs and hides accounted for an additional 300 pounds of agricultural produce on the market. As the physical work progressed, the doctor's correspondence highlights the continuance of several large, unpaid book debts,[1] the outstanding smuggling charges raised against the steamer *Beaver* and brig *Mary Dare*, and Simpson Moses's continued opposition to the Company in Oregon Territory.[2] Thus began Outfit 1853.

The pursuit of Lieutenant Hawkins' $1,500 debt continued to frustrate Tolmie. Steilacoom Barracks' Dr. John Haden had proposed exonerating himself (as co-signer) by paying $1,000 "as soon as possible" and then, on returning to the United States, "he should succeed in compelling Hawkins to cash up" for the balance. While the army doctor's effort to make a down payment was viewed as a good first step, his imminent departure to the United States was not. Tolmie realized that with both co-signers 3,000 miles away, the likelihood of his recovering the money would dwindle from slim to none.

Restitution of Collector Moses's $1,800-plus promissory note (that associated with the *Georgiana* rescue mission and the purchase of HBC goods in Victoria) proved equally challenging. The Haida's ill-fated hostages had been freed using HBC goods: credit James Douglas's humanitarian concerns for that quick turnabout. Quite possibly, however, the chief factor did so to placate his chief adversary (Moses). Following the rescue it appears that the collector's hands were tied by

1 With an aggregate total of nearly $104,000 (present day funds), the accounts represented no insignificant sum in the Company's ledger books.

2 Washington Territory was not organized as an incorporated territory of the United States until March 2, 1853.

Washington, D.C., politicians who refused to pay the bill outright.[3] The debt's retirement through 1852's "Civil and Diplomatic Appropriation Bill" then wending its way through Congress was promising. Unfortunately, multiple exertions to resolve this issue extended well beyond Oregon Territory, and the chronological scope of this present work. As if relishing the Company's predicament, Moses continued to press his "readiness to receive . . . payment of duties [for cargo entering the district] . . . as to put him in funds for current expenses" observed Tolmie. This, even as the collector produced his "most exorbitant bill of charges" against the *Beaver* and *Mary Dare*. Obscure, inflated assessments for warehousing, travel, and vague customs house actions connected to the "smuggled" goods shadowed the vessels' seizure. At this point, Tolmie weighed the difference between letting the cargo go to public auction or vigorously fighting the ballooning invoice through a lawsuit. Moses's property assessment ($600-plus) was also paid under protest as a percentage of the taxed land was under squatters' plows. New trespassers, like Louis Seton's[4] parcel on the Canadian Plain, meant the further issuance of impotent (though legally documentary) trespass notices. Serving these notices was dangerous work, and could lead to violence.

Recalling Douglas and Tolmie's previous deliberations on bribes and clandestine gifts to customs officials, this chapter's letters underline Fort Victoria's chief factor's refusal to give credence to Moses's so-called "understandings." Yet, requests for various inducements continued to emanate from Olympia's customs house. In one instance, Tolmie remarked about Moses's "repeated endeavors [during the summer months] to have a *private understanding* with the Coy that he, *for a suitable Consideration*," would allow the Company's ships free navigation on the Columbia River.[5] Within this chapter, the collector also attempts "under promise of Award" to influence the sworn testimony of a Victoria couple in the lawsuit against the *Beaver*. Today, the courts label such activity as witness tampering.

Speculation also persists (given the documented indiscretions herein) that news of Moses's misbehavior had by now reached Washington, D.C.[6] Thus, a surprise inspection tour in November by Charles Bradley,[7] the General Appraiser of U.S. Customs, raises the question: what was his real purpose? He announced his purpose as 1) the review the HBC's invoices connected with the *Georgiana*'s rescue mission, and 2) investigation of allegations made against the *Beaver* and *Mary Dare*. One need only stretch that mandate slightly to imagine a third (and undeclared) purpose: examine the extraordinary proceedings of Collector Moses.

---

3 Given the blatant and often negative attitudes held against the HBC by many "Washington City" politicians at this time, one might conjecture that the congressional appropriations committee that reviewed Moses's request for payment to the Company fell to a group possessing such biased opinions. Perhaps this possibility, or the exhaustively slow mail service of that day, influenced the somewhat leisurely progression of the HBC's payment through Congress.

4 No information was found regarding this squatter.

5 Euphemisms such as this are today typically used to describe acts of bribery.

6 I did not find the "smoking gun," a letter which may have been sent by one of the Company's American friends. Only Moses's corruption as it relates to the Company is known for sure, yet it remains likely that he was conducting himself similarly against his own countrymen. The government's later prosecutions of Moses, after he was tersely stripped of his office, seem to indicate that his downfall had its beginnings here.

7 This Massachusetts-born Bostonian had sailed up from San Francisco.

A number of vessels also visited "Port Nisqually" during this period. The appearance of Captain George Plummer's[8] brig *John Davis*[9] and its 40 to 50 tons of freight consigned to Bishop Modest Demers,[10] however, proved problematic. Tolmie had neither the means nor equipment to attempt the "very tedious and offensive operation" of landing and storing the cargo. So it was sent on to Victoria.

Tolmie's thoughts regarding the erection of a sawmill on Sequalitchew Creek brought Rudolph M. Walker[11] to the table as a potential partner. Walker, who already operated a mill in Tumwater, was a customer of Tolmie's throughout the 1850s. Walker now voiced an interest in expanding his lumber works to where Sequalitchew Creek emptied into the Sound. In late July, Tolmie ordered him to cut boards not only for Fort Victoria's use, but also in a speculative venture for San Francisco's building boom.

By now, Clerk Walter Ross's fall from a horse on the Nisqually Plains had sealed his fate. His injuries, which likely included multiple fractures in his legs and a badly fractured forearm, were of such a severe nature that they would eventually claim his life. Ross's misfortune opened the door for Thomas Dean Sr., who was given charge of the livestock and other wide-ranging duties as "bailiff of the plains."

By late November an unsettling rumor began to spread that "two Am[ericans] named Ellet and Davis, also two Indians belonging to [Nisqually were] supposed to be drowned, having left Olympia last Monday week for this place and no tidings having been received of them to the present day."[12]

Then on the evening of November 28, Vancouver's Edward Spenser arrived at Nisqually leading 14 men from east of the Rocky Mountains. A young clerk, Frederick W. Kennedy, who had been temporarily assigned to the Columbia River depot, arrived with that party. Having delivered these men, Spenser returned to his post near today's Kelso, Washington. Two Orkney Islanders, William Benston[13]

---

8 Plummer was the owner and master of the American brig *John Davis*, a ship that specialized in transporting lumber and general merchandise from Puget Sound to San Francisco. Captain A.W. Pray followed Plummer at the helm in the later 1850s.

9 *John Davis*, American brig. Captain George Plummer, master. 50-ton capacity for cargo including passengers, beef, vegetables, printing press, general merchandise and goods, window glass, and blankets.

10 A native of Quebec, Demers (1809–1871) was a Roman Catholic missionary (later bishop) in the Oregon Country. He arrived in the Pacific Northwest in 1838 and served parishioners from the Willamette Valley north to what became the Province of British Columbia, Canada. For more information: en.wikipedia.org/wiki/Modeste_Demers.

11 This Tumwater sawmill operator was involved in a number of business deals with Dr. Tolmie during the early 1850s. Not much is known about Walker, and the letter mentioned here, if it still exists, was not located.

12 Dickey, ed., *Nisqually Journal*, November 30, 1852.

13 Benston was a Scot HBC/PSAC employee born about 1830 and is associated with the ship *Prince of Wales II* (1851) as a passenger for the Puget Sound Company (1852). He was a laborer at Craigflower Farm on Vancouver Island. He was listed as having deserted in 1852. He returned south of the border, for, after declaring his intention to become a U.S. citizen, he secured 100 acres and settled in 1854 and 1855 in Pierce County, Washington. Twenty years later he was still active for, on July 15, 1874, ten days after the death of William Northover, Benston asked the probate court to appoint a guardian of Northover's children; his brother Adam was named. PS: BCA Diar-Rem Beinston; HBCA log of *Prince of Wales II*, 2; YFASA 32; FtVanASA 9; PPS: The *Journal of Occurrences…*; Washington Territory Donation Land Claims, 95; SS: Anderson, *The Physical Structure*, 2. Information courtesy of Bruce M. Watson.

and John Spencer Logan Moar,[14] remained at Nisqually along with Kennedy; the others were sent north to Victoria.[15]

Here then are Tolmie's letters and documents from the first half of Outfit 1853.

Document 6.01: A letter from William F. Tolmie, Nisqually, to George T. Allan & Archibld McKinlay, Oregon City, June 4, 1852.

Gentlemen,

Mr. C[hief] F[actor John] Ballenden has instructed me to inform you that he wishes the bearer, C. S[amuel] Parker Esqu[ir]e, to have his choice of any of the HB Coy's horses for sale at Champoeg at from forty to fifty dollars for each.

(Signed) W. F. Tolmie

Document 6.02: A letter from William F. Tolmie, Nisqually, to James Douglas, Victoria, June 14, 1852.

Dear Sir,

Antoine Gagnon having returned this afternoon from Cowlitz, proceeds at once to Victoria with all the Mail Matter accumulated here since last despatch. A list[16] is enclosed of the Indians accompanying Gagnon, and of the payments they are entitled to. I shall endeavor soon to send the Indians employed at sheep washing, &c., to Victoria for Payment, by which a considerable saving will be effected.

(Signed) W. F. Tolmie

Document 6.03: A letter from William F. Tolmie, Nisqually, to James Douglas, Victoria, June 15, 1852.

Dear Sir,

By the arrival of C[hief] F[actor John] Ballenden [last evening], I received Your communications of the 8th and 9th Inst and shall present the order on Father Beard tomorrow.[17] I enclose a letter from a Mr. [Rudolph M.] Walker,[18] stating his Plans with regard to the erection of a Sawmill on the Sequalitchew Stream. Mr. W[alker] Gives reference to Gov [John P.] Gaines and Surveyor Gen [John] Preston. He has a patent for this Territory for a planning machine &c., which he would attach to the mill.

14 Moar [var: Moore/More], an Orkney Islander born in 1830, was transferred to Nisqually from Vancouver Island on November 29, 1852. His wage was £17 per year as a general laborer, working mostly in the slaughter house, cleaning out stores, making candles, delivering beef to American settlements, and working with Indian crews at various manual labor. He disappears from the journal's entries in early October 1855.

15 Dickey, ed., *Nisqually Journal*, November 28–30, 1852.

16 This list was not found.

17 No further information could be found regarding this Catholic priest who was apparently working at the Mission of St. Joseph in what today is Olympia's Priest Point Park.

18 Walker, a Tumwater sawmill operator, was involved in a number of business deals with Dr. Tolmie during the early 1850s. Not much is known about Walker, and the letter mentioned here, if it still exists, was not located.

I am very sorry to learn that there has been so Great a loss on valuable Cargo of Cattle lately shipped by the Honolulu from this place for Victoria.[19] [Captain William R.] Pattle, when he comes in autumn for live Stock, should be strictly bound down [instructed] before leaving Victoria, as to the mode of stowing his Cargo, &c. He insisted when here [last], that all at Victoria concerned in the business were in favor of leaving the Cattle loose in the hold. Expecting an early opportunity of again addressing You I remain Sir, Your Very Obedt Servt,

(Signed) W. F. Tolmie

Document 6.04: A letter from James A. Grahame, Vancouver, to William F. Tolmie, Nisqually, June 17, 1852.[20]

Dear Sir,

I have drawn on you in favor of [the Reverend Father] François Blanchet[21] two orders dated 16th and 17th of this month for fifty dollars each which you will please honor when presented and oblige, Yours Respectfully,

James A. Grahame, HB Co

Document 6.05: A letter from Amory Holbrook, Oregon City, to William F. Tolmie, Nisqually, June 22, 1852.[22]

Dear Sir,

Enclosed, I forward you, as directed by the Solicitor of the Treasury, a copy of a letter[23] this day received from that officer, accompanied by the warrant of remission [for the *Mary Dare*]. I am directed, as you will observe, to retain that until the costs incurred are paid, but if you or Mr. [John] Ballenden send me an agreement to pay the same when taxed under the direction of the Judge, I will forward it to you. Publically, as an officer of the Government, I suppose I ought to regret the clemency Exercised by the Treasury Department, though privately & Sincerely I congratulate you on your success. I am truly yours,

Amory Holbrook, Asst Dist Attorney

---

19 Dickey, ed., *Nisqually Journal*, June 15, 1852. Chief Factor Ballenden reported that 40 head of cattle had died in transport from Nisqually to Victoria during the *Honolulu*'s last trip.

20 BC Archives, A/C/20/G 76.

21 Father Blanchet (1795–1883), Roman Catholic Archbishop of Oregon City, was born at St. Pierre de la Riviere de sud. P.Q., September 3, 1775. He was ordained a priest in 1819, served a year at the Cathedral in Quebec City, before spending seven arduous years as missionary to the Acadians and Micmac Indians of New Brunswick. He and Modest Demers came to Fort Vancouver in 1838 to minister to the French and mixed blood or *métis* in the Willamette Valley and Vancouver. He was consecrated bishop in 1843, and became Archbishop of Oregon City three years later. He went to Europe in 1846 and South America in 1855 in search of money and personnel for his remote jurisdiction. Blanchet died at Providence Hospital, Portland on June 18, 1883. Bischoff, *We Were Not Summer Soldiers*, 138.

22 UW Library, Tolmie Papers Acc. 4577-001, V0250e, Box #1, Folder #4. From a copy of the original.

23 This letter has yet to be located.

Document 6.06: A letter from John Ballenden, Vancouver, to William F. Tolmie, Nisqually, July 6, 1852.[24]

Dear Sir,

I enclose herewith a petition[25] to Judge [William] Strong, to be transmitted by him to the Secretary of the Treasury at Washington [D.C.], respecting the seizure, last autumn, of the trading goods on board the Steamer Beaver. This petition will have to be signed in duplicate by you. It will also be necessary that one be handed to the Collector (Mr. [Simpson P.] Moses) and that he certify that a true copy has been presented to him. Be kind enough to attend to this with all dispatch and send the original to me in order that I may obtain what other certificates are necessary as early as is possible.

I am exceedingly anxious to learn what has been done respecting Lieut [John] Dement's Bill on Mr. Collector Moses.[26] Until I hear from you on the subject I can take no further steps in the matter as they will be unnecessary should Mr. Moses honor the Bill.

I am sorry to inform you that Mr. [George W.] Hawkins's mortgage on the property in Oregon City transferred by him to Dr. [John] Haden is of no value. I called upon Mr. [Amory] Holbrook the other day and was informed by him that Lieut Hawkins had no claim to the land as, although apparently purchased by him, he never paid for it. He also told me that the property, even if sold, would not cover the amount of the mortgage. I regret much therefore to inform you that Dr. [John] Haden must devise other means to pay the amount of Lieut Hawkins's Bill endorsed by him. As my instructions on this subject are imperative, I must request you to explain the matter to Dr. Haden and to effect a settlement with him as early as is possible.

I called upon Mr. [John] Preston the other day and he informed me that it made no difference how the lines of the PS Company's claim were drawn. It is therefore unnecessary to make any alteration in your survey.

I also spoke to Mr. Preston regarding Mr. [Rudolph M.] Walker. He told me he only knew him while in Oregon City, but that they were not so intimate as to lead him to know anything regarding his pecuniary affairs. Gov [John P.] Gaines was absent from Oregon City while I was there.

Nothing further has been done towards a settlement of the seizure of the Mary Dare. Mr. Holbrook, the States' Attorney, has promised to ascertain the legal cost of the seizure as early as is possible, and I am at present in correspondence with Mr. [Maury?] Moreye[27] with hopes of inducing him to lessen his very exorbitant charge.

The Batteau with the property for Nisqually has not yet started. The arrangement of your waggons and fitting them for ocean [travel] takes longer time than I anticipated. She, however, will be sent off either tomorrow or next day.

---

24 UW Library, Tolmie Papers Acc. 4577-001, Box 1 Folder 1, letter #58.

25 A copy of this petition has yet to be located.

26 This is in regard to the Queen Charlotte Island rescue mission's promissory note to the HBC and made out by Moses.

27 H.J. Maury is either an unidentified attorney or a minor customs official of which little is known, here spelled as "Moreye" and who apparently served in the lower Puget Sound at this time.

Could you conveniently part with [John] McPhail? From what I have seen of him I like him much. The sheep are not so well taken care of as I would wish and I think I must make arrangements for taking them away. I am dear Sir, Yours very truly,

John Ballenden

Document 6.07: A letter from William F. Tolmie, Nisqually, to James Douglas, Victoria, July 8, 1852.

Dear Sir,

I duly received your letter of the 21st and 27th Ulto and have communicated your proposal regarding house-building on V[ancouver's] I[sland] to some Americans at Olympia whom I expect here today en route for Victoria. Having had letters to send, I have considered it best to forward an Express canoe and presume that the expense thereof should be divided between the Colony and General Charges. Enclosed is a list[28] of the Indians sent, and the article they will be entitled to on reaching their destination. I have made no terms with Mr. [Abraham] Way,[29] the spokesman of the American party, but have merely stated that he would meet with every encouragement and that white men on the Island charged two dollars a day for labor. The party will, I believe, consists of four and they are to have a free passage to Victoria, but find their own provision for the voyage.

The enclosed is a copy of a letter[30] lately received under cover from Mr. [Amory] Holbrook intimating to him the conditions on which the forfeiture of the Mary Dare is to be remitted. The expenses to be paid by the Company will, I fear, amount to a considerable sum. Did [our] business permit, it might be preferable to paying them to let the vessel and 230 [pounds of] crash Sugar be forfeited, and buy the former, or when sold at auction.

[Signed William F. Tolmie]

Document 6.08: A letter from William F. Tolmie, Nisqually, to John Ballenden, Vancouver, July 14, 1852.

Dear Sir,

By the present express are forwarded three letters to You addressed from Victoria, V[ancouver's] I[sland] and a Requisition of Goods for this post which please adopt in preference to that forwarded to You by post on the 22nd Ulto by Mr. [Edward] Huggins.

The Flour indented for is partly for use, and partly for Sale, and can be dispensed with should its Cost exceed $8.00 Per barrel.

I have diminished the indent for X.P. Plough Shares on the supposition that owing to the high price, the sale of them will not be so Great as anticipated.

There is a high demand for Blankets both from Americans engaged in the Fish & Oil trade and from Indians, so I trust that our Supplies may soon arrive.

---

28 This list has yet to be found.

29 Nothing on this settler or the identities of his associates, all of whom appear to be Americans seeking employment on Vancouver Island, was found.

30 See Amory Holbrook to William F. Tolmie, June 22, 1852.

Please advize me by return of bearer of the amount to be advanced Father Beard. He proposes drawing and Granting Bills for the same at once in case any political disturbances in France should destroy the source of his credit.

I have received from Mr. [Amory] Holbrook a Copy of his instructions from the Secretary of the Treasury, Washington, [D.C.] relative to the conditions on which the forfeiture of the Mary Dare is to be remitted, and fear that the expenses to be defrayed by the loss may be heavy. Mr. [Simpson P.] Moses could not inform me the other day what the amount of his charges would be. Mr. [Edward] Huggins forwarded to You, along with the Requisitions, a Copy of the Charges already paid Moses, and a duplicate thereof is herewith enclosed. It must be borne in mind that the charges of Two Hundred and Fifty Two dollars paid Moses, and entitled in his account "Warehousing consignment to W. F. Tolmie—42 days" was by his own admission in presence of Mr. Huggins, intended to cover his outlay in keeping Inspectors on board the Vessels, as the Consignment referred to remained on board the Mary Dare 'till landed at this place.

I forward this by express in order that You may get one Requisition as soon as possible. A Memo is enclosed of some things wanted by return of bearer. I remain Sir, Respectfully, Your Very Obedt Servt,

(Signed) W.F. Tolmie

Document 6.09: An invoice/letter from William F. Tolmie, Nisqually, to Lafayette Balch, Port Steilacoom, July 14, 1852.

Bought of W. F. Tolmie

2 Yoke Oxen—with yoke	$268.00
Driving said Oxen to Steilacoom	$5.00
	$273.00

Dear Sir,

The above is an Invoice of the Oxen Purchased by you recently and to be delivered today. Should it suit you to settle for them immediately pay the amount to Mr. [Walter] Ross whose receipt will be binding on me. If not, subscribe the accompanying promissory note and oblige.[31] Yours very respectfully,

S[igne]d W. F. Tolmie

Document 6.10: A letter from Lafayette Balch, Steilacoom to William F. Tolmie, Nisqually, July 14, 1852.[32]

Dear Sir,

I have just received your Communication together with the Oxen. I have concluded to Sign the Note as it would be a little more Convenient for me at present. And I have affixed the Signature of Balch and Palmer to the one you Sent. Should

---

31 A promissory note was "a written, signed, unconditional promise to pay a certain amount of money on demand at a specified time. The individual who promises to pay is the maker, and the person to whom payment is promised is called the payee or holder. If signed by the maker, a promissory note is a negotiable instrument." See: legal-dictionary.thefreedictionary.com/promissory+note.

32 Lafayette Balch to William F. Tolmie, July 14, 1852, UW Library, Tolmie Papers Acc. 4577-001, Box 1 Folder 1.

you prefer Mine Individually, you can have it changed. I am exceedingly obliged to you for your promptness in Sending the Oxen.

I wish to purchase from you Seven Blankets; [I prefer] Three Bales—please let me know the earliest opportunity [that] you can Supply me or, if not, whether you think I can obtain them at Victoria. I am Sir Very Respectfully,

Lafayette Balch

Document 6.11: A letter from William F. Tolmie, Nisqually, to William W. Miller, Olympia, July 15, 1852.

Sir,

In reply to your letter of today enquiring whether I could erect for you here a suitable building for a Surveyor of Customs Office and what rent would be charged for one year, I have to inform you that I will erect for you such a building at Nisqually Landing as soon as sawmill lumber can be obtained for the purpose and will charge no more than the customary rent for similar houses in this part of the Territory. Very Respectfully Yours,

(S[igne]d) W. F. Tolmie

Document 6.12: A letter from William F. Tolmie, Nisqually, to Simpson P. Moses, Olympia, July 15, 1852.

Sir,

In reply to your letter of the 12th Inst I beg to inform you that I have seen Mr. [William W.] Miller Surveyor of the Port of Nisqually and have agreed to erect a building for him at the landing here. Very Respectfully Yours,

(S[igne]d)W. F. Tolmie

Document 6.13: A letter from William F. Tolmie, Nisqually, to James Douglas, Victoria, July 21, 1852.

Dear Sir,

As Captain [Lafayette] Balch is sending the [American schooner] Damariscove, [Captain Eli Hathaway,] to Victoria, I avail myself the opportunity to send by that vessel the Mail accumulated here since I addressed you on the 8th Inst by the express canoe. Copy is also enclosed of a requisition lately sent to Vancouver. We are entirely out of blankets, and as the demand is brisk a supply is much to be desired. Perhaps should Mr. C[hief] F[actor John] Ballenden be unable to freight a vessel from the Columbia for Nisqually the Mary Dare might bring our goods down before going to Queen Charlotte's Island.

Captain Balch being in want of blankets for the [whale] Oil trade at Cape Flattery and being, for the moment, short of funds, has applied to me for a letter of credit for Five Hundred Dollars on you, to be expended in the purchase of blankets and other goods at Victoria. I have given him a letter of credit for the said amount and taken as security as bond on the Schooner Damariscove, copy of which is forwarded herewith and should the proceedings prove satisfactory to you I hope that Captain Balch may be accommodated.

As soon as I learn from Mr. C.F. Ballenden that he cannot freight our goods from the Columbia, I will notify you by express of the fact, in order that other measures may be adopted without delay for supplying the post. The return cargo would be Wool (about 7,000 lbs.), Furs, and a quantity of Hides wrapped up in salt—say 300 [pounds].

S[igne]d W. F. Tolmie

☙ Document 6.14: A letter from William F. Tolmie, Nisqually, to John Ballenden, Vancouver, July 24, 1852.

Dear Sir,

I have received your communication of the 6th Inst [document 6.06] accompanying two Copies of a Petition to Judge [William] Strong relative to the Steamer [*Beaver*]'s trade goods and now return one copy filled up with all the signatures and attestations [evidences] required.

Mr. Collector [Simpson P.] Moses asks a little more time in regard to the payment of the Bill he accepted from Lieut [John] Dement [regarding the Queen Charlotte Island Expedition] and expresses a confident expectation that he will soon have instructions from Washington [D.C.] to pay it and other claims of a like nature. The bill was not formally presented and protested, but that can be done whenever you may desire it. From the tenor of the correspondence shown me by Mr. Moses, I am inclined to think his expectation well-formed that govt will assume his liabilities incurred for the release of the prisoners on 2nd Aug.

I have seen Dr. [John M.] Haden respecting the [Lieutenant George W.] Hawkins Bill he endorsed, and regret to inform you that he declares his inability to pay the bill in full, but states that he will endeavor to make up any deficiencies that may remain after the Coy have instituted legal proceedings against Hawkins. The Doctor's idea is that both he and Hawkins should be sued by the Co and not himself alone.

[John] Macphail's services can be dispensed with here at Nisqually, but as Mr. [James] D[ouglas] has applied for him lately for [Edward E.] Langford's[33] farm, he, as head of the PS Coy in this Country will, I presume, decide on where [John] Macphail is to be sent to.

It will be necessary to ascertain 'ere the Mary Dare returns to Victoria, whether you can find it useful or not in the Columbia to send our goods round on, but I propose sending a boat to Victoria for some bales next week, Mr. Moses having issued a Circular to the Customhouse officers of the District to the effect that it is lawful to import goods in boats, rafts, &c.

S[igne]d W. F. Tolmie

---

33 On May 10, 1851, Langford arrived on the *Tory* from Brighton in 1851 with his wife and daughters. He became the bailiff or "manager" of the 600 acre Esquimalt Farm near Fort Victoria on Vancouver Island. He called the farm Colwood Farm and earned £60 a year and one-third of the profits generated. www.biographi.ca/en/bio/langford_edward_edwards_12E.html.

Document 6.15: A letter from William F. Tolmie, Nisqually, to James Douglas, Victoria, July 25, 1852.

Dear Sir,

The present is forwarded by Captain [George] Plummer of the Brig John Davis who, having brought some forty or fifty tons freight from San Francisco to this place for His Reverence Bishop [Modeste] Demers,[34] now proceeds with it to Victoria on the terms Specified in the accompanying copy of agreement.

Mr. Demers had consigned the packages to me and written requesting, as a favor, that they might be stored here and forwarded hereafter by the Coy's vessels to Vancouver's Island. I would have taken on myself to have stored the goods here had the generality of the packages not been too very large and weighty—that to have attempted landing and storing them, unprovided as we are with scows, boats or trucks, would have been a very tedious and offensive operation, involving much risk of injury to the goods and which we are unfitted to undertake, in the midst of harvest above all reasons.

Herewith is a Circular from Coll[ector Simpson P.] Moses to the officers on duty in his district intimating that goods can be imported otherwise than by vessels above 30 tons berthen & Mr. Moses has given a general order to Mr. ~~Ord~~ [William W.] Miller, Surveyor of the port, to enter at this place all goods coming in boats or canoes; and I had engaged a Large boat here to send for blankets but abandoned the intention on finding that the John Davis had to proceed to Victoria. Will you please send us either by return of the John Davis, or by your green boat, the bales as enumerated in the accompanying indent [charge]. Should the boat be sent, the person in charge of it should have Mr. Moses's circular at hand to present to any C[ustom] H[ouse] Officers he may meet en route to Nisqually and he should be careful about delaying unnecessarily in any way in coming along the US Coast.

I am to erect a house at the landing to be rented by Mr. Surv[e]y[o]r Miller, he having been instructed from Washington [D.C.] to reside at the port of delivery.

Mr. Moses desired information the other day as to whether it will be necessary for him to have a bonded Warehouse here wherein to store our goods. I said in reply that I saw no immediate necessity for such a measure, but that I would write you on the subject. He has an iron screw for pressing which he wishes to sell for $90 and says that is such as is used in the States for preparing Tob[acc]o and Wool. The screw is about 30 inches long and 3 inches in diameter or thereabouts. A copy of a drawing representing it in use is forwarded.[35]

Captain Plummer has just returned from Olympia where he has been making arrangements for entering here any cargo he may bring back from Victoria. I have agreed in that case to take his papers to the custom house, along with my own. He hopes you will unload him in the outer harbor preferring much to pay lighterage rather than take his vessel in. He asks $10 p[e]r ton for a return cargo, but will probably take less. Goods could, I think, be brought for much less in your large boat, but the risk would be greater. I have come under no obligation whatever to

---

34 See note 10 above.

35 No drawing of the screw press was present in the letterbook and it is believed to have been a separate document.

find Plummer a return cargo. "Padlock"[36] and his wife go passengers in the John Davis and their passage has been paid in beef and vegetables.

S[igne]d W. F. Tolmie

P.S. In making the agreement with Captain Plummer, I have acted on the supposition that Bishop Demers being about to establish on V[ancouver's] I[sland] will, of course, have funds to reimburse Fort Nisqually for the present outlay, and that the goods belonging to him will at all events be answerable for the freight paid on them. In the Bill Lading from San Francisco, of which Mr. Demers sent me no copy, are enumerated fifteen packages containing materials for a printing press and sixty nine packages of merchandize, but Captain Plummer and his mate affirm that only sixty eight or sixty nine packages were received on board in all. A pro-forma entry of merchandize is sent. 'Tis not required that the advance of 50/p[e]r cent should be made on any but English goods. Sandwich Island products may be invoiced at a very little over cost. S[igne]d W. F. T.

Document 6.16: A purchase order from William F. Tolmie, Nisqually, to Rudolph M. Walker, Olympia, July 29, 1852.

Dear Sir,

Subjoined is the Bill of Timber I spoke of yesterday. You will oblige by getting it Completed as early as Convenient.

600 feet Boards	1 inch Thick	20 feet long
600 [feet Boards]	1 [inch Thick]	11 [feet long]
5 M [feet Boards]	1 [inch Thick]	12 [feet long]

Very Respectfully Yours,
(Signed) W. F. Tolmie

Document 6.17: A letter from William F. Tolmie, Nisqually, to Father Beard, Olympia, July 31, 1852.

Dear Sir,

I received yesterday your note of the 26th and, as requested, send by the mail man the bills of Exchange &c., p[e]r Thom[a]s Tompice[37] Assuring as You unto £384.6/ Sterling to be equal to Ten Thousand Francs [f10,000.00] and deducting these from the Debt already drawn and paid for, your credit here will come to (£309.6/) Three hundred and nine pounds six Shillings St[erlin]g for which Amount the Bills are drawn. Against this Amount I now will apply in our books the 100 $ advanced Pere [Father] Temppart[38] [sic] at Victoria. Very Respectfully Yours,

Signed W. F. Tolmie

36 Padlock (an Indian). No other information was found regarding this individual or his wife.

37 Nothing was found on this individual who quite possibly was linked to St. Joseph's Catholic Mission in today's Priest Point Park, Olympia, Washington.

38 Nothing was found regarding this Catholic Mission priest who resided in today's Victoria, British Columbia.

Document 6.18: A letter from James Grahame, Vancouver, to William F. Tolmie, Nisqually, July 31, 1852.[39]

Dear Sir,

Accompanying, I beg to hand you [an] Invoice and Bill of lading of goods forwarded [to] you per Schooner Mary Taylor;[40] a priced Invoice will be sent by Post.

The freight, which you will perceive per "Bill of lading" amounts to nine hundred and nine 07/100 dollars ($909.07/100), you will pay to Captain [Hiram E.] Hutchinson[41] deducting amount supplied him at this place as per his receipt on "Bill of lading", say seventy four 50/100 dollars ($74.50) leaving an amount due him of eight hundred and thirty four 57/100 dollars ($834.57/100).

Mr. [Chief Factor John] Ballenden has requested me to inform you that he will write you by Mail. Yours respectfully,

J. A. Graham for HB Co

Document 6.19: A letter from William F. Tolmie, Nisqually, to James Douglas, Victoria, August 1, 1852.

Dear Sir,

By the bearer, Sclousin,[42] a Port Townsend Indian who says he has business at Victoria, I forward the accompanying letter to your address received by mail yesterday. Old Lucifer[43] and family obtain a passage from "Sclousin" the old man promising to repay the outlay on his account by working for the Company at Victoria. I have nothing fresh to communicate since addressing you on the 26th Ulto by the Brig John Davis.

Sclousin, on delivering the letters, will be entitled to a blanket 3 p[oin]ts; and each of his crew—five in all—will be entitled to a C[ommon] S[triped] Shirt ~~each~~ a piece.

Please to send by first opportunity 50 or more panes Window Glass of the

39 UW Library, Tolmie Papers Acc. 4577-001, Box #1, Folder #4.

40 *Mary Taylor*, American schooner. Captain Hiram M. Hutchinson, master (below). She ran cargo between Olympia and Victoria.

41 Likely born in Vermont, Hiram Edson Hutchinson, captain of the *Mary Taylor*, arrived with son Millard in the Pacific Northwest around 1848 and operated a freight service in Puget Sound. His first marriage to Vermont native Melinda Cutler had ended in her untimely death in 1843. Hutchinson eventually settled on Lopez Island where he established a trading post/post office. "Hi," as he was called by his close friends, "ran his business largely on the barter system, cash money being scarce supply. He had sugar, coffee, beans and nails which he purchased from Victoria. Since the British outlawed living on Lopez in 1853 it can be assumed that either he was not here then, or that he was in good relations with the government of Victoria (from where he purchased his goods for sale)." Later on, following the boundary settlement, Joseph Merril and Hutchinson ran about 650 head of sheep on Lopez Island for years. freepages.history.rootsweb.ancestry.com/~lopezislandhistory.

42 Sclousin (an Indian) [var: Slousin, or Bill.] Here, Tolmie describes the fort's steward and dairyman as "a Port Townsend Indian" which would affiliate him with the S'Klallam tribe. Alternately, Edward Huggins described him as "a short, but very stout and strong [Nisqually] Indian, a solid and [undemonstrative] man, who scarcely ever smiled and talked but little. He was brave, and a good fighter, and would not hesitate a moment to fight and would keep it up if necessary to the bitter end. He was in charge of the dairy and with the help of subordinate Indians was then milking between seventy and eighty cows, many of which were half wild, Spanish bred brutes and it required a courageous and strong man to handle them." For more see: Edward Huggins's "The Story of 'Bill' or 'Sclousin,'" unpublished typescript, October 13, 1900, UW Library, Edward Huggins Papers.

43 Old Lucifer (an Indian) was not identified or mentioned in any other Nisqually records.

kind ordered in the Requisition, and a bladder Putty. These articles are required for the house we are building for the Surveyor of Customs at the beach.

S[igne]d W. F. Tolmie

P.S. A manifest, Invoice and Entry should accompany the Window Glass [all the way into] port. The enclosed is from Dr. Bris [illegible].[44] More about him when I have the pleasure of seeing you. He has gone to Oregon City. T.

Document 6.20: A letter from William F. Tolmie, Nisqually, to John Ballenden, Vancouver, August 7, 1852.

D[ea]r Sir,

I duly received by return of Cush[45] your letter of the 27th Ulto and have lost no time in seeing Dr. [John M.] Haden about your last proposition—that he should pay the [Lieutenant George W.] Hawkins' bill by four tri-monthly installments, and grant bills for each of these. The Doctor reiterated his statement communicated in mine of the 24th Ulto, that he was not able to pay the full amount, but said he would do his utmost. He spoke of compromising the matter stating that if the Coy would exonerate him on payment of One Thousand dollars he would endeavor to pay them that amount as soon as possible, and that, if on returning to the States, which he expects to do in some three months hence, he should succeed in compelling Hawkins to cash up. He would thereupon pay the balance, which, with Interest, would amount to between five and six hundred dollars. He seemed uncertain, provided you acceded to his proposal, as to when he could muster $1,000, stating that it would depend on several contingencies, such as whether double pay would be continued to the US troops in Oregon or not, and whether or not he should be ordered home this fall, adding that if he went to the States he would be more speedily in funds.

A Mr. [Thomas] Maylor[46] residing near Olympia has enquired whether the Coy would cash a certificate of Bank Deposit from the British Bank of N[orth] America at Hamilton, Canada 88, for £200 Curr[enc]y. He also wishes to receive

44 The writing was faint on the photocopy received, so this could be Dr. John K. Bristow, who arrived from Illinois on the Oregon Trail in October 1852.

45 Though mentioned only once in this set of letters, the Snohomish Indian "Cush" (c. 1820–1858) was in fact a regular employee of Fort Nisqually. There, he had worked from at least 1849 as a general laborer, courier, foreman, and, principally, as cook. Edward Huggins, the fort's clerk, described Cush as "fat-faced . . . good-natured . . . jolly . . . possessing a fund of humor, and the powers of mimicry seldom seen among Indians . . . and was liked by everyone, whites and Indians [alike]. He had a way of speaking broken English, which was irresistibly funny." In a case of mistaken identity, "Cush was shot fatally [in 1858], and died a day or two afterwards." Edward Huggins, "A Trip from Fort Nisqually to Cowlitz in 1850," *Oregonian*, September 9, 1900. Parts I–9th & II– 23rd September 1900; Edward Huggins, "The Killing of Cush," *Oregonian*, August 19, 1900; and Steve A. Anderson, (ed.) *Fort Nisqually Indian Accounts Book; Commencing September 1849, Ending January 1851* as derived from the Huntington Library, Soliday Collection, Nisqually Papers, FN 1242, Volume 2 (San Marino, CA: Rampart Publications, Cape Carteret, North Carolina, 2012).

46 "In 1852, Irish immigrant Thomas Maylor Sr., and his brother Samuel canoed down Puget Sound and examined what would be called Alki Point. They kept paddling because there were too many Indians there. The Maylors pushed on to Oak Harbor where they bought land on the peninsula that separated Oak Harbor from Crescent Harbor. This became Maylor's, and later Forbes, Point." "Oak Harbor—Thumbnail History," HistoryLink.org Essay 8223; www.historylink.org.

remittances from Ireland through the Company, and is to direct his friends there to address Mr. Sec[retar]y [Archibald] Barclay on the subject.

Please to hasten the manufacture of the X.P. Plough shares at Oregon City as much as possible. Owing to their high price there, and the prospect of a supply from Victoria this winter my requisition for ploughshares might be reduced to 25 but [please] have the goodness to get more with all despatch, and forward to Mr. [Edward] Spencer for transmission by [Edward D.] Warbass's[47] boats. You would oblige me by laying in for Nisqually this fall while the article is abundant, forty or fifty pounds of good turnip seed. I would also take four or five pounds Carrot Seed.

Mr. [Simpson P.] Moses's bill will be protested unless paid next week, immediately after the arrival of the mail. I have the honor Sir,

S[igne]d W. F. Tolmie

Document 6.21: A letter from William F. Tolmie, Olympia, to Modeste Demers, Victoria, August 7, 1852.

D[ea]r Sir,

Your letter by Capt [George] Plummer [of the brig *John Davis*] came duly to hand, and I regret much that it was not in my power to land and store your goods at Nisqually, as we were at the time in the midst of harvest and besides had neither boats nor scows wherein to safely land the very large and heavy cases to your address.

I therefore became bound to Capt Plummer for the balance due of your freight from San Francisco, Three Hundred and Ninety Dollars, and agreed to pay him Four Hundred and Fifty Dollars additional to proceed with the goods to Vancouver's Island, making a total of Eight Hundred and Forty Dollars, which I shall have to pay on your account to Captain Plummer probably on the 10th Inst.

I hope, therefore, that when you come to Puget's Sound, you will be prepared promptly to reimburse me in the above named amounts, as you must be aware that in making the advance I have departed from the Company's usual mode of doing business. Hoping soon to have the pleasure of seeing you, [I remain, &c., &c.,]

S[igne]d W. F. Tolmie

Document 6.22: A letter from William F. Tolmie, Nisqually, to George W. Brown, the *Persia*,[48] August 12, 1852.[49]

Dear Sir,

The beef & Vegetables ordered by you last week are now sent on your acc[ou]nt

47 A New Jersey native, Warbass (1825–1906) traveled to California in 1849, where he was an auctioneer at Sacramento. With his health failing, he visited Oregon and settled at Cowlitz, there laying out Warbassport. Opening a store near present day Toledo, Washington, he engaged in the forwarding and commission business. He explored the Bellingham area for coal during this period (1850–1853). He continued to live on the Cowlitz until 1855, when he volunteered to fight in the Indian War. He became Post Sutler at Bellingham Bay and San Juan Island, where he lived. There, he was county auditor and member of the legislature from San Juan County. Bancroft, *History of Washington, Idaho and Montana* (see footnotes on 37, 167, 340, 381, 383). See also Edmund S. Meany, "News Department: History Sustains Losses," *Washington Historical Quarterly* 1, no.3 (April 1907), 176.

48 *Persia*, American ship. Captain George W. Brown, master. This vessel carried mail and sheep.

49 The location or station of Captain Brown's ship was not disclosed in the letter, but is believed to be Olympia. No biographical information could be found on this ship's captain.

herewith. Please return a note acknowledging receipt thereof and stating the quantity of both you will require next week. Very Resp[ectfull]y Yours,

S[igne]d W. F. Tolmie

Document 6.23: An incidental note at the end of William F. Tolmie's letterbook of 1852.

[The] Mail Steamer [to San Francisco?] leaves Oregon about the 10th & 25th of every month.

M[isters C. Samuel] Parker & [Stephen C.] Foster—Sacramento City, Box 24, California

Sheep to be deliver'd at St. Helens for 25 Cents each.

Tho[ma]s Carter—Portland.[50]

Document 6.24: A letter from William F. Tolmie, Nisqually, to John Ballenden, Vancouver, August 14, 1852.[51]

Dear Sir,

Your communication of the 2nd Inst accompanying Invoice and Bill Lading of your Shipment per "Mary Taylor" was received at Olympia yesterday.

The freight [charge] of $20 per ton is certainly very high, but it is the usual rate between [the] Columbia River and Puget's Sound, and our Sales will, I trust, be profitable nevertheless. I regret that Capt[ain Hiram E.] Hutchinson's base assertion that I promised him a cargo should have proved any obstacle to your making as good a bargain as possible for the conveyance of our goods; as had I come under any such obligation to him, I would immediately have notified you thereof. I merely sent Hutchinson a verbal intimation by a ship Captain who had purchased the last of our Blankets that there was freight at Vancouver for Nisqually to the amount of twenty five or thirty tons, and that if the "Mary Taylor" proceeded soon to Columbia River, she might probably be engaged to bring it around.

The Wedders for Vancouver will be sent across [the portage] early in September in charge of the party who go for the wild horses. Please inform me what number of horses you intend sending across and whether much difficulty may be anticipated in getting them away from Cattlepootle; also whether amongst the number there will be any horses fit for riding. Have the goodness also to mention the number of Sheep you propose transferring to Nisqually. These I shall expect to have charged against this P[uget] S[ound] Post at five shillings per head, the credit given by Mr. [Peter S.] Ogden for those sent from this to Vancouver last year. Herewith is forwarded a bill of Exchange from Father [Pascal] Ricard for £309.6/ Sterling with the letter of advance. Thereanent, the second and third sets of exchange remain here.

---

50 Document 6.23 denotes the conclusion of the HBCA's Fort Nisqually Correspondence Outward, 1850–1852 manuscript.

51 Document 6.24 denotes the start of the HBCA's Fort Nisqually Correspondence Outward, 1852–1854, Commencing August 14, 1852, Ending August 11, 1854, B.151/b/2. HBC Archives of Manitoba. From this point forward all documents not otherwise footnoted were acquired from this source.

Please to credit Ft Nisqually O[utfi]t [18]52 with the sum of Eight Hundred and forty Dollars, which charge to Mr. [Jean-Baptiste Abraham Brouillet][52] as p[e]r his [note] herewith.

I wrote you by mail on the 7th Inst and particularly requested your getting 25 [X.P.] 59 Plough Shares made for this place as soon as convenient.

I presented yesterday, in presence of witnesses, Mr. [Lieutenant John] Dement's Bill on Collector [Simpson P.] Moses, and the latter declined a payment "for want of public funds, and no instructions having been received from the Government to check upon any of its [suppositions] for the amount due." The Bill will be duly protested on the third day after presentation, it having been drawn payable three days after sign[in]g.

I start for Victoria today, Mr. [Alexander C.] Anderson remaining in charge during my absence.[53] I remain Sir, Your Very Obedt Servt,

(S[igne]d) W. F. Tolmie

Document 6.25: A letter from William F. Tolmie, Nisqually, to Daniel R. Bigelow,[54] Newmarket, August 14, 1852.

Dear Sir,

After completing the protest on the bill I left with you yesterday, please deliver it to the bearer under sealed cover to A[lexander] C. Anderson Esq[ui]re, Nisqually. I will be at [Vancouver's Island,] F[ort] V[ictoria] and with their [illegible] with you for as [illegible] trouble.[55]

---

52 Brouillet (1813–1883) was a native Canadian, born in the village of St. Jean-Baptiste de Rouville. After attending seminary he eventually worked in the Catholic Church and arrived in Oregon Territory in the later 1840s. By 1850 he was appointed vicar general of the newly created Diocese of Nesqually, which was headquartered in Vancouver. During that time he visited California, Mexico, and Europe, eventually moving back east where he passed away at the age of 48, in 1883. For more see Abing, Kevin, "Directors of the Bureau of Catholic Indian Missions: Reverend John Baptiste Abraham Brouillet, 1874–1884," www.marquette.edu/library/archives/Mss/BCIM/BCIM-SC1-directors1.pdf.

53 For Anderson see Watson, *Lives Lived*, 1:152–53.

54 Bigelow (1824–1905) was a native of New York, the youngest child of Jotham Bigelow and Cylindia Bullock Bigelow. He was educated at Union College in Schenectady, New York, and after teaching a year, entered Harvard where he read law and graduated in 1850. After graduation, Bigelow searched for a place to practice law; first to Indiana and then to Dodhevillee, Wisconsin, where he spent 16 months. On March 24, 1851, Bigelow set out for the Oregon Territory, arriving in Portland, on October 8, 1851. He noted in his diary that there were 20 to 30 lawyers in the city. Bigelow sailed from Portland with the Denny party on the schooner *Exact* on November 8, 1851. After a seasick trip and a stop at Alki Point in Seattle, he went to Olympia. Bigelow was among the first to practice law in the area, and at the first term of court for Northern Oregon in 1852, he along with Isaac N. Ebey, Quincy A. Brooks, Simpson P. Moses, and Elwood Evans were admitted to practice in the courts of Oregon Territory. At that time Bigelow was practicing law in partnership with Quincy Brooks. When he died, Bigelow was the oldest survivor of the first territorial legislature. Boyle, Wagner Architects, *The Bigelow House & Site: Condition Assessment, Potential Use Analysis & History* (Olympia, WA: September, 1991), 2–13.

55 From August 14 to September 8, 1852, Fort Nisqually was administered by Chief Trader Alexander C. Anderson while Dr. Tolmie was visiting Vancouver Island.

Document 6.26: A letter from Alexander C. Anderson, Nisqually, to Edmund A. Starling, Port Steilacoom, September 7, 1852.

Sir,

Acting upon information we had received, we have succeeded, after much trouble, in securing two Indians who are connected on the clearest evidence of having committed sundry depredations on our sheep flocks. The offenders are now in custody here; and as it is important that an adequate punishment should be inflicted in order to deter future offenders, I take the liberty of applying to you. Please to inform me by return of bearers, if it will be agreeable to you, that I should send the Indians to you in order that they may meet with their deserts under your authority at the [Steilacoom] Barracks; or whether, on the other hand we shall punish them summarily here, and dismiss them. Very Respectfully Yours,

Alex[ander] C. Anderson, C[hief] T[rader] H Bay Coy.

NB. For Mr. Starling's reply to the above; see [response] on flysheet of the book.[56]

Document 6.27: A letter from Edmund A. Starling, Port Steilacoom, to Alexander C. Anderson, Nisqually, September 7, 1852.

Sir,

I have just rec[eive]d your note in relation to the two Indians whom you state have been committing depredations on your sheep flocks. The right plan to persue would be to send them here; they would then have to be placed in confinement, and await the sitting of Court in this Country which, at times, is very indefinite. I would, therefore, in place of sending them here, have a good sound flogging administered to them at your place—explaining to them ostensibly the reasons for so punishing them. I am Respectfully, Your obt svt,

E. A. Starling, Ind[ian] ag[en]t

Document 6.28: A letter from William F. Tolmie, Nisqually, to John Ballenden, Vancouver, September 10, 1852.

Dear Sir,

On returning from Vancouver's Island on the 8th Inst, I received from Mr. C[hief] T[rader Alexander C.] Anderson your communication of the 14th Ulto, accompanying copy of your mem[orand]a to Mr. [Adolphus Lee] Lewes[57] regarding the wild horses to be driven to Cowlitz. The party from Nisqually with the Wedders will meet Mr. Lewes without fail on the 18th Inst at [Edward D.] Warbasses' [landing on the] upper Cowlitz. Should you decide on returning the Vancouver Sheep at that place, John MacPhail can be sent thither as soon as you may desire.

I enclose duplicate of a letter addressed to you on the 7th Ulto, being apprehensive that the original may have miscarried. I have not seen Dr. Haden since my return.

---

56 The note referred to here is the next letter in this series although it was originally located on the inside front cover "flysheet" of the original manuscript.

57 For Lewes see Watson. *Lives Lived*, 2:591–92.

Enclosed is a receipt from Capt [William] Howard[58] for Fifty Dollars /$50/ lent him by Mr. [A.C.] Anderson. Please advize when payment is made in order that the amount may be charged against Ft Vancouver Sale Shop. I remain Sir,

S[igne]d W. F. Tolmie

Document 6.29: A bill of exchange from William F. Tolmie, Nisqually, to John Ballenden, Vancouver, September 13, 1852.

D[ear] Sir,

Agreeably to your instructions I now forward the 2nd & third of Exchange of Pere [Pascal] Ricard's bill of Exchange for £309.6/.

S[igne]d W. F. Tolmie

Document 6.30: A letter from William F. Tolmie, Nisqually, to James Douglas, Victoria, September 15, 1852.

Dear Sir,

Herewith are forwarded the letters and papers for Victoria accumulated here since last mail, also copy of the Rev[eren]d R[obert] J. Staines' accounts, here with his order in favor of Captain [William R.] Pattle for $27.50 as a voucher.

Mr. Collector [Simpson P.] Moses expresses his readiness to receive his bill in payment of duties, provided an entry of goods be made to the deductible amount on duty of twenty-five hundred dollars, so as to put him in funds for current expenses.

I have seen Mr. [Rudolph] Walker about the lumber for Victoria, and will know in a day or two hence how soon he can commence preparing it. I remain, Sir,

S[igne]d W. F. Tolmie

P.S. A parcel of Pitsaw Files (2 dozen) are sent as requested. T.

Document 6.31: A letter from William F. Tolmie, Nisqually, to Rudolph M. Walker, Newmarket, September 16, 1852.

Dear Sir,

Will you please write one by return of bearer, or first opportunity, at what rate p[er] M [thousand] and by what date, you can supply the following bills of Lumber:

600 Boards 1 ½ in[che]s thick, 12 f[ee]t long, 12 in[che]s broad.

600 [boards] 1½ in[che]s thick, 12 f[ee]t long, 6 in[che]s wide.

58 Edward Huggins' recollection: "'Twas said that [William Howard, an] . . . ex United States Revenue officer . . . was in the celebrated Forrest divorce suit . . . [and] was a large, handsome, and highly accomplished man, and soon became very intimate with the leading men [at Fort Nisqually] of that early date and also with No. 1 people of Victoria, British Columbia, and especially with Mr. [James] Douglas. He spent many a day and night here [with me], and, of course, I had to share my room with him. He was the agent for the Bellingham Bay Coal Company, and I think superintended the opening of the coal mine. He tried very hard to get me to accept the position . . . person in charge of the store, the coal company intended to open at the mines. He was often present when I was trading with the down Sound Indians, and he had an idea that I was an infinitely smarter man than I knew myself to be . . . and as far as Howard, he quietly disappeared, some said he reentered the United States Government service, and became prominent in the [Civil War]." Edward Huggins to Ezra Meeker, May 3, 1903, WSHS Ezra Meeker Manuscript Collection T-145, Box 5/fo. 15, Washington State Historical Society, Tacoma.

20 M [thousand] feet Cedar Clapboards 6 in[che]s wide.
S[igne]d W. F. Tolmie

Document 6.32: A letter from William F. Tolmie, Nisqually, to Simpson P. Moses, Olympia, September 17, 1852.[59]

Sir,

In paying taxes on the Puget's Sound Agricultural Coy's lands, which you inform me the Board of County Commissioners have ordered to be assessed, I hereby declare that I pay under protest, the said taxes amounting to Six Hundred and Forty five dollars and Twelve Cents ($645.12/100). Very Respectfully Yours,

William Fraser Tolmie

Document 6.33: A letter from William F. Tolmie, Nisqually, to John Ballenden, Vancouver, September 27, 1852.

Dear Sir,

Herewith is forwarded a list of things required at this post in case there may be an opportunity of shipping them 'round by the vessel bringing the troops, or otherwise.

Mr. [Walter] Ross, as you would have perceived by his receipt given, only received 25 head of horses from Mr. Lewis, and five of these were foals of 1852. I hope that effectual means may be devised for rendering the wild geldings at Lewis's driveable, as thirty or forty good young horses would be a great acquisition here. Please to send me soon as convenient the Nisqually Servant's Accounts up to 1st June 1852.

(Signed) W. F. Tolmie

Document 6.34: A letter from William F. Tolmie, Nisqually, to John Ballenden, Vancouver, October 4, 1852.

Dear Sir,

Herewith is forwarded an "Abstract" lately received from Mr. Collector [Simpson P.] Moses of Custom house Charges against the "Mary Dare" on account of her seizure, he requested as a favor that immediate payment should be made, but I declined doing so before submitting the account to you. In the Charge "Custody of Vessel 55 days $330.00" it was understood between Mr. Moses and myself that an abatement would be made of the $252.00 mentioned in mine to you of July 7th/[18]52 and paid same to him under protest on the 20th May 1852. The said sum was then intended to cover the expense of keeping Inspectors on board the "Mary Dare" and has only been included on the present [account], Mr. Moses says, in case any protest which he duly forwarded should be favorably received at the Treasury Department at Washington [D.C.]. I remain Sir, Your Very obedient Servant,

(Signed) W. F. Tolmie

---

59 Here, Simpson P. Moses is credited with the title of office "Deputy Sheriff Thurston County, Oregon Territory."

P.S. I am prevented by a lame right land from writing privately. Please reply to the above as soon as possible. T.

Document 6.35: An Abstract of Charges by Simpson P. Moses, Olympia, to William F. Tolmie, Nisqually, October 4, 1852.

An Abstract of Custom House Charges against
the Brigantine "Mary Dare" on [the occasion] of her seizure.

To: paid W[illiam] W. Miller for riding express to Cathlamet & to hasten a special term of Court, such being not only my duty, but W[illiam] F. Tolmie, Esq, requesting me to use.

Requisition to procure a speedy adjudication	$225.00
The Clerke employed	$155.00
Custody of Vessel—55 days	$330.00
D[aniel] R. Bigelow's Fees	$100.00
To Clerk of Court—for [multiple] Copies of [letters] &c.,	$20.00
Postage	$2.00
Paid A[lonzo] M. Poe, for hire of boat	$50.00
Paid boarding Officers	$20.00
Paid boatmen	$250.00
	$1,152.00

Signed S[impson] P. Moses, Col[lector of Customs]

Document 6.36: A letter from William F. Tolmie, Nisqually, to James Douglas, Victoria, October 5, 1852.

Dear Sir,

Herewith is forwarded the Victoria mail with Memorandum of Articles required for this post by return of Canoe. Mr. [Rudolph] Walker, having rented the new Saw Mill at Newmarket, offers to Supply Pine lumber at $24.00 per Thousand [board] feet—deliverable at the point of embarkation below the [Deschutes] falls. He asks $31.00 per Thousand ft Cedar Clap boarding, and I have requested him to prepare the pine lumber first so as to maintain whether you are willing to give $31 for the Cedar before he commences sawing it. He would probably [trade a] large proportion of the amount to be paid for said lumber in Goods at 10 P[e]r Cent discount on our retail price. I've no prospect so far [for] Shipping the lumber to Victoria [and I have heard nothing/little] of the California T[rade in this article. If possible,] please to advize me by [return] whether or not [good coal is available for purchase and what we] can best time it at [for delivery to this place] and at what rate P[e]r Ton—as positive information on these points would be required on making a Contract p[e]r the Conveyance of the lumber. Have the Goodness also to state how much you would be willing to Give P[e]r Thousand feet for the transport of the lumber.

We have here for Shipment for Victoria 7,000 [pounds of] Wool, 5 Bales Furs and nearly 1,000 Green Hides salted and folded which, if carefully resalted at Victoria, could I think, be shipped to England with safety. The Collector of Taxes informed me lately that he had been directed by the County Court to [assess] Taxes on the lands Claimed by the Puget's Sound Agricultural Company and I accordingly paid him under protest $645.12, that being the Amount of Tax at 75 Cent p[e]r Acre on the extent of our lands, 224 square Miles, as shown by the late survey [by John Chapman]. At the December term of the County and [Territorial circuit] Court is the proper time for stating any reasons for objecting to pay the Taxes, and I can then, if it be thought advisable, do so.

Mr. Thomas Dean is [making] demands that his Son [Thomas] Aubrey [Dean Jr.][60] should be allowed to finish his time at this place, provided he would make a solemn promise to you of Good behavior whilst here. As one of our Englishmen left lately and some of the others are so intemperate and neglectful of duty as well, unless they reform, render their departure a desirable event, I am sure that [Aubrey] Dean, if steady, would be Very useful.

William Johnson,[61] formerly of Cowlitz, has begged as a particular favor to be allowed to go and work for the Company at Victoria; and I have made him the promise of employment there without any stipulation as to wages, rations, &c. Had he not been a Squatter on the PS [Agricultural] Comp's lands [at Cowlitz], I would not have given him a passage, and having already proved himself a slippery character, he is of course unworthy of much accommodation in the way of advances.

Please to send a Manifest, Invoice and Copy of the things to be sent by the Canoe in Charge of William Young. Instead of 70 Head of Horses comprising a fair proportion of unbroken Geldings, we have only received from Vancouver 25 head in all, all unbroken. and chiefly Mares and Young animals. I will consequently have to purchase horses from Indians to Supply the number You Request this fall. I shall therefore endeavor to purchase and hope to obtain them [in trade] for Goods.

---

60 Thomas Aubrey Dean (1831–1913) was an HBC sponsored settler, PSAC employee, of English descent. He was a farm laborer at Fort Nisqually 1852–1853. Shortly after Dean and his family (his father had been hired as a bailiff for the Fort Nisqually stock farm) received a cash advance in London, he sailed around the Horn and arrived at Fort Victoria on May 9, 1851. While his parents and brother George continued on to Nisqually, Thomas Aubrey stayed at Fort Victoria working as a laborer for the HBC until October 22, 1852 when he arrived at Nisqually to serve out the remainder of his term with his father working for PSAC. For the entertainment of others, he worked two Punch and Judy puppets which he made himself, sang comic songs and played a tin whistle which he also made himself. By June 18, 1853, he had had enough and quit before the end of his contract. By December he had settled on a claim of 160 acres in the Puyallup Valley; he was given a warning the same year by PSAC that he was squatting on PSAC land. On January 9 of the following year, he declared his intention to become a U.S. citizen. He was likely working there when, in November 1856 and January 1857, he was recorded as bringing in wheat and oxen to Fort Nisqually. At an unknown date, he took up homestead claims near Spanaway and raised cattle and sheep on purchased railroad land. After living on Tanawax Prairie he moved to Silver Lake on a 40 acre spread near the lake. There he died on October 24, 1913. Information courtesy of Bruce M. Watson, HBC Biographer. See also: www.gov.mb.ca/chc/archives/hbca/biographical/d.html, and www.voyagerrecords.com/arNWFiddlers.htm.

61 Johnson is likely the Cowlitz settler who, with wife Leona, moved to present day Winlock (then Cowlitz Farm lands) with his family in 1851, and who finally settled in the Ainsley District. It is doubtful that this squatter obtained a job in Victoria with Tolmie's less than glowing recommendation. Alma Nix and John Nix, eds., *The History of Lewis County, Washington* (Chehalis: Lewis County Historical Society, 1985), 224.

Mr. Walter Ross, who has unfortunately fractured his forearm by a fall from horseback, would not have proceeded to Victoria [if his injuries were not of such a serious nature. I might have been able to care for him as a] convalescent had I not been laid up with a Boil on the hand [which developed as I was] preparing attending to his Call. I particularly request to have the [supplies that I have ordered] sent by first opportunity. I Remain Sir, Your Most Ob St,

(Signed) W. F. Tolmie

[P.S.] Fifty Barrels of the Flour received from Victoria P[e]r "John Davis" are so Poor as I fear to be useless for me.

Document 6.37: A letter from James Douglas, Victoria, to William F. Tolmie, Nisqually, October 14, 1852.[62]

Dear Sir,

The Nasqually Indians arrived here on the 12th inst with the Vancouver mail, and your letter dated the 5th of October to which I shall now reply.

Mr. [Rudolph] Walker's removal to Newmarket will I fear prove an inconvenience to us, should lumber be purchased from him, as the increased distance will add considerably to the charge of transport to this place. In those circumstances I approve of your not giving him the order for the cedar clap boards, which can be prepared here at fully less expense; but I beg you will complete the order given for the inch [thick] deals [boards] which will all be required for the new farming establishments of the Puget Sound [Agricultural] Company.

In regard to the transport of that lumber to this place, we will be able to effect it by one or our own vessels as I shall send either the new Brigantine Vancouver or the Mary Dare to Nesqually about the beginning of December next, about which time the lumber should be brought down to meet the vessel there in order to avoid detention. A requisition for any goods required by that conveyance should therefore be forwarded to this place some time previously, that they may be put up in readiness for the vessel. The Nesqually Wool and Furs may also be shipped by the same conveyance. Should any earlier opportunity occur of forwarding the lumber, and other freight at a low rate of charge by any other vessel to this place, I have no objections to your taking that course, but I feel assured that chartering a vessel expressly for the purpose would involve a very serious expense which I do not feel disposed to incur.

I may reply to your enquiry concerning coal that [presently consists of] about 80 tons on hand at this place, which we will sell at 12 dollars a ton, and further that very large quantities may be procured at short notice from the mines at Nanaimo, where it is delivered along side for 10 dollars a ton. The coal is of excellent quality, and burns with a bright flame, and ardent heat, to a white ash leaving no dross or waste whatever.

The demand made by the Collector of Taxes for the levy on the Puget Sound Company's lands is, I suppose, according to law and the sum would have been levied by execution on the Company's property even if you had not consented to pay the demand; you had therefore no alternative but to pay the sum under protest which was the proper course. You remark that the sum paid was "645 dollars and

62 UW Library, Tolmie Papers Acc. 4577-001, Box #2, Folder #3, N. 979.413, D 741 #118.

12 cents, that being the amount of tax at .75 cents per acre on the extent of our land 224 square miles as shown by the late survey." By my calculations of the extent of that area, the rate of tax will not come to more than one half cent per acre or exactly 2 dollars and 88 cents a square mile, a matter to which I call your attention lest there should be a mistake in your statement.

Young [Aubrey] Dean is now sent to his father [Thomas Dean] with whom, I trust, he will behave better than he has done at this place and become a steady and useful man.

[The former Cowlitz squatter William] Johnson is here, but we have as yet entered into no arrangements with him, his terms being higher than we are disposed to give.

The supplies ordered in your note will be forwarded.

I am sorry that a better supply of horses has not been sent from Fort Vancouver, but I trust you will be able to purchase such as we want from the Indians, making the payments in goods, which will be charged at transfer price.

Mr. Walter Ross is now under the Doctor's hands, and I fear it will be some time before he is fit for duty.

The Mary Dare and Recovery[63] have been both dispatched to California with cargoes of coal, the latter the day before yesterday, and the former on the 6th inst.

Coal is very abundant at Nanaimo. In addition to the first discovery, a second 6 foot seam has been lately discovered at the distance of 1 ½ miles from the former and it is supposed we can take out about 10,000 tons by Indian labor alone. The coal is of excellent quality, superior as Mr. [John] Muir thinks to any Scotch coal he has ever seen, and fully equal to good English coal.

I will make no further comment on that discovery, lest I should say too much, as it is altogether so extraordinary that one can hardly think temperately on the subject.

We have not received the onion seed which you promised to send, and you will confer a great favour by forwarding it by an early conveyance. I remain, Dear Sir, Yours truly,

James Douglas

Document 6.38: A letter from William F. Tolmie, Nisqually, to John Ballenden, Vancouver, October 19, 1852.

Dear Sir,

I received on the 16th Inst Your Communication by mail of the 5th and, as you have decided on the removal of the Puget's Sound Co's Sheep from Vancouver to Nisqually, I think it preferable to send for them now, Rather than defer the matter 'till after Lammas 1853, as would necessarily happen were it postponed 'till next Year.[64]

John McPhail now proceeds for the Sheep to be transferred and is accompanied by four Sandwich Islanders and several Indians; Three of the former being engaged servants, their accounts are sent herewith and I would not recommend

63 *Recovery*, HBC brig [var: *Orbit*]. See Watson, *Lives Lived*, 3:1128–29.

64 "Lammas Day (Anglo-Saxon half-mas, "loaf-mass"), is a holiday celebrated in some English-speaking countries in the Northern Hemisphere, usually between 1 August and 1 September. It is a festival to mark the annual wheat harvest, and is the first harvest festival of the year. On this day it was customary to bring to church a loaf made from the new crop, which began to be harvested at Lammastide, which falls at the halfway point between the summer Solstice and Autumn September Equinox." en.wikip dia.org/wiki/Lammas.

advances being made to any for a higher amount than £3. St[erlin]g each beyond their Respective Credits. Cowie and Koemi or "Sam" proposes renewing their engagements at Vancouver as they did about this time last year in which case only will they be entitled to an advance. It would be desirable to engage them for two Years instead of one, these wages to be the same as at present Vitz; Cowie £25 P[e]r Annum and Koemi £20. [William] Tawaii[65] may also be engaged p[e]r £20 p Annum and allowed a small advance should he desire it. The Indians accompanying McPhail are not to be paid 'till their return to Nisqually. Please let him have two Common trading Guns and some ammunition for his return trip on Acc[ou] nt of the PS [Agricultural] Compy Nisqually.

Mr. [Simpson P.] Moses' Bill with the Debit is forwarded herewith, as [asked for] in Your last. Cash Sales Continue Good here. A list is enclosed of the horses transferred from Vancouver. They are for the Puget's Sound Coy. Have the goodness to inform me how they are to be priced, and by which post the expense of bringing them across is to be borne. I hope we may succeed in getting the remainder of the wild horses driven this way next year.

(Signed) W. F. Tolmie

P.S. Forty smoked Neat's Tongues are sent by [John] Macphail for Vancouver. Should opp[ortunit]y offer, please send for this post: 24 p[ai]rs Sea Boots and mention the retail price thereof at Vancouver.

Document 6.39: A letter from William F. Tolmie, Nisqually, to James Douglas, Victoria, October 20, 1852.

Dear Sir,

The present express is forwarded by direction of Mr. Ballenden, from whom a packet to your address has just been received.

Cash Sales continue pretty brisk here, and the business generally advances satisfactorily.

I cannot obtain a larger canoe hereabouts than the one sent, otherwise some Rams would have been sent for [Edward E.] Langford. Permit me to suggest our dispatching a boat or large Canoe for the Rams and please mention the number required.

Mr. Ballenden, having decided on not retaining the Puget's Sound Coy's Ewes at Vancouver, [John] Macphail, with a suitable party, has gone to bring them across—he will, on his return, be sent to Victoria.

Should there be any disposable salt salmon at Victoria please inform me p[e]r return of bearers of the quantity and price. I enquired in mine of the 5th Inst by Mr. [Walter] Ross the price of coal at Victoria, and the quantity obtainable there. Please also to mention the price of coal at Nanymo [Nanaimo]. Can Lime or Limestone be purchased at Victoria and at what cost? I enclose a San Francisco price List of September 30th.

(Signed) W. F. Tolmie

---

65 For Tawaii see Watson and Barman, *Leaving Paradise*, 413–14.

Document 6.40: A letter from William F. Tolmie, Nisqually, to James Douglas, Victoria, October 20, 1852.

Dear Sir,

Your letter of the 17th and 18th of Sept and 4th October came to hand this evening past as an express for Victoria was about to start and I detain the Indians for a short time to acknowledge receipt, and make a few enquires and remarks.

In the first place, please inform me whether it will be necessary to forward by express to Vancouver your reply to Mr. [John] Ballenden's letter. Such was his wish but probably your letter to him now received might convey the information he desires.

What would you consider a fair freight P[e]r M [thousand board feet] for lumber from Newmarket or Nisqually, to Victoria and would you think $10 P[e]r ton payable in Coal too high freight for the Wool and furs? There will be a transport with troops at Steilacoom in a few days hence, and an agreement might be made with the Capt to take the lumber . . . So Should a Vessel bring goods from Victoria in December, she will probably have to enter at Olympia, when the lumber could be shipped, or she came here to discharge. I have agreed with Mr. [Rudolph] Walker to take the Cedar Clapboard at $28 P[e]r M [thousand board feet] but, as he says, they sell readily at $30 he will probably take them back should you not want the Article.

Agreeable to recent instructions from Mr. Ballenden, I have sent Mr. Moses's Bill duly protested to Fort Vancouver whence [the bill] will be transmitted to the Secretary of the Treasury at Washington [D.C.] through Sir George Simpson. I shall suggest to Mr. B[allenden] to defer that proceeding 'till it be decided whether the Bill is to be employed, or not, in payment of duties. I shall address Mr. Moses on this subject again in a day or two. He wrote me very recently that he had had assurance from Senators [Gideon] Welles[66] and [Salmon P.] Chase[67] of their efforts to include the expenses of the "Queen Charlotte Island Expedition" in the "Civil and Diplomatic Appropriation Bill" and he hoped for definite information by next mail from Washington [D.C.] City.

I can meet a draft of $1,000 on favor of Mr. [Abraham] Way.

I shall endeavor to purchase the Oats for Victoria as soon as possible.

Please mention by return of bearers the number of Rams wanted for Victoria, and whether they are to be transported thither in our Canoe, or in a Victoria boat.

Mr. B[allenden] writes that there are only ten more Horses at [Adolphus Lee] Lewes's. I remain Dear Sir, Your Very Obedt Servant,

(Signed) W. F. Tolmie

Document 6.41: A letter from William F. Tolmie, Nisqually, to Simpson P. Moses, Olympia, October 20, 1852.

Dear Sir,

It would be completing the accommodation afforded us of obtaining Supplies from Victoria in canoes if you could permit the articles received in that way to be

66 For more on Gideon Welles (1802–1878), see millercenter.org/president/essays/welles-1865-secretary-of-the-navy.

67 For more on Salmon P. Chase (1808–1873), see www.history.com/topics/salmon-p-chase.

entered here instead of requiring their Entry at Olympia. I address You on this subject as Mr. Surveyor [William W.] Miller seems of opinion that he is not authorized by his instruction from you, to enter Goods here. Very Respectfully Yours,

(Signed) W. F. Tolmie

Document 6.42: A letter from William F. Tolmie, Nisqually, to Joseph Cushman,[68] Olympia, October 21, 1852.

Dear Sir,

I promised Captain [Albion Butler] Gove [master of the *George Wilkins Kendall*] to send you the earliest information obtained regarding the price of Coal at Victoria. There are 80 tons of coal at that place for Sale at $12—twelve dollars P[e]r ton. At Nanaimo 50 Miles North of Victoria, but easily accessible and safe for Shipping, the Coal will be delivered alongside at ten dollars P[e]r ton. Very respectfully Yours,

Signed W. F. Tolmie

Document 6.43: A letter from William F. Tolmie, Nisqually, to Amory Holbrook, Oregon City, October 23, 1852.

My Dear Sir,

Enclosed is Copy of account lately handed me by Mr. Collector [Simpson P.] Moses, which I am given to understand has to be submitted to and allowed by you, are justably presentable for payment.

I presume the first item in said account may as well be paid without demur altho' it is rather hard to be obliged to do so, as Mr. [William W.] Miller's expedition to Cathlamet was quite uncalled for. Mr. Moses had already written Judge Strong by post regarding the seizures, and might have again addressed him, or others, by the same conveyance. Moreover, I set out for Cathlamet about the same time as Mr. Miller, and offered to carry gratuitously any despatches the collector might desire to send.

With respect to the third charge of Three hundred and thirty dollars ($330), I paid Mr. Moses, under protest, on the 20th May 1852, Two hundred and fifty two dollars ($252) nominally for "warehousing" the Cargo on board the "Mary Dare", and so receipted for, altho' said cargo was never landed at Olympia. The said payment made under a threat of Sheriff's seizure was, in reality, exacted however, as Mr. Moses told me in presence of our Clerk Mr. [Edward] Huggins, to lower the expenses of keeping inspectors on board the Vessel, an outlay ~~then~~ he did not then probably see any other way of recovering.

On the 30th of last September, when Mr. Moses presented this account he explained that he had included the Two Hundred and Twenty two dollars aforesaid in his charges of Three Hundred and Thirty dollars for "Custody of Vessel" in case my protest should be favourably received by the Sec[retar]y of the Treasury [in] Washington [D.C.] and agreed that the proper deduction ($252) should be made in the event of the failure of the protest. With regard to the fourth charge of $100

68 Cushman is identified as being a representative within the Kendall Company of Olympia.

for D[aniel] R. Bigelow, I would merely enquire whether the Collector had a right to employ any other lawyers than the U.S. Attorney pro tempore.

The Charge for boatmen seems very high, but doubtless Mr. Moses has satisfactory Vouchers to produce in its support. I remain, Yours &c., &c.,

(Signed) W. F. Tolmie

P.S. Since writing the above, I have received the enclosed from Mr. Moses from which it appears that my protest proved unavailing. I expected no other result after learning Mr. Caruso's[69] decision on the Case of the Mary Dare. Mr. Moses will now, of course as he promised, deduct the $252 already paid for the Custody of the Vessel which will be reduce his account to $900, Supposing all the other charges [are] admissible.

(S[igne]d) W. F. T.

☙ Document 6.44: A letter from William F. Tolmie, Nisqually, to Henry N. Peers, Cowlitz Farm, October 23, 1852.

Dear Sir,

Judge [William] Strong having written me recently to notify Collector [Simpson P.] Moses that I should move for a hearing, at the ensuing term of Court, of my petition for a remission of the forfeiture of the Steamer "Beaver's" Goods seized by Mr. Moses, I sent the necessary notification expecting very soon some communication from Mr. [John] Ballenden on the subject, and hoping to be able to attend Court myself.

I have not heard from Mr. Ballenden about the petition, and it being impossible for me to leave home at present, I must request you to act for me as the Corp['s] Representative on the business, and shall now briefly state for the information of whatever legal gentleman may be employed, all that I would say if present at Court.

I put into the hands of Mr. [Simon B.] Marge at the May term of Court depositions on oath from Captn W[illiam] A. Mouat and myself to the effect that we had heard Captn C[harles] Stuart of the Steamer "Beaver" inform first the Dep[ut]y Coll[ecto]r, and on a second occasion [Simpson P. Moses] the Collector himself, that there were trade Goods on board the Steamer. It is to be hoped that the Compy's law agent may have these papers with him, and if admissible, they will constitute the only exculpatory[70] evidence to be produced unless A[ndrew] J. Simmons[71] should be at Court. That Gentleman was present when Captn Stuart mentioned to the Dep[ut]y Collector when he first boarded the Steamer that there were loose trade goods in the trade room. Mr. Simmons in Dec [18]51 told me that he remembered the circumstance and would testify to it when required. I remain Dear Sir, Your Very Obedt Servt,

(Signed) W. F. Tolmie

69 The editor could not find a federal judge with this name. This was apparently a lower court decision-maker who found a valid judgement against the Company's vessels.

70 "This type of evidence can exonerate a defendant in a case. Prosecutors are required to disclose to the defendant any exculpatory evidence they find or risk having the case dismissed." i-sight.com/resources/15-types-of-evidence-and-how-to-use-them-in-investigation.

71 The Simmons clan arrived in Oregon in 1847, with Andrew settling at Cowlitz Prairie. He died February 12, 1872, in Lewis County. *Seattle Post Intelligencer*, February 26, 1872, and the *Olympia Standard*, March 2, 1872.

P.S. Mr. [Amory] Holbrook, long the U.S. District Att[orne]y, cannot of course—altho' [at present] the Compy's legal advisor—act in Court for them on the present Case. But he will pass to me [information] of what Mr. Ballenden may have done on the matter, and relate what you ought to do in case no steps shall have got done later. Mr. Ballenden wishes the accompanying packet to his address to be sent by an Indian to the care of Edward Spencer;[72] only [the packets] ought to [be] forwarded express, as Mr. B[allenden] is anxious for news from V[ancouer] I[sland]. Please prepay and post the accompanying at Cowlitz and charge the Cost to Nisqually which advize in your next. (S[igned]) T.

Document 6.45: A letter from William F. Tolmie, Nisqually, to John Ballenden, Vancouver, October 23, 1852.

Dear Sir,

Your letters of the 11th Inst came to hand on the 20th and the accompanying mail for Vancouver Island was forwarded without delay. Agreeably to your instructions, the packets (4) and letters (8) to Your address and one packet to A[rchibald] Barclay Esq are sent to the Care of E[dward] Spencer, Monticello—under cover to You.

I have written Mr. [Amory] Holbrook about Collector [Simpson P.] Moses's bill and hope that some reductions may be made in it.

Judge [William] Strong, having written me to notify Coll[ecto]r Moses that I would move at next Court for a hearing of my petition for a remission of the forfeiture of the Steamer Beaver's Goods seized by Mr. Moses, I communicated the necessary notification and as I cannot with any propriety leave home myself. I have requested Mr. [Henry N.] Peers to see to the matter at Court and have given him all the information in my possession, suggesting that he should advize with Mr. Holbrook in case you should not have taken any steps in the business.

On receiving Judge Strong's letter, I expected to have heard from you regarding the petition. I remain Dear Sir, Your Very Obedient Servant,

(Signed) W. F. Tolmie

Document 6.46: A letter from William F. Tolmie, Nisqually, to John Ballenden, Vancouver, October 23, 1852.

Dear Sir,

Since forwarding to you on the 19th Inst by [John] Macphail Coll[ector Simpson P.] Moses's protested Bill, I have learnt from Mr. [James] Douglas that he wishes to employ it in payment of duties and that he thought of sending in a shipment after the arrival at V[ancouver] I[sland] of the Brigantine "Vancouver," expected in November. I mention this as it may alter your intention of sending said bill to Sir Geo[rge] Simpson and induce you to delay the proceedings for a post or two.

I understood verbally from [Simpson P.] Moses some time ago that, provided an entry of goods were made to the amount in duty of twenty five hundred dollars, he would take the bills he owes the Coy in part payment thereof.

(Signed) W. F. Tolmie

72 For Spenser see Watson, *Lives Lived*, 3:884.

Document 6.47: A letter from William F. Tolmie, Nisqually, to John Ballenden, Vancouver, November 1, 1852.[73]

Dear Sir,

The enclosed is a letter forwarded by me to Mr. [Amory] Holbrook in the expectation that it would find him at Cowlitz but, as I learn that owning to his absence the business it refers to has to be settled at the Vancouver term of Court, I enclose the letter to You, to be made use of as you may deem best.

Having learned that a delay has occurred on the departure of the troops from Vancouver, I have to Request You to forward for this place by their Transport, or any other opportunity;

One Hogshead Leaf Tob[acc]o or more, if abundant, say 3.
1 Coil Rope Taned 1½ in[che]s
3 doz drab Felt Hats for [Sale] to Am[ericans].
1 [coil] Ratline 12th
12 Gross Brass head[ed] Nails perhaps these may be found at a reasonable rate in Portland or O[regon] C[ity].
200 [pounds of] Brass Collar Wire
4 doz Black Ostrich Feathers
30 Gallons Rum
2 doz Children's Shoes
A small assortment of the N.Y. Goods

I Remain Dear Sir, Your Very Obedt Servt,
(Signed) W. F. Tolmie

Document 6.48: A letter from John Ballenden, Vancouver, to William F. Tolmie, Nisqually, November 1, 1852.[74]

Dear Sir,

I have to acknowledge the receipt of your letters of Oct 19th and 23rd, and after some consideration, considering you as the agent of the PS [Agricultural] Co, I have decided upon sending to Nisqually this autumn all the sheep (property of that Company) which still remain here. [John] McPhail, with the party of Kanakas and Indians, sent here by you, will start in the course of today, and I shall I feel rather anxious until I am made aware of their safe arrival at their destination. The portage is now very bad, and the season so far advanced, that I shall request Mr. [Henry N.] Peers to detain them at the Cowlitz Farm should there be, in his opinion, any doubt of the animals reaching Nisqually in safety.

I shall this year finally close the accounts of the PS [Agricultural] Co in so far as regards live stock or other property remaining at Vancouver, charging whatever

73 Although they reveal a great deal about the business of the fort, these letters rarely touch on the authors' personal lives. In its November 20, 1852, section titled "Births," the Olympia newspaper *The Columbian*, states: "On the 1st Inst, [there was the birth] of a son, the wife [Jane] of W[illia]m Fraser Tolmie, Esq, Hudson's Bay Co, Fort Nisqually." So it came to pass that on "All Saints Day," 1852, William Tolmie Jr., the couple's second child, was born.

74 UW Library, Tolmie Papers Acc. 4577-001, V0250e, Box #1, Folder #1. From a typescript copy.

wedders or wedder lambs—may then remain to account of Fort Vancouver—Western Department, Outfit 1853. I then shall forward to Nisqually the papers and accounts connected with that company, so that they may, in future, be made up wherever Mr. Douglas and you may agree upon.

I cannot help feeling glad to see the last of the PS [Agricultural] Co's stock taken away from the place as in consequence of the lawless population of this neighbourhood, and the impossibility of getting good and careful shepherds, [as] they have not received that attention during the last four years which they well merited. The number now sent to Nisqually is 840 of all kinds.

I shall forward by the vessel engaged for the transport of the troops to Nisqually the goods requested in your several letters but, as our plans are not yet arranged for the commencement of the Western Department accounts, the goods will be charged to Nisqually Outfit 1853, and will, therefore, have to be included in your inventory at the close of the current outfit. While on this subject allow me to request that all your accounts be closed and forwarded here not later than the 15th January, as otherwise it will put us to great inconvenience to close them previous to the departure of the express. I would also beg you to be particular in preparing your statement of men, so that we may know exactly who are on account of the HB Co, and who are on account of the PS [Agricultural] Co.

With respect to the horses delivered to Walter Ross by Mr. Lewis last summer, on the farther side of the Cowlitz River, I have charged to Fort Vancouver Depot the expense of sending them thence, but, the charge of taking them from thence to Nisqually must be borne by the PS [Agricultural] Co, and I debited that company with them at the lowest prices, I have yet received in this Territory, viz.,

Under 1 year old	$10.00
[Under] 2 [year old]	$30.00
[Under] 3 [year old]	$30.00

We have now no more disposable, as all we have left will be required for the use of Fort Vancouver.

I shall commence no further proceedings against Mr. [Simpson P.] Moses to enforce payment of Lieut [John] Dement's bill accepted by him until after the return of Mr. [Charles] Bradley from the Sound, or until I hear from Mr. Douglas. If the latter has any such intention as those you allude to in your letter of 23rd October he has never written me on the subject, and I, therefore, cannot help thinking you are mistaken, as after what occurred last winter, and the instructions given by the [Governors] in consequence, I can hardly think he would venture on such a step as that of sending goods to Nisqually in any of the Company's vessels without first obtaining the consent of the Gov and committee. I say nothing further about Mr. Moses's most exorbitant bill of charges as regards the seizure of the "Mary Dare" and "Beaver" until I learn the result of Mr. [Charles] Bradley's visit to the Sound.

Before taking any further steps respecting Lieut [George W.] Hawkins's bill, endorsed by Dr. [John] Hayden, I want to hear from Major [John S.] Hathaway after his arrival at Nisqually. The latter has promised to speak privately to the Dr on the subject, and I think the reasons which he, as a brother officer will urge, will bring about as early settlement. The vessel intended for the transport of the troops has not yet arrived, although hourly expected.

In any understanding you may have with Mr. Moses, I would place no confidence unless reduced to writing. I would, therefore, particularly caution you on this subject. Could the bill due by him be paid in the manner to which you allude in your letter of Oct 23rd, good and well, but 'till you receive his assurance to that effect in writing, the goods ought not to leave Victoria Harbour. I am, dear Sir, Your obedient servant,

John Ballenden

P.S. The Kanakas I have not been able to engage. I have, therefore, left them for you to settle with. Why do you not engage them for the Puget Sound [Agricultural] Company, and separate completely the accounts? It would prevent great confusion and much irregularity. J.B.

Document 6.49: A letter from William F. Tolmie, Olympia, to John Ballenden, Vancouver, November 3, 1852.

Dear Sir,

I have received your communication of the 26th Ulto which was delivered to me by Mr. [Charles] Bradley who, accompanied by Collector [Simpson P.] Moses, spent a night at Nisqually. I have come here for the purpose of seeing Mr. Bradley alone and have first had some conversation with him on the points referred to in your letter. Being much occupied, he could not examine the papers I was prepared to show, but suggested my addressing him at San Francisco on matters connected with the "seizures" which I shall do and send the letter open to you. Our Inventory being taken the goods ordered had better, I would suppose, be charged to O[utfi]t [18]53.

S[igned] W. F. Tolmie

Document 6.50: A letter from James Douglas, Victoria, to William F. Tolmie, Nisqually, November 5, 1852.[75]

My dear Sir,

I have barely a moment to inform you that one of our men [Peter Brown][76] was this day shot at the sheep station near the north dairy. The poor man was found there lifeless, near the hut, by his associate shepherd, who supposes the deed must have

75 UW Library, Tolmie Papers Acc. 4577-001, Box #2, Folder #3, N. 979.413 D 741 #118.

76 Not much is known of this murdered shepherd. Several days after the attack, Douglas wrote: "Our relations with the Native Tribes, continued in the most satisfactory state up to the 5th Inst, when . . . the foul and wanton murder of Peter Brown, a servant of the Hudson's Bay Company, by some Cowegin Indians, at one of the Company's sheep stations about 5 miles distant from this place, under circumstances of great atrocity. In such cases we are naturally led to suspect the existence of some [preexisting] cause, [such as] some previous injury or provocation that has tempted the untutored mind of the Savage to commit a fearful crime, but after the closest investigation of that case I have not been able to discover any mitigating circumstance whatever, which can be urged in extenuation of its guilt. The murder of Peter Brown may be therefore regarded in the light of a mere wanton outrage, as this unfortunate victim, of savage treachery was known to be a remarkably quiet and inoffensive young man, the only son of a respectable widow in Orkney." govlet.ca/en/pdf/cc4-blm-6.pdf, Despatch from James Douglas, Victoria, to Sir John Pakington, London, November 11, 1852. 933, CO 305/3, p. 147; received in London on January 29, 1853, [No. 8].

been committed by 2 Cowegen [Cowichan] Indians when he left at the hut with poor Brown that morning when the sheep were driven out to pasture. Very truly yours,
James Douglas

[P.S.] We have stopped the sale of [gun]powder. J. D.
[P.S.S.] Charles Ross [Jr.] might come and live with his poor mother [Isabella Ross]. J. D.

Document 6.51: A letter from William F. Tolmie, Nisqually, to William W. Loring, Corpus Christi, Texas, November 7, 1852.

Dear Sir,

Lieut G[eorge] W. Hawkins, when about to leave Oregon in May 1851, being indebted to the Hudson's Bay Co and unprepared to pay, granted his bill for the amount and procured endorsement from Dr. [John] Haden of the 1st Artillery, Steilacoom [who was] then on a visit to the Rifle Regiment at Vancouver.

The note was made payable to M[isters] Mainland, Phelphs & Co, New York,[77] and when due was returned protested. Since then, notwithstanding repeated enquiries, nothing has been heard of Mr. Hawkins, and as the securities he gave Dr. Haden have proved worthless, I am anxious to learn whether Mr. Hawkins still belongs to the Rifle Regiment and where he is stationed. May I request you to have the kindness to inform me, by letter on these points?

Fort Nisqually and its neighborhood have not altered much since we had the pleasure of seeing you in this quarter two years ago. Several new settlements have been formed however, since that period, on other parts of the seacoast. I am Dear Sir, With Much Respect, Your Obedient Servant,
Wm Fraser Tolmie

Document 6.52: A letter from William F. Tolmie, Nisqually, to George Simpson, Lachine, November 15, 1852.[78]

My dear Sir,

I write in haste to inform you that Collector [Simpson P.] Moses of Olympia, showed me very recently a letter addressed to him, dated "State Department, Washington [D.C.], 27th Augt [18]52" signed "Daniel Webster"[79] and to the effect that inasmuch as the U.S. Government had in contemplation the buying out the rights and privileges of the Hudson's Bay and Puget's Sound Companies as secured by

77 In 1852, the New York-based merchantile firm of Mainland, Phelps & Company was comprised of a partnership involved in merchandise, stock market, and investments. The firm was known to be active into the middle 1880s.

78 HBCA, Governor George Simpson Loose Inward Correspondence, D.5/35 fos. 171–171d.

79 A native of New Hampshire, Webster (1782–1852) graduated from Dartmouth College with a law degree, an education he applied while working in a Boston law firm. Turning to politics, he became the leader of the conservative Whig Party. He served as a congressman from New Hampshire, senator from Massachusetts, and Secretary of State under Presidents William Harrison, John Tyler, and Millard Fillmore. He oversaw the enforcement of the Fugitive Slave Act and died in Marshfield, MA, in 1852. www.biography.com/people/daniel-webster-9526186#synopsis.

Treaty, and had not yet obtained sufficient information as to the nature, extent and value of their possessions, President [Millard] Fillmore had recommended Mr. Moses to the Secretary of State, as a person whose opinion on these points would be valuable.

Mr. Moses is requested to consider, as a distinct matter, the propriety of extinguishing the Hudson's Bay Co's right to the free navigation of the Great Northern branch of the Columbia River. As Mr. Moses without the least encouragement from me, has been making repeated endeavors this summer to have a private understanding with the Coy that he, for a suitable Consideration[80] in the event of success, should draw up and obtained signatures throughout the Territory to a Petition that Congress should buy us out. I looked at first with suspicion on this new announcement of his, but am now inclined to think that the letter he produced is genuine. Mr. Webster's signature is in a small cramped and rather illegible hand and such, I have been informed, is the character of his autograph.

The Puget's Sound Coy's claim was surveyed [by John Chapman] last Spring and amounts to 224 square miles. Three fourths of the Oak timber on or near Puget's Sound is to be found upon the claim which greatly enhances its value; squared oak timber being now worth 40 cents p[e]r cubic foot for shipping to California. All are well here, and the business progressing Satisfactorily. I remain Dear Sir, Your very obedt Sert,

Wm Fraser Tolmie

Document 6.53: A letter from William F. Tolmie, Nisqually, to John Ballenden, Vancouver, November 15, 1852.

Dear Sir,

I now forward a mail from Victoria as p[e]r Packet List, and the letters addressed by me to Mr. [Charles] Bradley open for your perusal, after which, please to seal and mail them. I have said nothing to him about [Simpson P.] Moses's refusal to land the Vessels immediately being of opinion that he had legal justification for the course he adopted. Neither have I made allusion to the Company's leniency in not prosecuting Moses, not knowing what to say on that sore subject. All are well here and business progresses satisfactorily. I remain Dear sir,

(Signed) W. F. Tolmie

Document 6.54: A letter from James Douglas, Victoria, to William F. Tolmie, Nisqually, November 17, 1852.[81]

My dear Sir,

I now dispatch a canoe for the purpose of bringing on any letters for this place that may have accumulated at Nisqually, and I transmit by the same conveyance a letter for the Colonial Office, which I will now thank you to forward by the earliest mail as I am anxious it should reach the hands of the Colonial Secretary as soon as possible.

80 Moses's suggestion of a "private understanding" and "suitable consideration" could, in this instance, be interpreted as a bribe to be made under the table to this public official.

81 UW Library's Tolmie Papers Acc. 4577-001, Box #2, Folder #3, N. 979.413 D 741 #107.

All is quiet here at present though much alarm is felt by the settlers for which there is no cause; the murderers [of Peter Brown] have fled to Nanaimo, and we propose giving them chase as soon as the steamer arrives here, it being the intention to send a sufficient force to take them wherever they may be found.

The Cowegins [Cowichans] appear to regret the untoward event very much, and have sent in word that they will not harbour nor screen the murderers, and will apprehend them if possible. This is satisfactory provided they keep their promise, which I think they intend to do.

There is no word of the Mary Dare or Recovery from California, and we are rather anxious for intelligence from abroad. Please send a few rams for Mr. [Edward E.] Langford by the return canoe. With best wishes, I remain, dear Sir, Yours truly,

James Douglas

Document 6.55: A letter from William F. Tolmie, Nisqually, to John Ballenden, Vancouver, November 20, 1852.

Dear Sir,

Enclosed is a deposition[82] from Mr. [Hugh A.] Goldsborough [of] Olympia which may be of service at Court when the case of the Steamer [*Beaver's*] trade Goods is to be tried. A[ndrew] J. Simmons informed me lately that he had given his testimony at the last session of Court at Cowlitz. If you can ascertain please give me particulars thereof.

A man and his wife (Teal), recently from Victoria, have been openly accusing Mr. [Simpson P.] Moses in Olympia of having urged them last May—under promise of Award—to go to Court and swear that the St[eamer] Beaver had been a month at Victoria last Autumn and had Consequently Abundant time to discharge her Cargo before towing the "Mary Dare" to Puget's Sound.

Mr. Moses mentioned, incidentally, the other day that foreigners had no right to Charter or freight American Vessels in the Coasting Trade, altho' in the Case of the Mary Taylor he had not noticed the infringement of law. He read some enactments[83] which did not seem to me Very applicable. Nevertheless, it might be well to have Mr. [Amory] Holbrook's opinion on the matter. I remain dear Sir, Your Very Obedt Servt,

(Signed) W. F. Tolmie

P.S. I have requested a Gentleman in Olympia, Mr. [Quincy A.] Brooks,[84] to take Teal and his wife's depositions regarding the matter above alluded to, and to forward them to you, to be employed, or not—as you may deem most advisable. T.

---

82 Goldsborough was prominent in Washington's territorial activities. He witnessed the signing of several Indian treaties and was connected with activities not only at Fort Steilacoom, but also in Olympia/Tumwater. Gary Fuller, *Nothing Worthy of Note Transpired Today: The Northwest Journals of August V. Kautz* (Tacoma, WA: Tacoma Public Library, 1978), 417.

83 An "enactment" is a legislative term, meaning endorsements or legitimizing statements.

84 A native of Pennsylvania and educated at Duquesne College, Pittsburgh, Brooks (b. 1828–c. ?) graduated from law school in 1849. Immigrating first to Oregon in 1851 he eventually moved to Olympia. His jobs included inspector of customs, deputy collector of that port, and prosecuting attorney in 1852, and clerk of the Superintendent if Indian Affairs. In 1858 he moved to Salem, Oregon, where he married Lizzie Cranston in 1858, and then to Portland, where he remained until 1861. He acquired a mercantile business in Walla Walla, and afterwards moved to Auburn, Washington Territory. Bancroft. *History of Oregon*, 1:768. See also Hines, *Illustrated History of Washington* (Chicago: Lewis Publishing Company, 1893), 2.

Document 6.56: An agreement between William F. Tolmie, Nisqually, & William P. Wells, James McAllister[85] & William Berry,[86] Nisqually Bottoms, November 22nd, 1852.[87]

It is agreed between the undersigned that W. F. Tolmie is to supply M[isters] Macalister, Wells and Berry with beef at eight cents p[er] lb., and other goods at market prices, they [McAllister & Wells] defraying the cost of delivery.

Macalister, Wells and Berry are to pay W. F. Tolmie for such supplies as they may receive from him, in good merchantable pine lumber at Twenty five dollars p[er] M [thousand board feet], as soon as the Sawmlll they are now constructing at Shudadam, may be in operation, but should said Mill, from any cause not produce lumber sooner than the first day of June 1853, W. F. Tolmie will there have the option of taking cash instead of lumber in payment of supplies rendered to the undersigned.

[Signed] James McAlister, William Berry, William P. Wells, Wm F. Tolmie

Document 6.57: A letter from William F. Tolmie, Nisqually, to James Douglas, Victoria, November 25, 1852.

Dear Sir,

I have to acknowledge receipt of your communications of the 5th and 14th Novr and, as requested, send by return of your Canoe 6 S[outh] Down Rams P[e]r Mr. [Edward E.] Langford. I have also the pleasure of sending a San Francisco Herald reporting the safe arrival of the "Recovery"` and "Mary Dare" at that port.

Herewith are forwarded a Requisition ~~to be~~ for Fort Nisqually to be forwarded P[e]r first Company Vessel bound this way, and made on the Supposition that the Goods ordered from England will not be out before February [18]53. Also, Copy of our Charges against Fort Victoria Outfit 1852, and the Vessels seized here in December last.

Please inform me how soon you are likely to send for the Oats and lumber in order that they may be in readiness.

Lumber having risen to a high price in California, owing to the burning of Sacramento City,[88] I shall probably sell the Clapboarding ordered for Victoria should a good offer be made for it. If you wish the boards also sold, please advize and state the lowest price. The lumber at Newmarket & Steilacoom Mills has been engaged for some time to come by a San Francisco Merchant.

'Tis almost certain that while the excitement regarding lumber lasts, the Mill stream here will be taken possession of by some of the many now in search of mill sites.

---

85 Born in Greenup County, Kentucky, McAllister (1811–1855) came west with his family in the Michael Simmons party in 1845. He made an attempt to go to the California gold mines but returned and farmed until the Indian War of 1855–56, where he was killed by the Indians on October 27, 1855.

86 Other than the fact that Berry was a millwright of some repute, no other biographical information could be found regarding his life.

87 UW Library, Tolmie Papers Acc. 4577-001, Box #2, Folder #5.

88 Sacramento City caught fire November 4, 1852; almost 85 percent of it was destroyed.

I beg your attention to the enclosed Copy of a letter lately addressed by me to Sir George Simpson and also to a Copy of a letter &c., from me to a Mr. [Charles] Bradley, Genl appraiser, who has been on a Visit of Inspection to the different U.S. Custom houses along the Pacific. I sent the letter open to Mr. [John] Ballenden who was to have mailed it to Mr. Bradley at San Francisco.

It will not be advizable to import any more odds and ends of wantages in Canoes, as Mr. [William W.] Miller insists that Canoes bringing Goods must proceed direct to Olympia and enter there. Mr. Miller's reasons for this [additional obligation] is that he cannot persuade on Mr. Moses to give him written instruction to enter Canoes here. Please state P[e]r first opportunity how we are to charge the livestock sent P[e]r first trip of the "Mary Dare" and by the Steamer [*Beaver*], also by the "Honolulu" and "Alice". Direct also how the livestock Supplied Mr. [John] Work in exchange for his Horses is to be charged. I presume it will be against the HBC at the old transfer price of 4 P[e]r Cent.

Any Shipmaster coming this way in the Coy's Vessel must be Very Careful to have a Correct Manifest &c., as Mr. Collector [Simpson P.] Moses is just as ready as ever to take advantage of any oversight. A packet from England to Your address received by last mail is sent herewith. I remain Sir, Your Very Obedient Servant,

(Signed) Wm. F. Tolmie

Document 6.58: A letter from William F. Tolmie, Nisqually, to James Douglas, Victoria, November 29, 1852.

Dear Sir,

By the present opportunity are forwarded the Y[ork] F[actory] Express and eleven engaged men as P[e]r list enclosed. Having had one case of desertion here, Pierre Ansio[89]—a worthless little Canadian, I hurry the party off with all dispatch which must excuse my not writing at greater length. I remain Dear Sir, Your Very Obdt Sert,

W. F. Tolmie

89 No further information on Ansio was found.

CHAPTER SEVEN

December 1st, 1852–May 31st, 1853

"Among other articles, we have shipped . . . 4 Barrels of [salmon] which you will please to present without charge to Mr. Collector Moses, as his letter of application to you implies that a gift of that kind will not be unacceptable, and to refuse it might expose us to inconvenience and trouble."

—James Douglas to William F. Tolmie, January 26, 1853

In March 1853, a Fort Vancouver colleague reported that "[t]he business of Nisqually as managed by Chief Trader Tolmie does him great credit. This year the result of the trade shows a very handsome profit—more than £1,000. Should the Hudson's Bay Company for any length of time be compelled to retain their Possessory Rights [south of the boundary line], I would recommend that more attention than usual be devoted to that section of the country. It is settling fast by Immigrants of a superior class, and the access is at all times easy from Vancouver's Island; so that supplies of goods can at any time be forwarded with very little risk."[1]

For several years Tolmie had pressed his superiors for advancement in rank. To his disappointment, the doctor's ardent self-promotion, backed by a 20-year tenure and his colleagues' affirmation, proved insufficient in swaying his superiors. The rank of chief trader would therefore remain his throughout the latter half of Outfit 1853.

While many successful business transactions took place and are described in this work, those that collapsed demanded far more of Tolmie, and the correspondence proves this out. These failed ventures, along with old and new tribulations with settlers, squatters, and corrupt customs officials, continued to plague him and Douglas into the new year. In response to Collector Simpson Moses's "letter of application" to Tolmie, four barrels of salmon were eventually sent to the collector's private residence for his personal use. As noted above, Moses implied that a "gift of that kind" would "not be unacceptable," with Douglas adding that "to refuse it might expose [the Company's vessels] to inconvenience and trouble." This was, in essence, a bribe asked for and given.

1 John Ballenden to George Simpson, March 22, 1853, HBCA, Fort Vancouver Correspondence Outwards, B.223/b/42, p. 110.

The longstanding Hawkins debt remained a burden on Steilacoom Barracks' Dr. John Haden. Tolmie's ability to collect on the debt continued to diminish until just one option remained: a lawsuit. This placed both physicians in an awkward situation. Even as he tried to patch together a payment plan that Haden could accept, the chief trader continually sought new business opportunities whenever he felt they might benefit the Company. As the Hawkins case illustrates, even seemingly good deals could, and did, occasionally go sideways.

French physician Dr. L. C. Broy[2] entered into a new business partnership with Tolmie in December 1852. During the previous nine months Broy had helped establish Portland's first hospital. The French physician's speculative venture included Tolmie's purchase of milled lumber on Puget Sound that would then be bought and resold by Broy in San Francisco's booming construction market.[3] Others had succeeded in similar stratagems, so (mistakenly) Tolmie entered into a verbal agreement with Broy; principally to sell the Frenchman 20,000 board feet of cedar and fir siding for $1,000—siding that Tolmie had already acquired from Rudolph Walker for half that price. A second offer involved 16,000 board feet of flooring lumber for a similar amount. This Broy did not take. The French doctor's unexpected disappearance just days after his agreement was struck foreshadowed the many incongruities that arose over the next eight months. Other setbacks included: miscommunications with Tolmie's colleagues in Vancouver; shifting interpretations on the verbal agreement's major points; missed payment deadlines; altered conditions; Broy's being incommunicado when important decisions were to be made; the use of Father Pascal Ricard as escrow agent; the unexpected involvement of (and misplaced trust in) a rather designing Frenchman, Pierre Dumilatre;[4] a ship's sailing without warning; promises made, then broken, then made again. On and on it went.

Ultimately, Dumilatre gained possession of not only Broy's cash (meant for Tolmie), but both orders of Tolmie's lumber. Applying the funds "to other business" concerns, Dumilatre had engaged Lafayette Balch and Dr. John Webber's[5] brig *Cyclops*[6] (Captain William Perkins), then anchored in Olympia's harbor. Tolmie's

---

2 Little is known of this early Portland doctor, including what his initials "L.C." represent.

3 Eight months would pass before Tolmie freed himself of this debacle.

4 Not much is known about this owner of Dumilatre and Company in San Francisco. He apparently had business contacts in Portland, Olympia, San Francisco, and Steilacoom, but dealt primarily in the importation of dry goods and tobacco.

5 Dr. Webber was the first citizen physician to locate and practice medicine in Steilacoom and the surrounding neighborhood, arriving there in company with Lafayette Balch on the brig *George Emery* in the fall of 1852. He was also partner in the mercantile firm of Balch and Webber, the first general store opened in Steilacoom. Little is known of the early life of Webber other than he graduated from Brunswick Medical College, having read medicine with Dr. N. Smith, whose eldest daughter Martha Z. Smith became Webber's wife. Two sons were born to the couple. Soon after the second son was born Martha died. The doctor then came to Puget Sound. Webber also brought a stock of drugs and established a drug store, which he put under the competent management of a Mr. Beddington, who unfortunately met an untimely death. Webber remained in Steilacoom until his death, which occurred in 1868. Lauri Downey Bartlett, "Dr. John Webber," Steilacoom Historical Society [Unpublished].

6 The *Cyclops*, Captain William Perkins, was one of five "windjammers" running between San Francisco and the Pacific Northwest coast and owned by Lafayette Balch and John Webber, who were owners of a mill on Puget Sound. Jack McNairn and Jerry MacMullen, *Ships of the Redwood Coast* (Redwood City, CA: Stanford University Press, 1946), 13.

lumber was somehow loaded aboard the *Cyclops*. Once again, Tolmie faced the all-to-familiar, but "disagreeable necessity" of taking "legal measure to secure payment." Then, without notice to any of the principals in this deal, the *Cyclops* departed from Puget Sound. The Frenchman had privately secured Captain Perkins' demurrage costs through a "conditional bill of sale" which transferred ownership of the lumber to the ship's master. Any hope Broy or Tolmie had of recovering their money or the lumber was gone. This chapter ends with Broy describing the affair as "disagreeable ... annoying ... unauthorized" all the while casting blame on his shady compatriot.[7]

A typically cold, overcast winter greeted 1853's arrival. Celebratory traditions persisted as the fort's journal recorded the "men enjoying themselves dancing." The traditional regale of rum and cakes was undoubtedly served.[8] Sharing in the festivities was Captain William Mouat and his crew of the brigantine *Mary Dare*, then anchored at the roadstead.

In early February, a large canoe party from Vancouver (via Olympia) arrived at the Nisqually roadstead. And while their personal belongings were carted to the fort, three boxes containing an estimated $70,000–$80,000 in gold dust and coins remained at the beach store.[9] With Tolmie absent on customs house business, it fell to apprentice clerk Edward Huggins, to play host to the Earl Charles W. Fitzwilliam,[10] his personal valet, two experienced hunters, and a Company clerk named John Miles[11]—who came from the HBC's London office. Huggins remembered: "[A]t first I took the London Clerk to be the son of the English Earl, because of his overbearing manner. He, [Miles], in a loud kind of a way told me to ... 'Get the gold!' I gave orders [for three or four men] to go down with the cart and I would follow after. I then went to the hall and [began] to eat my supper with Mrs. [Jane] Tolmie and her sister Miss [Letitia] Work (now my wife). [Then] the door suddenly opened and in stalked Mr. Miles and, without a word of apology to the ladies or taking any notice of them, in a loud coarse voice exclaimed: 'Why don't you do as I order you!?! Go down to the beach and take charge of the gold I brought from Vancouver! I'll report you and have you removed!'"[12]

Indignantly, Huggins "rather peremptorily, ordered [Miles] from the room and threatened to put him out [by force], but he went at once and I followed, telling him what I thought of him. He made all manner of threats, and said he'd have me removed, &c."[13] The Earl Fitzwilliam was, according to Huggins, "a very quiet,

7 Ultimately, Broy disappeared altogether. The chief trader's last attempt to contact him occurred in late July 1853. Dumilatre's fate raises even more questions. What happened to the lumber? Was it unloaded and/or sold? Who received that money? Given the conflicting ambiguities of this whole sordid tale, it remains highly unlikely that Tolmie ever received a dime, and simply had to write off the whole affair.

8 Dickey, ed., *Nisqually Journal*, January 1, 1853.

9 Edward Huggins to Clarence B. Bagley Jr, May 12, 1906, UW Library, Clarence B. Bagley Papers, Accession #0036-001, 1864–1931, 2/4-17. See also Dickey, ed., *Nisqually Journal*, February 3, 1853. The value of $70,000–80,000 in today's currency is approximately $2,243,169. That February, the *Mary Dare* sailed off for Victoria with the vast treasure in her hold.

10 Sir Charles William Wentworth Fitzwilliam (1786–1857) was "3rd Earl Fitzwilliam in the peerage of Great Britain, and 5th Earl Fitzwilliam in the peerage of Ireland." For more see: en.wikipedia.org/wiki/Charles_Wentworth-Fitzwilliam,_5th_Earl_Fitzwilliam.

11 For Miles see Watson, *Lives Lived*, 2:686.

12 Edward Huggins to Clarence B. Bagley Jr., May 12, 1906, UW Library, Clarence B. Bagley Collection.

13 Ibid.

unassuming man" and he called Huggins aside and "told me to take no notice of [Miles . . . who] had been drinking too much Hudson's Bay Brandy."[14] Within two days the party left for Victoria, due principally to Miles who was "anxious to proceed onwards."[15] The Earl Fitzwilliam's entourage (without Miles) returned on April 16, but this time attended by a young clerk named Frederick Kennedy, who stayed to work for Dr. Tolmie.[16]

New squatters also made their presence known. Three of them, Thompson, Rosencrants, and a third unidentified person "at the instigation of old [Thomas M.] Chambers, have jumped the claim at the mouth of the Sequalitchew [Creek]" noted one journal entry.[17] Additionally, Hugh Hunter, Henry Chapman, John Sechy, and H. John had all been issued new trespass notices.[18]

Another late comer was J. W. Balance whom Huggins described as a "diminutive, feeble-looking man who . . . had carried on a [tanning] business in Portland."[19] Balance "came to the fort and introduced himself to Tolmie as an experienced tanner and said that he had heard the Doctor had accumulated a large number of hides . . . [and that there] was now a great demand for tanned leather in the settlements in Oregon and California, and with our hides, turned into leather here, [they] would be a source of great profit to the company. Dr. Tolmie listened to the little man's proposal with a great deal of interest and . . . [after spending nearly $1,000 of the Company's money] the tannery was soon constructed, a rough little house, about twenty-five by fifteen feet and three or four tanning vats made—holes in the ground made water-tight with cedar puncheons caulked tight. The tanner, who often used unnecessarily coarse language, appeared to get along very well with Dr. Tolmie . . . except when Balance wanted money." When the tanner failed to produce a viable product, Huggins remembered, "no one appeared to know what had become of him. Dr. Tolmie took possession of all he could find at the tannery, and that was not much, only a few half-tanned hides and a few tanner's tools."

Nearby, Steilacoom Barracks had experienced a change of command. Lieutenant John Dement, Captain Bennett Hill, Sergeants Robert,[20] and James Hall had all been ordered back to the United States. One of their replacements was young Lieutenant William Alloway Slaughter[21]—another of Tolmie's leading correspondents in this chapter and beyond.[22]

---

14 Ibid.

15 Dickey, ed., *Nisqually Journal*, February 5, 1853. In 1906 Edward Huggins recalled Miles' fate: "When [Miles] arrived at Victoria, he soon found his proper place working at a desk. Misters [James] Douglas, [John] Work and [Roderick] Finlayson were too many for him, and instead of being a man of importance amongst them as he supposed, [he was no more than] green hands in the Victoria office." Edward Huggins to Clarence B. Bagley Jr., May 12, 1906, UW Library, Clarence B. Bagley Collection.

16 Dickey, ed., *Nisqually Journal*, April 16, 1853.

17 Dickey, ed., *Nisqually Journal*, February 9, 1853.

18 Dickey, ed., *Nisqually Journal*, February 21, 1853.

19 All quotes in this paragraph are from Huggins, "The Balance Tannery and an Early Trip to Olympia," Portland *Oregonian*, September 2, 1900.

20 This is probably the Scotsman Robert M. Hall who is noted in the 1850 census for Lewis County, Oregon Territory, as 23 years of age.

21 William Alloway Slaughter (1826–1855) was born in Kentucky and appointed to the Military Academy at West Point in 1844. In May 1851, Lieutenant Slaughter met and married Mary Wells, of Port Huron. In April 1852, the whole regiment was ordered to the Pacific Coast. Mrs. Slaughter, a bride of less than a year, was the only woman to accompany the troops. Bonney, *History of Pierce County*, 1:189.

22 Lieutenant Slaughter's name would become seared into the territory's collective memory at the outset

Also introduced is Major Albert J. Smith, U.S. Army paymaster on the Pacific slope.[23] Though stationed in San Francisco, Smith made regular trips to the lower Columbia and Steilacoom Barracks, for army regulations required him to personally disperse pay to the troops. And though previously alluded to, the forthcoming correspondence illustrates the HBC's part in providing Major Smith with hard currency. In the following two years, Smith endorsed several advances (checks)[24] to the HBC, some exceeding $7,000 dollars. All went smoothly as long as ready cash remained available. Later on, however, when the Company's cash reserves dried up, Smith was forced to either delay payday or find his funds elsewhere.

Towards the end of this fiscal cycle, rumors surfaced that Collector Moses's job was in peril. The Britons and settlers greeted the development with mixed views. Even so, the Company's vessels now operated within tight, new customs regulations on Puget Sound's waters. Penalties from previous seizures had been refunded, and no new threats from Olympia lay on the immediate horizon. The Company's possessions at Nisqually had finally been professionally surveyed/mapped—a copy now in the hands of Washington Territory's Surveyor General John Preston. Given such positive developments, Dr. Tolmie likely viewed the upcoming year with increased optimism.

Far to the east, however, a fresh batch of antagonists were working westward over the Rocky Mountains. Within this brigade of travelers was one who was professionally, personally, and politically committed to extinguishing the Company's operation south of the international boundary line. This man was Washington Territory's first governor: Isaac Ingalls Stevens.

Here then are the documents from the last half of Outfit 1853.

Document 7.01: An excerpt from a private letter from William F. Tolmie, Nisqually, to George Simpson, Lachine, approximately Winter/Spring, 1853.[25]

[Sir,]

With regard to my own prospects of advancement [in the Company], I leave it to anyone conversant with the circumstances to say whether the post I have occupied during the last ten years, conducting a new and comparatively untried business, has not involved more anxiety and responsibility, and required quite as much skill and tact, as the management of a Fur trading district or of a set of accounts where the minutest details and arrangements are reduced to rule, and routine.

---

of the upcoming Indian War.

23 A Tennessean, Smith received the United States Army rank of major in 1849. While in the Pacific Northwest, he was the army's paymaster stationed in San Francisco—and serving as payroll clerk for both Steilacoom and Vancouver Barracks in 1853–1854. After being reassigned to Fort Union (Santa Fe, NM, area) in around 1855–56, Major Smith was eventually reassigned to Key West, FL. There, in the summer of 1861, he deserted and became the paymaster of the Army of Tennessee—fighting for the south during the Civil War. Sources: www.santafetrailresearch.com/fort-union-nm/fu-oliva-4b.html; archive.org/stream/officialarmyregi1856unit/officialarmyregi1856unit_djvu.txt; www.dtic.mil/dtic/tr/fulltext/u2/a258518.pdf; proust.library.miami.edu/findingaids/?p=collections/findingaid&id=851.

24 In those days, checks were referred to as an order, advance/advice, or note.

25 BC Archives, MS-0557, Box 2. From a typescript copy. This excerpt does not identify the recipient, but from the tenor and mention of "jealousy existing on the eastside" in the letter, it is assumed that he is writing to the HBC's North American Governor Sir George Simpson.

Be it remembered too that amidst troubles with Indian cattle thieves in the earlier years, and with Americans, deserting servants, &c., subsequently, I have been entirely alone 'till 1846, and since [then] have had the assistance only of youths scarcely out of their teens. The gentlemen in charge at Vancouver had divers [sic] troubles of a similar nature and weightier interests at stake, but I doubt wether [sic] their anxieties were greater, and they could consult together when occasion required and had zealous and experienced clerks as aids and subordinates.

I regret that the jealousy existing on the eastside towards the Puget's Sound Company should have an injurious influence on my prospects [for a raise]. I am going by this post to address Govr [Eden] Colvile and Mr. [Henry Hulse] Berens[26] regarding my promotion. I have to ask from you an effectual word to them on my behalf. I remain, My dear sir, very truly yours,

[Signed] W. F. Tolmie

Document 7.02: A letter from William F. Tolmie, Nisqually, to John Ballenden, Vancouver, December 5, 1852.

Dear Sir,

I have now to acknowledge receipt of your letters of Novr 1st & 25th the [contents of which] I was glad to learn that Mr. [Charles] Bradley would receive my letters at Vancouver.

Ft Nisqually Inventory was taken on the 1st Novr as has been customary for some years past and, should you still intend that the supplies to be forwarded from Vancouver by the transport vessel are to belong to Outfit 1852, have the kindness to send an account of them p[e]r first mail in order that they may be put in Inventory. Every exertion shall be made to have the Nisqually accounts at Vancouver by the 15th January as you direct.

Signed Wm F. Tolmie

Document 7.03: A letter from James Douglas, Victoria, to William F. Tolmie, Nisqually, December 6, 1852.[27]

Dear Sir,

The York Factory party arrived here on the 4th inst and delivered the packet safely, also your letter of 29th November.

We have not yet succeeded in purchasing a canoe for Nisqually as there are none of the right description within reach. But we shall endeavour to procure one at the first favourable opportunity. The Indians have been, therefore, paid for the trip in order to save the expenses of paying them at Nesqually.

We shall see what can be done for you in the way of Flour by the first ship that proceeds to Nesqually; but I hardly think it will be in our power to send you any, as we have not a large stock on hand.

---

26 Henry Hulse Berens (1804–c. 1863) was a director of the Bank of England, 1849-50. He became a member of the Committee of the Hudson's Bay Company in 1833, Deputy Governor in 1856, and Governor in 1858, a position which he held until 1863. www.gov.mb.ca/chc/archives/hbca/biographical/b/berens_henry.pdf.

27 UW Library, Tolmie Papers Acc. 4577-001, Box 2, Folder 3, N. 979.413 D 741#123.

The Mary Dare and Recovery have both returned from California. The market was unfortunately over-stocked with coal before their arrival at San Francisco, and purchasers hesitated on bidding for an article whose qualities had not been thoroughly tested.

The cargoes were, therefore, sold at a low price, the one at 15 and the other at 16 dollars per ton. The experiments since made with that coal have proved, I am informed, very satisfactory, and the opinion is expressed that it will answer well for steamer's use.

The news from Nanaimo is good. The miners struck coal in the shaft at the depth of 45 feet. This proved to be a bed of excellent coal measuring rather over 72 inches from roof to pavement, and great things are expected from it.

The Recovery sailed yesterday for a supply of potatoes at Cowetchen [Cowichan]. The Mary Dare will be detained at least 15 days in port for repairs. No word of the Steamer [*Beaver*] as yet. Indians all quiet. Have not yet attempted to catch the [Cowichan] murderers [of Peter Brown, our shepherd], reserving that duty 'till the arrival of the Steamer. With Best wishes, Yours sincerely,

James Douglas

P.S. Please mail the accompanying letters for England by first opportunity.

Document 7.04: A letter from William A. Howard, Olympia, to William F. Tolmie, Nisqually, December 14, 1852.[28]

Dear Sir,

Enclosed I send you advises [advances] of M[isters] Adams & Co of Five hundred ($500) Dollars [which presently is] in their hands to my credit, an informality of the D[ra]ft [which] obliged it to be sent back per last Steamer to San Francisco (which sailed on the 4th inst) and will be here probably on the 20th inst again. I have workmen waiting for pay due them [who wish] to go away and are consequently very clamorous. I also have some goods, provisions, &c., in store that I require money to make available. Can you accommodate me with Four hundred Dollars until I can receive the cash from the Draft? If so it will confer on me a very great favour. The roads between here and the Cowlitz are almost impassible, but I hope to get the money next week. Mr. [Captain Eli] Hathaway took the business in hand, has gone to San Francisco & will remit per Steamer. The Mary Taylor has arrived from Vancouver at Port Townsend [and] sailed from Victoria on the 30th November. I hope to receive letters from Mr. Douglass [sic] by her—have you? I am dear Sir Very truly Yours,

W. A. Howard

Document 7.05: A letter from William F. Tolmie, Nisqually, to John Ballenden, Vancouver, December 15, 1852.

Dear Sir,

I have to acknowledge receipt on the 6th Inst <u>by mail</u> of your communications bearing date 4th and 8th November; also of a packet for Mr. [James] Douglas mailed at V[ancouve]r prior to the arrival of the Y[ork] F[actory] Express.

28 UW Library, Tolmie Papers Acc. 4577-001, Box 1 Folder 4.

Having sold lumber to Dr. L.C. Broy to the amount of One Thousand Dollars I have requested him to pay that amount to you which, on receipt, please credit to F[ort] Nisqually O[utfi]t 1852.

I forward this by Dr. Broy who expects to see you at Vancouver very soon. Please advize as soon as he has paid the above amount. I will write soon again.

S[igne]d W. F. Tolmie

Document 7.06: A memoranda by William F. Tolmie, Nisqually, to himself, December 15, 1852.

Mem[orand]a:

Wrote Dr. L.C. Broy requesting him to pay the amount due for lumber 1,000$ to J[ohn] Ballenden, Esq[ui]re.

Document 7.07: A letter from William F. Tolmie, Nisqually, to John Ballenden, Vancouver, December 20, 1852.

Dear Sir,

I wrote you on the 15th by Dr. Broy, that I had sold him lumber to the amount of One thousand Dollars ($1,000) which he was to pay to you. I have now 16 M [thousand board feet of] fir flooring boards to offer him at $45 P[e]r M [thousand board feet], the price he pays at Olympia making an amount of $720, which, if he pays you, please advize me of [the transaction] without delay. I shall write Dr. Broy by this post.

(Signed) Wm F. Tolmie

Document 7.08: A letter from William F. Tolmie, Nisqually, to Dr. L.C. Broy, Portland, December 20, 1852.

Dear Sir,

In addition to the Cedar and fir siding I have already sold you, I have now to offer you Sixteen Thousand [16,000 board] feet of Lumber 12 foot [long and] inch and a half [thick] boards and flooring boards. I subjoin a copy of the order as handed to Mr. [Rudolph] Walker, and enclose copy of a receipt from him to show that he is bound to deliver said lumber to my order. You can have the lumber at the market price $45 P[e]r M [thousand board feet] and if you take it please pay the amount ($720) Seven hundred and twenty Dollars to Mr. Ballenden who will immediately notify me thereof.

(Signed) Wm F. Tolmie

Document 7.09: A letter from William F. Tolmie, Nisqually, to Hugh A. Goldsborough, Olympia, December 29, 1852.

Dear Sir,

Herewith is enclosed a priced invoice of goods you have agreed to sell for me at Seven Percent Commission. Please acknowledge receipt of the goods by return

of bearer, and have the goodness to return the box, of which the key is enclosed.
(Signed) Wm F. Tolmie

P.S. The goods are in ~~two~~hree packages—a box & 2 bales.

Document 7.10: A letter from Hugh A. Goldsborough, Olympia, to William F. Tolmie, Nisqually, December 31, 1852.[29]

Sir,

My Yesterday's hasty note acknowledged the receipt of three parcels of goods, forwarded by you for sale on commission by me. Since then I have examined them and find all correct but the striped cotton shirts; of these there were received only 48 instead of 60 as per your priced Invoice.

On the next page I send you a Receipt in form. Col [Michael T.] Simmons desires me to Request you to send him regularly, if practicable, a quarter of Beef each week, until he may advise you to the contrary. About half of the blankets are already sold. With best regards, Yours very Respectfully,

H. A. Goldsborough

Document 7.11: A letter from George Gibbs, Portland, to William F. Tolmie, Nisqually, December 31, 1852.[30]

Dear Sir,

I beg have to call to your remembrance the haiqua [dentalium shells] which you were good enough to promise to get for me some time since. I do not know indeed, but you may have forwarded it as I have been in the interior of Northern California where we rarely had opportunities of hearing [from anyone]. May I ask of you the favor if you have not already purchased it, to obtain the longer kind only, if it is to be had, or if not, to remit the money to Fort Vancouver for me. But if it is possible to procure some of the really large shells, say 2 ¼ inches long and upwards, I wish to have them to send back to my friends at Humboldt Bay. I have myself returned to Oregon to remain ~~at last~~ for a time at last, having received the appointment of Collector at Astoria. If you send by Mr. [Edward D.] Warbass, it will do. Wishing you the compliments of the Season in a happy New Year, I am, Very truly, your obt sert,

George Gibbs

[P.S.] Judge [William] Strong & Mr. [Archibald] Mckinley who sit with me over a glass of "arf and arf" join in good wishes.[31]

29 UW Library, Tolmie Papers, Box 1, Folder 4, Acc. 4577-001, VO250e/4577.

30 Ibid.

31 Gibbs's reference to "arf and arf" is what today is called a "half-and-half" or "black and tan" style of serving beer. In this way, the barkeep mixes two beers of contrasting color and density, like a pilsner/porter combination or pale lager/stout mixture. In either case, one beer must be of a lesser density than the other to stay afloat. Today, a common mixture of the less dense Guinness over a Bass Ale, or a Guinness over a Harp Lager is favored.

Document 7.12: A letter from William F. Tolmie, Nisqually, to Simpson P. Moses, Olympia, January 5, 1853.

Dear Sir,

I have deputed W[illiam] A. Mouat Esqu[ire] to present to You, &c., the Brigantine "Mary Dare's" Manifest Outwards. Will you please inform me by Mr. Mowat's return, whether the Mary Dare on her ensuing trip, and when entering at Olympia, could without infringement of law, Ship some thirty thousand feet of lumber from the New Market Mill, and take in the remainder of her Cargo here? Yours &c., &c.,

(Signed) Wm F. Tolmie

Document 7.13: A letter from William F. Tolmie, Nisqually, to Hugh A. Goldsborough, Olympia, January 5, 1853.

Dear Sir,

Having learnt from Capt [Charles] Thomas[32] [of the American bark *Brontes*][33] that you are nearly out of Blankets, I send you by Captn [William A.] Mouat one bale containing 50 blankets 3 p[oin]ts Best which please sell at $4/ four dollars each as heretofore. Out of the proceeds of your Sales, please bring to Pere [Georges] Blanchet[34] of [Pascal] Ricard's [Oblate Catholic] Mission the sum of Three Hundred and forty-five dollars Eighteen Cents ($345.18/100) and take his receipt for the amount paid him.

Have the goodness to send by return of the canoe the keg of nails and hinges (3 dozen) left for me by Captain Thomas.

(Signed) W. F. Tolmie

Document 7.14: An extract from a letter by William F. Tolmie, Nisqually, to Lafayette Balch, Port Steilacoom, January 8, 1853.

[Sir,]

I would not object to your cutting Oak Timber on the Puget's Sound Company's lands, provided a fair stumpage were paid per tree . . . the amount of stumpage would depend on some measure on the locality you might select. In fixing the stumpage, we would, I presume, be guided by the custom in other parts of the United States, and on this point I am not well informed.

---

32 No biographical information could be found regarding this ship's captain.

33 *Brontes*, American bark. Skippered by Charles Thomas at this point, the vessel's primary cargo was milled lumber and piling materials. The vessel was docked at Seattle's waterfront when the Indian War of 1855 erupted and the settlement was attacked.

34 Georges Blanchet (1818–1906), referred to as a "scholastic" in the Oblate order, had accompanied Father Ricard to the Olympia Mission from the beginning. Georges remained a Brother for a long time and was not ordained to the priesthood until November 1, 1892. For more see www.omiworld.org/en/dictionary/historical-dictionary_vol-2_o/1871/oregon-united-states-1847-1860/.

Document 7.15: A letter from William F. Tolmie, Nisqually, to James Douglas, Victoria, January 8, 1853.

Dear Sir,

I acknowledge receipt of your letters of the 2nd, 18th, & 21st, December 1852.

Enclosed are Invoice and Bill Lading of the Cargo Shipped by the Mary Dare, which owing to the Very bad weather experienced here, has been delayed much longer than would otherwise have happened.

I have sold the Cedar siding to Dr. [L.C.] Broy of Portland at $50 P[e]r M [thousand board feet] and have offered him the flooring lumber at $45, but his answer has not yet arrived. Altho' disposable, the lumber could not have been got ready for this trip of the vessel, as [Rudolph] Walker had no means of Getting it to the landing [at] Newmarket.

I hope the requisition of Goods may be forwarded by the next Vessel sent to Nisqually, and should there be no X.P. Plough Shares, please send some C[ast] M[etal] ones as soon as possible.

Not having succeeded in purchasing horses for Victoria from the Indians, I have sent P[e]r "Mary Dare" the best of the Marrons received from Vancouver this Summer.

John Macphail goes [as] passenger in the Brigantine [*Mary Dare*]. I do not think he has any Credit on the Company's Books. Matthew Hanus[35] and William Barret[36]—two of Mr. [Edward] Langford's men who Commenced work on the [space left blank by Tolmie]—now return to him, under promise of indemnity for past doings.

I am fully convinced that nothing will prevent squatters from taking possession of the [Sequalitchew Creek] mill site here but [the act of] our commencing in earnest to erect a saw mill here ourselves.

Having been questioned on the subject by several parties, I have to request information as to the wholesale price of Blankets, Baize and Shirts at Victoria.

Captain [Lafayette] Balch has written to enquire whether I would consent to his cutting Oak Timber in this vicinity on condition of his paying a stumpage for each tree. I have replied that I would not object provided he paid a fair stumpage.

There has been no mail for three weeks past, and Captain [William A. Mouat] Mowat, who has just returned from Olympia, has brought none.

S[igne]d W. F. Tolmie

P.S. Mr. [Simpson P.] Moses has asked to have 3 [barrels of] Salmon sent for him by next vessel from Victoria. I enclose Moses's letter[37] asking for Salmon. T

---

35 Bruce Watson, via March 24, 2016, email to editor notes: "I went through my whole data base for both Matthew Hanus and William Barret and could find neither hide nor hair of anyone resembling their names." No mention is made of either man in the fort's journal.

36 See previous footnote.

37 This letter has yet to be located.

Document 7.16: A letter from William F. Tolmie, Nisqually, to John Ballenden, Vancouver, January 17, 1853.

Dear Sir,

I wrote you on the 15th Decr regarding lumber sold to Dr. [L.C.] Broy for one Thousand Dollars payable to you, and on the [option] regarding lumber offered for sale to him. I expected a reply to mine of the 15th Decr by last mail, but was disappointed [when I did not get one]. Please inform me by return of posts whether the letters referred to have reached you.

(Signed) W. F. Tolmie

P.S. All well here and business good for the season. Loss of stock so far not great. T.

Document 7.17: A letter from Joseph Hardisty, Vancouver, to William F. Tolmie, Nisqually, January 18, 1853.[38]

Dear Sir,

In balancing the Abstract the other day I noticed that the sum of £41.9.8 was charged against Montgomery, John (B) for Book Debits at Nisqually Outfit 1851. On the 1st June 1851, John Montgomery (A) had a credit Balance of £50.19.10 and John Montgomery (B) to whom the book Debits were charged had a debit Balance of £10.8.9. The Book Debits above alluded to should therefore in my opinion have come against John Montgomery (A). Ought they not?

Please inform me as soon as possible in order that if it be a mistake it may be rectified prior to our sending off the accounts [per York] Factory. In haste, Yours, &c.,

Joseph Hardisty

Document 7.18: A letter from William F. Tolmie, Nisqually, to John Ballenden, Vancouver, January 19, 1853.

Dear Sir,

Referring you to the enclosed Draft, I have to request you to credit Ft Nisqually Outfit [18]53 with Sixty Five Dollars ($65) which charge to account of Bishop [Modeste] Demers, should he have funds in your possession, otherwise please return the Draft as soon as convenient.

(S[igne]d) Wm Fraser Tolmie

Document 7.19: A letter from William F. Tolmie, Nisqually, to John Ballenden, Vancouver, January 20, 1853.

Dear Sir,

Enclosed is a Draft for One Thousand Dollars ($1,000) on Captain T[homas] L. Brent[39] Columbia Barracks in your favor from L[ieutnant John] Dement, U.S.A.

38 BC Archives, A/C/20/H21. From a typescript copy.

39 At this time, U.S. Army Captain Brent lived with Captain Rufus Ingalls and Brevet Captain Ulysses S. Grant at Columbia Barracks/Fort Vancouver. There, "Brent served as Assistant Adjutant Quarter Master . . . . [and] lived in a two-story prefabricated house Ingalls had had built in the Quartermaster

Steilacoom [Barracks]. Please credit the amount when paid to Fort Nisqually O[utfi]t [18]53 or advize by earliest opportunity should Captain Brent have already remitted (as in his letter authorizing him to draw for $1,000 he spoke of doing) to Mr. Dement, and consequently declined; paying the Draft.

Please inform me what premium the Coy should have for Drafts on London? The amount at present asked for is only $100.

S[igne]d W. F. Tolmie

Document 7.20: A letter from William Brotchie, Port Steilacoom, to William F. Tolmie, Nisqually, January 20, 1853.[40]

My dear Sir,

On Friday last I saw all the good folks at Victoria. They told me of you, Mrs. [Jane] Tolmie, and [of] your livestock being well. I have entered into some arrangements with [Roderick] Finlayson about my Spars. He mentioned to me [that] if I saw you, to purchase [for him] four head of American Oxen if possible. (I hope no impediment [stands] in the way, you must strain every nerve to do this). Finlayson will write you [all the] particulars by the Mary Dare. [Captain William Mouat] was to have left Tuesday for here.

I shall be delighted to see you and Jane. I have to take up this Ship to Olympia and after that I hope to be on my way back to Fort Rupert. We have had very bad weather lately. We left San Francisco on the 27th Dec [1852] and on the 2nd Jany off Cape Flattery Gales commenced from [the] S[outh] E[ast] which drove us as far as Scott's Islands. We have lost nearly one suit of Sails; in fact we are nearly a wreck and worst of all, Leaky. Mr. [Thomas] Lowe is on board, also another partner of the vessel—a regular Down Easterner, such a lot as the devil never shook a stick at. If an opportunity offers, send me a Beef Steak or a few Tongues. I want some to cope with these Yankees. Of course, you have all the news by Walter Ross. My respects to Mrs. Tolmie also to Mr. [Edward] Huggins, and believe me, Yours sincerely,

(Signed) W. Brotchie

[P.S.] I have been up now two nights otherwise I would come and see you. W. B.

Document 7.21: A letter & memoranda from William F. Tolmie, Nisqually, to John Ballenden, Vancouver, January 21, 1853.

Dear Sir,

The Victoria & Nisqually accounts are now forwarded in charge of Mr. Kenneth Logan who will, I trust, reach Vancouver speedily and safely.

Considering it be fair that the Puget's Sound Co should pay freight on other supplies, I have debited their account with £150, half the sum charged this post at Victoria for two supplies of goods P[e]r Mary Dare amounting together to £1091 Sterling.

Depot area of the post in 1850. In 1854, the timber in the immediate vicinity of the now reduced Military Reservation was pretty much depleted: Captain Brent, assistant quartermaster, purchased forage and firewood for the post from nearby settlers." See www.nps.gov/parkhistory/online_books/fova/clr/clr2-3c.htm for more information.

40 UW Library, Tolmie Papers Acc. 4577-001, 10250, Box 1, Folder 1. From a typescript copy. At this time, the former HBC skipper was privately employed and not with the Company.

I have charged the PS Coy 33⅓ percent for duties instead of 25 p[e]r cent as formerly to cover their share of the extra duties charged at Olympia on goods imported from Vancouver's Island.

The money ($50) lent Captain [William] Howard is charged against Ft Vancouver Sale Shop, in case that gentleman may have had the amount fixed there, as he promised when accommodated with the loan.

I have credited the estate of the late C[harles] Forrest with the proceeds of the Sale of his personal effect here, as [the] Coy's ser[van]ts were the principal purchasers.

Agreeable to instruction in a circular from Sir George Simpson dated Lachine Decr 1st 1852, I forward to Vancouver the papers, &c., of the late C[harles] Forrest. The money ($199.50/100) on the Inventory of his effects will be forwarded to Victoria for the use of his daughter [Annie][41] unless you should see fit to place it to the credit of his estate, in which case, please advize me by return of bearer.

I wrote you by mail on Decr 15th and Jany 7th notifying that I had sold Dr. [L.C.] Broy of Portland lumber to the amount of $1,000 which he was to pay to you immediately on his return from Puget's Sound. I wrote on the 20th Decr stating in addition that I had offered Dr. Broy lumber to the amount of $720 for which, if he took it, he was to make prompt payment.

Please [provide] information on these matters at your earliest convenience. Should Broy pay for the Lumber please credit the amount to Ft Nisqually O[utfi]t 1852 or, if not, put on Inv[entor]y lumber to the amount of $1,944. See Mem[orand]a enclosed for full particulars. I remain sir, Your very obet sert,

W. F. Tolmie

Mem[orand]a regarding Fort Nisqually Acc[ou]nts, Outfit 1852

Should Dr. Broy not pay for any of the Lumber referred to in my letters to Mr. C[hief] F[actor John] Ballenden, Ft Nisqually [is] to be credited with the following as on Inventory:

16,000 feet fir flooring $24.	$384.00
20,000 [feet] Cedar Siding $28	$560.00
	$944.00

Should Dr. Broy take & pay for the Cedar Siding as he agreed to, but decline purchasing the flooring, Ft Nisqually O[utfi]t '52 [is] to be credited with $1,000 cash and on Inv[entor]y with the 16,000 feet fir flooring; $384.

W. F. Tolmie

Document 7.22: A letter from William F. Tolmie, Nisqually, to James Douglas, Victoria, January 23, 1853.

Dear Sir,

Mr. Walter Ross arrived here on the 19th with the Victoria accounts which, along with those from this post, were forwarded yesterday morning in charge of Mr. [Kenneth] Logan. I have detained Mr. Ross 'till the arrival of the mail and he

41 Annie Forrest, who now lived in Victoria, was the teenaged métis daughter of the deceased Cowlitz Farm postmaster, Charles Forrest.

now takes all the postal matter accumulated for V[ancouver] I[sland]. Expecting to write soon again, [I am, &c., &c.,],

S[igne]d W. F. Tolmie

Document 7.23: A letter from William F. Tolmie, Nisqually, to John Ballenden, Vancouver, January 24, 1853.

Dear Sir,

I beg to advize having this day drawn on you for fifty Dollars ($50) in favor of George Gibbs Esq[ui]re, Astoria, and in favor of T[homas] Lowe Esq[ui]re of San Francisco for two hundred Dollars; all of which please charge to Ft Nisqually O[utfi]t 1853. Some Hyquas [detalium shells] received from Victoria for Vancouver are forwarded in charge of Mr. [Thomas] Lowe.

(Signed) Wm F. Tolmie

Document 7.24: A letter from James Douglas, Victoria, to William F. Tolmie, Nisqually, January 26, 1853.[42]

Dear Sir,

I have to acknowledge receipt of your letter of the 8th January covering an additional requisition for articles required from this place; and also your letter of 23rd January—received this day by the arrival of Mr. Walter Ross from Nisqually. As neither of these communications requires further remark I will proceed to the notice of other matters.

The Mary Dare is again about to proceed to Nisqually with the supplies as per invoice herewith, including a great part of the goods ordered by you for that place. Among other articles, we have shipped Forty Barrels of Flour, and Thirty Barrels of Salmon, besides 4 Barrels of the latter which you will please to present without charge to Mr. Collector [Simpson P.] Moses, as his letter of application to you implies that a gift[43] of that kind will not be unacceptable, and to refuse it might expose us to inconvenience and trouble.

We presume that the Flour will fetch at least $40.00 p[e]r Barrel, at which price we can replace it by a better article at the Sandwich Islands.

I beg that the Mary Dare may receive as speedy a despatch from Nisqually as possible, and that you will send by her as much Beef, dead and alive, as you can manage to ship, and also the seed oats, formerly ordered, with as many inch deals as you have on hand, provided that you have not previously sold them.

The "Norman Morison" arrived here on the 10th inst with her passengers all in good health. She had a very pleasant passage out, and completed the voyage in five months, less one day.

I returned safely from Comegin [Cowichan] and Nanaimo on the 19th inst and am happy to inform you that we succeeded in capturing both [of] the murderers [of the shepherd Peter Brown] who were executed by hanging in the presence of

---

42 James Douglas to William F. Tolmie, January 26, 1853, UW Library, Tolmie Papers Acc. 4577-001, V0250e, Box 1, Folder 2. N 979.514, D74e, #113. From a typescript copy.

43 Moses's "gift" is a euphemism for the more accurate expression of "a bribe."

the whole tribe, without any other loss of life—either on our part or on that of the Natives. We had a good deal of trouble in affecting our object, and had to carry their villages sword in hand, but the Almighty disposer of events favoured the just cause, and the land is now cleansed from the pollution of innocent blood.

Her Majesty's Ship "Thetis"[44] sailed last week for California, and we soon expect another of Her Majesty's ships to replace her.

The Brig Vancouver[45] will sail in a few days for Fort Langley for a cargo of Salmon which she will take on to the Sandwich Islands.

I beg that you will forward the accompanying letters for England and Vancouver by the first opportunity. With Best Wishes, I remain, Yours Truly,

James Douglas

P.S. Many thanks for your private favours, to which I will reply as soon as time permits. I have no authority to lay out large sums of money in improvement for the Puget's Sound Company, nor to be held responsible for such outlays with my own means. I have addressed them repeatedly on the subject without eliciting a satisfactory reply. Adieux for the present.

Sincerely yours, James Douglas

Document 7.25: A letter from William F. Tolmie, Nisqually, to John Ballenden, Vancouver, January 30, 1853.

Dear Sir,

I received only yesterday your communication of the 8th Decr [18]52, accompanying a packet for Mr. Douglas bearing the Columbia City post mark of Decr 20 [18]52 on the envelope to my address. There seems so far to be no improvement in postal arrangements between Vancouver and this quarter.

The arrival of the Norman Morison at Victoria has recently been reported here on pretty good authority. No direct news from that quarter since the arrival of the accounts. Having nothing of importance to communicate I now conclude and remain,

(Signed) Wm Fraser Tolmie

Document 7.26: A letter & memoranda from William F. Tolmie, Olympia, to John Ballenden, Vancouver, February 5, 1853.

Dear Sir,

Enclosed is a certificate of deposit for One Thousand Dollars ($1,000) payable to you by [William H.] Barnhart & Co, Portland,[46] which I have cashed for a premium of Two Per Cent having also obtained good security in Olympia for its payment. Please credit the amount to Nisqually O[utfi]t 1853.

S[igne]d William Fraser Tolmie

44 *Thetis*, HMS frigate. "This 36-gun fifth-rate frigate of the Royal Navy was commissioned in 1846. After nearly a decade of service with the British, she was transferred to Prussia in exchange for two steam gunboats." en.wikipedia.org/wiki/HMS_Thetis_(1846).

45 *Vancouver*, HBC steamer/schooner. See Watson, *Lives Lived*, 3:1134.

46 As of the fall of 1852, the William H. Barnhart & Company was agent for the Wells, Fargo & Company in Portland. *The Federated Philatelist: Newsletter of the Northwest Federation of Stamp Clubs*, No. 205, December 2013, 4.

Mem[orand]a: the above forwarded by posts and another letter notifying to Mr. B[allenden] the transaction forwarded by Captain B[enjamin] P. Barstow[47] who made the deposit of $1,000 with [William H.] Barnhart. T

Document 7.27: A letter from William F. Tolmie, Olympia, to John Ballenden, Vancouver, February 11, 1853.

Dear Sir,

I have to acknowledge receipt of your letters of 26th and 31st Ulto and 1st Inst.

Having been absent at Olympia Getting the "Mary Dare" cleared, I had not the pleasure of seeing Mr. [John] Miles when he passed. The three Cases [of gold] Specie are safe and will be forwarded by the Brigantine [*Mary Dare*].

In reply to the enquiry of Yours of the 26th January, I have to state that there are about Five Thousand dollars Cash on hand. I will retain in my Coffers Three thousand Dollars, as you direct, and Ship the remainder to Victoria by the "Mary Dare."

On the 5th Inst I cashed a Certificate of Deposit for One Thousand dollars, which is payable to you, on order by William H. Barnhart & Coy, Portland. This is the last transaction of the sort I will engaged in. I forwarded the Certificate to you by mail and should it be lost have still recourse on the parties Concerned.

I am sorry to learn that the Nisqually Accounts have failed to give you satisfaction. They are made out in the manner prescribed by Mr. Dugald Mactavish[48] who was Accountant at Vancouver in 1843 when I took Charge here, and from whom I obtained [the] formula before leaving Vancouver.

Explanations on the points referred to in Your memorandum are forwarded and will, I hope, be understood. I shall arrange to set out for Vancouver, O[regon] T[erritory] on or about the 21st Inst when Mr. [John] Miles may be expected back from V[ancouver's] I[sland] as he was understood to say while here that he would Complete his business there in three days.

You enquire how I make out the Charge for freight against the Puget's Sound Coy. It is as follows: Ft Nisqually has to pay 33⅓ P[e]r Cent advanced on the English Cost of its Supplies and, in addition, heavy freights on the Shipments ~~of~~ from the Depots. Now, I know of no reason why the Puget's Sound Compy should not pay its proportion of these freights as well as of the duties. If as Mr. [Thomas] Lowe informed me, after the Accounts were made up, the PS Co is entitled by its original agreement with the HB Co to Goods at 33⅓ P[e]r Cent, the Case is altered. But now that the PS Co's business is prosperous and paying, a more equitable adjustment of burthens should be made.

I shall see Dr. [John] Haden tomorrow and, should he decline paying [the George W. Hawkins bill]—which is I believe his intention, shall Commence suit against him forthwith. Having been laid up with sprained ancle [sic] for a few day, I have already written him on the subject, but have heard no answer.

With regard to the transport of Goods across the Cowlitz Portage for the Supply of this Post; the trial made last Summer satisfied me of its undesirability on

---

47 It is speculated that Barstow was a New England ship builder and sea captain making the Puget Sound to San Francisco run at this time.

48 For Mactavish see Watson, *Lives Lived*, 2:611–12.

a large Scale, and I hope to succeed on Convincing you of this when we meet and converse on the Subject.

The Mary Dare has just brought us a supply of the most necessary articles of trade goods, but salt was omitted of which the PS Coy's requires a large supply. I remain Dear Sir, Your very Obedt Sert,

William Fraser Tolmie

P.S. I wrote you on the 19th Jany enclosing a Dr[af]t on you for Sixty five dollars from Bishop [Modeste] Demers which I cashed here. The amount to be refunded by Pere [Pascal] Ricard should the Bishop have no funds in your possession. Please inform me whether you have received my letter of Jany 19th.

Document 7.28: A letter from William F. Tolmie, Nisqually, to Joseph Hardisty, Vancouver, February 11, 1853.

Dear Sir,

In reply to yours of the 18th Jany, I have to inform you that I cannot find in any of the documents at this place any affixed a "B" to John Montgomery's name. Our [John] Montgomery [(a)] has been stationed here since [18]41 or [18]42 and had a pretty large Cr[edit] Balance when he deserted in 1849. He returned in 1850 and drew a considerable part of his balance in 1851. In that year his [account] as priced in the Nisqually Ser[van]ts Acc[oun]t Book amounts to £44.6/8 as there can be no doubt but that your amount £41.9/8 should appear against John Montgomery "A", i.e. the Nisqually M[ontgomery].

[Signed] William F. Tolmie

Document 7.29: A letter from L.C. Broy, Portland, to William F. Tolmie, Nisqually, February 14, 1853.[49]

Dear Sir:

I have the pleasure to acknowledge the receipt of your letter of 20th December last in which you offered me for sale 16,000 feet of lumber at $45 p[e]r M [thousand board feet] in addition to that which I have previously purchased of you; the purchase of this I beg leave to decline.

I presume you are aware of the verbal contract entered into between us in the house of Father [Pascal] Ricard at Olympia, by which I purchased of you 20,000 feet of lumber at $50 p[e]r M [thousand board feet] to be paid when the lumber was shipped. As the vessels are daily expected at Olympia for the same [destination—San Francisco], I hope soon to have the pleasure of liquidating the debt. I was a little surprised a week or two since at a request from Mr. Ballenden for the sum of $1,720 for the payment of lumber purchased of you, $1,000 for that I purchased of you when at Olympia and to be paid for when shipped, and $720, I presume, for that which you offered me but which I decline. I explained the matter satisfactorily to Mr. Ballenden, and trust that it is clearly understood by yourself.

49 UW Library, Tolmie Papers Acc. 4577-001, V0250e, Box 1, Folder 1. From a typescript copy.

With sentiments of high regard, I have the honour, Dear Sir, to be very Respectfully, Your Obedt Servt,

(S[igne]d) L.C. Broy

Document 7.30: A letter & forwarded documents from William F. Tolmie, Nisqually, to James Douglas, Victoria, February 19, 1853.

Dear Sir,

By the arrival of the "Mary Dare" I received Your communication of the 26th January, Accompanying Invoice, &c., of Goods shipped for this place by the Brigantine, as said Goods have been entered at the Custom house without trouble and the "Mary Dare" with a Cargo of Cattle, Beef, Oats, &c., is now almost ready for Sea.

I regret much that a Good Supply of Salt was not forwarded by last trip of the "Mary Dare", as we are now almost out of that indispensable article. In a requisition forwarded on the 24th Novr 1852, One thousand bushels were indented for, but if Convenient, fifteen hundred or more might be sent to accommodate the probable demand during the Salmon Salting season. Last Year, we might have sold an advantageous twenty five hundred bushels or more.

Please [know that I received a letter from] Mr. Ballenden today stating that Dr. Broy would pay for the Cedar Siding ($1,000 as agreed on) as soon as Notified that it had been Shipped P[e]r California. This is not according to agreement and from what is reported at Olympia, I am inclined to Suppose that Broy repents of his Lumber speculation on Puget's Sound, and does not mean to fulfill his engagements. He declined taking the flooring boards. Please direct me by first opportunity what to do with the lumber, whether to sell it at Cost, or ship to Victoria by next opportunity.

I am sorry to inform you that our mill site (the Sequallitchew) has been taken possession of by two men, who have built a hut here, and are making preparations for the construction of a dam. The usual warning has been handed to them.

A few barrels of Flour have been sold at Forty Dollars, but as a better Article than ours is coming into ~~from~~ marked from California, the demand is slackening.

I wish much to obtain for the Puget's Sound Co here two or three sober, honest, Young men of rather light weight, thin otherwise, to be employed about the Horses & Cattle. The latter require increased attention now that the demand for Beef is so great. [Charles F.] Gallion wishes to return to Victoria, but Cannot be spared 'till some new hands arrive. W[illia]m Hunt,[50] one of Mr. [Edward] Langford's men, would answer here if Mr. L[angford] could spare him.

There are forwarded P[e]r "Mary Dare" three Cases "Specie" left here by Mr. [Robert] Miles, and another Case Containing $4,143.44/100 from this post, and $380.20/100 in a separate bag belonging to Captain [David] Wishart. The goods remaining here are not worth to the Coy more than $200, but it would save us trouble here if they were purchased at that price. Should he show you this list, you will perceive that a Great many of the Articles on it are unsaleable.

50 Hunt was apparently one of Langford's better hands at Colwood Farm. Aside from the fact that his is listed as a farmer/voter in British Columbia's 1880 census, no other information could be found concerning his time with the PSAC.

The accompanying is a Copy of a letter[51] lately received from Mr. Ballenden. I have the honor to be, Sir, Your Very Obedt Sert,

(Signed) W. F. Tolmie

P.S. I have had an offer of one Dollar P[e]r Salted Hides for all I Can deliver at the beach. I send a sample of leather manufacture here, which can be supplied at 37½ P[e]r [pound]. Should it give satisfaction, You will perhaps order some for V[ancouver] I[sland].

Documents forwarded

Copy Letter from J. Ballenden Esq[ui]re; Invoice of Shipment P[e]r Mary Dare; Invoice of Cash; Bill Landing P[e]r Mary Dare; Cash ac[count] Fort Nisqually Outfit [18]52; Steamer Beaver ac[count] with Fort Nisqually.

Document 7.31: A letter from William F. Tolmie, Nisqually, to James Douglas, Victoria, March 29, 1853.

Dear Sir,

On returning from Vancouver, I had the pleasure to receive your communication of the 21st Inst by which I was gratified to learn that Nisqually Wool continued to rise in the estimation of the London buyers.

When at Oregon City, I was informed by Surveyor General [John] Preston that he would require from Mr. [Henry N.] Peers and myself within a month, a statement of the PS [Agricultural] Coy's land claims at Cowlitz and Nisqually, sworn to by us, and corroborated by affidavits from persons, if possible, unconnected with the Co. Will you please direct me as to the manner in which the statement is to be drawn up whether it is to be positive and unqualified, or to be clogged with any reservations. It seems to me of great importance to obtain a full recognition from Mr. Preston of the extent of our claim.

Of the flour lately received from Victoria in [the] return barrels; [these] were from the [illegible] and not Oregon produce. These were purchased at V[ancouve]r at a govt sale, and shipped 'round in the Mary Dare. Please send me by first opportunity, affidavits to the effect that said flour was received from Vancouver by the Mary Dare.

I will send by an early opportunity an account of P[uget's] S[ound] Cash Sales from the beginning of the Outfit, which will be continued monthly thereafter. I have had many applications for Wedder Sheep to be taken to the [California] gold mines, but have declined selling 'till the beginning of June, when I hope to obtain $10 a piece for them. Beef sells in Portland at 00.25 P[e]r [pound] and is scarce at that price.

The millsite jumpers seem to be in earnest, and are advancing briskly in their operations.

In reply to your remarks on the making [of] Nisqually entirely a P[uget's] S[ound Agricultural Company] Post, I have to observe that its Cr[edit] Balance for Outfit [18]52 amounts to £1045; which sum will, I hope, be exceeded in the current Outfit and as long as Cash prices are so high at Victoria and we have a full supply of goods, a profitable business for the Fur trade may be carried on here. If,

---

51 It could not be determined which letter Dr. Tolmie sent.

however, goods were sold cheaper at Victoria than either here, or at Fort Vancouver, The Fur trade would sustain but trifling loss were Nisqually made a P[uget's] S[ound] Post. I remain Dear Sir, Your very obt Servt,

Signed W. F. Tolmie

P.S. I made a requisition while at Vancouver and expect goods 'round immediately by an Am[erica]n Vessel, freight $13 P[e]r ton. Your letters will be forwarded as directed. Some goods intended for the use of Cloverdale [Farm][52] & rec[eive]d at V[ancouver] by the Norman Morison were sent here by mistake. I would like them exchanged at Victoria for similar articles—Baize, Printed Cotton, and Green Blankets, and shall send a list in my next.

Document 7.32: A letter from William F. Tolmie, Nisqually, to L.C. Broy, Portland, April 4, 1853.

Dear Sir,

I forward herewith a receipt from [Monsieur Pierre] Dumilatre, Supercargo of the Brig "Cyclops", for the Twenty thousand [20,000 board] feet of Lumber you purchased from me last autumn, also an order on you from Mr. Dumilatre for $1,000 in payment of said lumber. The order in question I have made payable to P[eter] S. Ogden Esq[ui]re or any Agent he may appoint, and you are, I trust, prepared to cash it immediately as if not, the disagreeable necessity will be forced upon me to take legal measures to secure payment before the "Cyclops" leaves Olympia. Mr. Dumilatre has appropriated to other businesses the five hundred dollars you directed Father [Pascal] Ricard to retain as part payment for me.

(Signed) W. F. Tolmie

P.S. By yours of Feby 14, [18]53 in reply to mine of Decr 20th, [18]52, I find that there had been a misapprehension as to the terms of our verbal contract regarding the lumber you purchased from me. You, it seems, understood that it was to be paid for only after shipment, whereas I considered that it was from the time of sale at your disposal, and that on returning home you were to make immediate payment to [John] Ballenden at Vancouver which you said would suit you much better than sending the money overland to Nisqually. T

Document 7.33: A letter from William F. Tolmie, Nisqually, to Peter S. Ogden, Vancouver, April 4, 1853.

Dear Sir,

Enclosed is a certificate of Deposit N°. 54 on Adams & Co for Five Hundred Six & 35/100 Dollars which amount please, on receipt, to credit to Fort Nisqually O[utfi]t 1853.

52 Dr. Tolmie's private estate, Cloverdale, consisted of 1,100 acres north of Victoria. Eventually, it included a 15-room house constructed of stone and California cedar redwood. The house was demolished in 1963. *Journal of William Tolmie*, 369.

I also enclose a receipt for Lumber delivered on ac[count] of Dr. Broy, and an order on him for One Thousand Dollars, in payment thereof. Knowing nothing of Dr. Broy's means, nor of his credit as a businessman, I think it advisable that he should either pay or give satisfactory security for the amount before the "Cyclops" leaves. May I therefore request you to send someone to Portland expressly to obtain payment or make a settlement with Broy to whom he may present my letter accompanying this or not, as circumstances may dictate. Should Broy pay, the letter will be unnecessary. But if not, it should be handed to him, and advice of the result sent to me with as little delay as possible.

The other letter to Broy herewith is from a Mr. [Rudolph] Walker of Newmarket who has sold Lumber to Broy and partner [Pierre Dumilatre], and is not to deliver any more unless paid immediately or [he will not accept all future orders] on Ft Nisqually. Please to have Walker's letter delivered to Broy by the gentleman who calls on the Coy's account, and as Walker is to be at half the expense of the present express, have the goodness to let me know by return of bearer what the cost may be at Vancouver.

(Signed) Wm F. Tolmie

Document 7.34: A letter from William F. Tolmie, Nisqually, to John B. Preston, Oregon City, April 8, 1853.

Dear Sir,

I write to inform you that a statement of the Boundary lines of the Puget's Sound Company's claim at Cowlitz and Nisqually, with Affidavits &c., as you direct, will be handed to you about the 19th or 20th of the Current month. I have the honor to be Dear Sir, Very Respectfully, Your Obedient Servt,

Signed Wm Fraser Tolmie

Document 7.35: A letter from James Grahame, Vancouver, to William F. Tolmie, Nisqually, April 9, 1853.[53]

Dear Sir,

I received yesterday a packet from you marked immediate and, in the absence of Mr. [Peter S.] Ogden, I opened it and sent a gentleman to Portland as soon as I possibly could with your letters to L. Broy. He returned last evening and handed me a sealed letter from Broy to you which I now enclose. It appears he had sent money to his partner [Pierre Dumilatre] in the Sound who has applied it to a different use; the Doctor accepts the order and is willing to pay as soon as he can, perhaps in three weeks. [John M.] Breck & [William Seton] Ogden[54] would not become security for him and I did not know anyone else we could depend upon. I hope you may receive this Express before the vessel sails in order that you make all safe. The draft on Adams & Co has been left with Breck & Ogden and is all right.

53 UW Library, Tolmie Papers Acc. 4577-001, V0250e, Box #1, Folder #4.

54 This refers to John M. Breck and William Seton Ogden's General Store in Portland. Breck, who was born in Philadelphia, Pennsylvania, in 1828, was 16 years old when he left his home state for Wisconsin. In 1850 he left there for Oregon on the vessel *Columbia.* He served as purser for the voyage. In 1857 and 1858 Breck was elected Assessor of Portland, and then mayor from 1861 to 1862. See en.wikipedia.org/wiki/John_M._Breck.

All the information about the expense of the Express is this; the trip to Portland £.6.00 and a canoe and three Indians now dispatched to the Cowelitz. Your packet came by the Steamer. Yours Respectfully,

J. A. Grahame

Document 7.36: A letter from L.C. Broy, Portland, to William F. Tolmie, Nisqually, April 9, 1853.[55]

Dear Doctor,

I have just received your note of the 4th Inst and am much surprised that Mr. [Monsieur Pierre] Dumilatre, without my authorization, has disposed of the $500 I have left for you in Mr. [Pascal] Ricard's hands. This incident puts me in a very disagreeable situation with you and I am indeed sorry to be so very annoyingly circumstanced. Mr. [Neil] McArthur[56] of Fort Vancouver came today to receive a bill of $1,000 signed by Mr. Dumilatre, and this latter Gentleman gives me no notice of it. At his passage in Portland he told me that the Money he received for his Goods in Olympia would be to pay you and as he had not done so, I am indeed sorry that at this moment it is utterly impossible for me to pay at present. I have just seen Mr. [William] Seton Ogden and have made arrangements with him to pay your account as soon as possible. Mr. Ogden has accepted my word and I will do honor to it, and I trust, dear Doctor, that soon I shall be able to satisfy you.

As you are now acquainted with the disagreeable situation in which Mr. Dumilatre has placed me, I trust you will let the ship sail, otherwise its' retard will cause me considerable loss as I shall have your bill paid immediately on the ship's arrival in San Francisco. Excuse all the delay and trouble I have unawaredly been cause of through Mr. Dumilatre's fault, but confide in my word dear Doctor and you shall soon be paid. Your humble Servant,

(S[igne]d) L.C. Broy

Document 7.37: A letter from William F. Tolmie, Nisqually, to John B. Preston, Oregon City, April 11, 1853.

Sir,

I herewith forward a statement from myself on Oath of the boundaries of the Puget's Sound Agricult Company's land Claim at Nisqually with Affidavits from three Citizens, (Messrs [Michael T.] Simmons, [Thomas] Linklater & [John] Edgar) [who are] in no ways interested in said Company's Concerns; to the effect that the said boundary lines include no more land than the Company—by its agents—actually occupied long prior to the date of the Oregon Boundary Treaty.

I also forward a map, or plan[57] of the said claim, the outline or boundary lines of which were surveyed and marked out—in summer 1852, and the sketch now sent you is therefore more Correct than the topographical outline of the same

55 UW Library, Tolmie Papers Acc. 4577-001, V0250e, Box #1, Folder #1.

56 For McArthur see Watson, *Lives Lived*, 2:632.

57 This is believed to be the John B. Chapman map now in the Washington State Archives, and reproduced on page 254 of this book.

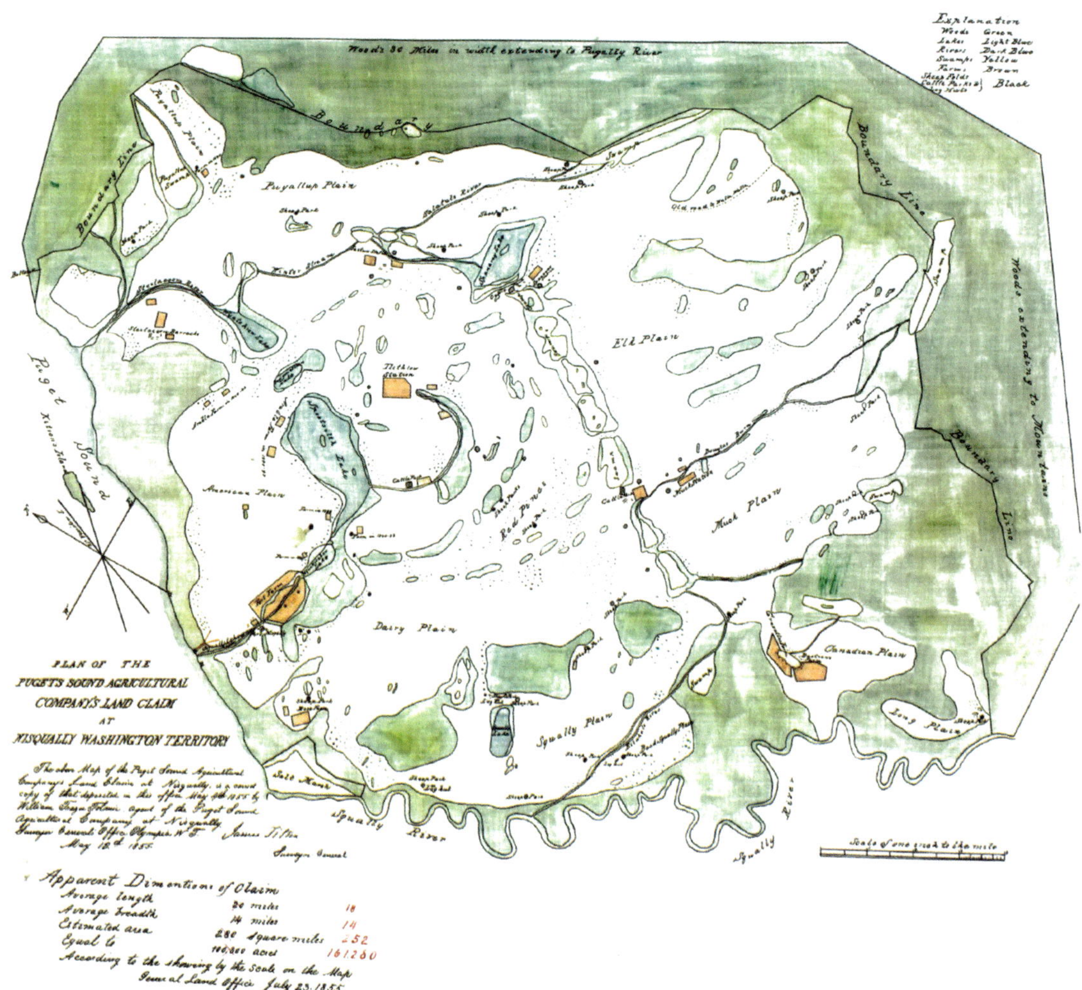

American immigrant John Chapman contracted with Dr. Tolmie to create this map of the HBC/PSAC's holding on Puget Sound during spring 1852. While not geographically accurate, the map depicts known land features and period tree lines. Image AR270B-3459AR_mapPSAgricCo1855. *Courtesy of the Washington State Archives, Olympia, Washington*

"An Accurate Map of British Possessions in Pierce County, 1852." Using Chapman's map, others of the period, and online USGS maps, the editor pieced together natural features, landmarks, and hidden clues left by surveyor Chapman, Huggins, and Tolmie to create this map of the actual possessions of the HBC/PSAC as provided by the Treaty of 1846. *Research and initial design by Steve A. Anderson; map by Chelsea Feeney., cmcfeeney.com.*

tract of Country handed to you in August 1851. I have the honor to be, Sir, Very Respectfully, Your Obedt Servt,

(Signed) William Fraser Tolmie

Document 7.38: An affidavit by William F. Tolmie, Nisqually, describing the Puget's Sound Agricultural Company's Claim, April 11, 1853.

I, William Fraser Tolmie of Nisqually, Pierce County, O[regon] T[erritory], on oath declare that the Puget's Sound Agricultural Company, by its Agents, were in the occupancy and use, as its farms & lands, or otherwise as property on the Fifteenth day of June 1845, and for a long time previously, of the tract of land Comprised within the following described boundary lines, which have been duly traced out and marked Vizt;

The boundary line Commences at the N[orth] W[e]st Corner of the claim from a Stake in the Ground near high water mark on the shore of Puget's Sound and within ascertain and bearings Distances of certain Fir Trees in its neighborhood. Said Stake is about one and one third (1⅓) Miles N[orth] by E[ast] of the Entrance of Steilacoom Creek and about half a mile S[outh] of Mr. B[ill] Bolton's house.

The boundary line runs thence in an easterly direction altho' Zig-Zagging more or less as all the lines do, about four miles to a Stake at the N[orth] W[est] Corner of Paleilah Swamp, including the round plain N[orth] of Steilacoom Creek as well as Palelilah prairie and Swamp; thence about S[outh] E[ast] by E[ast] one and a quarter miles; thence in a General Course of S[outh S[outh] E[ast] fourteen miles to a Stake in the Ground near the road to Walla Walla; Thence in a S[outh] W[este]rly direction, to a Stake in the Ground at Nisqually River fourteen and a half miles; Thence in a N[orth] Westerly direction following for most of the Course the meanderings of the Nisqually river about sixteen and a half miles to a Stake in the Ground on the Shore of Puget's Sound; Thence to the point of commencement about eleven and a half miles, along the shore of Puget's Sound.

Document 7.39: A letter from John Breck & William Seton Ogden, Portland, to William F. Tolmie, Nisqually, April 11, 1853.[58]

Dear Sir,

We herewith enclose you a due bill of Captain C.P. Dryden[59] of Brig "J[ohn] S[ebastian] Cabot"[60] for the sum of One Hundred & Eighty-three 75/100 Doll[ar]s [$183.75].

Captain Dryden understands that he is to pay it out of his freight money at Nisqually. Will you therefore oblige us by retaining the amount from the freight

58 UW Library. Tolmie Papers Acc. 4577-001, V0250e, Box #1, Folder #1.

59 C. P. Dryden (1813–1871). Master of the *John Sebastian Cabot*, "Captain C.P. Dryden was one of the best known of the pioneer sailing masters on the Sound. He was born in Pennsylvania and came to California in 1849, entering the coasting trade soon after his arrival." *Lewis & Dryden's Marine History of the Pacific Northwest*, 94.

60 *John Sebastian Cabot*, American brig, Captain C.P. Dryden. In October 1852, Thomas Coupe was skipper. In 1860 off Mendocino, California, the brig dragged anchor and capsized.

due by you to the vessel & inform us of the payment in order that we may collect the money at Vancouver. We are Very truly, Your Obt Servts,
Breck & Ogden

P.S. Dr. L.C. Broy desires us to say to you that he will pay an amount which he owes you immediately on his return from Olympia. B & O.

Document 7.40: A letter from William F. Tolmie, Nisqually, to Thomas Lowe, San Francisco, April 18, 1853.

Dear Sir,

Please to send by the "G[eorge] W[illiam] Kendall" or any other seaworthy vessel bound to this part of Puget's Sound, the following articles, consigned to me, and to be landed at this place.

100 [barrels of] Flour—sound & good—should the price not exceed Eleven dollars P[e]r [barrel].
15 [pounds of] Corrosive Sublimate, or Muriate of Mercury—price not to exceed $5 P[e]r [pound]. N.B. p[rice per] c[ase] in London about 5/. St[erlin]g.
1 o[unce] Strychine—best.

Write to me by post as soon as you may have purchased the above articles in whole or in part, stating prices, &c., and the amount due you, in order that I may take measures to have early payment made from Ft Vancouver.

Please inform me by return at what price P[e]r [pound] salt can be purchased wholesale at San Francisco. I would not want the best quality as it would chiefly be used in salting hides, and throwing to Cattle.

I was sorry to learn the other day that the "John Adams"[61] at Dungeness was making considerable daily leakage. I remain, Dear Sir, Very Respectfully Your's,
W. F. Tolmie

P.S. Please inform Mr. [Peter S.] O[gden] by post of the amount you may expend as I have requested him on hearing from you thereanent, to refund forthwith. T

Document 7.41: A letter from William F. Tolmie, Nisqually, to T[homas] Fox, Steilacoom Barracks, April 18, 1853.[62]

Sir,

I reply to your note enquiring the date of the Contract for the four buildings rented at Steilacoom. I have to state that said Contract commenced from the date

61 *John Adams*, American bark. In 1851, the vessel's master was Captain Henry Jewell and later, Captain McKelmer.

62 Originally, this was incorrectly copied into the letterbook as the 15th and not the 18th of April 1853. Private Thomas Fox was discharged from Steilacoom Barracks at the end of his U.S. Army service on June 18, 1855.

of the arrival of the Artillery Co (M) at Steilacoom in fall 1849. The Contract was verbal between Captain [Bennett H.] Hill & myself.

S[igne]d W. F. Tolmie

Document 7.42: A letter from William F. Tolmie, Nisqually, to Peter S. Ogden, Vancouver, April 18, 1853.

Dear Sir,

By the Hon[oura]ble Mr. [Charles] Fitzwilliam now proceeding to Fort Vancouver are forwarded letters received by him from V[ancouver's] I[sland] for Oregon and England.

Having written Mr. [Thomas] Lowe of San Francisco to purchase for this place Flour and other things, which may amount to from two to twelve hundred dollars, and requested him to inform you by the earliest opportunity of the sum he may expend, I have to beg of you to remit him the money as soon as possible thereafter, and charge to Fort Nisqually Outfit 1853, advising me thereof in due course. The flour ordered is for use and sale likewise should the state of the market here warrant it. I remain Sir, Your very Obedt Servt,

Wm Fraser Tolmie

Document 7.43: A letter & sales statement from William F. Tolmie, Nisqually, to James Douglas, Victoria, April 18, 1853.

Dear Sir,

I received on the 16th Instant your communications of the 2nd and 12th and regret that the former was not forwarded sooner as it has come to hand too late to admit of my adaption of your form of a letter to Mr. [John B.] Preston. Copies are sent herewith of my letter to the Surveyor General as well as of the affidavits accompanying it, all of which I handed to Mr. [Henry N.] Peers at Olympia on the 12th Inst and he proceeded with them to Oregon City forthwith, taking at same time a Sketch, and definition of the boundaries of the Cowlitz Claim, which is supposed to contain Eighty Thousand acres or thereabouts.

The affidavit regarding the seventeen Barrels Flour spoken of in yours of the 2nd as those transmitted, has not been received. Please forward it by the earliest opportunity, as I am under bond of one Hundred Dollars either to produce affidavits, or pay duties, within three months, which period will soon expire.

I was happy to learn from Collector [Simpson P.] Moses the other day, that the Treasury Dept had remitted the forfeiture of the Steamer Beaver's trade goods.

There having been London letters for you here for some time, I have thought best to send off Mr. Fitzwilliam's Indians at once particularly as I know not when Mr. Simpson may arrive.

Please give at least a fortnight's warning before sending here for livestock so that we may have some Large oxen caught in advance.

It would be very advantageous if we could have a tannery established here, and would add to the value of the property in case of our selling out. I enclose a proposition[63] made by a person [just] arrived, [a man named J.W.] Balance, engaged in tanning in Nisqually bottom.[64]

Subjoined is a statement of the Puget's Sound Coy's monthly Sales since the commencement of Outfit 1853. I have already been offered $4 p[e]r head for all dispensable Sheep, and hope for better offers yet Would it not be advisable to advertise here and in California that by the 10th June, about 1,000 Sheep will be for sale at this place? I remain, Your very Obedt Servant,

W. F. Tolmie

Puget's Sound Agr[icultur]al Company's Sales at Nisqually

1852	November $	594.31
	December	828.53
1853	January	759.90
	February	1594.89
	March	1145.43
		$4906.65

Document 7.44: A letter & list from William F. Tolmie, Nisqually, to James Douglas, Victoria, April 23, 1853.

Dear Sir,

Mr. [George] Simpson, having arrived from Vancouver [on the 20th], is to start for Victoria today as soon as the foreign mail arrives.

The Victoria Indians lately have stole[n] before leaving, the articles enumerated in the accompanying list, and I hope, that with a view to prevent the recurrence of such speculations, a noise may be made about the present theft and restitution of the stolen goods insisted on. The fellows were well treated here, and housed inside the pickets.

I had more difficulty than heretofore in getting Nisqually Indians to go to Victoria on the present occasion, and had to promise them a 3 p[oin]t blanket each, and the same for the canoe. They begged hard that I should request you to permit them to live inside the Fort during their detention at Victoria & I promised to use my influence to obtain them that boon. The grievance of living outside exposed to the pilfering and plundering of the Victoria Indians is of long standing, and has often been complained by our voyaging hands.

Having written you recently on the 16th, I have nothing further to communicate at present and remain Sir, Your very obedient Servant,

W. F. Tolmie

P.S. I have subscribed for a paper ("Columbian") but through some oversight, it has not been sent to you. Enclosed is the answer to your enquiry regarding printing. T

63 This proposition was not found attached to this letter.

64 In 1848, Balance, along with a settler named Ebson, purchased the Portland tannery of D. H. Lownsdale, who had arrived in Oregon in 1845, and established a tannery on the west side of town. Other than that, Balance is mentioned in the fort's journal just twice, in 1853 and 1854, and nothing more could be found out about him. See www.accessgenealogy.com/oregon/founders-of-portland-oregon.htm.

List of Articles stolen by the Victoria Indians who Conveyed Mr. Fitzwilliam to Nisqually:

2 tin Pots
1 large oval tin Pan
1 tin Baking [pan] long and narrow

Document 7.45: A letter from William F. Tolmie, Nisqually, to Thomas Lowe, San Francisco, April 25, 1853.

My Dear Sir,

I have to acknowledge receipt of yours of March 31st and April 9th as well as of the consignment of Flour &c., P[e]r "Rowena".[65]

I tried three houses, but could prevail on none of them to take the Flour on commission, as they all had a sufficiency of their own for sale and I have taken it on a[ccount] of the Co for $16 P[e]r barrel at which price I have been offered 30 [barrels] delivered here. [Captain Warren] Gove[66] offered me $16.50 for a ton of yours delivered at Olympia, but that would not suit, as we charge $1.50 for delivering a [barrel] of salmon there. I have sold 3 doz of the hats at $6 P[e]r doz. The bread I shall endeavor to dispose of this week. I would not recommend you sending any more consignments to me as I cannot do them justice without neglecting the Co's business.

Referring to what you propose regarding Capt [William R.] Pattle and the Honolulu Packet, I would observe that if I understand the Revenue Laws right, Pattle would infringe them by taking cargo from the Sound to S[an] Francisco, his [schooner *Honolulu*] being a British vessel. We have no pure bred Sheep, i.e., Sheep directly descended from English stock, for sale, but [in] abundance equally as large and in whom the California blood has been eradicated by crossing. I am this morning to sell thirty of our ordinary Ewes (dry) without lambs for $10 each to a Californian from San Jose Valley. Would it suit you to give so much? Please say by return of post and state also what else you would wish purchased in case of not liking the Sheep.

---

65 *Rowena*, American bark. This three-masted bark had square sails on the fore and mainmasts but rigged with fore-and-aft sails on the mizzen. Port Steilacoom's Lafayette Balch had a quarter interest in this vessel which, for a time, hauled pilings and squared timber from Puget Sound to San Francisco.

66 Warren Gove (1816–1892) was born at Edgecomb, Maine, in 1816. His early life was spent at sea and he rose to the rank of captain, but again and again suffered shipwreck and disaster. By way of Cape Horn, he reached California in 1853. He captained one of the earliest sailing vessels to enter Puget Sound, the bark *Sarah Warren.* He quit the sea and went to the Puget Sound country to live. In 1854, his wife joined him, having come from Boston. They established their new home at Steilacoom, where they afterward lived and died. He brought the first American steamboat, the *Fairy*, to Puget Sound. Captain Gove figured prominently in the events of pioneer times in the Northwest. Gov. Isaac I. Stevens, the first governor of Washington Territory, appointed him quartermaster of volunteers in 1855, when the whole country was aroused over the Indian troubles, martial law having been declared. He held various offices of honor and trust, including that of government inspector of customs prior to 1860, while the office was maintained at Steilacoom. He was afterward in charge of the Puyallup Indian Agency. William Henry Gove, *The Gove Book: History And Genealogy of The American Family of Gove and Notes of European Goves* (Salem, MA: Sidney Perley, 1922), 268n. Viewed at archive.org/stream/govebookhistoryg00gove/govebookhistoryg00gove_djvu.txt. This Captain Gove is often confused with his brother, Captain Albion B. Gove, who arrived in 1851 aboard the schooner *George Wilkins Kendall.* Herbert Hunt, *Tacoma, Its History and Its Builders: A Half Century of Activity* (Chicago: S.J. Clarke Publishing Company, 1916), 356; Gordon Newell, *Ships of the Inland Sea* (Portland: Binford and Mort, 1960), 13.

I wrote you by post on the 18th Inst to purchase for Nisqually 100 [barrels of] Flour if to be had at $10. By last mail we heard that it was down to $8. Please get the Flour in [barrels] rather than sacks as in arrival it will be stored in a house abounding in rats. Excuse haste & bad pen, and believe me My dear sir, Very Truly Yours,

W. F. Tolmie

Document 7.46: A letter from Winfield S. Ebey, Port Townsend, to William F. Tolmie, Nisqually, April 30, 1853.[67]

D[ea]r Sir,

A Canoe has arrived here from Victoria having a few small articles aboard for you. The Iroquois Called at the Custom House and I have made out an entry of the things they have. I send the Entry to you for your Signature. Please assign and return it to this office at your first Convenience.

I have retained the original Invoice as we are required to Keep these on file at this office. I send a Copy. The duties are so very small, an Affair you can send by the Indians if you deem it safe. Or, it can be paid over when Convenient. With respect, I am Your Obt Servt,

W. S. Ebey, D[eput]y C[ollector]

Document 7.47: A letter from William F. Tolmie, Nisqually, to Peter S. Ogden, Vancouver, May 9, 1853.

Dear Sir,

I am happy to inform you that the "[*John Sabastian*] Cabot" has delivered her cargo for this post in good condition. The captain of the "Cabot" having left the sum of One Hundred and Seventy five dollars here for M[isters John] Breck & [William Seton] Ogden, I have sent these gentlemen a draft on you for said amount which please honor & charge against Fort Nisqually Outfit 1853.

There being more opposition now than during the winter months, our Sales are not quite so good, as they then were, but improvement may be looked for when the fishing season begins.

I regret that I cannot send you any beef cattle as requested. Our beef cattle are now too wild that they have to be hunted like Buffalo, and seldom appear in the plains except at morn[ing] and evening. I remain Sir, Your very obedient Servt,

(S[igne]d) W. F. Tolmie

P.S. Please let me know as soon as convenient whether you a[c]ceded to Dr. [John] Haden's proposal mentioned to you in a former letter—to pay $500 this summer and $500 as soon thereafter [on the Hawkins bill] as he can muster funds for the purpose. T

67 UW Library, Tolmie Papers Acc. 4577-001, V0250e, Box #1, Folder #3.

Document 7.48: A letter from William F. Tolmie, Nisqually, to Misters John Breck & W. Seton Ogden, Portland, May 9, 1853.

Gentlemen,

Captain Dryden of the "J[ohn] S[ebastian] Cabot" having left with me the sum of One Hundred and Seventy Five dollars payable to you, I enclose an order on P[eter] S. Ogden, Esq[ui]re Vancouver for said amount.

Having been advised from San Francisco that the sum of Ten Dollars has been deposited for me with Snow[68] and Savior[69] of Portland, an order on them in your favor is enclosed. On receipt please credit Fort Vancouver with the ten Dollars, and advize me thereof, in order that I may apply the amount to its destined purpose here.

In acknowledging receipt of this Please inform me whether you may have made any arrangement with Dr. Broy for the payment of his partner's note to me for $1,000 and which Broy, I understand, accepted. Broy, when lately at Olympia, gave out that he had effected a settlement with you. I remain Gentlemen, Respectfully, Your Obedt Servt,

(S[igne]d) W. F. Tolmie

Document 7.49: A letter from William F. Tolmie, Nisqually, to James Grahame, Vancouver, May 9, 1853.

My dear Sir,

The "Cabot" has arrived and delivered her cargo in good condition except the Flour which I presume was sour when shipped.

Enclosed are some memoranda regarding the goods P[e]r "Cabot". Please send the 50 P[e]r Cent and selling price of the Coals, Comforters, and Caps enumerated in the memo sent. Have the goodness also to send by return of post, the requisition I left with you in March, as I did not have it copied. Capt [C.] Dryden of the Cabot will be at S[an] Francisco in from 15 to 20 days from this date and hopes to obtain freight from Mr. [George T.] Allan for Portland, in which case he will bring the remainder of our Outfit 'round & will return the requisition to you by the post following its receipts.

Send me also, if you please, a copy of my private account at Vancouver for Outfit 1853 and by mail on Co's a[ccount] a box of Dean's two hold pens. I remain, Dear Sir, Yours Sincerely,

(S[igne]d) W. F. Tolmie

68 This is presumed to be Lucien Snow, "a Maine man having the thrift and enterprise of New England" who owned a business between Pine and Oak streets in Portland's Sellwood District. He was reportedly involved in a number of business deals at this time. Harvey Whitefield Scott, ed., *History of Portland, Oregon: With Illustrations and Biographical Sketches of Prominent Citizens and Pioneers* (Portland: D. Mason & Company Publishers, 1890), 140.

69 No information could be found on this individual, or the financial firm of "Snow & Savior" in Portland in 1853.

Document 7.50: A letter from William F. Tolmie, Nisqually, to Thomas Lowe, San Francisco, May 9, 1853.

Dear Sir,

Yours of the 23rd April has just come to hand, and in reply I am sorry to inform you that the [barque] "John Adams" by last accounts was aground at Dungeness with part of a cargo on board. [Captain Henry] Jewell[70] had left, and taken all his property. I wrote [Archibald] MacKinley forthwith enclosing a report from [McAlmonds], sailing master, asking for instructions and money, &c. I presume your decision will now be to abandon the Vessel. The "J[ohn] S[ebastian] Cabot" having discharged cargo here from Ft Vancouver will be at [San] Francisco in about 20 days when the Captain hopes to obtain freight from Mr. [George T.] Allan for Portland, after which, he will bring the remainder of the Nisqually Outfit from Vancouver. Being interrupted by visitors I must conclude and remain, Dear Sir, Very truly Yours,

(S[igne]d) W. F. Tolmie

Document 7.51: A letter from William F. Tolmie, Nisqually, to Peter S. Ogden, Vancouver, May 14, 1853.

Dear Sir,

I have partly cashed an order from Mr. [Nathaniel] Coe, Postal Agent, on the Treasury Department Washington [D.C.], for $284.48 and would like to know from you by return of post what would be a fair discount for such an accommodation? The draftee being bound to allow for my trouble &c., here, and whatever trouble expense and delay you may incur in getting the order cashed or otherwise disposed of. I enclosed the said order retaining a duplicate here, and remain, Sir, Your very Obedt Servt,

(S[igne]d) W. F. Tolmie

Document 7.52: A letter from William F. Tolmie, Nisqually, to Peter S. Ogden, Vancouver, May 20, 1853.

Dear Sir,

I wrote on the 14th Inst stating that I had partly cashed an order from Govt Postal Agent [Nathaniel] Coe on the Treasury Dept Washington [D.C.] for

70 No information could be found regarding Jewell's personal life. However, H. H. Bancroft reveals that: "The first vessel that came into the harbor of New Dungeness for a cargo was the *John Adams* in the spring of 1853. Jewell, her master, started with his steward [a man named Church] to go to Port Townsend in a small boat, and never was seen again. The Indians admitted that two of their people had murdered the two men, but as it could not be shown that they were dead, the accused were never tried. McAlmond, who was a competent shipmaster, sailed the vessel to S[an Francisco]. An eccentric man, who obtained the soubriquet [nickname] of 'Arkansas Traveler' by his peregrinations [trips] in the region of Dungeness in 1854, was shot and killed by Indians while alone in his canoe." Bancroft, *History of Washington, Idaho, and Montana*, 93.

$284.48 and enquired what would be a fair discount for such an accommodation, having had an understanding with the recipient of said order, that he should make a fair allowance for whatever trouble, expense, and delay might be incurred "in getting the order cashed or otherwise disposed of."

Will you please inform me as soon as convenient whether you accede to Dr. [John] Haden's offer, already mentioned, to pay five hundred dollars of the [George W.] Hawkins bill in June or July 1853, and five Hundred more as soon as he can muster funds for the purpose, his understanding being that, on payment of $1,000, the said bill should made over to him.

Father [Pascal] Ricard wishes as soon as possible to draw on Marseilles, [France] for his annual allowance of 10,000 francs and having understood that Mons[ieu]r [Jean-Baptiste Abraham] Brouillet obtained a more favorable rate of exchange from Mr. Ballenden last year, than he himself to here, he wishes me to ask you to put him this year on the same footing as Brouillet. He had last year a credit of £309.6.0 in dollars at $4.84 to the pound sterling. Please write me regarding [Pascal] Ricard's credit as soon as convenient, as the old gentleman desires to obtain the money immediately. Business is improving since the goods P[er] "Cabot" have been opened. I remain sir,

(Signed) W. F. Tolmie

P.S. On the 9th April, I forwarded by Major [Albert J.] Smith his bill payable on demand for $1500, the amount advanced him here for the payment of the troops at Steilacoom. Please advize in your next whether said bill has been received or not.

W. T.

Document 7.53: A letter from Thomas Lowe, San Francisco, to William F. Tolmie, Nisqually, May 23, 1853.[71]

Dear Sir,

Enclosed you will find Invoice of flour shipped by the Bark "Sarah Warren",[72] [Captain Warren Gove] and Bill Lading of the same, also a duplicate of my Letter to you by the "Mary Melville"[73] of the 17th Inst. The "Sarah Warren" sailed before I had time to write by her, and the Invoice and bill Lading had to be sent by the "Melville."

On the 19th Inst I had the pleasure of receiving your two favors of the 18th April, which I had given up for lost. By this mail I have written Mr. Ogden stating the amount of the Invoice by the "Sarah Warren", and he will probably remit by return of the Steamer. Any arrangement you can make to diminish the commission on purchases will be satisfactory to us, as the universal practice here is to buy only when there are funds in hand, and I believe we are the only parties who make advances, and we long do so to the Company, Knowing that they are Sound. We cannot, however, borrow money here ourselves for a short time at less than 5 per cent p[e]r month, as we have no real estate in the City to mortgage, but as yet we have never been under the necessity of applying for a loan. Why can't you write to Mr. Ogden when you

71 UW Library, Tolmie Papers Acc. 4577-001, V0250e, Box #1, Folder #4.

72 *Sarah Warren*, American bark. This vessel was built at Freeport Maine, and was listed as slightly over 188 tons, and Captain Warren Gove was her master.

73 *Mary Melville*, American bark. Captain Barston. No other information could be found other than the captain was known to be "big-hearted."

want anything from here and let him to send down the supposed amount of the Invoice? I think that would be the best plan, and it would come cheaper to you.

The corrosive Sublimate will cost $2.50 p[e]r [pound] and the Strychnine $7 p[e]r [ounce]. They will be sent up by the next vessel to the Sound. The Books you want are not to be found here, but I will send to the States for them.

I think it would be well to write Mr. Ogden to remit us the amount of the consignment p[e]r "Rowena"; at least of what has been sold of it, also any money that may be received from [Lafayette] Balch. I have already written to him on the Subject, and he may probably send down by next mail.

I wrote you in a former Letter that Captn [William] Brotchie owed me more than the amount of his Wages in the "John Adams" for Cash advanced him. Besides this, he has a gold watch of mine valued at $80 which I left with him for sale and Capt [William Alexander] Mouat tells me that Brotchie sold 12 suits shepherd's plaid Clothing for $180.00.

I enclose to you a Package for Mr. Douglas containing Accounts of the Shipment P[e]r Mary Dare, and today's Prices Current. From it you will see that Goods are very low compared to what they have been, and that trade is dull, money scarce, and the market overstocked with Goods. I remain, Dear Sir, Very truly Yours,

Thomas Lowe

Document 7.54: A letter from William F. Tolmie, Nisqually, to James Grahame, Vancouver, May 23, 1853.

Dear Sir,

Will you be kind enough to send me by return of post a statement of Adam Beinston's and Tho[ma]s Linklater's accounts, also of William Benston's—one of the express men of 1852 who deserted this Spring from this post.

Please inform Mr. [Peter S.] Ogden that [L.C.] Broy made no settlement with me here and that having forwarded to Vancouver the order on him, original as well as duplicate, I had nothing to show whereon to institute legal proceedings, moreover, [Pierre] Dumilatre had, previous to Broy's arrival, executed a conditional bill of sale of the cargo as security to the Captain [William Perkins] of the "Cyclops" for freight dem[ur]rage. Is it supposed that Broy will return to Portland, or have we seen the last of him? Yours truly,

(S[igne]d) W. F. Tolmie

P.S. Please credit Breck & Ogden with $8.45 recd for them from [Captain] Dryden. T

Document 7.55: A letter from William F. Tolmie, Nisqually, to John Breck & W. Seton Ogden, Portland, May 23, 1853.

Gentlemen,

I have received yours acknowledging receipt of the $145 from Captn Dryden transmitted through the HB Co, Ft Vancouver. Your letter of April 17th [18]53 by Broy, containing Dryden's note, came to hand quite recently and the Captain [who] turned up quite unexpectedly paid the additional $8.75 without demur, and

I have by the present post requested Mr. [James A.] Grahame to credit you with the amount. Do you think Broy will return to Portland and has he any property or a good business there? Information on these points will greatly oblige. Gentlemen, Yours Respectfully,

(S[igne]d) W. F. Tolmie

Document 7.56: A letter from William F. Tolmie, Nisqually, to James Douglas, Victoria, May 25, 1853.

Dear Sir,

I have to acknowledge receipt of your letters of the 14th and 23rd Inst, the latter of which came to hand yesterday. The mail from V[ancouver] I[sland] for England has been duly posted at Olympia.

I have advertised in the Columbian 1,000 Wedders and 200 Ewes, or thereabouts, as for Sale about the 25th June, and have written to have advertisements to this effect made in Oregon and California. As squatters on the Co's Claim are increasing in Numbers and holdings, we will, I fear, soon be much circumscribed[74] in regard to available sheepwalks, as each squatter insists on preventing our Sheep from pasturing on his claim.

Thompson, the person improving the Sequallitchew Millsite, has lately taken as partners Captain Balch of Steilacoom and a millwright named [William] Berry, and intends, I am informed, laying off a town forthwith.

Having finished potatoe planting, we Commence Sheepwashing on the 30th [of May].

Puget's Sound Cash Sales for April: $800.37. I remain, Dear Sir, Your very Obedt Servant,

Signed) W. F. Tolmie

Document 7.57: A letter from Archibald McKinlay, Oregon City, to William F. Tolmie, Nisqually, May 25, 1853.[75]

Dear Sir,

My friend McArthur[76] is at length about to start to see you, and I hope you and he will be able to come to terms about the sheep. I told you all about him when you were here and have nothing further to add than to say that any attention you can shew him will be much appreciated by me.

I am glad to inform you that by the last mail I had letters from [Thomas] Lowe [of San Francisco] stating that the "John Adams" had reached that port in safety but he says nothing about [Henry] Jewell. I do not know therefore, whether he was on board or not. It is very fortunate however that she has got down as she will not be a total loss. [George T.] Allan has gone to establish a branch in the Umpqua and will not be back for at least six months.

74 Tolmie's use of "circumscribed" can be translated as "restricted, constrained, and/or hemmed in" by the squatters.

75 UW Library, Tolmie Papers Acc. 4577-001, V0250e, Box #1, Folder #6. From a typescript copy.

76 This friend of Archibald McKinley is quite possibly John Macarthur, an early Oregon City settler.

Compliments to Mrs. [Jane] Tolmie. My wife desires me to say that she hopes the next time you come to Oregon, you will bring her with you. Our family, with the exception of Janet, are well. I believe [Dr. Forbes] Barclay[77] has at length found a cure for my complaint in the chest. Yours ever,

Arch. McKinlay

Document 7.58: A letter from William F. Tolmie, Nisqually, to James Grahame, Vancouver, May 30, 1853.

My Dear Sir,

Your favor of the 16th accompanying the Req[uisitio]n is at hand.

We shall soon have a thorough search for the two Bales Blue Blankets and the Bale of Red Baise and advize you of the result. I shall by next post send an additional Requisition. [In the] meantime, please bear in mind that we shall want several baskets of tin kettles.

(Signed) Wm F. Tolmie

Document 7.59: A letter from William F. Tolmie, Nisqually, to Thomas Lowe, San Francisco, May 30, 1853.

Dear Sir,

Having written you on the 18th April to purchase Flour &c., as per copy of letter above given, I feel rather surprised at your not having acknowledged receipt and should it have miscarried, have to request you to make the desired purchases as soon as possible.

Mr. [Peter S.] Ogden writes that your order on him for the amount purchased will be attended to. Please say what you wish done with the proceeds of the Flour you consigned to me P[e]r Rowena. The Bread is still unsold.

(Signed) W. F. Tolmie

---

77 For Barclay see Watson, *Lives Lived*, 1:174.

Appendix

Treaty between Her Majesty and the United States of America, for the Settlement of the Oregon Boundary[1]

Signed at Washington, June 15, 1846 (Ratifications exchanged at London, July 17, 1846)

Her Majesty the Queen of the United Kingdom of Great Britain and Ireland, and the United States of America, deeming it to be desirable for the future welfare of both countries, that the state of doubt and uncertainty which has hitherto prevailed respecting the sovereignty and government of the territory on the Northwest Coast of America, lying westward of the Rocky or Stony Mountains, should be finally terminated by an amicable compromise of the rights mutually asserted by the two parties over the said territory, have respectively named Plenipotentiaries to treat and agree concerning the terms of such settlement, that is to say:

Her Majesty the Queen of the United Kingdom of Great Britain and Ireland has, on her part, appointed the Right Honourable Richard Pakenham, a member of Her Majesty's Most Honourable Privy Council, and Her Majesty's Envoy Extraordinary and Minister Plenipotentiary to the United States; and the President of the United States of America has, on his part, furnished with full powers, James Buchanan, Secretary of State of the United States; who, after having communicated to each other their respective full powers found in good and due form, have agreed upon and concluded the following Articles:

Article I

From the point on the 49th parallel of north latitude, where the boundary laid down in existing treaties and conventions between Great Britain and the United States terminates, the line of boundary between the territories of Her Britannic Majesty and those, of the United States shall be continued westward along the said 49th parallel of north latitude, to the middle of the channel which separates the continent from Vancouver's Island; and thence southerly, through the middle of the said channel, and of Fucas Straits to the Pacific Ocean; provided however that the navigation of the whole of the said channel and straits, south of the 49th parallel of north latitude, remain free and open to both parties.

1 British & Foreign State Papers, 34: 14, web.archive.org/web/20091113034143/http://www.lexum.umontreal.ca/ca_us/en/cus.1846.28.en.html.

Article II

From the point at which the 49th parallel of north latitude shall be found to intersect the great northern branch of the Columbia river, the navigation of the said branch shall be free and open to the Hudson's Bay Company, and to all British subjects trading with the same, to the point where the said branch meets the main stream of the Columbia, and thence down the said main stream to the ocean, with free access into and through the said river or rivers; it being understood, that all the usual portages along the line thus described, shall in like manner be free and open.

In navigating the said river or rivers, British subjects, with their goods and produce, shall be treated on the same footing as citizens of the United States; it being, however, always understood, that nothing in this Article shall be construed as preventing, or intended to prevent, the Government of the United States from making any regulations respecting the navigation of the said river or rivers, not inconsistent with the present Treaty.

Article III

In the future appropriation of the territory south of the 49th parallel of north latitude, as provided in the 1st Article of this Treaty, the possessory rights of the Hudson's Bay Company, and of all British subjects who may be already in the occupation of land or other property lawfully acquired within the said territory, shall be respected.

Article IV

The farms, lands, and other property of every description, belonging to the Puget's Sound Agricultural Company, on the north side of the Columbia river, shall be confirmed to the said Company. In case, however, the situation of those farms and lands should be considered by the United States to be of public and political importance, and the United States Government should signify a desire to obtain possession of the whole or of any part thereof, the property so required shall be transferred to the said government at a proper valuation, to be agreed upon between the Parties.

Article V

The present Treaty shall be ratified by Her Britannic Majesty, and by the President of the United States, by and with the advice and consent of the Senate thereof; and the ratifications shall be exchanged at London at the expiration of six months from the date hereof, or sooner if possible.

In witness whereof the respective Plenipotentiaries have signed the same, and have affixed thereto the seals of their arms.

Done at Washington the 15th do of June in the year of our Lord, 1846.

[L.S.] RICHARD PAKENHAM.
[L.S.] JAMES BUCHANAN.

Declaration between Her Majesty and the United States of America, approving the Boundary Maps, prepared by the Joint Commissioners appointed under Article I of the Treaty of 15th June, 1846.[2] Signed at Washington, February 24, 1870

The Undersigned, Edward Thornton, Esquire, Her Britannic Majesty's Envoy Extraordinary and Minister Plenipotentiary to the United States, and Hamilton Fish, Secretary of State of the United States, duly authorized by their respective Governments, having met together;

The set of maps, 7 in number, which have been prepared by the Commissioners appointed by the two Powers to survey and mark out the boundary between their respective territories under the first Article of the Treaty concluded between them at Washington, on the 15th of June, 1846, having been produced;

And it appearing that they do correctly indicate the said boundary from the point where the boundary laid down in Treaties and Conventions prior to June 15, 1846, terminates westward on the 49th parallel of north latitude to the eastern shore of the Gulf of Georgia, which boundary has been defined by the Commissioners by marks upon the ground;

The Undersigned, without prejudice to the rights of their respective Governments as to the settlement and the determination of the remainder of the said Boundary, hereby declare that the said maps certified and authenticated under the signatures of Colonel John Summerfield Hawkins, Her Britannic Majesty's Commissioner, and of Archibald Campbell, Esquire,[3] the Commissioner of the United States, and of which duplicate copies similarly certified and authenticated are in the possession of the Government of Her Britannic Majesty, have been duly examined and considered, and, as well as the marks by which the [Page 30] boundary to the eastern shore of the Gulf of Georgia has been defined upon the ground, are approved, agreed to, and adopted by both Governments.

In witness whereof, the respective Plenipotentiaries have signed the same, and have affixed thereto their respective seals.

Done at Washington, the 24th day of February, in the year of Our Lord, 1870.

[L.S.] EDWARD THORNTON.
[L.S.] HAMILTON FISH.

---

2 British & Foreign State Papers, 63: 1053, web.archive.org/web/20091113034143/http://www.lexum.umontreal.ca/ca_us/en/cus.1846.28.en.html.

3 Campbell was one of the original commissioners for the United States on the 1846 Treaty. He died in Washington, D.C., July 27, 1887.

Bibliography

Archives

Clarence B. Bagley Papers, University of Washington Libraries Special Collections, Seattle.

Edward Huggins Manuscript Collection, Washington State Historical Society, Tacoma.

Edward Huggins Papers, University of Washington Libraries Special Collections, Seattle.

Eva Emery Dye Papers, Oregon Historical Society, Portland.

George W. Soliday Collection of Western Americana, Nisqually Papers, The Huntington Library, Art Collections and Botanical Gardens, San Marino, California.

Hudson's Bay Company Archives, Archives of Manitoba, Winnipeg, Canada.

James Robert Anderson Papers, Royal British Columbia Museum & Archives, Victoria, British Columbia.

John Work Papers, University of Washington Libraries Special Collections, Seattle.

Lucile C. McDonald Collection, University of Washington Libraries Special Collections, Seattle.

Washington State Archives, Olympia.

William Fraser Tolmie Letterbook, Royal British Columbia Museum & Archives, Victoria, British Columbia.

William Fraser Tolmie Papers, Royal British Columbia Museum & Archives, Victoria, British Columbia.

William Fraser Tolmie Papers, University of Washington Libraries Special Collections, Seattle.

Articles, Books, Papers

Abing, Kevin. "Directors of the Bureau of Catholic Indian Missions: Reverend John Baptiste Abraham Brouillet, 1874–1884," Milwaukee: Marquette University, 1994. www.marquette.edu/library/archives/Mss/BCIM/BCIM-SC1-directors1.pdf.

Adams, John. *Old Square-Toes and His Lady: The Life of James and Amelia Douglas.* Victoria, BC: Horsdal & Schubart, 2001.

Anderson, Steve A. "A Crofter's Tale: Adventurous John of the Clan MacLeod."

Columbia: The Magazine of Northwest History 24, no. 2 (Summer 2010): 27–34.

———. "The Forgetting of John Montgomery: Spanaway's First White Settler, 1845–1885." *Pacific Northwest Quarterly*, Spring 2010.

———. *Fort Nisqually Indian Accounts Book: Commencing September 1849, Ending January 1851*. Newport, North Carolina: Rampart Publications, 2010.

———. *Fort Nisqually Indian Accounts Book: Commencing November 1850, Ending November 1852*. Newport, North Carolina: Rampart Publications, 2012.

———. "A New Look at an Old Map: Deconstructing Chapman." *Columbia: The Magazine of Northwest History* 25, no. 4 (Winter 2011): 22-27.

———. *The Physical Structure of Fort Nisqually: A Preliminary Study on the Structural Development of a Hudson's Bay Company Site, 1843–1859*. Tacoma: Metropolitan Park District, 1988.

———. "Shipwright, Storyteller & Stone Blind: James Scarth of the HBC." *Occurrences: The Journal of Activities of Fort Nisqually Historic Site*, Summer 2006.

Asher, Brad. *Beyond the Reservation: Indians, Settlers, and the Law in Washington Territory, 1853–1889*. Norman: University of Oklahoma Press, 1999.

Bancroft, Hubert H. *History of Oregon, Volume 1: 1834–1848*. San Francisco: The History Company. 1886.

———. *History of the Northwest Coast Volume I & II, 1543–1846*. The History Company, San Francisco, 1884, 1886.

———. *History of the Pacific States of North America*. San Francisco: A. L. Bancroft & Co., 1882-1890.

———. *History of Washington, Idaho and Montana, 1845–1889*. San Francisco: The History Company, 1890.

Bartlett, Lauri Downey. "Dr. John Webber." Unpublished manuscript. Steilacoom: Steilacoom Historical Society, n.d.

Bischoff, William N. *We Were Not Summer Soldiers: The Indian War Diary of Plympton J. Kelley, 1855–1856*. Tacoma: Washington State Historical Society, 1976.

Blankenship, Georgiana M., ed. *Early History of Thurston County, Washington; Together with Biographies and Reminiscences of those Identified with Pioneer Days*. Olympia, WA: n.p., 1914.

Bonney, William P. *History of Pierce County, Washington*. Chicago: Pioneer Historical Publishing Company, 1927.

Bowsfield, Hartwell, ed. *Fort Victoria Letters, 1846–1851*. Winnipeg, MB: Hudson's Bay Record Society, 1979.

Boyle, Susan, and Robert C. Wagoner. *The Bigelow House & Site: Condition Assessment, Potential Use Analysis & History*. Olympia, WA: 1991.

Callum, George W. *Officers and Graduates of the U.S. Military Academy at West Point, N.Y. from its Establishment in 1802 to 1890 with the Early History of the United States Military Academy*. Boston and New York: Houghton, Mifflin and Company, 1891.

Carey, Roland. *The Sound of Steamers*. Seattle: Alderbrook Publishing, 1965.

Crooks, Drew. "The Life of Thomas Linklater." *Occurrences: The Journal of Activities of Fort Nisqually Historic Site*, Fall 1991.

———. "The Story of John Edgar." *Occurrences: The Journal of Activities of Fort Nisqually Historic Site*, Spring 1993.
Dickey, George. "Company M: 1st Artillery in Oregon Territory, 1849–53." Unpublished manuscript. Fort Nisqually Living History Museum, Tacoma, n.d.
———, ed. *The Journal of Occurrences at Fort Nisqually: Commencing May 30, 1833, Ending September 27, 1859.* Tacoma: Metropolitan Park District, 1988. [referred to in notes as *Nisqually Journal*]
———. "The Outstations." *Occurrences: The Journal of Activities of Fort Nisqually Historic Site* Vol. 12, no. 1 (Spring 1994), 3–7. Tacoma: Metropolitan Park District.
Eckrom, Jerry. "Reconstructing Willie." *Occurrences: The Journal of Activities of Fort Nisqually Historic Site*, Fall 1999.
Gibbs, George. *Indian Tribes of Washington Territory.* Fairfield, WA: Ye Galleon Press, 1967.
Gibbs, James A., Jr. *Pacific Graveyard: A Narrative of the Ships Lost Where the Columbia River Meets the Pacific Ocean.* Portland: Binfords and Mort, 1950.
Gough, Barry M. *Gunboat Frontier: British Maritime Authority and Northwest Coast Indians, 1846–1890.* Victoria: University of British Columbia Press, 2011.
Gove, William Henry. *The Gove Book: History and Genealogy of the American Family of Gove and Notes of European Goves.* Salem, MA: Sidney Perley Publisher, 1922.
Halpenny, Francess G., ed. *Dictionary of Canadian Biography: Vol. 8, 1851 to 1860.* Toronto: University of Toronto Press, 1985.
Hines, Harvey K. *An Illustrated History of the State of Washington.* Chicago: Lewis Publishing Company, 1894.
Hirch, Mirjam. "Trading across Time and Space: Culture along the North American 'Grease Trails' from a European Perspective." Paper presented at the Canadian Studies International Interdisciplinary Conference: Across Time and Space, Visions of Canada from Abroad, University College of the Cariboo, Kamloops, September 2003.
Huggins, Edward. "The Balance Tannery and an Early Trip to Olympia." *Portland Oregonian*, September 1900.
———. "Donation Land Claims in Pierce County." *Tacoma Sunday Ledger*, February 1892; and *Tacoma Weekly Ledger*, March 1892.
———. "The Killing of Cush." *Portland Oregonian*, August 1900.
———. *Reminiscences of Puget Sound.* Edited by Gary Fuller Reese. Tacoma, WA: Tacoma Public Library, 1984.
———. "The Seizure, Condemnation and Sale of the British Ship *Albion*, by the Puget Sound Customs." *Portland Oregonian*, October 14, 1900.
———. "The Seizure of the Hudson's Bay Company Schooner *Cadboro*." *Portland Oregonian*, October 28, 1900.
———. "A Trip from Fort Nisqually to Cowlitz in 1850." *Portland Oregonian*. September 9, 1900.
Hunt, Herbert. *Tacoma, Its History and Its Builders: A Half Century of Activity.* Chicago: S.J. Clarke Publishing Company, 1916.

Lang, Frank A. "John Jeffrey in the Wild West: Speculations on His Life and Times (1828–1854?)." *Kalmiopsis: Journal of the Native Plant Society of Oregon* 13 (2006): 1–12.

Lang, William L. *Confederacy of Ambition: William Winlock Miller and the Making of Washington Territory*. Seattle: University of Washington Press, 1997.

Large, R. G., ed. *The Journals of William Fraser Tolmie, Physician and Fur Trader*. Vancouver BC: Mitchell Press, 1963.

MacEachern, John. "Elwood Evans, Lawyer-Historian." *Washington Historical Quarterly* 52, no. 1 (January 1961): 15-28.

McDonald, Lucile C. "Brush-off at Olympia Led to Founding of Steilacoom." *Seattle Times*, June 25, 1950.

———. *Washington's Yesterdays (Before There Was a Territory) 1775–1853*. Portland: Binfords and Mort, 1953.

McNairn, Jack, and Jerry MacMullen. *Ships of the Redwood Coast*. Redwood City: Stanford University Press, 1946.

Meany, Edmund S., "News Department: History Sustains Losses," *Washington Historical Quarterly* 1, no. 3 (April 1907), 176.

Milliken, Emma. "Choosing between Corsets and Freedom: Native, Mixed-Blood, and White Wives of Laborers at Fort Nisqually, 1833–1860." *Pacific Northwest Quarterly* 96, no. 2 (Spring 2005): 95–101.

———. "The Thornhill Story." *Occurrences: The Journal of Activities of Fort Nisqually Historic Site*, Winter 2002.

Morgan, Murray C. *Puget's Sound: A Narrative of Early Tacoma and the Southern Sound*. Seattle: University of Washington Press, 1981.

Neufeld, Carol. "John Rigney." *Steilacoom Historical Museum Quarterly* 22, no. 2 (Summer 1993), 1, 6–9.

———. "Lafayette Balch, Founder of Steilacoom." *Steilacoom Historical Museum Quarterly* 14, no. 3 (Fall 1985): 1, 4–6.

Newell, Gordon. *Ships of the Inland Sea*. Portland: Binford and Mort, 1960.

Nix, Alma, and John Nix, eds. *The History of Lewis County, Washington*. Chehalis: Lewis County Historical Society, 1985.

Osness, Richard D. *From Wilderness to Suburbia. An Illustrated History of Parkland Washington.* Northglenn, CO: Western Media Printing Inc., 1976.

Patera, Alan H. "Expresses Serving Oregon City, Oregon." *The Federated Philatelist: Newsletter of the Northwest Federation of Stamp Clubs* no. 205 (December 2013): 4–5.

Rathbun, John C. *History of Thurston County, Washington from 1845 to 1895*. Olympia: Paladium Publishing, 1895.

Reese, Gary Fuller, ed. *Nothing Worthy of Note Transpired Today: The Northwest Journals of August V. Kautz*. Tacoma: Tacoma Public Library, 1978.

Sampson, William R. *Dr. McLoughlin's Business Correspondence, 1847–1848*. Seattle: University of Washington Press, 1973.

Scott, Harvey Whitefield, ed. *History of Portland, Oregon: With Illustrations and Biographical Sketches of Prominent Citizens and Pioneers*. Portland: D. Mason & Company Publishers, 1890.

Simpson, George. *Narrative of a Journey Round the World, During the Years 1841 and 1842*. London: Henry Colburn, 1847.

Sinclair, Donna L. *"Our Manifest Destiny Bids Fair for Fulfillment": A Historical Overview of Vancouver Barracks, 1846–1898, with Suggestions for Further Research*. Vancouver: Center for Columbia River History, U.S. National Park Service, 2004.

Skeckela, Theresa. "Isaac Bastian: A Link to Local History." *Nisqually River Notes: A Bimonthly Publication of the Nisqually River Council.* Olympia, 1993 Vol. 6, no. 5.

Steele, Harvey. "Fort Nisqually Besieged," *Occurrences: The Journal of Activities of Fort Nisqually Historic Site*, Fall 1994.

———. "Hyas Tyee: The United States Customs Service in Oregon, 1848–1889," Department of the Treasury, United States Customs Service, *Pacific Region Newsletter*, Portland, 1990.

Stevenson, Shanna B. *Lacey, Olympia, and Tumwater: A Pictorial History*. Norfolk: The Donning Company, 1985.

Strong, Harry McElroy. "The Adventures of a Pioneer Judge and His Family." *Columbia: The Magazine of Northwest History* 16, no. 4 (Winter 2002–2003): 18–24.

Vincent, Mary Ann Lambert. *The House of the Seven Brothers: A Genealogical Story of the Olympic Peninsula Indians*. Port Townsend: Self Published, 1960.

Watson, Bruce M. *Lives Lived West of the Divide: A Biographical Dictionary of Fur Traders Working West of the Rockies, 1793–1858*. Kelona: The Centre for Social, Spatial, and Economic Justice/University of British Columbia, 2010.

Watson, Bruce M., and Jean Barman. *Leaving Paradise: Indigenous Hawaiians in the Pacific Northwest, 1787–1898.* Honolulu: University of Hawai'i Press, 2006.

Watson, Bruce M. Unpublished biographical research on Puget's Sound Agricultural Company Servants, collected and printed here courtesy of Mr. Watson. Vancouver, British Columbia.

Wright, E. W., ed. *Lewis & Dryden's Marine History of the Pacific Northwest: An Illustrated Review of the Growth and Development of the Maritime Industry, from the Advent of the Earliest Navigators to the Present Time, with Sketches and Portraits of a Number of Well Known Marine Men*. Portland: The Lewis and Dryden Printing Company, 1895.

———. Obituary of Andrew J. Simmons, *Seattle Post Intelligencer*, February 26, 1872; *Olympia Standard*, March 2, 1872.

———. *The Reports of Committees 1852-United States Congress. Senate: 30th Congress, 1st Session-48th Congress, 2nd Session*, US Government, Washington D.C.

Index

About the Editor

For the past four decades editor Steve A. Anderson has worked in the field of heritage and local history. His passion for the history of the British fur trade in the Pacific Northwest was sparked as he served as administrator of Fort Nisqually Living History Museum in Tacoma, Washington, from 1980 to 1990. Since then he has been a museum consultant; director of the Renton History Museum, Washington; and a researcher of Fort Nisqually's voluminous records.

Anderson's articles have appeared in the *Pacific Northwest Quarterly*, *Columbia: The Magazine of Northwest History*, *Cowlitz Historical Quarterly*, *Renton Historical Quarterly*, and *Occurrences: The Journal of Activities of Fort Nisqually Historic Site*, of which he is the founding editor.

His books include *The Physical Structure of Fort Nisqually: A Preliminary Study on the Structural Development of a Hudson's Bay Company Site, 1843–1859* (Metropolitan Park District, Tacoma, WA, 1988); *Angus McDonald of the Great Divide* (Museum of North Idaho, 2011); *Fort Nisqually Indian Accounts Book, 1849–1851,* Vol. I, and *Fort Nisqually Indian Accounts Book, 1850–1852*, Vol. II (self-published, Newport, NC, 2012).

Since 2012 Anderson has served as the director of the History Museum of Carteret County, Morehead City, North Carolina. He lives in Cape Carteret, North Carolina, with his wife Lynn Doggett Anderson and their dog Cami.